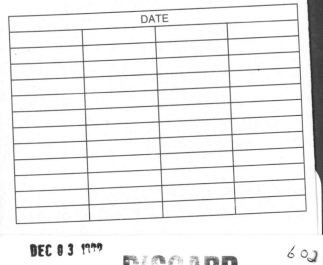

270
COL

Collins, Michael,
1960-

The story of
Christianity.

$29.95

DATE			

THE STORY OF
CHRISTIANITY

THE STORY OF
CHRISTIANITY

FATHER MICHAEL COLLINS
MATTHEW A. PRICE

DK PUBLISHING, INC.

A DK PUBLISHING BOOK
www.dk.com

Project Editors	Caroline Hunt
	Susannah Steel
Art Editor	Dawn Terrey
Senior Editor	David Pickering
Senior Art Editor	Claire Legemah
Senior Managing Editor	Anna Kruger
Deputy Art Director	Tina Vaughan
DTP Designer	Robert Campbell
Picture Research	Julia Harris-Voss
	Mariana Sonnenberg
Production	David Proffit
	Louise Daly
US Editors	Jim Bolton, Claudia Volkman,
	Chuck Wills
Editorial Consultant	Luci Collings
Historical Consultant	Mark Galli (Editor,
	Christian History magazine)
Index	AD Publishing Services Ltd.

First American Edition, 1999

2 4 6 8 10 9 7 5 3 1

Published in the United States by DK Publishing, Inc.
95 Madison Avenue
New York, New York 100116

Copyright © 1999 Dorling Kindersley Limited, London
Text copyright © 1999 Michael Collins
Text copyright © 1999 Matthew A. Price

Library of Congress Cataloging-in-Publication Data
Collins, Michael.
  The story of Christianity: 2,000 years of faith / Michael Collins
& Matthew Price. — 1st American ed.
       p.   c.m.
  Includes index.
  ISBN 0-7894-4605-7 (alk. paper)
  1. Church history.   I. Price, Matthew Arlen.   II. Title.
BR145.2.C63 1999
270—dc21   99–23294
                                                        CIP

Scripture quotations are taken from four different translations: the *New Living
Translation*, the *New International Version*, the *King James Version*, and the *New Revised
Standard Version*. The *New Living Translation* copyright © 1996 Tyndale House
Publishers, Inc., Wheaton, Illinois 60819, USA, is used by permission. All rights
reserved. The *New International Version*® (NIV®) copyright © 1973, 1978, 1984 the
International Bible Society, is used by permission of Hodder & Stoughton Ltd., a
member of the Hodder Headline Plc Group. All rights reserved. The *New Revised
Standard Version* copyright © 1989, 1995 the Division of Christian Education of the
National Council of the Churches of Christ in the United States of America, is used by
permission. All rights reserved.

ISBN 0-7894-4605-7

Color reproduction by Colourscan, Singapore
Printed and bound by L. Rex Printing Company Limited in China

CONTENTS

THE ROOTS OF CHRISTIANITY
❖

CHURCH & EMPIRE
❖

CHRISTIAN EMPIRE
❖

AUTHORS' PREFACE

AS WE LOOKED AT ONE ANOTHER across the table at the publisher's offices in London to plan the content and layout of this book – one of us a lifelong Protestant, the other a Catholic – the irony was not lost that we were attempting to create a truly ecumenical project that would harmonize hundreds of years of acrimonious, sometimes deadly, theological differences. And we were laboring on English soil, where both sides raged against one another for centuries after King Henry VIII decided he needed a younger, presumably more fertile, bride to replace the wife who had been unable to bear him a male heir. Yet, despite our divergent lineages, we were able to work together easily, believers willing to put aside differences of tradition and doctrine to strive for the greater good.

This, we believe, is not only the spirit of this unique book – a work that examines Christianity from a global perspective – but will also be the church's legacy from the twentieth century. Against the backdrop of great advances in learning, two world wars, and the proliferation of other religions, Christianity – through the efforts of such people as Pope John Paul II, Billy Graham, Archbishop Desmond Tutu, Mother Teresa of Calcutta, and countless others – has regained its vitality by diminishing the importance of its many branches and returning to its earliest roots, the life and teachings of Jesus Christ.

We hope that you will find *The Story of Christianity* both fascinating and inspiring. More importantly, however, we pray that you will find in its pages the true spirit of Christianity and the essence of the One to whom millions have dedicated their lives over the past 2,000 years.

Matthew Price

Michael Collins

INTRODUCTION

FOR CHRISTIANS and non-Christians alike, the story of Christianity is a major part of the world's history. The Christian faith has affected every sphere of life, from morality to politics, from art to literature, from science to philosophy. Today one-third of the world's population call themselves Christians. Twenty centuries separate us from the time when the little-known and enigmatic Jesus walked the dusty roads of Galilee, preaching his message of repentance and salvation. This book sets out to explore those centuries – how the followers of Jesus, who believed he was God, tried to live out his teachings.

For Christians, their faith and the history of their religion center on Christ. As Blaise Pascal stated, "Jesus Christ is the center of all and the goal to which all tends." No account of Christianity can be complete without describing the emotional, intellectual, and spiritual impact of this historical figure on the untold numbers of people who have followed and believed in him.

CHRIST IN MAJESTY
Christians believe that Jesus Christ ascended to heaven after his death and reigns as king. So much Christian art depicts him as faith pictures him to be in the heavenly realms.

Christians believe that when Jesus was born "the Word became flesh" – God came to earth. Subsequently Jesus experienced both adoration and open contempt during his ministry. His power and authority inspired awe and trust in the crowds that followed him and intense anger among his adversaries. The most powerful statement of his identity, recorded in the Gospel of Matthew, came when Jesus turned to his earnest disciple, Peter, and asked him, "Who do you say that I am?" The fisherman answered instinctively, "You are the Messiah, the son of the living God" (Matthew 16:15-16). A similar faith still drives his followers. The motivation for Christians to love others and to live better lives comes from gratitude to Jesus Christ and the desire to be like him. Their motivation to undertake missions comes from his command to his original followers to "go and make disciples of all nations" (Matthew 28:18).

❖

" I AM THE WAY AND THE TRUTH AND THE LIFE "

JESUS CHRIST (JOHN 14:6)

EARLY CHRISTIAN MARTYRS IN ROME
Since the days of Roman rule when those who refused to worship pagan deities were put to death, countless Christians from every continent of the world have had the courage to face death and die for Christ rather than to renounce their faith.

Since the life, death, and resurrection of Christ, Christianity has become one of the most prominent faiths in the world. Countless martyrs have given their lives to spread the gospel on every continent; glorious works of art, architecture, and music have given expression to what words alone could not communicate; theologians and preachers have conveyed the

" ALL OUR POWER FOR GOOD IS DERIVED FROM GOD "

CYPRIAN, THIRD-CENTURY BISHOP

simple yet limitless meaning of Christ's message in innumerable ways; and reformers have fought zealously to ensure that core Christian beliefs not be lost to the convictions of an individual or institution.

❖

The history of Christianity can be divided into a number of epochs, each of which is explained in this volume. Christianity is firmly rooted in the promises God made to the great leaders, or patriarchs, of the Old Testament; it is a religion with distinctly Jewish origins. At the time of its advent, Palestine, the home of the Jews, was a tiny outpost of the Roman empire. There, according to his followers, the long-awaited Messiah of the Jews came to redeem God's

A CHRISTIAN KING
Often the religion of the king has been the religion of the people; and kings have usually had immense influence over religion in their lands. The devout Christian ruler Charlemagne, who ruled over much of Europe in the ninth century, enforced a number of mass conversions.

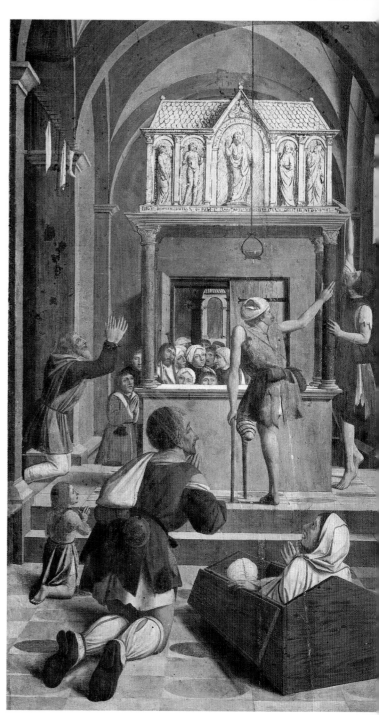

MEDIEVAL PILGRIMS PRAYING AT A SAINT'S TOMB
In a superstitious age, the tombs of saints were regarded as places of healing and cures. They frequently became sites of pilgrimage, where the sick came to touch a tomb, hoping for a miraculous cure, and "sinners" came as an act of penance.

people. Through three centuries the early church survived external hardships, persecution, schisms, and heresies. Beginning with Nero, generations of Roman emperors carried out sporadic persecutions of Christians. Despite this, a standard form of church government was established, headed by bishops, presbyters, and deacons. Foremost among the bishops were those of Antioch, Alexandria, and, most of all, Rome. Forms of worship, most importantly the Mass, or the Lord's Supper, were also developed which bound the community together in the face of adversity and even death. The task of the church was to remain faithful to the teachings of Jesus and the apostles, and to present those teachings to the world around it.

PURITANS GOING TO CHURCH IN COLONIAL AMERICA
The Puritans, the devout and solemn English Protestants who first colonized New England, did much to shape the entire religious ethos of what was to become the United States.

The pagan empire was vanquished and the cause of Christ won after 311 when religious freedom was granted in the Roman Empire. With this stability came a need to codify the basic tenets of the Christian church to protect it against a threat more dangerous than the sword – the poisoned pen of the heretic. The church utilized its newly acquired authority to call all the church's bishops together for this purpose: between 325 and 451 four general church councils affirmed for all future believers the nature and work of Christ and the Godhead.

During the early Middle Ages the church weathered threats from barbarian invasions and the rise of Islam. A schism in 1054 split the Western and Eastern halves of the orthodox Christian church, which subsequently became known as the Catholic and Orthodox churches respectively. Although the essential doctrines held by East and West remained the same, the church has never again been unified, at least not in the first two millennia of its existence.

The fabric of the church would further rend in the sixteenth century when a German friar named Martin Luther nailed his criticisms of corrupt Catholic church practices to the door of his parish church in Wittenberg, and in so doing launched the Protestant Reformation. In the centuries that followed, the church would both shape and be shaped by the revolutions of science, philosophy, and politics that have driven civilization into the modern era.

During the sixteenth and seventeenth centuries the Christian faith expanded far beyond Europe. In the eighteenth century charismatic personalities, such as the Wesley brothers, George Whitefield, and Jonathan Edwards initiated religious revivals in the United States and Britain. By the end of the nineteenth century, Christianity had spread to every continent and to almost every country, becoming the most popular and the most widespread religion in the world.

" THE CHURCH IS LIKE A GREAT SHIP POUNDED BY THE WAVES ... OUR JOB IS NOT TO ABANDON SHIP BUT TO KEEP IT ON ITS COURSE "

BONIFACE, EIGHTH-CENTURY MISSIONARY MONK

CHRISTIANITY IN THE HOME

For the devout believer, Christian faith is a central part of home life, and prayer is a part of the normal routine of the day. Saying grace, or giving thanks, before and after a meal has always been learned from a young age (above).

" CHRISTIANITY IS A LIVING TRUTH "

J.H. NEWMAN, NINETEENTH-CENTURY CATHOLIC CARDINAL

❖

As the world marks 2,000 years since the birth of Jesus, no one can remain indifferent to the impact of Christianity. Although Christians can rejoice in much that has been achieved, there is also cause for regret. Many persecutions and wars have been undertaken in the name of Christ. Often, those who have called themselves Christians have been shockingly indifferent to the sufferings of others. Jesus said that he had come to bring freedom, yet for most of the last 2,000 years, Christians retained the practice of slavery. The world has been scarred by battles fought by Christian factions, all claiming to fight under the banner of the one

" IN PRAYER IT IS BETTER TO HAVE A HEART WITHOUT WORDS, THAN WORDS WITHOUT A HEART "

JOHN BUNYAN, SEVENTEENTH-CENTURY PURITAN

God. Christians have also massacred and tortured those who did not share their belief, which led the great pacifist and religious leader Mahatma Gandhi (1869–1948) to declare, "I love your Christ, but not your Christians."

While the story of Christianity has often been marred by selfishness and greed, care of the poor, the sick, and the needy has always been a hallmark of the true Christian. The early church was so renowned for its works of charity that one of its greatest foes, Emperor Julian the Apostate (r. 361–63), complained that it was hard for him to restore paganism when the Christians "care not only for their own poor but for ours as well." Such organized campaigns of love have continued to the present day, producing an endless succession of Christian schools, hospitals, and programs to help the poor, the broken, and the oppressed.

Christianity has also had a remarkable impact on the worlds of art and thought. Some of the greatest artists and composers have been inspired by their Christian faith: Michelangelo, Fra

AN ETHIOPIAN MAN AT PRAYER
In many regions of Africa over half of the population is Christian. This is largely a result of missionary activity in the modern era, originally from the West, and then from within Africa. In Ethiopia this figure also reflects the survival of the original Ethiopian (or Abyssinian) church, established in the fourth century and important to the country ever since.

Angelico, Dürer, Bach, and many others. Tradition records that when Handel composed the "Halleluiah Chorus," he exclaimed, "I did see heaven laid open before me!" Many others have felt the same. Who cannot marvel at the majesty of the Gothic cathedrals of Europe, nor gaze in awe at Michelangelo's frescoes on the ceiling of the Sistine Chapel? Great thinkers such as Augustine, Anselm, Aquinas, Luther, Locke, Pascal, Kierkegaard, and Dostoevsky have all, in different ways, been inspired and shaped by Christian faith.

✤

The last century has seen a great change in the composition of the Christian church. The greatest numbers of Christians are now found not in traditionally Christian Europe, but in

"THE CHURCH IS CALLED TO REFLECT GOD'S CHARACTER IN THE WORLD"

DAVID SHEPPARD, TWENTIETH-CENTURY ANGLICAN BISHOP

RELIGION AND POLITICS
The twentieth century saw a rise in political activism among Christians of all denominations. The struggle for human rights and political justice has been fought all over the world, and often led by those with a strong Christian faith. The devout and inspirational Baptist pastor Martin Luther King, Jr. (left), for instance, led campaigns for racial equality in the United States in the 1950s and 1960s.

Africa, Asia, and South America. In the face of growing secularism, the churches and Christian communities that have long been satisfied to remain divided are now learning to work together. Other challenges continue to present themselves, such as the role of women in the leadership of the church and the urgent need to care for the environment. Whatever the future holds for the global church, however, Christians will still derive their inspiration and example from Christ. For them, the story of Christianity continues to be a dialogue between human beings, with all their strengths and imperfections, and a loving Savior.

The Roots of Christianity

2000 BC–AD 64

CHRISTIANITY is deeply rooted in the past, and it is only by examining the Jewish roots of Christianity that modern readers can fully understand the depth and breadth of the Christian faith. Many central Christian beliefs, indeed many of the categories within which Christians think, were shaped by the events, great leaders, and texts of the Old Testament.

Palestine, the setting for much of the Old Testament, was an outpost of the Roman Empire at the time of Jesus' birth. Yet as the grown Jesus began his short ministry declaring the revolutionary message of God's peace and salvation, the news of his miracles and teaching spread quickly and attracted so many followers that the authorities were incensed. Jesus was brought to trial and crucified. After Jesus' death and resurrection his followers willingly risked beatings and even death to spread his gospel message.

The three kings offer gifts of gold, frankincense, and myrrh to the baby Jesus

THE OLD TESTAMENT: THE STORY OF ISRAEL

THE FERTILE CRESCENT

The land of Abraham's birth was in the northern part of the region, then known as the Fertile Crescent. Owing to its benevolent climate, which was conducive to many forms of agriculture, this area was one of the earliest cradles of human civilization, and trade and travel were often possible through the region from early times. The world's first known cities were thriving here by c. 8,000 BC. By the time of Abraham's birth, probably around 2,000 BC (the date is disputed), the area had already seen a number of early civilizations rise and fall. Abraham's journeys took him through most of these settled and civilized lands but not to the wild and little-known countries beyond.

✤

WHEN WE SEARCH for the roots of Christianity, the Bible is the major source for our historical knowledge of Christianity's Jewish heritage. Besides this, we have archaeological evidence and surviving written fragments from other books, but the Bible is easily the preeminent, and in many places the only, source for the events it records.

The historical validity of every part of the Bible has been endlessly debated for several centuries, and the debate may well go on for several more. As far as the history of Christianity is concerned, however, it is the actual biblical text that counts and not the scholarly controversies. Therefore, in this book, we will confine ourselves to considering only the biblical narrative and its effects on the story of Christianity and leave the debates over its historicity to others.

✤ THE BEGINNING OF THE STORY ✤

While Genesis, the first book of the Bible, opens with the story of Creation and the lives of such intriguing figures as Adam and Eve, Cain and Abel, Enoch, and Noah, the immediate ancestry of Judaism and Christianity begins in the eleventh chapter, with what appears to be a simple notation about an obscure Mesopotamian clan: "This is the history of Terah's family" (Genesis 11:27).

About 2,000 years before the birth of Christ, a man named Abram, the son of Terah, later renamed Abraham, heeds the calling of God and moves his family from the prosperous region of his birth (Ur in Iraq) and journeys to the eastern edge of the Mediterranean Sea.

Seemingly unimportant events involving unimportant people. Yet, for believers, the Old Testament narratives are not measured like ordinary history. The life of this insignificant Mesopotamian traveler is the beginning of the great epic of "salvation history," for Christians see in the events of the Bible the calling and care of God for his people. More than that, for both Christians and Jews the history of this man and his family is their own history. These people are among the earliest and greatest heroes of the faith. Abraham, his son Isaac, and his grandson Jacob are the Patriarchs, the founding fathers of the Jewish people. Their very obscurity is taken as evidence that God uplifts the humble to the highest place, as the Bible says he does.

Much of the framework of Christian thought derives from the Old Testament: a God who is active in history, not far away and uninvolved, who steps in to redeem his people; the Scriptures as the Word of God, eternally valid; a divine law that binds even kings, that emperors and peasants alike must obey. These and many other key ideas derive from Christianity's Jewish heritage.

✤ THE PATRIARCHS ✤

The land to which Abram traveled was known at that time as Canaan and later called Palestine. It is now mostly part of the state of Israel. Although less than 10,000 square miles (26,000 square kilometers) in size, its location – the region where Africa, Asia, and Europe meet – made it a major focal point for trade and ideas in both the ancient and modern worlds. By any normal criteria, it would seem that Abram made a hasty and foolhardy decision to leave his homeland and move to a place that was completely foreign and hostile to him. Genesis indicates that he was a clan chief and came from a wealthy family, suggesting that he was not motivated by the desire that drives many immigrants to seek their fortune in a new world.

With everything to lose and nothing to gain, Abram's sole impetus would seem to have been his faith in God and his conviction that God's promises to him would be fulfilled. These promises, known as the Abrahamic Covenant, are first spelled out in the twelfth chapter of Genesis: "The LORD told Abram,

UR: THRIVING METROPOLIS, ADVANCED CITY, AND ABRAHAM'S BIRTHPLACE
Most scholars believe that the city of Ur was the site excavated between 1922 and 1934 about 230 miles (370 km) southwest of Baghdad. Ur was an important Bronze Age trade center with expansive homes, a vast library, well-planned boulevards, and a temple tower, or ziggurat (above). Of particular interest to biblical scholars are the many variations of the name Abram found on clay tablets that date to a century or two after his death.

ABRAHAM PREPARING TO SACRIFICE ISAAC

Abraham's supreme obedience to God was put to the test when God commanded him to sacrifice his long-awaited son. Even then, Abraham was ready to obey. This sixth-century AD floor mosaic shows Abraham preparing Isaac for the sacrifice. Genesis tells how an angel appeared in time to tell Abraham, "Lay down your knife. … for I know that God is first in your life" (Genesis 22:12).

" ALL PEOPLES ON EARTH WILL BE BLESSED THROUGH YOU "

GENESIS 12:3

'Leave your country, your relatives, and your father's house, and go to the land that I will show you. I will cause you to become the father of a great nation. I will bless you and make you famous, and all peoples on earth will be blessed through you' " (Genesis 12:1-3).

Genesis then relates that, at the age of 75, Abram left for Canaan with his family, as the Lord had instructed. By the time Abram was 99 years old God had restated and reaffirmed his covenant twice, but by now Abram had despaired of ever becoming a father. The Lord appeared to him and said, "I am God Almighty; serve me faithfully and live a blameless life. … I will make you the father of not just one nation, but a multitude of nations! … now you will be known as Abraham, for you will be the father of many nations" (Genesis 17:1-5). Thus, when Abraham was 100 years old and his wife Sarah 90, they had a son and named him Isaac. Isaac grew up to become a person of great integrity and patience. He married Rebekah, who gave birth to twin sons, Jacob and Esau. However, through deceit, Jacob stole the birthright that belonged to his brother Esau as the firstborn and inherited the covenant God had made with Abraham.

Later Jacob had a life-changing encounter with God and became a devout and honorable man. God then changed Jacob's name to "Israel," the name by which the Jewish nation has since been known.

❖ JOSEPH IN EGYPT ❖

Jacob had 12 sons, but favored his youngest son, Joseph, in particular. This favoritism provoked a dangerous sibling rivalry, and eventually, out of jealousy, Joseph's brothers sold him into slavery in Egypt. By so doing, the brothers set the stage for one of the greatest and most frequently told events in Israel's history, the Exodus.

Although Joseph was brought to Egypt as a slave and was unjustly imprisoned by the false accusations of the wife of his master, Potiphar, the head of the royal guard, his wisdom and favor with God secured his release. Joseph rose in stature to become prime minister

PHARAOH OF THE EXODUS

Some of the most spectacular examples of ancient Egyptian art are the four 67-ft (20-m) statues of King Ramses II on the site known as Abu Simbel. Reigning from c. 1279–1212 BC, Ramses is believed by many to have been the despotic ruler who oppressed the Israelite people, thus initiating the great exodus led by Moses.

❖

and second in command to the king. His divinely given insight and piety served him and the Egyptian people well during a severe famine that devastated the region for seven years. Through careful and prudent management, he had prepared for this disaster by ordering that grain be stored for a seven-year period prior to the famine. Not only was Joseph able to save his adopted nation, but, after a dramatic reunion with his brothers, he was able to save his entire family by moving them to Egypt.

Joseph's family were made welcome by the Egyptians. This warm reception was due in large part to Joseph's important status but was helped by the sympathetic ruling class that, historians believe, governed Egypt at this time, the Hyksos. The Hyksos were an Asiatic people who had successfully invaded Egypt around 1710 BC. The fact that they, like the Israelites, were of Semitic ancestry probably placed Joseph's people in a favorable position, and they were allowed to settle in the fertile Goshen region of Egypt.

Over 200 years later, the Hyksos were overthrown, and a native Egyptian dynasty returned to power. Then, according to the book of Exodus, an unnamed pharaoh of the new dynasty was alarmed by the ever increasing number of Israelites and, believing them to be a threat, turned them into slaves. The Israelites were forced to build the cities of Pithom and Rameses for the king.

✥ MOSES AND THE EXODUS ✥

After many generations of abject poverty and severe oppression, it must have seemed to the Israelites that God had forgotten his promises to their patriarchal forefathers. But God was to send a deliverer in the unlikely form of a reluctant and painfully shy Hebrew named Moses. Moses was raised in the Egyptian royal court, where he lived for 40 years as the adopted son of one of the pharaoh's daughters. After killing an Egyptian who beat an Israelite slave, Moses fled to the wilderness. He spent many years living in the desert as a shepherd. During this time he married, raised a family, and settled into a comfortable if uneventful life.

One day, while tending his father-in-law's flocks near Mount Sinai, Moses had a dramatic encounter with God. Here he saw a burning bush that was not consumed by the fire. God ordered Moses to return to Egypt and to deliver his people. Moses hesitated at first but eventually obeyed God's command. With the assistance of his brother Aaron, whom Moses insisted accompany him, he went to Egypt and demanded that the pharaoh release the Israelites so they could return to the land of their ancestors. The pharaoh repeatedly refused. Finally, after God caused the deaths of the first-born son of each household in Egypt, the pharaoh relented, and the

MOSES RECEIVES THE TEN COMMANDMENTS
Ten commandments or laws were handed down to Moses from God on Mount Sinai. The book of Exodus records that they were inscribed on tablets of stone and passed on to the Israelites.

Israelites were freed. The final blow to Israel's former oppressors came after they crossed the Red Sea. Exodus tells us that God parted the waters so that the entire Hebrew nation could walk safely through on dry land. The pharaoh, who had changed his mind about their release and was now pursuing the Israelites with a great army, ordered his soldiers to follow the people between the walls of water. After the Israelites had arrived safely on the far shore, God closed the sea around the Egyptian troops.

With God directing the Israelites through Moses, they marched across the desert to Mount Sinai, where they received the Ten Commandments, rules for daily conduct and religious practices, and instructions for building the Tabernacle. The tablets of stone bearing the Ten Commandments were carried by the Israelites in an Ark, a small wooden chest that came to symbolize the presence of God with Israel (*see side column*).

❖ THE PROMISED LAND ❖

After receiving the Law, the people of Israel were to march directly to Canaan, the Promised Land, and seize the region God had promised to Abraham. However, because they complained and built idols to false gods along the way, God punished the Israelites, and they were sentenced to wander in the wilderness for a period of 40 years. At the end of that time, Moses died

> ❝ I AM THE LORD YOUR GOD, WHO BROUGHT YOU ... OUT OF THE HOUSE OF SLAVERY; YOU SHALL HAVE NO OTHER GODS BUT ME ❞
>
> DEUTERONOMY 5:6-7

in Moab, within sight of Canaan, the Promised Land. He is remembered as the greatest leader in Israel's history. When the people finally crossed over the River Jordan into the land of Canaan, it was a new generation led by Joshua, the man God called to replace Moses. On account of their sins, the Hebrews had wandered in the desert for an entire generation, spending 40 years on a journey that can take only 11 days by foot on the direct route.

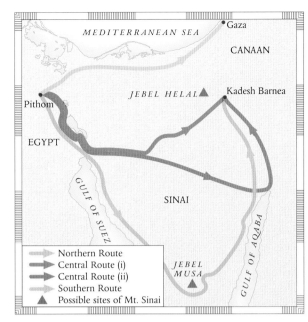

POSSIBLE ROUTES OF THE EXODUS
Biblical scholars have proposed numerous routes for the Israelites' journey from Egypt to Canaan. The difficulty comes in identifying with confidence the precise locations for the major events along the way.

❖ THE RISE AND FALL OF ISRAEL ❖

Joshua proved a capable moral leader and military strategist. He quickly made ready the Israelite army and gained victories in the central highlands, the southern city-states, and then the northern regions of Palestine. So Israel finally claimed the lands that had been promised to them through the Covenant God had made with Abraham centuries before. Israel was divided up into 12 Israelite tribes and ruled by a series of judges rather than monarchical rulers. For nearly 200 years, the Israelites thrived under theocratic rule that was mediated by the laws God had laid down for them through Moses prior to his death.

Yet, as well as often falling into the idolatrous ways of other nations, the Israelites became obsessed by the idea that they needed an earthly king to govern them. Despite prophetic warnings that an absolute ruler would burden them, they insisted on having a king.

The first king of Israel was Saul, who, according to the Bible, was the tallest and most handsome man in the country. Unfortunately, Saul's physical attributes were not matched by his character: he was to show a lack of moral direction, unbridled paranoia, and willingness to defile the holy places of the land of Israel.

After his death on the battlefield, Saul was replaced by David, Israel's greatest king and one of the most beloved figures in the Bible. Although deeply flawed, David ushered in a period of great spiritual and political stability. His faithful and intimate relationship with God has been recorded in many of the hymns

> ❝ As the mountains surround Jerusalem, so the LORD surrounds his people ❞
>
> PSALM OF DAVID
> (PSALM 125:2)

BAAL
The Canaanite god of storms and guardian of the rains, Baal was one of the many gods associated with fertility. It was believed that worship of him brought fertile soils and a good crop. The Israelites were often tempted to worship Baal and other Canaanite gods. The biblical writers saw this as idolatry and unfaithfulness to the God of Israel.

❖

ISRAEL'S KING JEHU PAYING TRIBUTE TO THE ASSYRIANS

The expansionist Assyrians finally reached Israel in c. 722 BC. They plundered the land and amassed tribute from the people. The panel above is from the monument known as the "Black Obelisk

of Shalmaneser." It shows King Jehu of Israel lying prostrate before Shalmaneser III and is believed to be the only surviving contemporary depiction of an Israelite king.

THE BOOK OF PSALMS

Very different from most of the Old Testament, much of which provides historical records, genealogies, and laws, the book of Psalms is a deeply moving collection of 150 songs and poems. While nearly half (73) of the Psalms are attributed to David; others are credited to Moses (Psalm 90), various Temple musicians, and writers from the post-Exilic period. Many of the Psalms were used in communal worship; others are more personal expressions of joy and sorrow. They cover to pics ranging from thanksgiving for God's mighty works to pleas for a messianic deliverer.

❖

found in the book of Psalms. David was succeeded by his son Solomon, who, although a person of great ability and wisdom, turned away from the high road of moral leadership and obedience to God, preferring narcissism and hunger for physical pleasure.

After Solomon's death, the nation of Israel was divided into two kingdoms, Israel in the north and Judah in the south. Israel was the larger kingdom representing ten of the tribes, while Judah retained only two. Despite the strength of numbers, Israel was conquered over a century before Judah. In 722 BC Assyria swept through and destroyed the northern kingdom, dispersing the people and settling foreigners on the land. In 597 BC Judah was invaded by the Babylonians under their powerful ruler, Nebuchadnezzar. A decade later Judah rebelled, and Nebuchadnezzar ordered the destruction of Jerusalem, razed the

Temple, and led most of the remaining population into exile. Israel and Judah had repeatedly disobeyed the Torah, the prophets, and the judges God had established to rule over them. Even their kings had abandoned their faith, and many engaged in such heinous practices as sacrificing children to pagan gods, murdering priests who demanded faithfulness to God and the Torah, and plundering the Temple treasury to finance their own interests and further the practice of other religions. Yet, while in captivity in Babylon, a small group of pious Judean believers maintained their cultural and religious identity and prayed for the day when they could return home.

❖ CYRUS AND THE RETURN ❖ FROM EXILE

After Nebuchadnezzar died, the Babylonian Empire began a steady decline, and within a few years it had been conquered by Cyrus of Persia. Cyrus issued a decree that allowed captive peoples to return to their homelands. Although most of the Jewish exiles had settled comfortably into the cities of the Persian Empire and decided to remain, in 539 BC about 50,000 Jews returned to Palestine.

What the Jewish exiles found in Jerusalem was disheartening. The Temple and the city walls needed rebuilding, the Jews were threatened by enemies, and the inhabitants had very few resources. Soon, in despair, the people turned to the ways of their ancestors,

CYRUS THE GREAT

THE Persian king, Cyrus (r. 559–529 BC), played an essential role in Israel's history. After defeating Babylonia, Cyrus inherited its empire, which included Syria and Israel. His lenient attitude towards subject peoples and his tolerance of their religious beliefs led him to allow the Israelites, along with other exiled peoples, to return home. Cyrus was welcomed as a deliverer of the people and even as God's "anointed," chosen to release them (Isaiah 45:1-6). An account surviving from this period records that those held captive in Babylon were free to return to their native country, though it does not refer to the Jews specifically.

abandoning the Torah and practicing pagan religions. When Nehemiah, cup-bearer to the Persian king Artaxerxes I, learned about what was happening in Jerusalem he was greatly troubled. After fasting and praying for several months, he asked Artaxerxes if he might go to his homeland. The king granted his request and gave him full authority as a royal commissioner. Nehemiah was a highly competent administrator and united the people in the rebuilding of the Temple and the city walls. Despite local opposition, Jerusalem's walls were rebuilt in 52 days. Later, together with Ezra the priest, Nehemiah initiated spiritual reform and revival.

Ezra, in fact, is recognized by many as the father of Judaism. His scribal work with the Torah, his struggle for national revival, and the trust Artaxerxes placed in him not to squander the fortune he had been given to rebuild the Temple are all evidence of his fine character. These achievements also confirm his status as a great spiritual leader at a time when the Jewish people were struggling to maintain their unique identity.

❖ A NEW JUDAISM ❖

Although there was hope among the Hebrews that Israel could be reunited as one nation, eventually Judea became part of Coele-Syria and was ruled by the Syrian government. Yet the period of the conquest and exile was not entirely devastating to the Hebrew culture and religion. In fact, many of the practices of Judaism we are familiar with today developed in this period. Since there was no Temple, synagogues came into existence as "temporary" places of worship. The Torah was gathered and edited with great care since the Jewish people had lost virtually everything else that gave them a national identity. The priestly class was given an elevated status, and a strong sense of separateness developed as rituals and laws unique to the Jewish people and their monotheistic beliefs were emphasized and cherished.

Also, Aramaic – the common language of Palestine at the time of Jesus – first came into widespread use among the Jews during the Babylonian captivity. Aramaic was the major trade language of the Middle East at the time, and, while in Babylon, the Jews came to speak it in everyday life. By 300 BC, Jewish rabbis were writing their biblical commentaries in Aramaic, and synagogue worship included both the traditional Hebrew and the then more universally understood Aramaic.

This was a period in the history of the Jews that could well have seen their beliefs and culture erased. Instead, their convictions were tested and their theology was refined. One scholar notes that before the Exile, idol worship was a persistent feature of Israel's life; it has never had the same prominence since. The Jews became a more united and far stronger people than they had been before.

THE DEAD SEA SCROLLS

In 1947 a shepherd boy discovered a collection of nearly 500 scrolls in a cave near the Dead Sea, which lies between Israel and Jordan. The works contained, among other writings, fragments of every Old Testament book except Esther. Believed to have been written between 250 BC and AD 68 by a Jewish sect called the Essenes, the scrolls confirmed the reliability of the Hebrew Scriptures that had been handed down through the centuries from one scribe to another. Of particular interest was the book of Isaiah, found in its entirety – the oldest manuscript of a complete book from the Old Testament, dating to about 100 BC.

❖

THE IMPORTANCE OF MUSIC

❖

JUDAISM included music in its worship from early times, and musical instruments were important tools in Jewish religious life. The Hebrew term for musical instruments, *kelim*, was also the word for such essential implements as dining utensils and weapons. Instruments, then, were not intended to be a showcase for the skills of the musician but were necessary equipment for the Israelite community.

For example, they were played during warfare, in times of celebration, at funeral processions, and, in particular, during worship, whether in the Temple, the synagogue, or on pilgrimages. The Bible provides us with several

THE SHOFAR
On special occasions in the Jewish calendar, particularly New Year's Day and the Day of Atonement, the shofar (a ram's horn) is blown. In biblical times the shofar was also sounded during military maneuvers.

CYMBALS, C. 2100 BC
Cymbals were used as percussion instruments in the earliest forms of Jewish worship in the Temple.

lists of musical instruments used by the people of Israel, including wind instruments (horns, pipes, and trumpets), percussion instruments (cymbals, the tambourine, bells, and gongs), and stringed instruments (the lute, the harp, and the lyre).

Christianity later followed Judaism in its manner of worship: congregational singing and, where possible, music with instruments have always been important parts of much Christian worship.

Instruments were also used symbolically in the Old and New Testaments by such writers as Isaiah, who states that the Israelites will "keep time" on their musical instruments while God destroys Assyria (Isaiah 30:31-32). Paul likens a life devoid of love to a "meaningless noise like a loud gong or a clanging cymbal" (1 Corinthians 13:1). Jesus compares the actions of hypocrites who boast about their good works to the sound of a blaring trumpet (Matthew 6:2).

BETWEEN THE OLD & THE NEW TESTAMENTS

THE GREEK LANGUAGE

Greek, the primary language of the writers of the New Testament, is a precise tongue that allows for deeply subtle shades of meaning. By adding various prefixes, suffixes, and stem changes, a single verb can have hundreds of meanings in Greek. Classical Greek, which flourished in the fifth century BC prior to Alexander's conquests, was simplified into a dialect known as *Koine* to allow for easier communication between the various conquered lands. This common language aided early Christian missionaries in spreading the gospel among disparate ethnic groups and classes of people.

✢

THE HISTORY OF THE intertestamental period is marked by the appearance and lasting influence of a number of key military, political, and religious figures. The first of these individuals to step boldly onto the world stage was Alexander the Great. In 336 BC, at the age of 20, Alexander succeeded his father, Philip, as king of Macedon. Philip had amassed a coalition of Greek city-states for the express purpose of invading Persia. His untimely death thrust his over-achieving son onto the throne, and in 334 BC, after gaining control of Europe, Alexander embarked on a series of brilliant military campaigns against King Darius and his Persian Empire.

Alexander achieved stunning victory after stunning victory. He continued south, taking first the city of Tyre and later sweeping into Egypt, where he founded Alexandria, the famous city that bears his name. In 331 BC Alexander became the new ruler of the Persian Empire, and by the time of his death, in 323 BC, he had control of lands that stretched from Greece to the northern borders of India.

While the military conquests of Alexander are extra-ordinary, his lasting influence came through the spread of Greek philosophy, language, and culture. The Hellenization of the Eastern world was so complete that, 100 years after his death, 70 Jewish scholars in Alexandria were sponsored to translate the Old Testament into Greek. Their effort is known as the Septuagint, a work that was often used by New Testament writers when quoting the Old Testament and that has helped scholars understand the meaning of many obscure Hebrew phrases by comparing them to known Greek terms.

Alexander was succeeded by his generals, Ptolemy and Seleucus, who played a key role in the history of the Jewish people. Ptolemy, who ruled Egypt, and Seleucus, who controlled Babylonia, and their

THE APOCRYPHA

✢

A NUMBER of Jewish religious books written between the end of the Old Testament period and the beginning of the New are collectively known as the Old Testament Apocrypha. These books are: Tobit, Judith, the Wisdom of Solomon (also called Wisdom), Ecclesiasticus (also called Sirach or the Wisdom of Jesus Ben Sirach), Baruch, the Epistle of Jeremiah, 1 and 2 Maccabees, and additions to the books of Esther and Daniel. The Prayer of Manasseh and 1 and 2 Esdras have sometimes been included in their number. Some of the books, such as Maccabees, are historical; others, such as Ecclesiasticus, fall into the category known as Wisdom Literature.

These books were included in the Septuagint translation of the Old Testament and hence came into use in the early church, which used the Septuagint as its Old Testament. However, when the Jewish canon was determined at the Council of Jamnia (c. AD 90), the Apocrypha was excluded. The church continued to treat it as part of the Old Testament, and the earliest surviving Bibles, dating to the early fourth century, all contain the Apocrypha.

By that century, however, its canonicity had been strongly questioned by important theologians such as Athanasius and Jerome. (Jerome later withdrew his objections, after being rebuked by the pope.) The main objection was that it did not form a part of the Hebrew canon. Another ground for complaint was that the New Testament writers never actually quote from the Apocrypha, although they do quote from the Septuagint which contains it. Nevertheless, after various councils and decrees had defined the Old and New Testament canons late in the fourth century (*p. 61*), all parts of the church kept the Apocrypha in the Bible. It has remained part of Catholic and Orthodox Bibles ever since (these churches refer to it as the "deutero-canonical" books). At the time of the Reformation Luther and others, raising once again the objections voiced by Athanasius et al, banished it from Protestant Bibles, leaving the various branches of Christendom with slightly different Old Testaments.

JUDITH AND HOLOFERNES
One of the most famous episodes in the Apocrypha is the story of Judith's assassination of the Assyrian general Holofernes. Her courageous actions enabled the Israelites to regain confidence and defeat the Assyrians.

ALEXANDER THE GREAT

ALEXANDER (356–323 BC) was one of the greatest generals in history. On his campaign against the Persians, he won great battles successively at Susa, the capital; at Persepolis, the site of the empire's treasury; and, finally, at Babylon. When the Persian king Darius was murdered, Alexander named himself the new ruler of the Persian Empire. In 327 BC, Alexander was once again on the move, but his weary troops refused to go farther than northern India after conquering what is now Afghanistan. Alexander returned to Babylon, where he died prematurely at the age of 33 from what is believed to be an excess of alcohol. The empire he had so quickly gained was divided between his generals.

descendants, fought for control of the neutral lands of Phoenicia and Palestine, which lay between their empires. The Seleucids eventually gained power over this territory in 198 BC. Under the Seleucid reign of Antiochus III, better known as Antiochus the Great, the Jews were treated fairly and with respect. However, his successor, Antiochus IV Epiphanes, was determined to Hellenize his empire completely.

✦ THE JEWISH REBELLION ✦

While some wealthy Jews welcomed these changes, most commoners suffered greatly during the reign of Antiochus IV. Not only were the city walls of Jerusalem destroyed, many Jewish people were persecuted and killed. The Temple was used for pagan religion, and the practice of Judaism was outlawed. The unrest caused by this oppression finally boiled over into open rebellion when a priest named Mattathias killed a royal officer who had demanded that the local temple be used for pagan sacrifices. Mattathias and his five sons fled the region but soon built a guerrilla army of sympathizers. After the death of Mattathias, his son Judas assumed leadership of the rebellion. Known as "Maccabee," or hammer, because of his keen military instincts and ability to strike the enemy quickly and decisively, Judas achieved a series of stunning victories over larger and better-equipped armies.

By 165 BC the Maccabean Revolt had restored religious freedom for the Jewish people. The Temple in Jerusalem was cleansed of the idol worship that had commenced three years earlier, and sacrifices

were once again made to God. This event is celebrated today by Jewish communities and is called *Hanukkah* or "Feast of Dedication." The Maccabeans, also known as the Hasmoneans, ruled Palestine for nearly a century until incompetence, corruption, and civil war eventually eroded the internal strength of the country.

By the middle of the first century before Christ's birth, the nation was ripe for conquest, and in 63 BC the Roman general Pompey easily assumed control of Jerusalem. The Roman government soon gained complete authority over the territory. In 47 BC a young man with an appetite for destruction and cruelty named Herod, later known as Herod the Great, became governor of Galilee. Within ten years, after a bloody campaign against his rivals, he was named king of the region.

HANUKKAH

During this annual eight-day winter festival, lights are rekindled in each Jewish household to commemorate the Maccabean victory in 165 BC.

✦

"THE TRIUMPH OF JUDAS MACCABEUS" BY PETER PAUL RUBENS

When Antiochus IV Epiphanes placed a statue of Zeus in the Jerusalem Temple, demanding that sacrifices be made to it, Judas Maccabeus and his guerrilla army of Jews marched on Jerusalem, occupied Mount Zion, and purified the Temple. Religious freedom was subsequently restored to the Jews, and an independent Jewish state was established, otherwise known as the Hasmonean kingdom.

THE JEWISH TABLE

Although Jewish law had strict guidelines as to which foods were and were not permissible, meals were far from the dry, tasteless affairs one might expect. Since animals and fowl were an important source of milk, wool, and eggs, meat was usually reserved for special occasions such as holidays and weddings. Fish, however (at least the fish that was not considered unclean), was a common source of protein. Food was often roasted over an open fire – usually in the courtyard so that smoke would not fill the house. Like Christians today, Jews offered thanks to God prior to the meal.

❖

The religious climate of this era in Palestinian history was also fraught with turbulence. There were five major religious parties, each of which would play a role in the life of Christ and the development of the early church. These were the Pharisees, the Sadducees, the Essenes, the Herodians, and the Zealots.

Three of these groups were more political than religious in nature. The Sadducees and the Herodians were typically wealthy and aristocratic. The Sadducees dominated the Temple and the Sanhedrin, the highest judicial, religious, and administrative council of the Jews. The Herodians, the party gathered around King Herod, were more interested in maintaining the status quo with the Roman government than the Sadducees, but both shared a common goal of maintaining their elite place in the community. The Zealots, however, were at the opposite end of the political spectrum. Founded by Judas the Galilean, they preached the bloody overthrow of Rome and a return to Jewish authority in Palestine.

The Pharisees and Essenes were also polar opposites, although both were deeply religious. The Pharisees were an extremely devout, legalistic, and self-righteous group who despised anyone they believed fell short of their scrupulous interpretation and observance of religious and ceremonial practices, believing that the traditional interpretation of the Torah was binding. Jesus repeatedly condemned them as hypocrites and slaves to the laws they labored to fulfill. The Essenes were also extremists in their observance of the Torah. Yet, because they isolated themselves and dedicated their lives to prayer and scholarship, they had very little influence on the day-to-day activities of the Jewish community.

❖ THE RISE AND POWER OF ROME ❖

Despite the religious and political skirmishes that dotted the landscape of Palestine in the decades before Christ, few questioned that the real seat of power lay in Rome. Eight centuries, according to legend, after it had been founded on seven hills near the banks of the Tiber River, the Roman Empire had become a singular world power.

Initially governed by a succession of Etruscan chieftains, the Roman people eventually overthrew their harsh rulers in 509 BC and established a republican system of government. Rome soon forged a number of alliances that furthered its rise as a dominant commercial power. Its chief rival, the North African state of Carthage, launched three separate wars against Rome, known as the Punic Wars, which together spanned more than 100 years. In 146 BC Roman armies destroyed Carthage and forced its

HEROD "THE GREAT"

KING Herod the Great was descended from Idumean generals who had been defeated by the grandson of Mattathias, John Hyrcanus. The Idumeans were nominally Jewish, having been forced to be circumcised and follow the Jewish religion after Hyrcanus's conquest. They were still seen as outsiders, however, and not really trusted. Herod himself was a great Hellenizer, building theaters and stadia for athletics, and sponsoring plays and athletics contests, all of which were extremely offensive to Jewish sensibilities. He consolidated his power in a variety of ways, including murdering three of his sons, two of his ten wives, and anyone else he perceived as a threat to his absolute authority. Yet, ironically, Herod was a competent administrator who brought prosperity to the region and undertook the biggest building program in its history.

vast territories to recognize Roman authority. By this time Rome also ruled over Italy, Sicily, Sardinia, Corsica, and parts of Spain. The Roman armies next moved east toward Asia, taking Illyria, Macedonia, and a sizable portion of Greece. By 50 BC Rome controlled the entire Mediterranean region and had extended its reach north to seize Gaul (modern-day France) and establish fortifications in Britain.

Julius Caesar, the Roman general, statesman, and historian who had invaded Britain, sought to establish himself as the sole ruler over the scattered Roman provinces. He accomplished this by crushing his enemies, including Pompey, and suppressing the republican form of government. On March 15, 44 BC, Caesar was murdered by Brutus, Cassius, and other republicans who had opposed his ascension to unfettered power. Alliances, betrayals, and wars ensued. Mark Anthony, who had assumed power, was defeated by Caesar's great-nephew, Octavian, in 31 BC. Octavian was then named the first Roman emperor, thus permanently abolishing the republic, and designated himself Augustus or "the revered one."

Herod's political instincts served him well during this turbulent period. He allied himself with Anthony, who controlled the eastern half of the empire, and was given authority over Syria, Galilee, and Judea. Later, after Octavian defeated Anthony at Actium in 31 BC, Herod managed to curry favor with the newly established supreme ruler and retain his crown as "King of the Jews."

Herod's cruel reign came to a bloody end in 4 BC, and his kingdom was divided between his surviving sons. As his life came to a close, Herod's lifelong paranoia and depravity spiraled out of control. Five days before his death he ordered the murder of Antipater, his son and designated heir. He also imprisoned prominent Jewish leaders and scholars, ordering that their executions should commence upon his death and thus ensure that the nation would be in mourning after he was gone.

THE AQUEDUCT OF CAESAREA-MARITIMA
One of the most astonishing architectural feats of the ancient world was the construction by Herod the Great of the great harbor city of Caesarea-Maritima, home to over 40,000 people. A 6-mile (10.5 km) tunnel through Mount Carmel tapped into underground springs, and a connecting aqueduct of the same length provided fresh water for the inhabitants.

WORKING THE LAND
Most Jews in Palestine were part of a largely poor, rural peasant or artisan class. The majority of them did not belong to any of the religious groups but followed a simple form of Judaism that incorporated magic and charms to help them through the trials of everyday life. Apart from the paying of taxes, the Romans' arrival would have had little effect on the daily lives of these Jews.

❖

HOUSES IN PALESTINE
Dwellings in biblical times were almost as varied as houses today. Most families lived in small, one- to four-room structures made of stone or mud brick. The interior walls were sealed with plaster while the roof had wooden beams that bore the weight of branches and mud. Densely packed clay covered the floor. In cities, the doorways of many houses faced a common open space or courtyard.

❖

"FOR UNTO US A CHILD IS BORN"

THE WISE MEN

In Matthew we read that after the birth of Christ "some wise men from eastern lands arrived in Jerusalem, asking, 'Where is the newborn king of the Jews? We have seen his star as it arose, and we have come to worship him'" (Matthew 2:1-2). These men were probably astronomers from Mesopotamia. The "star" they followed may have been a comet or a supernova. Regardless of the light's source, in the Gospel story it is regarded as a divinely inspired beacon whose significance was not lost on a perceptive band of Eastern scholars.

❖

GOLD, FRANKINCENSE, AND MYRRH

The gifts the wise men, or Magi, brought to Jesus were of such value in the ancient world that a poor family from Judea would have considered them treasures. Gold, of course, continues to be a consistently valuable commodity. The practical use of myrrh and frankincense, however, is less familiar to modern consumers. Both are processed from aromatic plants and are used to make perfumes, incense, and other scented products. Frankincense was sometimes used for religious ceremonies and myrrh for funerals, so some have seen symbolic meanings in the gifts.

❖

IN THE OBSCURE TOWN of Bethlehem in the desolate province of Judea in the great empire of Rome, a baby was born in about 4 BC to a young woman named Mary and her fiancé, Joseph. Although the infant's lineage is traced to Abraham and David in the first chapter of the Gospel of Matthew, there would have been little to suggest to the casual observer that this child was the promised Messiah, the King of kings and Lord of lords. Yet his life, death, and resurrection are the central events of Christian history.

❖ JESUS' CHILDHOOD ❖

We are told very little about the child's mother, other than that she was a young virgin who had conceived by the power of the Holy Spirit. We know even less about Jesus' "adoptive" father, Joseph, except that he was a carpenter and a man of great integrity. When Joseph found out that Mary was pregnant prior to their marriage, he decided quietly to break the engagement. In a dream he was told by an angel that the child was from God and that he should proceed with the marriage.

When Jesus was about two, an angel again appeared to Joseph to warn him of Herod's extermination of all male infants in Bethlehem. Joseph and his family escaped to Egypt. Following Herod's death, the angel instructed Joseph that it was safe to return, and the family settled in the Galilean town of Nazareth. The Gospels provide very little information about Jesus' childhood and young adulthood. Luke's Gospel tells us that a righteous man named Simeon and a prophetess named Anna recognized him as the Messiah. We also read in the same chapter that Jesus was "filled with wisdom beyond his years" (Luke 2:40) and that when he was 12 years old the religious teachers in Jerusalem "were amazed at his understanding and his answers" (Luke 2:47) when Jesus met with them during a Passover festival.

THE FLIGHT OF THE HOLY FAMILY INTO EGYPT

According to Matthew's Gospel, Herod the Great ordered the killing of all Jewish boys in and around Bethlehem under the age of two in an attempt to kill the Messiah he had heard about and feared (an event known as the "Massacre of the Innocents"). Jesus' family was forced to flee to Egypt to escape Herod's wrath. They stayed there until Herod's death, when they moved north to settle in Nazareth.

❝ *I hear the voice of someone shouting, 'Make a highway for the LORD through the wilderness'* **❞**

ISAIAH 40:3

THE WILDERNESS OF JUDEA

Lying between the Dead Sea and Jerusalem, the Judean Desert was the harsh wilderness where John the Baptist received his prophetic calling from God. He baptized people and urged them to repent from sin. According to the Gospels, Jesus withdrew into this arid, stony land after his baptism by John. Here, Jesus encountered Satan and was tempted three times.

❖ JESUS' BAPTISM AND TEMPTATION ❖

The Gospel narratives concerning Jesus' life and ministry begin in earnest when he is about 30 years of age. His initiation onto the world stage begins with his baptism by John the Baptist. John was the child of Elizabeth, Mary's cousin, and was a renowned prophet who baptized repentant sinners in the muddy waters of the River Jordan. John's ministry had been prophesied by the prophet Isaiah: "I hear the voice of someone shouting, 'Make a highway for the LORD through the wilderness'" (Isaiah 40:3). John also preached an apocalyptic message concerning the judgment and wrath of God and the coming Messiah, who, he proclaimed, was already among them.

When Jesus stepped onto the banks of the Jordan and asked to be baptized, John recognized him as the promised Savior and initially refused, stating, "I am the one who needs to be baptized by you … so why are you coming to me?" (Matthew 3:14b). But Jesus insisted that it was the right thing to do. When Jesus came up out of the water, the heavens opened, and the Spirit of God descended like a dove and settled on him. A voice from heaven could be heard saying, "This is my beloved Son, and I am fully pleased with him" (Matthew 3:17).

After his baptism, and prior to his public ministry, Jesus went into the desert and was tempted by Satan. This confrontation between good and evil, occurring after the physically weakened Jesus had fasted for 40 days and nights, represented the struggle that has existed since Creation between the kingdoms of light and darkness. The first temptation Jesus faced from Satan was to use his divine powers to satisfy his earthly hunger. Jesus responded that only the Word of God can truly meet human needs. The second temptation concerned physical safety. Satan told Jesus to throw himself off the Temple roof and allow the angels to protect him, thereby proving that he was the Son of God. Jesus responded by quoting from Deuteronomy, "Do not test the Lord your God" (6:16). Finally, Satan showed Jesus the nations of the world and said, "I will give it all to you … if you will only kneel down and worship

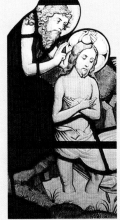

JOHN THE BAPTIST

JOHN the Baptist is one of the most enigmatic figures in religious history. According to the Bible, he was born to parents who were too old to have children, and it was prophesied that he would be "filled with the Holy Spirit" from birth. When his public ministry began, John lived in the wilderness, wearing a garment of camel's hair and a leather belt and eating locusts and wild honey. He emerged from the desert to call the people of Israel to repentance and to predict the coming of the Messiah. We are told in Mark 6 that King Herod Antipas imprisoned John for speaking out against him and his wife Herodias. Some time later, the daughter of Herodias danced so well that Herod promised her anything she asked. At the prompting of her mother, she asked for the head of John the Baptist, and her request was granted.

THE SEA OF GALILEE – VIEW FROM THE MOUNT OF BEATITUDES

Also known as Lake Gennesaret, or the Sea of Tiberias, the Sea of Galilee was an important source of revenue for local Galileans as many worked as fishermen. According to the Gospels, Jesus called together his disciples on these shores and performed great miracles.

me" (Matthew 4:9). Jesus refused to compromise with evil and ordered the tempter to leave immediately. Jesus' response to temptation and his rejection of Satan's deceit reaffirmed God's plan for his life and ministry.

✤ DISCIPLES OF JESUS ✤

For the next three years, from about AD 27–30, Jesus preached and ministered throughout Palestine. He gathered around him a core group of followers, or disciples. Except for Matthew, who was a tax collector, and those whose occupations were not recorded, these men were not learned scholars but ordinary fishermen. Their coarse attitudes and inability to grasp the message Jesus repeated to them sometimes frustrated him. They often quarreled needlessly and at times created dissent around them. Yet Jesus knew of the trials and tribulations that lay ahead, and he needed individuals who could withstand persecution and who would be willing, after he was gone, to embark on treacherous missionary journeys. Except for Judas, who betrayed him, Jesus' disciples matured and eventually laid the foundation for the church around the world.

Although Jesus spoke with great authority and knowledge – even those who opposed him referred to him as "Rabbi" – he used simple homilies to teach, correct, and edify his followers. The essence of his message was, "Turn from your sins and turn to God, because the kingdom of heaven is near" (Matthew 4:17).

Jesus did not hold the attention of either his disciples or broader audiences by employing technical theological discourse. Instead, he told stories, or parables, that were entertaining as well as instructive. Each parable explains a specific concept such as obedience, prayer, humility, wealth, God's love, thankfulness, and the return of Christ to gather up the faithful. In his parables and other teachings, Jesus frequently attacked the false piety of the religious leaders. Pharisees and teachers of the religious law had often complained that he was associating with such despicable people as tax collectors and other notorious sinners – even eating with them. Another theme of Jesus' teaching is the kingdom of God, or of heaven, a kingdom like no other where God is the ruler; here, the humble and meek are exalted and the mighty are brought down, and he who would be first must be the servant of all. One modern writer even referred to it as "The Upside Down Kingdom," because it reverses all the realities of human empires and kingdoms.

✤ THE MIRACLES OF JESUS ✤

Jesus also performed numerous miracles, healing the sick and lame and giving people hope and assurance that the man they had come to hear was more than just another teacher. His miracles fall into two basic categories: to meet the immediate physical and emotional needs of those around him, and to prove his divinity. Interestingly, his first recorded miracle

> " ... EVERYONE WHO EXALTS HIMSELF WILL BE HUMBLED, AND HE WHO HUMBLES HIMSELF WILL BE EXALTED "

LUKE 18:14

was at a wedding feast in Cana, where, at his mother's request, he changed water into wine. With this gesture, Jesus was able to overcome a potentially embarrassing situation for the host. Later miracles – from feeding the 5,000 to healing the blind and lame – further demonstrated his great compassion for humanity. Such miracles as raising his friend Lazarus from the dead and calming a stormy sea also confirmed his divinity and his power over all creation.

Jesus' words and actions, and the crowds who followed him, increasingly incensed the scribes and Pharisees. They saw him as a threat to their authority, and his rebukes were an affront to them. What outraged them most was Jesus' message that he was the

promised Messiah – God incarnate who fulfilled the Torah and the Prophets. Together they plotted against Jesus and devised a plan for his destruction. Popular support for Jesus also began to wane when it became apparent that he was not a political messiah who would break the shackles of Rome. He repeatedly insisted that his kingdom was not of this earth, that indeed he was subject to the laws and taxes of those in authority. John notes that "at this point many of his disciples turned away and deserted him" (John 6:66).

Yet Jesus' core group of followers, the twelve men he had initially selected, remained with him. They had witnessed his miraculous signs and had been present during the Sermon on the Mount in which Jesus described the blessings that await those who earnestly follow him. The Twelve were joined by other believers, including Mary Magdalene and the sisters Mary and Martha, in preaching and striving to gain new converts throughout the Galilean region.

The most infamous of those who turned against Jesus was Judas Iscariot. His betrayal was revealed by Jesus at the final meal Jesus shared with his disciples

THE BEATITUDES
In his Sermon on the Mount (Matthew 5-7), Jesus outlined the Beatitudes, or states of blessedness, enjoyed by different members of God's kingdom. For instance, those who mourn will be comforted (5:4), those who are merciful will be shown mercy (5:7), the peacemakers will be called the children of God (5:9), and those who are persecuted for their devotion to God will inherit the kingdom of heaven (5:10).

✤

HEALING OF THE PARALYZED MAN
As Jesus' popularity grew, so did the number of people who sought his healing powers. While Jesus was in Capernaum, a paralytic had to be lowered gently through a hole in the roof in order to reach him.

CRUCIFIXION AT THE TIME OF JESUS

In 1968 archaeologists discovered the body of a young man named Jehohanan, identified by lettering on his ossuary (container for burying human bones), who had been crucified in the time of Jesus. The trauma of Jehohanan's ordeal is evident in his skeletal remains and reflects something of the suffering Jesus endured on the cross.

While his hands are undamaged, the lower forearms show marks where the nails were driven through. His legs had been forced together, twisted to the side, and pushed upwards into a sort of squatting position. His feet were secured by a single nail hammered into both heels. The heelbone, (*above*), shows the nail still in place. After he had hung on the cross for a period of time to prolong the agony, his legs would have been fractured by a single blow, and death would have followed quickly as the lack of skeletal support would have prevented him from inhaling and exhaling.

❖

before his crucifixion. The meal was held to honor the Jewish Passover. Appropriately, Jesus chose this solemn occasion to offer bread and wine, representing his body and blood, to the disciples. This Eucharist, or "thanksgiving," is still offered today in churches around the world to commemorate Jesus' death on the cross and the new Covenant he offers believers.

❖ ARREST AND TRIAL OF JESUS ❖

After the meal Jesus went with the remaining disciples to the Garden of Gethsemane to pray. Judas, who had been bribed with 30 pieces of silver, led a group of soldiers to Jesus who arrested him as the disciples fled into the night. Even Peter, who had pledged his support to Jesus only hours earlier, later denied that he had ever known him. In the end, Jesus was completely alone.

After his arrest Jesus was taken first to Caiaphas, the high priest. Accused of blasphemy when he refused to deny his divinity, Jesus was then led before the Sanhedrin. Although they condemned him, they were unable to carry out his execution

without the approval of the Roman governor, Pilate. Pilate, who is portrayed in the Gospels as a man struggling with his convictions, saw no justifiable reason for Jesus to be condemned. Yet the religious leaders had stirred the crowds into such a frenzy against Jesus that Pilate was afraid of their reaction if he released him. After discovering that Jesus was from Galilee, Pilate decided to pass the problem on to Herod Antipas, the tetrarch of Galilee. Herod refused to handle the matter, however, and returned the prisoner to Pilate. Reluctantly Pilate condemned Jesus to death by crucifixion, but only after he had symbolically washed his hands of any guilt in the matter.

Prior to his execution, Jesus was cruelly tortured and belittled by the Roman soldiers. After scourging and beating him, they placed a crown of thorns on his head, gave him a reed scepter, and mockingly hailed him as "king of the Jews." He was then taken to Golgotha, or the "skull," a place of execution a short distance outside Jerusalem. There he was nailed to a cross and placed between two criminals. The Gospels

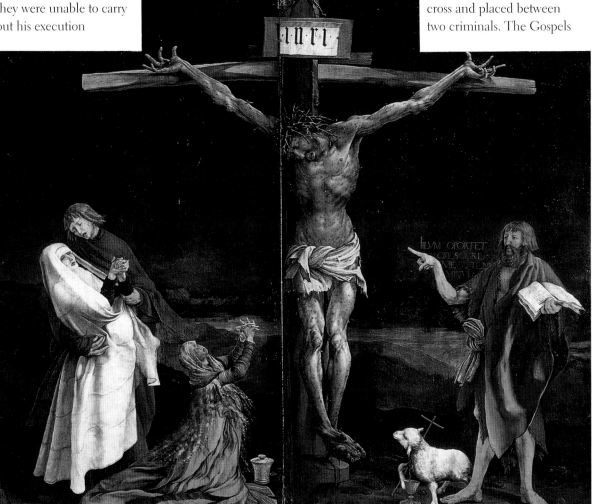

"THE CRUCIFIXION" BY GRUNEWALD

The harrowing picture of Jesus nailed to the cross has become the most universal of Christian images. The Crucifixion has been depicted by artists throughout the centuries to show the immense suffering and agonizing torture endured by Jesus.

give us a vivid portrayal of Jesus' final hours. Most in the crowd jeered at him. At his feet were his family and a few followers who stood and wept. Below him the Roman soldiers gambled for possession of his garments.

❖ JESUS DIES ON THE CROSS ❖

The Gospels give us Jesus' final statements or, as they are commonly known, his "seven final words." He asked God to forgive his tormentors (Luke 23:34); he consoled the penitent thief who hung beside him (Luke 23:43); he asked John to look after his mother (John 19:26-27); he cried out to God (Matthew 27:46; Mark 15:34); he expressed his physical suffering (John 19:28); he declared the end of his mission (John 19:30); and, finally, he committed himself to God (Luke 23:46).

Upon his death a great darkness fell over the land, and an earthquake tore apart the Temple curtain separating the Holy Place and the Holy of Holies (the outer chamber and the inner sanctuary). Many of those who had previously doubted and scorned Jesus began to say that he must have been the Son of God. However, the religious leaders hoped to end the story of Jesus by placing guards outside his tomb to ensure that no one would steal the body and claim that he had risen. Yet on the third day, his disciples reported that Jesus was no longer in his grave.

❖ "AFTER THREE DAYS I WILL COME ❖ BACK TO LIFE AGAIN"

Witnesses to the Resurrection numbered in the hundreds. After three days in the tomb Jesus appeared to, among others, Mary Magdalene, Peter, two of his followers walking to Emmaus, 500 people on a mountain in Galilee, the 11 surviving apostles (Judas

> ❝ GOD HAS GIVEN US NEW BIRTH INTO A LIVING HOPE THROUGH THE RESURRECTION OF JESUS CHRIST ❞
>
> 1 PETER 1:3

had hung himself after betraying Jesus), and other people at various times prior to his ascension into heaven.

The question of whether these reports were true has long been debated by scholars from all parts of the theological spectrum. What cannot be denied is that all of these people believed that what they witnessed

THE RESURRECTION OF JESUS
The morning after the Sabbath a few of Jesus' female followers came to anoint Jesus' body and discovered the empty tomb. An angel appeared to them and reminded them of Jesus' promise that he would rise again after three days.

was not a spirit or someone who had revived in the tomb but was the actual risen Lord. In fact, at first even the disciples were skeptical. Yet, if they had not truly believed, trusting what their eyes beheld, their ears heard, and their hands touched, then they would not have risked their lives to spread the gospel message, especially among hostile contemporaries who could dispute their claims.

The mandate for evangelism, called the Great Commission, was given by Jesus to his disciples immediately prior to his ascension: "Go and make disciples of all the nations, baptizing them in the name of the Father and the Son and the Holy Spirit. Teach these new disciples to obey all the commands I have given you. And be sure of this: I am with you always, even to the end of the age" (Matthew 28:18b-20). Armed with this exhortation, together this hardy band set forth to become a witness to all they had seen and heard.

BURYING THE DEAD
Unlike the Greeks, who believed in the immortality of the soul but not of the body, the Jews held in reverence the remains of those who had died. Caves were the first tombs, followed later by family crypts carved out of rock (usually limestone) and constructed with shelves to hold boxes called ossuaries. After the body had been prepared for burial by wrapping it in linen, spices and perfumes were applied to reduce the odor during decomposition.

❖

THE INFANT CHURCH

THE FIRST TASK FOR THE disciples, as instructed by Jesus, was simply to wait. He had promised that in Jerusalem they would receive the Holy Spirit, who would give them new power. On the first Pentecost after Jesus' resurrection, about 120 believers gathered in Jerusalem to pray and seek God's guidance. Early in the morning the apostles, Jesus' mother, and his brothers were gathered in a house in the city when they were suddenly consumed by the power of the Holy Spirit. They each heard the sound of a mighty rushing wind, saw tongues of fire, and were able to speak in the languages of all the people who had come to Jerusalem in order to celebrate Pentecost. Shortly after, Peter delivered the first Christian sermon, whose outline became the standard

PENTECOST – DETAIL FROM THE VERDUN ALTAR, TWELFTH CENTURY
The name Pentecost comes from the Greek word for "fiftieth," which was originally used to refer to the Jewish Feast of Weeks (Shavu'ot) that fell 50 days after Passover. The Greek term was later used to refer only to the feast celebrating the descent of the Holy Spirit on the disciples. Another popular name for this Christian feast day is Whitsunday.

for the early church: Jesus Christ was the promised Messiah; the religious leaders were guilty of his unjust execution; the grave had not conquered Jesus, instead he had risen from the dead; and salvation was free to anyone who believed in him. That day, Peter was able to persuade about 3,000 people to be baptized into the new Church.

Not surprisingly, the words and actions of the disciples invoked the wrath of the high priest. But, we are told, the newly emboldened believers declared that they obeyed God and God alone. No longer would they deny Christ.

As the church grew, it became apparent that wise helpers would need to be put in place to assist the apostles by administrating the needs and welfare of the beleaguered converts. These individuals came to be known as "deacons." The first of these was a young man named Stephen. After a brilliant sermon and defense of the faith before the Sanhedrin, Stephen was condemned to death by stoning – the first Christian martyr. Stephen's death led to the dispersal of the believers, who were now open to persecution. Rather than stamping out the Christian faith, however, the religious leaders helped it to spread as the scattered church gained new converts wherever the disciples went.

✤ THE CONVERSION OF SAUL ✤

As Stephen lay dying, a young man named Saul stood nearby holding the cloaks of the executioners. Saul, a Jew from Tarsus in Asia Minor, had studied under the great teacher Gamaliel. A Roman citizen, he enjoyed many privileges and seemed destined for greatness in the Pharisaical community. After Stephen's death he pursued other Christian believers (or "followers of the Way," as they were known until the term "Christian" was first used for believers, in Antioch) with a vengeance. While traveling on the road to Damascus, however, he was struck down by a blinding light and heard the voice of the Lord, who asked, "Saul! Saul! Why do you persecute me?" (Acts 9:4b). Trembling on his knees, Saul asked who was addressing him. The voice replied, "I am Jesus, the one you are persecuting! Now get up and go into the city, and you will be told what you are to do" (Acts 9:5-6).

The blinded Saul, later known as Paul, became a believer and went on to Damascus just as he had been commanded. There he was baptized by a man named Ananias. Paul's blindness immediately left him, and he went to Arabia for a time of prayer and preparation for

SAUL'S CONVERSION ON THE ROAD TO DAMASCUS

The Acts of the Apostles gives three accounts of the conversion of the apostle Paul, who was still called by his Hebrew name of Saul. The most dramatic of these is found in Acts 9, where Paul is described as "breathing threats and murder against the disciples" (Acts 9:1). All three versions mention a supernatural light and a voice that causes Paul to fall to the ground, but, although most depictions of Paul's conversion show him falling from a horse, there is no biblical reference to support this.

A GLIMPSE OF PAUL

The second-century Roman writer Onesiphoros gives a description of Paul in his "Acts of Paul and Thecla." Paul is referred to as being "rather small in size, bald-headed, bow-legged, with eyebrows that met, and with a large, red and rather hooked nose. Strongly built, he was full of grace, for at times he looked like a man, at times like an angel." The fresco above is believed to portray Paul and dates to the third century. Paul was probably born in AD 6 and is thought to have died in AD 64.

❖

his ministry. When he returned to Jerusalem he was initially treated with suspicion by those he had formerly persecuted. He was eventually accepted and was sponsored by a man named Barnabas, with whom he traveled on much of his first missionary journey.

Paul returned to Tarsus, where he stayed for a number of years. Later Barnabas asked Paul to join him in Antioch in Syria, which soon became the center for Christian mission work. Joined by Barnabas's cousin John Mark (who would later write the Gospel of Mark), the three men undertook their first missionary journey together. John Mark left them early in the campaign and returned to Jerusalem, a situation that later caused friction between Paul and Barnabas and resulted in them separating during their second missionary journey.

The first journey took the two men through the island of Cyprus and across the southern coast of Asia Minor. They were thrown out of Antioch in Pisidia, headed east into Lyconia to the city of Lystra (where Paul was stoned by local Jews and left for dead), and traveled 50 miles (80 kilometers) to Derbe before retracing their steps by sea to the port of Antioch in Syria.

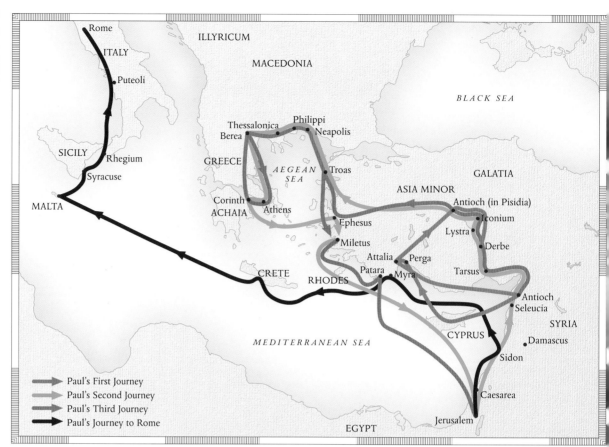

PAUL'S MISSIONARY JOURNEYS

Paul undertook at least three journeys on his mission to spread the gospel, each of which brought opposition and adversity. He was stoned and left for dead at Lystra; he came up against black magic and sorcery in Ephesus; and he was imprisoned in Rome. Yet there were also several successes when Paul's message encouraged many to convert to the new Christian faith.

> **❝** *I was … in danger from rivers, danger from bandits … danger in the wilderness, danger at sea* **❞**
>
> **PAUL'S DESCRIPTION OF HIS JOURNEYS (2 CORINTHIANS 11:26)**

❖ THE JERUSALEM COUNCIL ❖

While Paul and Barnabas were in Syrian Antioch, a dispute arose concerning the custom of circumcision. Some preached that unless a man had been circumcised, according to the law of Moses, he could not be saved. Paul and Barnabas strongly disagreed with this doctrine. Finally, a delegation from both sides went to Jerusalem to present the two cases to the apostles and elders.

Paul, who had decided to focus his mission work on the Gentiles after repeatedly being rejected by Jewish leaders, argued that faith in Christ was the only requirement for salvation. The Jewish Christians stated their case that Gentiles must conform to Jewish law, including circumcision, before they became eligible for salvation. Two of the apostles, Peter and James, argued for Paul's position, and the conservative Jews were defeated. James, the brother of Jesus, recommended that Gentile believers should strive not to offend their Jewish brothers and sisters as a way to appease both sides. The council ended on a positive note as Paul and Barnabas shared stories from their missionary travels. The elders voiced their approval of the work the two men were doing among the Gentiles and encouraged them to continue in their efforts.

Upon their return to Antioch in Syria, Paul suggested another trip to the new churches in Galatia, a plan Barnabas endorsed. However, when Barnabas decided to bring John Mark along, Paul refused to go, and the two men went their separate ways. Barnabas and John Mark set sail for Cyprus while Paul, accompanied by a believer named Silas, headed overland through Syria and Cilicia to Galatia. In Lystra the latter were joined by a young believer named Timothy, and together the group journeyed to the city of Troas.

❖ THE FIRST EUROPEAN CHURCH ❖ IS ESTABLISHED

In Troas Paul had a vision of a man asking him to come to Macedonia, a region located across the Aegean Sea that was part of the continent of Europe. Paul's decision to follow this call was the first step towards spreading Christianity from Asia Minor into Europe. The first European church Paul and Silas established was in the city of Philippi, and the first convert was a wealthy merchant woman named Lydia.

From Philippi the missionaries headed west to Thessalonica, where they established another new church. Persecution from local religious leaders forced them to flee to Berea, however, where they were warmly received but were pursued by a group of Thessalonians. The Berean Christians sent Paul to Athens while Silas and Timothy remained behind with plans to join him later.

While Paul was waiting in Athens he became troubled by all the idolatry he saw. Wherever he went he would debate with Jews, God-fearing Gentiles, and Epicurean and Stoic philosophers, sharing with each the message of salvation through Jesus Christ. The philosophers invited Paul to come and speak at the Areopagus on Mars Hill, where his famous sermon about the true identity of the "Unknown God" he saw worshiped in Athens was greeted with mixed reactions.

Although a few people converted, Paul was unable to establish a church, and he decided to go west to Corinth. Known for its immorality, Corinth seemed an unlikely place for a thriving church. Yet Paul was very successful in converting a number of key citizens, and established churches in Corinth and the surrounding towns. After spending more than a year there, Paul sailed eastward to Ephesus, the capital of the Roman province of Asia, then across the Mediterranean Sea to

JOSEPHUS, THE JEWISH HISTORIAN

BORN into a prominent Jewish family about 40 years after the birth of Christ, the historian Joseph ben Mattathias, better known as Flavius Josephus, was a notable student of Judaism. He also became a Pharisee prior to joining the Jewish war against the Romans in AD 60 as a commander. He was captured but was later made a Roman citizen and enjoyed the favor of the emperor. Josephus became a historian and wrote such works as the seven-volume *Jewish Wars* and the 20-volume *Antiquities of the Jews*. His writings include references to Jesus and the early Christian believers. Without his works, very little of the period would be known to us today.

> **"** *Ananus [the high priest] ... assembled a council of judges, and brought before it the brother of Jesus the so-called Christ, whose name was James ...* **"**
>
> JOSEPHUS,
> ANTIQUITIES XX 9:1

THE DESTRUCTION OF JERUSALEM AND ITS TEMPLE

❖

THE Jews had always been regarded as a slightly unusual minority within the Roman Empire. The Jewish diaspora had scattered them to most corners of the empire, and they formed a significant community in many places. They stood out somewhat: they refused to participate in any of the normal religious rites, preferring to stick to their own religion, and indeed tended to stay fairly separate from the world around them.

Some accused them of unfriendliness: the Roman satirist Juvenal, whose business it was to be rude about most people, accused them of being a race so surly and morose that if you asked one of them the way in the street, he would not answer unless you were one of his own community. Others, however, saw much to admire. In a world in which the old Roman family ties were loosening, the strength of Jewish families and communities stood out, and the unchanging certainties of their religion held a great

attraction in the flux of first-century paganism. The scattered synagogues around the empire often had a large fringe of sympathetic Gentiles trying to learn about and live by the laws of the Jewish God. All this time Jewish nationalism had lain quiet. The emperors had seen no reason to fear disloyalty. This was to change in the AD 60s. The standard of rebellion was raised, and it took four years, from AD 66 to AD 70, to tear it down.

The last stand was in the far south of Palestine, on a rocky fortress called Masada, where 4,000 Jewish men, women, and children committed suicide rather than surrender to the forces of Rome. Nearly 2,000 years later, "Never again Masada" remains a rallying cry for the nation of Israel. The emperor Titus was so determined to stamp out the problem for good that, after taking Jerusalem in AD 70, he had the Temple razed to the ground. Today only the western wall of the Temple remains.

THE TRIUMPHAL ARCH OF TITUS, ROME
This relief shows the spoils brought home from the ruined Jerusalem Temple. One of the spoils held aloft is the menorah, the sacred seven-branched candlestick.

GOSPEL AND POSTAL SYSTEM

Initiated by Darius I of Persia (522–486 BC), the first known postal system was not for the benefit of the general populace. It began as a courier network, which was devised as a means of sending official documents to the various outposts of his empire. Later, the Romans created stations or inns that provided food and fresh horses for official couriers. Personal correspondence was, for the most part, sent from one location to another when a traveler happened to pass by. Letters distributed among the early churches were carried by the numerous missionaries who moved from city to city. These epistles helped to foster a sense of community among far-flung believers.

✥

Caesarea. He later stayed for a short time in Jerusalem and concluded his journey by returning to Syrian Antioch. Paul's third missionary trip took him once again through familiar territory, and he spent much of his time encouraging local believers. He journeyed west to Ephesus, where he remained for two years preaching daily at the lecture hall of Tyrannus.

✥ THE EPISTLES OF PAUL ✥

While living in Ephesus, Paul wrote his epistle, or letter, to the Galatians, in which he summarized the doctrines of grace. He also wrote letters to the churches in Corinth after learning of their internal problems. From Ephesus Paul went to Troas, Macedonia, and Corinth, where he composed his *summa theologica*, a letter to the Christians in Rome that summarized the basics of the faith.

From Corinth Paul eventually made his way back to Jerusalem. Here he was accused of bringing Gentiles into the Temple, which led to his arrest and trial before the Sanhedrin. He was sent to Caesarea after it was rumored that there was a plot to assassinate him, and remained in prison for two years until he successfully appealed that as a Roman citizen he should be tried in Rome. A shipwreck near the island of Malta delayed his journey for nearly a year.

When he finally arrived in Rome, Paul was placed under a form of house arrest that allowed him to receive visitors and write letters. During this time it is believed that he wrote the epistles to the churches in Ephesus, Colosse, and Philippi (part of the collection known as the "Prison Epistles"). Paul also wrote personal letters to Philemon, Timothy, and Titus.

We are not certain about Paul's fate after this. The book of Acts closes with him still waiting for his case to be heard before Caesar. Some traditions hold that he was released and continued his mission work. Others assert that he was beheaded on the orders of Nero. Whatever the case may be, there is little doubt that Paul was more influential in establishing the Christian religion, both in practice and theology, than any single person other than Jesus Christ.

✥ THE CLOSE OF THE APOSTOLIC AGE ✥

The first period of the Christian church, the apostolic age, essentially ends as the first century AD draws to a close. Although the New Testament canon was not officially recognized until the end of the fourth century *(see side column)*, each part of it had been completed by the close of the apostolic age. The first Gospel, written by Mark in about AD 65, used much of the same source material as the other two synoptic Gospels, Matthew and Luke. John's Gospel came later in the century, as did the book of Revelation, an apocalyptic vision that was meant to encourage

HOW GRECO-ROMAN CIVILIZATION HELPED THE SPREAD OF CHRISTIANITY

✥

DESPITE the persecution endured by the infant church under Roman rule, extensive highway systems, an open-minded and educated populace, and relative peace all helped in the spread of the gospel message. The first emperor, Octavian (later Augustus), emerged as the sole ruler in 27 BC after a period of civil war. His reign began a period of peace called the *Pax Romana*. In this orderly, peaceful state the Romans imposed on their empire, governed by the clear rules of Roman law, it became possible for trade, the arts, agriculture, most other kinds of culture, and for civilization generally to flourish.

Peace made travel and communication possible, and the Roman roads made it as easy as it would be until the nineteenth century. The network of roads was well planned and constructed so that they ran on as straight a course as possible. While their primary

THE APPIAN WAY – A ROAD TO ROME

function was to serve the military, these roads promoted the expansion of trade and commerce and allowed citizens to travel with relative ease and safety. In addition, the Roman navy usually kept the Mediterranean free of pirates, who had often ruled the sea. The ability to move freely about the empire was important for the dissemination of ideas and was an invaluable tool for the growth of the early church. Christians particularly benefited from these conditions as they sought to spread their message.

The term "Greco-Roman" refers to the influence the Greek culture had upon the Roman Empire, particularly in the arts and literature. Many Roman citizens were literate, and the exchange of ideas, influenced by the Greek tradition of free debate, opened the door for early missionaries to share their faith and convictions.

PETER

PETER, the simple Galilean fisherman who was one of Jesus' key disciples, was born Simeon bar-Jonah (Matthew 16:17). Later he was more commonly referred to as Cephas, the Aramaic equivalent for the Greek Peter, meaning "rock." Peter lived up to his designation, both during Jesus' life when he was often at the center of key events and after Jesus' ascension when he was the first disciple to bring the gospel to the Gentiles. He was the preeminent leader of the early church and wrote two very important epistles. Peter holds special significance to Catholics as the first bishop of the Roman church and the first in the unbroken line of apostolic succession that extends to the present pope. This conviction is based on Jesus' words to Peter as recorded in Matthew: "Now I say to you that you are Peter, and upon this rock I will build my church" (Matthew 16:18). Although we don't know for sure when or how Peter died, tradition holds that he was martyred in Rome during the reign of Nero.

the persecuted church. The book of Acts, the letters of Paul, James, Peter, and John, and the letter to the Hebrews complete the New Testament.

The cities of Jerusalem, where the great commission was given, and Antioch, where Paul based his missionary efforts, figure prominently as centers from which the early Christian faith spread. Ephesus, too, played

> ## "...YOU ARE PETER, AND UPON THIS ROCK I WILL BUILD MY CHURCH"
>
> MATTHEW 16:18

an important role in the early church after the apostle John moved there and wrote his Gospel and epistles.

As with Paul, we know little about the fate of the original disciples other than what has been passed down through tradition. We know from Acts that James,

the brother of John, was martyred in AD 44 on the orders of King Herod Agrippa. Peter, according to Eusebius, was crucified upside down in Rome. Andrew is venerated in Russia as the apostle who ministered and died in what was then known as Scythia. Thomas is identified with India, as is Bartholomew. Matthew may have gone to Ethiopia, Thaddeus to Persia, and James, the brother of Jesus, to Egypt.

Whatever the individual cases of the apostles may be, these dedicated men witnessed events that launched them on a crusade that is reverberating to this day. Regardless of where they went or how they died, they left behind a new generation of believers that was willing to take up the cause and continue to spread the message of Christ despite the many obstacles that lay before them.

THE CRUCIFIXION OF PETER
According to Eusebius, a fourth-century Christian bishop, Peter was crucified upside down at his own request, saying that he was not worthy to die as his Lord had done.

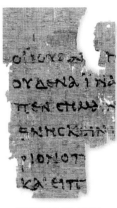

NEW TESTAMENT FRAGMENT
There are about 5,000 surviving fragments of the New Testament. The oldest, a brief snatch of the Gospel of John, has been dated to about AD 125. The earliest listing of the 27 books that make up the New Testament was in a letter written by Athanasius, the bishop of Alexandria, in AD 367. The New Testament canon was officially recognized by councils at Rome in AD 382 and at Carthage in AD 397 (*p. 61*).

❖

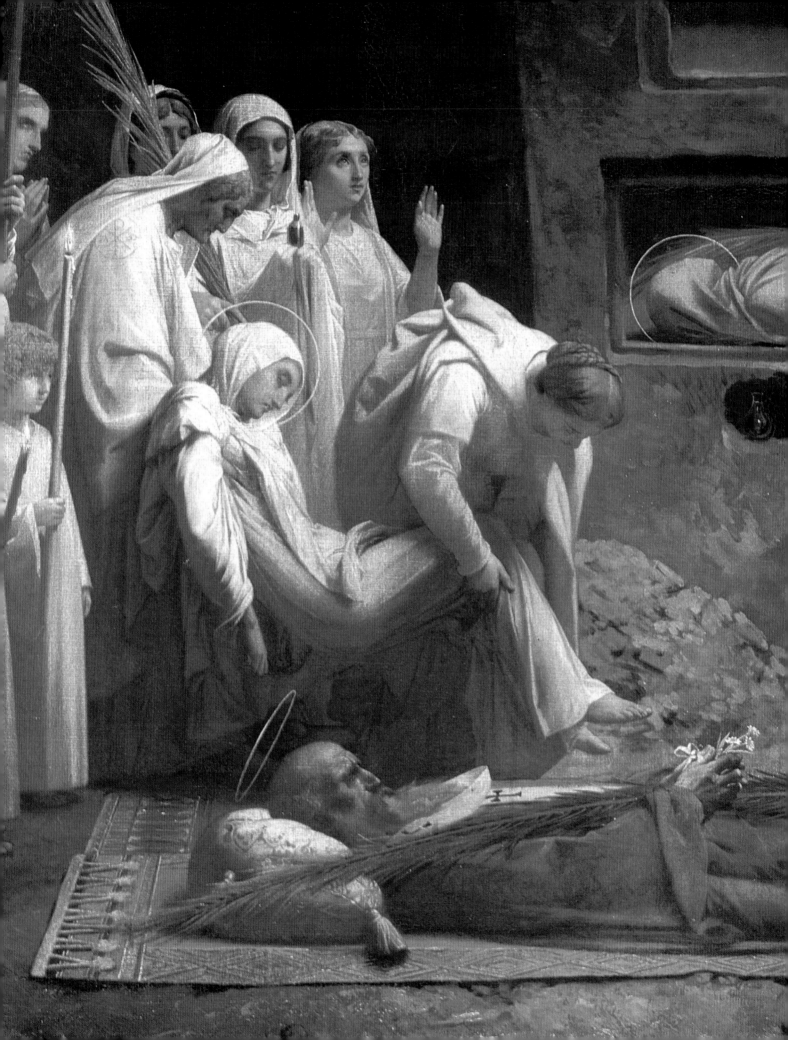

Church & Empire

64–313

ENCOURAGED BY THE teaching and example of the apostles, the first Christians appointed bishops, presbyters, and deacons to govern their communities and ensure their development. These ecclesiastical leaders also had the responsibility of teaching and handing on their faith. Christians soon came under attack from the state, which saw the new religion as a threat; some Christians chose to die as martyrs rather than renounce their new faith.

In spite of this persecution, the church spread rapidly throughout the Roman Empire and beyond. Christian thinkers and writers emerged who were capable of conversing with the often hostile, pagan and Jewish world. Further challenges were to be found within the Christian community itself, as some individuals began to develop doctrines that conflicted with the teaching of the apostles. This was a time of flux and a time of trial. In response, Christians came to depend on the teachings of the bishops, especially those of the most important cities of the East and West.

The burial of early Christian martyrs in Rome

A NEW RELIGION

THE CHRISTIAN church was born in the high summer of the Roman Empire into an immensely cosmopolitan world. Under the Roman peace, myriad peoples of Europe, North Africa, and the Middle East, their goods, their ideas, and their religions, all mingled in a way that they never had before.

For religion, in particular, it was a time of curious restlessness. The ancient Roman religion was still adhered to by most in the West, although many were influenced by skeptical philosophers. In addition a number of "mystery religions" seem to have been growing in popularity (p. 43), and there was considerable interest in the Jewish religion, which had large settlements in many cities, including Rome itself.

Meanwhile the emperors had begun the cult of emperor worship, largely as a way of increasing

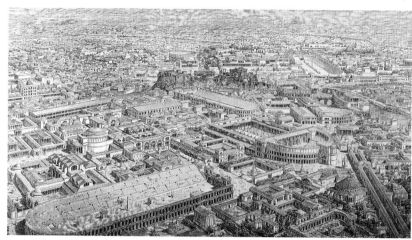

THE ETERNAL CITY, THE "HEAD OF THE WORLD"
In the first century, Rome was the greatest city in the world. The Roman Empire stretched, at its peak, from Scotland to Syria and from the Sahara in the south to the Rhine and the Danube in the north. It remained preeminent in the third century, the era shown (above).

EASTERN CULTS

The Romans were culturally eclectic, willingly embracing a wide variety of styles and customs. In particular, they were fascinated by all that came from the Near East. Egypt attracted the greatest interest. (People had been traveling to see its monuments for centuries before the Romans got there – the world's first tourists?) Its art and hieroglyphics were unlike anything the Romans had seen before. Many in the upper classes embraced Egyptian cults, especially the mystery religion centered on the mother-goddess and life-giver Isis (*above, with her son Horus*).

❖

"SEE HOW THOSE CHRISTIANS LOVE ONE ANOTHER!"

PAGAN SAYING, QUOTED BY TERTULLIAN

the loyalty of their subjects; in modern terms, it was more a political than a religious practice. Julius Caesar was the first ruler to be deified, and, after him, so were all the emperors (some cared less about their divinity than others). People were obliged to attend the ritual sacrifices to the emperors as part of their religious duties, regardless of whether they believed in them or not. Romans also venerated the memory of their ancestors. And each religion could be held in combination with any of the others. One could have joined them all, if one had the money. It was therefore with a certain amount of suspicion that people regarded Christians and their refusal to take part in any religious observances but their own. Indeed, when disasters happened, they were apt to blame the impious Christians for angering their gods.

❖ THE CHURCH'S STRENGTHS ❖

At first Christianity must have seemed just another new religion from the Near East, one among many. As such, it may have aroused the opposition of more conservative Romans such as the historian Suetonius (69–140), who said, "All that is loathsome comes from the East." He viewed Christians as "a class of men given to a new and malevolent superstition."

The birth of this new religion did not, however, seem that important – a merely local sensation in an obscure and backward province. So how did Christianity make any headway into society amid so much competition, given the precarious position of the Christians? How did the church convert the early pagans who confronted Christianity with either apathy or hostility?

Perhaps it was the force of its teachings and of its preachers. Perhaps the story of the life, death, and resurrection of Jesus was so compelling that it challenged disbelief. For the hearer new to Christianity, its teachings were exciting. God, the

God above all other gods, had become a human in the person of Jesus in order to persuade people to worship a loving God. Here was a compassionate deity none need fear. And the longing for immortality was answered by the promise of the risen Lord Jesus that his followers would join him in eternal life.

Many were also impressed by Christian community life, with its strong emphasis on family and on charity. Even some of the church's enemies commented on the Christians' love – the Christian apologist Tertullian *(see also p. 47)* was pleased to assert that many pagans said, "See how those Christians love one another!" The unity of the church was also a strength. Again, its enemies bear reluctant witness. The pagan critic Celsus, writing in c. 170, commented of Christians: "Their agreement is quite amazing, the more so as it may be shown to rest on no trustworthy foundation."

✥ THE CHURCH'S ORGANIZATION ✥

Maintaining unity was one of the main concerns of the church's leadership, now exercised by bishops, who drew their authority from what was later called "the apostolic succession." This term refers to the fact that the first bishops had been appointed by the apostles and had in their turn appointed successors, who were thus seen as the rightful heirs of the apostles as the senior leaders of the Christian community. To keep the church united, the bishops communicated with each other as much as they could. (Since the Reformation, many Protestants have disputed this view of the importance of the bishop; the preeminence of bishops was, however, unchallenged in the early church.) In addition the apostles had appointed others to help in the work of spreading the gospel, known as presbyters or elders, and had established the order of deacons to help the church leadership in practical matters, such as dispensing charity. In the first centuries there were also deaconesses.

In the time of the apostles, these leadership structures appear to have been fairly fluid. By the end of the first century, a standard pattern had emerged wherever the church had become established. In each city one bishop was in overall charge of the Christian community; he was assisted by presbyters, who were increasingly known as priests. Deacons still assisted in practical matters, although their role diminished. After the Jerusalem church had been destroyed in the Jewish War of 66–70, the bishops of the leading cities of the empire, Rome, Alexandria, and Antioch, had the greatest prestige and influence among all the bishops.

CHRISTIANS MADE INTO TORCHES – AT THE WHIM OF THE EMPEROR

In 64 the emperor Nero was blamed for starting a great fire that destroyed much of Rome. "Therefore, to scotch the rumor," wrote the historian Tacitus, "Nero substituted as culprits a class of men whom the crowd style Christians … vast numbers were convicted … derision accompanied their end: they were torn to death by dogs, or they were fastened on crosses, and, when daylight failed, were burned to serve as lamps by night" in the emperor's garden (as pictured above).

WORSHIP & LEADERSHIP

B Y THE END OF THE FIRST century, Christians had developed a clearly defined way of worshiping. The church was growing fast and was becoming increasingly involved with the world beyond its Jewish roots. As it did so, it had to grapple with a stream of theoretical and practical questions.

✤ THE FIRST CHURCH SERVICES ✤

The early Christians' pattern of worship was very similar to that of their successors today. They met on Sunday, the day of the Resurrection, rather than Saturday, the Jewish Sabbath. When they met they celebrated the Eucharist, studied the Scriptures, prayed, and sang hymns together. Buildings created specifically for Christian worship did not appear until Christianity became officially tolerated in 313, and so, having no other choice, the early Christians met in one another's houses. As time went by, some large houses were specially modified to accommodate church meetings (*p. 49*).

Groups generally met very early in the morning. They read from the Jewish prophets as well as from the writings of the apostles and evangelists. The leader of the liturgy commented on the texts that had been read, and those present may have added their own thoughts and observations. Prayers were also offered for people in need and on behalf of the sick, and Pliny tells us (*pp. 44-45*) that they "sang a hymn to Christ as God."

Writing in the 150s, Justin Martyr (*p. 46*) gives us some idea of how the Christians gathered for worship: "On the day called after the sun there takes place a meeting of all who live in towns or in the country. The memoirs of the apostles are read, as are the writings of the prophets, insofar as time will allow. When the reader has finished, the president, in his speech, admonishes and urges all to imitate these worthy examples. Then we all stand and pray together aloud. When the prayers are ended, we greet one another with a kiss. At that point, as we have already said, bread is brought, with wine mixed with water to the president," who accepted them and prayed, offering up "praise and glory to the Father of the Universe, through the name of the Son and the Holy Spirit," and then giving thanks "for our being deemed worthy to receive these things at his hands." When he had concluded the prayers and thanksgivings, "the people consent by saying Amen – so be it."

The bread and wine over which the thanksgiving had been said were then distributed by deacons, who later brought the bread and wine to those who could not be at the meeting. Justin said that participation in the Eucharist was limited: "None is allowed to share unless he believes the things which we teach are true, and has been washed with the waters that bring the remission of sins and give a second birth, and lives as Christ ordered us so to live. For we do not receive them as ordinary bread and ordinary wine, but as Jesus Christ our Savior."

The form of liturgy Justin describes, centered on Bible reading, sermon, prayers, and Communion, has often been elaborated on, but in outline it has remained unchanged, the basic pattern of worship for most Christians, for 2,000 years.

BAPTISM: A UNIVERSAL RITE OF INITIATION
Baptism, in which the believer is sprinkled or washed with water, is seen by nearly all Christians as the sign of God's forgiveness of the new Christian. Catholic and Orthodox Christians also see the ceremony of baptism as the instrument through which that forgiveness is imparted.

AN EARLY CHRISTIAN AT PRAYER
The early Christians stood to pray. The practice of kneeling, which did not become common until the 800s, began when people started to kneel as the priest pronounced the words "This is my body, this is my blood" at Communion.

❖ THE APOSTOLIC FATHERS ❖

Every Sunday the fast-growing congregations needed to be taught. There were many different interpretations of the Scriptures, and, if Christians were not to be led astray, false teachers had to be rebuked, discipline maintained, and complicated questions of theology resolved. Was Jesus in fact God, in human disguise, or was he truly both God and man? Which pagan customs were acceptable for Christians, and which must be rejected? Could Christians who grievously sinned be forgiven and restored to full fellowship?

Searching the Scriptures for answers to these questions, different teachers disagreed. It fell to the bishops to decide on the basis of Scripture and of the oral tradition passed down to them from the apostles; both were equally valued. As Papias (c. 60–130), bishop of Hierapolis in Asia Minor, put it, "I shall not hesitate to set before you, along with my own interpretation, everything I carefully learned from the elders and carefully remembered. … It seemed to me that I could profit more from the living voice than from books."

The most famous post-apostolic leaders became known as the Apostolic Fathers for their proximity to the era of the apostles and their fidelity to the doctrine of the apostles. The earliest is Clement, perhaps the third or fourth successor of Peter as bishop of Rome. Writing in c. 85 to the same community at Corinth to

which Paul had once addressed his letters, Clement reproved a number of Christians: "You will please us greatly if, being obedient to the things which we have written through the Holy Spirit, you will root out the wicked passion of jealousy, in accord with our call for peace and concord." Other Apostolic Fathers included Bishop Polycarp of Smyrna (*p. 44*), and Papias, who wrote the five-volume *Expositions of the Sayings of the Lord*, of which only fragments remain. Figures such as these provide a human link back to the apostles, whom they knew – Polycarp claims that the boy who offered Jesus loaves and fish to perform a miracle later became bishop of Tours, in France.

Ignatius, bishop of Antioch in Syria, was another highly influential figure. He is known through the seven letters he wrote on the way to his martyrdom at Rome in c. 107, in which he defended the Incarnation, insisting that Christ is both divine

> ## " FAITH IS THE BEGINNING AND LOVE IS THE END "
>
> **IGNATIUS OF ANTIOCH**

and human, "both flesh and spirit, born and unborn, God in man, true life in death, … first subject to suffering and then beyond it." He also taught that the bishops guard the unity of the faith, so that "we ought to regard the bishop as the Lord himself." As he went to be martyred, he wrote, "It is better to die for Jesus Christ than to rule over the ends of the earth."

Ignatius had an exalted view of Communion, writing of it as breaking "one bread … the medicine of immortality." This view was shared by the unknown author of the *Didache*, or *The Teaching of the Twelve Apostles*, which decreed: "On the Lord's own day gather together and break bread and give thanks, having first confessed your sins so that your sacrifice may be pure." Indeed, the Apostolic Fathers were as one in their view of the church and its worship: one united body, focused on baptism, Communion, prayer, and study of the Scriptures, under the rule of bishops.

SECRET SIGNS
The persecuted early Christians used secret symbols to avoid unwelcome curiosity. The dove was a reminder of the dove from Noah's ark. The anchor was a symbol of the Cross, and of Christ as anchor in the tempests of the world. The Chi-Rho symbol (*above*) was the first two letters of Christ's name in Greek. The fish could stand for Christ: *ichthus*, Greek for "fish," can be an acronym of the Greek for "Jesus Christ, Son of God, Savior."

❖

COMMUNION
Like baptism, Communion has always been practiced by nearly all Christians. The meaning of the biblical teaching on Communion is disputed, but the post-apostolic generation and those who followed them certainly believed that Christ was really present in the bread and wine, the spiritual food of his people.

❖

CHALLENGES TO THE EARLY CHURCH

GNOSTIC BELIEFS

Gnostics believed that they had discovered what had been hidden from others. The material universe, they believed, was created by a malevolent divinity, whom they identified with the God of the Old Testament. The Supreme Being was good, and had instilled in the hearts of the elect a spark that sought release from the prison of the flesh. Only these chosen few were predestined to a high destiny; the rest of humanity had no reason for hope.

✦

FROM THE BEGINNING, the church met with many challenges to its beliefs, both from within and without. First, the fledgling church had to avoid being swallowed up by some of the influential religions of the day. Then it had to face major divisions within its own ranks.

✦ GNOSTICISM ✦

The most significant of these internal challenges came from the Gnostics. The name is an umbrella term for a number of groups, each of which thought that it had obtained the secret key to religion. In each case, this hidden knowledge (Greek *gnosis*, hence the name) centered on the belief that the material world is evil but that the souls of the elect few could struggle to escape it, as well as various esoteric recipes for so doing. Beyond that, each group believed that it alone held the truth, and despised all other Gnostics and all other religions, which were but shadows of the truth.

Gnostic beliefs possibly entered the church in the time of the apostles, and Paul may have been opposing such teaching in his letters to the churches at Colosse and Corinth. From the late first century to the middle of the second, orthodox leaders repeatedly clashed with about a dozen different Gnostic groups, each of which tried to convert the church to its own secret religion.

All Gnostics rejected the Incarnation, owing to their belief that matter is evil. The leaders of two Gnostic

groups, Basilides in Egypt and Valentinus in Rome, taught, as the "true" Christian teaching, that Jesus had only appeared to be a man but had, in fact, been a spirit all the time. This heresy came to be known as Docetism, from the Greek *dokesis*, "appearance."

> ❝ AS CHILDREN OF THE LIGHT OF TRUTH, FLEE FROM DIVISION AND FALSE TEACHING. WHERE THE SHEPHERD IS, THERE FOLLOW LIKE SHEEP ❞
>
> **IGNATIUS OF ANTIOCH**

✦ MARCION AND THE BIBLE ✦

The learned Greek convert Marcion, who came from Asia Minor and was prominent in the church at Rome by 137, combined some Gnostic beliefs, without the emphasis on secrecy, with his own radical biblical criticism. Marcion sought to make Christianity more acceptable to Greek thought by rationalizing it and

GNOSTIC ETHICS

The Gnostics followed two distinct philosophies. Some were extremely ascetic, and strove to escape the temptations of the flesh – they regarded marriage as evil; others freely indulged in physical pleasures, declaring that this had no effect on the soul. Their emphasis on secret knowledge led to a whole series of bizarre rites of initiation and secret doctrines. In contrast, the church encouraged family life and taught that salvation was open to all. Its teachings were public, not secret, and it had no exclusive elite, unlike the Gnostics.

✦

GNOSTIC AMULETS

In the Roman world, belief in evil spirits was universal, and many wore amulets, such as these (above), which may have been intended to protect the wearer or to help his soul after death.

Gnostics believed that after death the soul must ascend through the seven (known) planets, controlled by evil powers, to reach its fulfillment beyond the material world, in the world of pure spirit.

THE CHALLENGE OF THE EXOTIC
Many mystery religions were popular in the first and second century, most now forgotten. The cults of Attis and Cybele, Isis (p. 38), and Mithras were particularly important. The Egyptian religious ceremony above shows the drama and glamour that were a part of the mystery religions' appeal.

have a new revelation, adding to the biblical one; inspiring, charismatic leadership; the very high standards of behavior demanded of members, much more stringent than the rest of the church; and the claim to be the only true Christians, so that to reject them was to reject God (all these features were to recur in many other heretical groups). The content of their "New Prophecy" seems strange today: they believed that the kingdom of heaven would shortly descend to earth in their home province of Phrygia in Asia Minor. The purity of their lives, however, and the strength of their Christian witness was such that they won a large following, including the fiery African apologist Tertullian (*p. 47*), who, fed up with the laxity of his orthodox brethren, ended his life a Montanist.

cutting it loose from its Jewish heritage. In Marcion's judgment Paul was the only true Christian among the biblical authors, and he deleted the rest of the biblical text from his own personal canon. Having thus disposed of all the elements of Christianity he considered problematical, and having spelled out a system of beliefs that was largely Gnostic, except that it was not secret, Marcion was surprised to find himself thrown out of the Roman church in 144. He retreated to the Middle East, where he founded a large and successful sect.

Persuasive though they were, Marcion and the Gnostics were divided and offered salvation only to an elite few. The church was universal and united; the gospel offered forgiveness to all. By the end of the second century, Gnosticism was a spent force, and the church was stronger than ever.

❖ MONTANISM, THE NEW PROPHECY ❖

In the 170s, in Asia Minor, an inspiring Christian leader called Montanus claimed to have a major new revelation. He and his two female lieutenants began a thriving cult that was to remain a force in Asia Minor for a century. Its cardinal features were: the claim to

❖ DEFINING ORTHODOXY ❖

There were very many other cults and sects at the edge of the church, such as the Ebionites, Jewish Christians who refused to abandon Jewish customs and rites. The number of such groups increased with time, as those defeated in theological debates frequently formed their own sects. In the 390s, Filastrius, bishop of Brescia, listed 156 distinct heresies, all still flourishing. The orthodox view on such groups was summed up by Cyprian in the 250s: "He cannot have God for his Father who does not have the church for his Mother." Augustine was even more succinct: "There is no salvation outside the church." This view explains the ferocity with which heresies were fought: they were robbing people of eternal salvation.

Controversies with heretics did, however, have a positive effect in encouraging the church to clarify its beliefs. Against Marcion and the Gnostics, for example, the church reaffirmed its faith in the Old Testament, and began to define what was and was not in the New Testament canon. Against Montanus, church leaders declared the priority of the biblical revelation over subsequent private revelations.

PERSECUTION

IMPERIAL FEARS

Christians were often from the poorer classes and sometimes met at night, something that worried the authorities. The imperial powers, fearful of conspiracies and popular uprising, had expressly forbidden nocturnal gatherings in the Law of the Twelve Tables. So the Christians appeared potentially subversive, through no fault of their own.

❖

IN THE YEARS after the crucifixion of Jesus, many of his followers were faced with the prospect of suffering a violent death, as had their Lord. Dire rumors circulated about them. The authorities mistrusted them. They had no legal right to exist.

The Roman Empire normally tolerated religions, if their adherents were willing to sacrifice to the emperor. It was a loyalty test. The Jews refused but, being long established, were still tolerated so long as they remained loyal. As Celsus put it, "The religion of the Jews may be highly peculiar, but it is at least the custom of their fathers." The Christians could offer no such defense.

❖ AN OUTLAW RELIGION ❖

As long as Christianity remained illegal, Christians were at the mercy of imperial disfavor and popular enmity. Fortunately, no emperor regarded them as enough of a threat to institute a systematic, empire-wide campaign against them until 249. There were, however, a number of local, temporary persecutions and many martyrs – the word comes from the Greek, "to bear witness." Misunderstandings clouded the image of Christianity in the popular mind. Eucharistic

POLYCARP

POLYCARP (c. 70–156) was taught by John the Evangelist as a youth. He was bishop of Smyrna in Asia Minor by c. 107 and remained so until he died there. The second-century account of his martyrdom is the oldest in existence. It records that the mob shouted against him, "This is the father of the Christians, the destroyer of our gods, who teaches many not to sacrifice or worship." The magistrate urged him, "Have respect for your age. Revile Christ and I will release you." Polycarp replied, "For 86 years I have been his servant, and he has done me no wrong. How can I blaspheme my King who saved me?" He was burned at the stake.

teaching about feeding from "the body and blood of the Lord" was misinterpreted as cannibalism, and references to Communion as a "love feast" gave rise to rumors of incest, orgies, and infant sacrifice. The Roman historian Tacitus, writing in c. 115, describes Christians as "a class of men loathed for their vices" and says that after the fire of Rome in 64 (p. 39) they were "convicted, not so much for the crime of arson, as for hatred of mankind."

These attitudes endured. Writing in c. 170, Celsus claimed, "There is a new race of men born yesterday, with neither homeland nor traditions, allied against all religious and civil institutions, pursued by justice, universally notorious for their infamy, but glorying in common execration: these are Christians."

Popular anger led to many persecutions. At the time that Tacitus was writing, Pliny the Younger, governor of Bithynia in northern Asia Minor, was asking the emperor Trajan, by letter, for

UNKNOWN IN LIFE, FAMOUS IN DEATH

The Martyrdom of Polycarp *records: "The martyrs we love as disciples and imitators of the Lord, as they deserve, on account of their matchless devotion to their own King and Teacher." This picture reflects the same reverence, which has* persisted in every century. A few early Christians took readiness for martyrdom to extremes: Ignatius of Antioch wrote, "Grant me nothing more than to be poured out as an offering to God. ... I am passionately in love with death."

advice on dealing with the increasing number of Christians who refused to worship an image of the emperor. He explained that he had been confronted with complaints against the Christians, because of whom the temples were "almost deserted." This left Pliny with a problem: what to do with Christians who were denounced to him as unfaithful subjects of the emperor?

He wrote to Trajan: "Meanwhile this is the course I have taken with those who were accused before me as Christians. I asked them whether they were Christians, and, if they confessed, I asked them a second or third time with threats of punishment. If they kept to it, I ordered their execution; as for Roman citizens, I noted these down to be sent to Rome." The emperor replied, approving of Pliny's tactics, while urging that the Christians be not hunted, but punished only when denounced by informers. Other emperors were less kind: Nero, Domitian, and Marcus Aurelius all persecuted the church in Rome.

❖ PRECARIOUS EXISTENCE ❖

Things did not improve for the Christians. In 177 up to 48 Christians were killed at Lyons in Gaul after rumors of immorality. Three years later, 12 were martyred at Scilli in North Africa. In 202 the emperor Septimius Severus, worried at the growth of the church, prohibited conversion to the Christian faith, leading to a major persecution.

Respite came during the reign of Alexander Severus (r. 222–35), whose mother was sympathetic to the Christians. The emperor may himself have had a statue of Christ in his home, along with images of Abraham and the deified emperors. The emperor Philip of Arabia (r. 244–49) was also a sympathizer and maintained an active correspondence with noted Christian writers. His death in 249 was the signal for vicious persecutions throughout the empire.

" THE BLOOD OF THE MARTYRS IS THE SEED OF THE CHURCH "

TERTULLIAN (TRADITIONAL TRANSLATION)

VESTED INTERESTS

Many of those who denounced Christians to the authorities seem to have had a vested interest in pagan religions. Power, prestige, and money were involved in pagan ritual. The priesthood, the preserve of the upper class, was exercised largely for financial gain, and those who made a living from animal sacrifices, or who made idols, would not give in easily to a new cult that opposed these activities. The many anonymous victims of such opposition included five stonecutters of Sirmium (in modern-day Hungary), who were executed at the beginning of the fourth century for refusing to make an image of the god Aesculapius.

❖

THE DIARY OF PERPETUA

❖

PERPETUA was a young woman who was martyred in Carthage, with several companions, early in the third century, probably for converting to Christianity in spite of the decree of Septimus Severus. While awaiting execution, she kept a diary, in which she wrote about her faith, her father, and the birth of a child during her imprisonment.

She touchingly writes that when she received permission for her baby to stay with her, "my prison had suddenly become a palace, so that I wanted to be there rather than anywhere else." Her father was inconsolable, saying to her: "Daughter, have pity on my grey head … if I have favored you above all your brothers. … Do not abandon me! Give up your pride!" She replied,

"It will happen as God wills." Her father left her in great sorrow. Hilarianus the governor then pleaded with her, "Have pity on your father's grey head; have pity on your infant son. Offer the sacrifice for the welfare of the emperors." She and her companions refused. She wrote: "We were condemned to the beasts and returned to prison in high spirits." A fellow Christian finished their story: "The day of their victory dawned, and they marched from prison to the amphitheater joyfully as though they were going to heaven, with calm faces, trembling, if at all, with joy rather than fear."

THE MARTYR'S CHOICE
This painting dramatizes the choice of sacrifice or death, as faced by a young woman like Perpetua, in a Roman court.

DEFENDING THE FAITH

PAGAN CRITICS

The apologists for
Christianity sought to give
it intellectual credibility by
reasoning with critics such
as the pagan intellectual
Celsus, who claimed,
c. 170, that Christians
avoided the educated, the
wise, and the sensible but
rather preyed on "anyone
stupid, anyone uneducated,
anyone who is a child." He
felt this showed that "they
want and are able to
convince only the foolish,
dishonorable and stupid,
and only slaves, women,
and little children." The
apologists were anxious to
show that the rational basis
for Christianity was strong
enough to convince the
best educated and
the wisest.

I
N THE FACE OF PERSECUTION, ignorance, and
hostility, the church needed to provide a stout
defense of its practice and beliefs. The writers
who provided this defense are sometimes referred
to as the apologists (meaning those who explain or
defend their beliefs, rather than apologize). Their aim
was to provide a rational explanation to people more
acquainted with Greek philosophy and to persuade
the Jews to accept Jesus as their Messiah.

✤ EARLY APOLOGISTS ✤

Among the earliest apologists were Aristides and
Quadratus, who wrote to the emperor Trajan
offering a rational explanation of their beliefs.
More famous is Justin Martyr, who taught
Christian philosophy in Rome in the 140s and
150s and worked to express Christian doctrines in
philosophical terms. Justin was aware of the outlandish
accusations leveled against the Christians by pagans,
such as illicit sexual relations and cannibalism. He
refuted these in his two "apologies," and defended the
Christians against the charge of offending the gods
and of not being true patriots. The fact that he could
address the emperor and the senate shows the important
position Christians were assuming within the empire
a little over a century after the lifetime of Christ.

Perhaps the most poetic of early apologists was the
unknown author of the *Epistle to Diognetus*, which
was probably written in the late second century to

JUSTIN MARTYR

B
ORN of pagan parents in c. 100, Justin Martyr
experimented with various philosophies before
being baptized c. 130. After this, he taught at Ephesus,
then went to Rome, started a school
of Christian philosophy, taught with
considerable success, and was
ordained a presbyter. He wrote two
apologies to correct errors about
the Christian faith. The first was
addressed to the emperor
Antoninus Pius c. 151, the
second to the Roman
senate in 162. Justin
was finally executed by
the emperor Marcus
Aurelius, c. 165, with
several companions.

explain the Christian religion to an interested pagan.
"Christians," the author writes, "are not distinguishable
from other people, neither by origin, by language nor
by mode of dress. They do not live in their own cities,
nor do they have their own language, nor indeed do
they live any special style of life. They live in their own
countries, but as foreigners; every foreign land is their
homeland, and their homeland is as a foreign country.
They live their lives on earth, but are citizens of
heaven. They obey the laws of the land, but by the

THE EARLIEST PICTURE OF THE CRUCIFIXION
*Scribbled in army officers' quarters on the Palatine Hill in Rome
in the early 200s, this satirical graffiti shows a man with the head
of a donkey being crucified. The caption reads, "Alexamenos
worships his god." The apologists fought prejudice such as this.*

tenor of their lives, they live above the law. They love
everyone, but are persecuted by all. They are unknown
and condemned; they are put to death and gain life.
They are poor and yet make many rich. They are
dishonored, and yet gain glory through dishonor. They
are attacked by Jews as aliens, and are persecuted by
Greeks; yet those who hate them cannot give any
reason for their hostility. To put it simply, the soul is
to the body as Christians are to the world … The soul
is in the body but is not of the body; Christians are in
the world but not of the world."

Several of the apologists were also important church leaders and theologians. Irenaeus (140–202) was the second bishop of Lyons, in the south of Gaul (modern-day France). An energetic opponent of Gnosticism (*p. 42*) and various other heresies, he wrote extensively, his most important work being the hugely influential five-volume *Against the Heresies*. Irenaeus was also an important theologian, who worked to clarify the canon of the New Testament and whose *Presentation of the Apostolic Preaching* became a standard work.

He sought to clarify what was truth and what was error by appealing to and trying to define "the Rule of Faith," the basic core of Christian faith, as a rule by which the truth or otherwise of heretical and orthodox teaching could be judged. This core of faith was eventually to be summarized in the great creeds of the fourth century (*pp. 60-63*).

❖ THE APOLOGISTS' ACHIEVEMENT ❖

Irenaeus and most of his fellow apologists sought to place Christianity right at the heart of contemporary culture. In so doing, they assimilated many philosophical and cultural elements of Greco-Roman civilization. They were largely pragmatic and embraced the attitude of adapt and adopt: pagan festivals were taken over to become Christmas and Easter, and a place was found for pagan philosophy and literature in Christian thought, as a preparation for the gospel. When pagans argued that Christianity would weaken the state, the apologists countered that, rather, it would strengthen the State against the immorality that attacked it.

Some objected that in adopting so much of Greco-Roman culture, Christians were also taking on its flaws. Tertullian, in particular, opposed the marriage of Greek philosophy and Christian theology, saying, "What has Athens to do with Jerusalem?" Rather than giving rational explanations of his faith, he preferred to say, "I believe because it is absurd." His was a lone voice. The apologists' adoption of philosophy was effective and it was to dominate the future. Christian theology was increasingly to be expressed in philosophical terms – as it still very often is today.

TERTULLIAN

ONE of the most gifted of Christian apologists, Tertullian (c. 160–225) was born in Carthage near modern Tunis in North Africa. Trained as a lawyer at Rome, he returned to Carthage and used his sharp intellect and biting wit to attack the enemies of the faith. "We are but of yesterday and we have filled all you have – cities, islands, forts, towns, assembly halls, even military camps, tribes, town councils, the palace, senate, and forum. We have left you nothing but the temples." In addition to his apologetic work and many controversies with other Christians, he was a major theologian, one of the first to write in Latin. His work developing the concept of the Trinity remains seminal.

Although the apologists' writings failed ultimately to convert the Roman world to Christianity, they nevertheless offered a sober defence against the sometimes hysterical attacks of their enemies, and contributed in no small way to the Church's developing understanding of Christian doctrine.

> *If the Tiber rises too high or the Nile too low, if the sky remains closed or the earth moves, if plague or famine come, the cry is 'The Christians to the lion.' All of them to a single lion?*
>
> **TERTULLIAN**

PHILOSOPHER, EMPEROR, PERSECUTOR
The emperor Marcus Aurelius (r. 161–80) was also a philosopher (shown above, fourth from left). He taught: "Do what you have in hand with scrupulous and unaffected dignity, with love, independence and justice." However, this philosophy did not prevent him from persecuting Christians, angered by their "simple spirit of opposition."

THE TRIUMPH OF FAITH

LEADERSHIP

Theophilus (*above*), who was bishop of Antioch by 170 and died in 180, is typical of the high quality of leadership in the early church. With only persecution for their earthly reward, such leaders had the purest of motives. Many of the best early theologians were bishops; Theophilus himself was the first to use the word "Trinity" of God.

❖

❝ *I have believed in the Son of God ... for he alone is the end of salvation, and the basis of immortal life; for he is a refuge to the tempest-tossed, a solace to the afflicted, a shelter to the despairing* **❞**

THECLA, EARLY CHRISTIAN

NDER THE ROMAN EMPIRE, a person could travel and preach in every land from Scotland to Syria if they knew just two languages: Latin and Greek. In addition, the Roman peace, the Roman roads, and the trade and prosperity of the times were all extraordinarily propitious for the spread of ideas. Yet these factors alone do not explain why Christianity, out of all the hundreds of religions of the empire (*pp. 38-39*) should have outgrown all the rest.

❖ A RELIGION OF SLAVES ❖

If we trace the initial spread of Christianity, we find that it was welcomed particularly by slaves and by the poorer members of society, so much so that pagan critics accused Christians of being able to convince only "slaves, women, and little children" (*p. 46*).

In fact, the slave trade may have played a valuable part in the spread of the gospel. Second-century Spanish lists of slaves include Palestinian names, some of whom may have been Christians, and in the Italian coastal town of Pompei, which was destroyed by a volcanic eruption in the year 79, what may be a cross was found, hung on the wall of a slave's bedroom. This scattered evidence reflects another major factor in the spread of Christianity: its international nature.

The church welcomed all races and all classes into a unified and caring community (*pp. 38-39*). Belief in

❝ CHRIST HAS TURNED ALL OUR SUNSETS INTO DAWN ❞

CLEMENT OF ALEXANDRIA

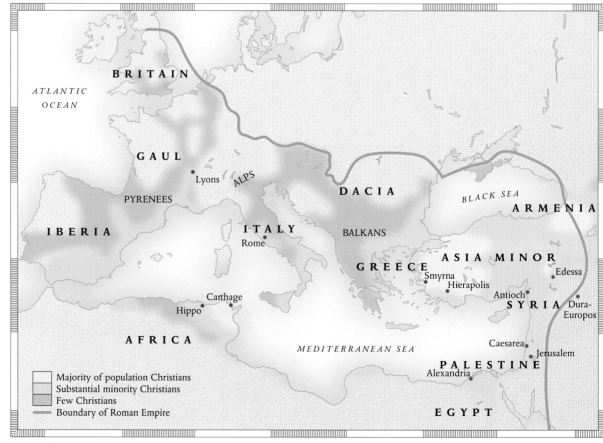

AN ESTIMATE OF THE SPREAD OF CHRISTIANITY BY 300
We have a general idea of which areas were more or less strongly Christian. North Africa and Asia Minor were then the areas with the highest proportion of Christians. Beyond the Roman Empire, Christianity had spread into present-day Armenia, Iraq, and Iran.

Map legend:
- Majority of population Christians
- Substantial minority Christians
- Few Christians
- Boundary of Roman Empire

Map labels: BRITAIN, ATLANTIC OCEAN, GAUL, Lyons, ALPS, PYRENEES, IBERIA, ITALY, Rome, DACIA, BALKANS, BLACK SEA, ARMENIA, GREECE, ASIA MINOR, Smyrna, Hierapolis, Edessa, Antioch, SYRIA, Dura-Europos, Carthage, Hippo, AFRICA, MEDITERRANEAN SEA, Caesarea, Jerusalem, PALESTINE, Alexandria, EGYPT

THE EARLIEST SURVIVING CHURCH BUILDING

IN 1921 a team of archaeologists working on the banks of the Euphrates in modern Syria discovered the remains of the earliest surviving Christian church. It was situated in what had been an ancient Roman garrison town named Dura-Europos, on the eastern frontier of the empire. Abandoned by the Romans in 257, the ruins had remained undisturbed until the twentieth century. Within the town itself were temples to Mithras, Adonis, Tyche, Artemis, Baal (in a Syrian form), several local deities, three temples to Zeus, the garrison's own temple next to the military headquarters, a Jewish synagogue, and a Christian house church. The Christian building had begun its life as a middle-class house, with the rooms arranged around an internal courtyard as was then customary. Within this domestic building was a worship room with space for an altar and a chair and some sixty people. To one side was a smaller room decorated as a baptistery chapel, with simple scenes of the Resurrection (the oldest surviving depictions of it) and miracles of healing. This *domus ecclesia*, or house church, is part of a tradition going back to New Testament times in which Christians met in the houses of the richer members of their congregations (for example, the house of Prisca and Aquila, mentioned in Romans 16:3-5). The remains *(below left)* suggest that by the third century many of the houses in which churches met may have been converted for worship in a similar way.

SYNAGOGUE, DURA-EUROPOS
The town's synagogue, which had been rebuilt in 245, was richly decorated with frescoes depicting Old Testament scenes. Followers of many deities met within a few minutes' walk of each other for their various ceremonies.

THE PLACE OF BAPTISM
The basin at the end of this room was created for baptism. Set in a columned niche decorated with a starry sky, it is the focus of the baptistery chapel. The style of painting is similar to that of the synagogue (above). The picture within the niche is of Christ healing the paralytic. Possibly the earliest surviving depiction of Jesus, it shows him young and beardless.

Christ was not an individual affair. In the lonely confusion of the city, with its anonymity, there was comfort in belonging to a community that cared, and this emphasis on communion and unity found practical expression in care for widows, orphans, and the poor. Even Julian the Apostate *(p. 59)*, who hated Christianity, admitted that it had been "specially advanced through the loving service rendered to strangers, and … care for the burial of the dead."

❖ A NEW VISION IN A DARK WORLD ❖

Christianity was almost alone among the religions of Rome in being a missionary faith whose members believed that they had been commanded to communicate their faith to others and that it was a faith infinitely worth sharing. It is difficult to explain the impact of Christianity without considering the emotional effect this religion had on its adherents. Their writings often claim that it gave them new hope, new love, and new joy – a transformed vision of life. The views of Clement of Alexandria *(p. 52)* are typical: "All our life is a celebration for us.… We sing while we work, we sing hymns while we sail, we pray while we carry out all life's other occupations."

Even when Christians were faced with persecution, their faith sustained them with the hope of eternal life. This gave tremendous hope and encouragement, as did their feeling that he was present with them. In the words of one early martyr, Genesius of Rome, who died in c. 205, "Were I to be killed a thousand times … I should still be his man. Christ is on my lips, Christ is in my heart; no torments can take him from me."

FIRST CHRISTIAN KINGDOM
St. Gregory the Illuminator (c. 257–332) went to Armenia at a time when the king, Tiridates III, was persecuting the church, and in 301 persuaded Tiridates to embrace Christianity. The king then encouraged his people to follow him into the new faith, which they did en masse – the first time that Christianity had become the official religion of a country.

❖

THE DEVELOPING CHURCH

B Y THE END OF THE SECOND century, the
church had spread across much of the empire
(p. 48). We get a glimpse of its size and influence
when we read the bishop of Rome, writing c. 250
that in his church "there are 46 priests, seven deacons,
seven sub-deacons, 42 acolytes, 52 exorcists, readers and
doorkeepers, more than 1,500 widows and beggars, all
of whom are supported by the grace and love of the Lord."

✤ DEBATES AND DIVISIONS ✤

The church's understanding of the deep and mysterious
truths at the heart of the gospel was gradually hammered
out through a series of internal debates. The greatest of
these were the attempts to understand the Trinity and
the Incarnation. The Bible teaches that God is one,
and that Father, Son, and Holy Spirit are God. It also
teaches that Christ is man and Christ is God. It does
not spell out how to understand these paradoxes.
The effort to do so took centuries and eventually
required the creation of a whole new vocabulary,
because the natures of the Trinity and of the
Incarnation are unique.

The orthodox descriptions of these mysteries were
finally to be fully developed at the great councils of
the fourth and fifth centuries (pp. 60-63). Previously,
a number of attempts to describe them lost sight of
Christ's humanity in their efforts to do justice to his
divinity, or vice versa, and so fell into heresy. Two
such attempts were made by the advocates of the two
schools of Monarchianism, a heresy which began in
Rome in c. 190. The name refers to the fear that
talking about Jesus as God endangered the *monarchia*,
the unity and authority of God the Father. One school
of monarchianists, in response, tried to make Jesus less
than God. Theodotus of Byzantium was expelled from
the church at Rome in c. 190 for asserting that Christ
was a mere man, in whom God was specially present.
His heresy did not end there. It was powerfully put
forward by Paul of Samosata, bishop of Antioch from
260, who was condemned by a synod in his own city
in 268 for suggesting that Christ was only a man, pen-
etrated by the divine *ousia*, or "substance."

Others tried to preserve the *monarchia* by uniting
Christ to the Father so closely that his distinct personhood
was lost, as the Roman Sabellius did early in the third
century when he asserted that Father, Son, and Spirit
were simply different modes of the same being. This
school of Monarchianism became known as
Modalism, Sabellianism, or Patripassianism (from the
Latin for "father suffers") – the last because, if true, it
would mean that the Father suffered on the cross.

The debate occupied the energies of many, including
two Roman presbyters, Hippolytus and Callistus, who
clashed over their views on the Trinity. They were to
clash again when Callistus, having become bishop of
Rome in 217, had to face one of the thorniest problems
of the early church: what to do with the Christians who
had briefly reverted to paganism in the face of imperial
persecution?

Some bishops refused to readmit them, others simply
imposed penance. Callistus took the generous attitude;
Hippolytus opposed him. In response to the crisis, a
group of Hippolytus's followers met and elected him

THE CRYPT OF THE POPES
*Nine popes of the mid-third century are buried in the Crypt of the Popes, in the catacomb of St.
Callistus in Rome. In the center is the tomb of Pope Sixtus II (r. 257–58). The crypt lay abandoned
for almost 1,500 years until rediscovered by Giovanni Battista de Rossi in the late 1800s.*

THE CATACOMBS

LIKE their pagan ancestors, the Christians at Rome considered the burial of their dead a most sacred duty and the responsibility of the whole church. Collections were made regularly to pay for the burial of members of the community. For reasons of hygiene and space, Roman law prohibited burial within the city precincts, so the Christians of the early centuries adopted the pagan practice of burial in underground chambers, outside the city limits.

One set of burial chambers was at a place called Kata Kumbas, "at the hollows," just outside Rome on the Appian Way. From that name, such chambers have since come to be called catacombs. Although not unique to Rome, the greatest number of catacombs is found near the precincts of the imperial city, and to this day over 60 have been explored by archaeologists.

The catacombs give us much precious information about the life and death of the early Christians. By reading their sepulchral inscriptions, we can know what rank they occupied in society, what the average life expectancy was, as well as their occupations. This opens up to us the world of the early Christians, and their art speaks eloquently of their faith in the risen Christ.

In general such cemeteries were excavated below the property of wealthy Christian families. Most cemeteries contained the bodies of several martyrs venerated for the

EQUAL IN DEATH
At first Christians buried their dead in long tunnels or galleries in which little distinguished the wealthy from the poor because they prized their equality before God. As time passed, however, the rich constructed small chambers where several members of a family could be buried together.

witness of their lives to the point of death. Such tombs became the sites of pilgrimage. In time, after the end of the imperial persecutions of Christians at the beginning of the fourth century, special churches were built above or near the tombs of saints, most famously St. Peter's Basilica. The majority of those buried in the catacombs, however, were simple Christians. The burial rites were carried out at night. Sometimes the Eucharist was celebrated. On the anniversary of their death, relatives gathered at the tomb to share a meal and remember them.

LATER HISTORY

The third century was a period of expansion for the catacombs, as many members of Rome's aristocratic class were converted to Christianity. The numbers swelled even further after the accession of Constantine in the early fourth century, and three-quarters of the catacombs date from this time. When Roman power declined thereafter, the catacombs became vulnerable to theft. In 537 the Goths raided and sacked several of the subterranean cemeteries. In 755 Pope Stephen II (r. 752–57) gave orders for the bodies of the martyrs to be brought from the catacombs to the safety of churches within the city walls, where they were interred with very great reverence and where they still remain. Henceforth it was deemed unsafe to continue the practice of burial in the catacombs, and they gradually fell into disuse.

CATACOMB ART FROM THE VIA LATINA CATACOMB
Due to the dark, cramped space, the art of the catacombs was simple and perfunctory. Though basic, it served to record the memory of the dead and, with simple biblical scenes, to inspire the living. This picture shows Moses and the Israelites crossing the Red Sea, with the Egyptians behind them (p.17).

❝ Daily we read the scriptures and experience dryness of soul until God grants food to satisfy the soul's hunger ❞

ORIGEN

bishop of Rome. Thus Hippolytus became the first "antipope." The schism continued through the pontificates of Urban and Pontianus, who succeeded Callistus in 222.

In order to restore unity, both the legitimate pope, Pontianus, and the antipope, Hippolytus, resigned in 235, when the two were exiled to Sardinia by the emperor Maximin Thrax. Reconciled on the island, they soon met their death as martyrs. The issue of what to do with the lapsed was to raise itself again, with more intensity, in future persecutions.

✦ THE ALEXANDRIAN FATHERS ✦

In the early third century, Christian theology was taken to new heights of intellectual sophistication by two theologians based in the great city of Alexandria, on the north coast of Egypt. The site of the most famous library in the ancient world – containing over half a million volumes – Alexandria had been an intellectual center for centuries. By the late second century, it was the site of a great school for catechumens (those studying the faith to prepare themselves for baptism). Yet Christianity was still on the defensive against pagan philosophy and religion.

This began to change from 190, when Clement of Alexandria (c. 150–215) began to direct the school of catechumens. He was more at home in the world of Greek philosophy than any Christian teacher before him and continued the work that the apologists (pp. 46-47) had begun, going beyond them to create an entire Christian philosophy of a depth and subtlety that pagans had to respect. His learning did not conflict with his faith: Clement looked to

Christ as the great teacher, the *logos* or "Word of God." "Just as night," Clement wrote, "would cover everything in spite of the stars, if the sun did not exist, so also, if we had not known the Word, and been illuminated by him, we would not have been any different from the fowls which are fed in darkness, and prepared for death."

After Clement comes the greatest name associated with the city of Alexandria: the theologian Origen (185–254). Most of his enormous output takes the form of sermons and commentaries on Scripture, on which he brought to bear his deep learning in Platonic and other philosophy. He developed the theory that

ORIGEN

A NATIVE of Alexandria, the son of pious Christian parents, Origen was greatly affected when his father, Leonidas, was martyred in 202 and as a young man decided to become a teacher of the faith. Origen studied in his native city and taught there for 28 years, becoming legendary for his learning. He lived on little food or sleep, studying the Bible for hours every day until he knew most of it by heart. He was a famously prolific writer; Jerome claims he wrote some 2,000 works, saying, "Who could ever read all that Origen wrote?" The bishops of Jerusalem and Caesarea ordained him in 230. His own bishop objected, as his permission had not been asked, and two synods at Alexandria stripped Origen of his license to teach as a priest. Humiliated, he stayed at Caesarea, still writing voluminously. Tortured in the persecution of Decius in 250, he was then released, dying in 254.

CHRISTIANS IN PRAYER – A THIRD-CENTURY FRESCO

Clement of Alexandria described prayer, simply, as "conversation with God." St. John Damascene later said that it was "the raising of heart and mind to God." In a book such as this it is easy to forget that the heartbeat of the church has always been the life of prayer of its members. History can record the doings of bishops and theologians, but, for Christians, the primary reality is the relationship of the church with Christ, an unseen reality wherever Christians follow their Lord's injunction to "worship in spirit and in truth." For the believer, this worship is at the heart of the "work of God," of which history books record only the surface.

THE FATAL LIBELLUS
The words on this libellus *read: "Here present and conforming to the order I have made a libation. I, Aurelia Demos, present this declaration. I, Aurelius Irenacus, wrote it for him as he is illiterate." Failure to make the sacrifice was cause for execution.*

each biblical text has multiple levels of meaning – the literal, the moral, and the spiritual – partly as a way of coping with passages whose literal meaning is obscure or seemingly contradictory. This approach was to be enormously influential.

He also wrote *Contra Celsum*, a long, carefully argued treatise against a pagan critic of Christianity, Celsus of Alexandria, and a book on the problem of evil. Although Origen was posthumously challenged on grounds of orthodoxy, he was quite aware of the need to be faithful to the traditions handed down in the church. He wrote, "The teaching of the church has been handed down through an order of succession from the apostles, and remains in the churches even until the present day. That alone is to be believed which is not at variance with the ecclesiastical and apostolic tradition." He went through torture to witness to the orthodox faith.

The persecution in which Origen was tortured was the first empire-wide crackdown on the church. It was the work of Emperor Decius, who gained power in 249. Threatened by war on the borders, he wished to return to the ancient gods of Rome and ensure the loyalty of his subjects.

❖ PERSECUTION ACROSS THE EMPIRE ❖

Decius issued a decree whereby all who offered sacrifice to an image of the emperor were given a letter attesting to their obedience, called a *libellus*. Those who did not possess such a letter were liable to torture and execution. Among the casualties were the bishops of Rome, Antioch, and Jerusalem. Others, including the bishops of Carthage and Alexandria, fled into hiding. Several bishops abandoned their positions. Cyprian of Carthage records how bishops Martialis and Basilides in Spain bowed to pressure to offer sacrifice to the image of the emperor.

Decius was killed in battle in 251, which the church saw as divine retribution, but the persecutions did not end. Cornelius, the bishop of Rome, was sent into exile by the emperor Valerian in 253, and in 257 a decree was issued: "The most sacred emperors Valerian and his son Gallienus command that there shall be no meetings [of Christians] in any place, and that they shall not frequent the cemeteries. If anyone fails to observe this beneficial precept, he shall be beheaded." Which is exactly what happened to scores of Christians.

At the same time, the emperor demanded that bishops, presbyters, and deacons offer sacrifice to the gods. In 258 Sixtus, the bishop of Rome, and six of his deacons were arrested while carrying out the sacred liturgy and were immediately executed. Bishop Cyprian of Carthage, one of the greatest leaders and theologians of the early church, was beheaded.

During these years the problem of how to treat those who lapsed in the face of persecution raised its head once more. After the persecution of Decius, Novatian, a presbyter of Rome, took exception to the perceived leniency of Pope Cornelius. Novatian succeeded in having himself elected antipope in 251 and went on to found a sect. He was martyred in 258, but his sect survived in Rome until it was outlawed through the determination of Pope Innocent I (r. 401–17), and even longer in Constantinople.

Fortunately the next emperor, Gallienus (r. 260–68), published an edict of toleration in 261, ending the penultimate persecution of Christians in the Roman Empire and giving the church 40 years of peace.

GRIDIRON MARTYR
Of all the victims of the persecutions of the 250s the most famous now was one of the humblest then. He was a lowly deacon called Lawrence, arrested with Pope Sixtus in 258. The sixth-century account of his martyrdom relates that he was condemned to be roasted alive over a grill. After a few minutes, Lawrence said to his captors, "You can turn me over now, I am done on that side." Those few words, whether apocryphal or true, have earned his memory undying fame.

❖

CHRISTIAN CENTER
In the third century North Africa was one of the most heavily Christianized areas of the Roman Empire. Its leading church center was at Carthage, near modern Tunis (*above, now only a ruin*). North Africa was the first Latin-speaking church – the churches in Rome and Gaul were still largely Greek speaking in 200 – and produced some of the greatest early theologians, including Tertullian and Augustine.

❖

THE GREAT PERSECUTION

PRELUDE TO TRAGEDY

The ferociously anti-Christian neo-Platonist philosopher Porphyry led an intellectual assault on Christianity from 270 onwards. He wrote a 15-volume work *Against the Christians*, c. 280–90, saying, "The evangelists were the inventors, not the historians, of those things they record about Jesus." Other influential pagans such as Hierocles, the bitterly anti-Christian neo-Platonist governor of Bithynia in Asia Minor, encouraged the junior emperor Galerius in his desire to "correct all things according to the ancient laws and public discipline of the Romans."

❖

THE FOUR EMPERORS

Diocletian divided the empire between four emperors *(above)* with himself as their chief. One of the four, Galerius, led the attacks on the church, but then on his deathbed in 311 revoked the edicts of persecution, decreed that Christians might "exist again," and asked them to pray "for our good estate."

❖

IN 298, DURING pagan sacrifices at a temple in Antioch, the pagan priests accused the Christians of disrupting the ceremony. An ugly scene took place, and in the end the troops had to intervene. It was the prelude of the bloodiest persecution of all.

❖ DIOCLETIAN AND GALERIUS ❖

Diocletian, the senior emperor, had been tolerant of the Christians for the 20 years of his reign, as his wife and daughter were probably Christians. Galerius, the caesar (junior emperor), was bitterly opposed to the Christians. After he won a decisive victory over the Persians in 296, his influence increased. In 300 an imperial edict commanded all soldiers to offer

> ## "SO MANY SUFFERED THAT THE MURDEROUS AXE WAS DULLED, AND THE EXECUTIONERS GREW WEARY"
>
> ### EUSEBIUS OF CAESAREA

sacrifices, an order that at once compromised the numerous Christians in the army. Death was the ultimate punishment. Three years later, further edicts were published, demanding the destruction of the places of worship, the confiscation of the Scriptures, and the arrest of the ecclesiastics. Still, Diocletian restrained Galerius: there was to be no bloodshed. Finally in 304, with Diocletian ill, Galerius extended the edict to all citizens of the empire, who were ordered to offer sacrifices to the gods on pain of death. Throughout the empire executions took place, and several Christian communities were wiped out in Africa, Egypt, and Palestine.

Such was the public backlash to the bloodbath that in 305 Diocletian was obliged to resign. In the West the new emperors, Constantius and Maxentius, revoked the edicts and granted toleration once more. In the

East Galerius, who had succeeded Diocletian as senior emperor, redoubled the persecution. It was still not enough: he could not stamp out Christianity. One contemporary Christian writer, Lactantius, even saw God's hand in the troubles: "There is another cause why God permits persecutions to be carried out against us, that the people of God may be increased."

Despite his continued hatred of the Christians, in 311 Galerius was forced to proclaim a Protocol of Toleration, which restored the rights of the Christians to meet in public and worship throughout the East. To the Christians who had suffered through the years of persecution and uncertainty, this was a new dawn of a golden era. Little could they have imagined the privileges they would soon enjoy under the new emperor,

THE MARTYRS OF THE CATACOMBS
This painting attempts to imagine the persecutions. Because Christians held to their faith, people asked why "neither loss of goods, nor of the light, nor bodily pain or tortures deter them."

Constantine (*pp. 58-59*). As with previous persecutions, in the aftermath there was a debate about how to treat those who lapsed under persecution. Unfortunately, this debate after the Great Persecution was to lead to a permanent split in the North African church.

❖ SCHISM WITHOUT HEALING ❖

Eighty North African bishops objected to the ordination of Caecilian, bishop of Carthage, in 311 because it had been performed by a bishop who had handed over the sacred books to the persecutors. They elected a rival bishop. This was the beginning of a permanent schism that still divided the church in North Africa when the Muslims invaded (*pp. 88-89*).

Both sides appealed to the emperor Constantine. He declared for Caecilian and against his rival, Donatus. The Donatists saw this as persecution, asking, "What has the emperor to do with the church?" and founded a church that was to have, at its peak, 500 bishops.

The new sect skilfully took advantage of an existing split between the rich, Latin-speaking citizens of the coastal cities and the poor Punic speakers of the hills and the hinterland. By having services in Punic instead of Latin, the Donatists were able to take on a mantle of local patriotism. They also exploited practical resources such as control of the main bakery in the city of Hippo to reward their supporters. In addition, they claimed that theirs was the true church. Augustine (*pp. 68-69*) summed up the orthodox response to this: "The clouds roll with thunder that the House of the Lord shall be built throughout the earth; and these frogs sit in their marshes and croak – 'We are the only Christians!'"

Nevertheless, the Donatists flourished. They were to survive an attempt by the imperial commissioner Count Macarius to crush them by force in 347. It took Augustine, backed by the power of the state, to break their strength; the church had to turn persecutor to do it, in a last ironic postscript to the Great Persecution.

> *The servants of God are those who are hated by the world*
> **DONATIST SLOGAN**

Christian Empire

313–590

AFTER ALMOST two and a half centuries of persecution by Roman emperors, Christians were given permission to worship in public for the first time in 311. Then Constantine, the first Christian emperor, became a generous patron and protector of the church; when it was threatened by the Arian heresy, Constantine convened his bishops to meet at a "general council" of the church, the first since the council held by the apostles at Jerusalem. Further councils were assembled at moments of grave theological and pastoral tension to resolve problems that affected the wider church.

Emperors and bishops worked hand in hand as the church, benefiting from the patronage of Christian emperors, was increasingly modeled along imperial lines. The arts (architecture, sculpture, mosaic work, and music) flourished, while the sees (of Rome, Constantinople, Jerusalem, Antioch, and Alexandria) increased in prestige. Theology developed through the contributions of such intellectual giants as Basil, Gregory, and Athanasius in the East, and Ambrose and Augustine in the West. This era also saw the development of monasticism and remarkable evangelistic efforts by missionaries who preached the gospel in lands as far apart as Ireland, India, Ethiopia, and Georgia.

Emperor Justinian I, champion of Christian orthodoxy

CHRISTIANIZING THE EMPIRE

FEW, IF ANY, of the Christians suffering persecution as the fourth century began could have imagined that before a hundred years had passed, pagan temples would be closed and Christianity would be the official religion of the empire. Before that could come about, there were problems to be resolved.

✤ CONSTANTINE THE GREAT ✤

The son of the tolerant emperor Constantius Chlorus and his Christian wife, Helena, Constantine the Great (r. 306–37) succeeded his father as coemperor of the western part of the Roman Empire. As coemperor, he ruled alongside his rival Maxentius, who had already occupied the city of Rome.

In 312 Constantine defeated Maxentius at the Battle of the Milvian Bridge, outside Rome. Constantine's Christian sympathies became apparent just before the battle when, as a result of a vision he had (*see caption, below left*), he ordered the monogram of Christ to be painted on his soldiers' shields. On entering Rome as the victorious sole emperor of the West, Constantine set about establishing religious toleration and ending persecution by the pagan Roman Empire. In 313 he met with Licinius, emperor of the East, and issued a decree that was published at Milan. The "Edict of Milan" granted freedom of conscience and worship to all religions and restored Christian property.

> **"[AT THE VICTORY OF CONSTANTINE] THERE WAS TAKEN AWAY FROM MAN ALL FEAR OF THOSE WHO HAD FORMERLY OPPRESSED THEM"**
>
> BISHOP EUSEBIUS OF CAESAREA, CHURCH HISTORIAN

However, the two emperors soon clashed, and Licinius, a pagan, retaliated by resuming his persecution of Christians in the East. The political situation now took on the mantle of a religious war, with Constantine finally defeating Licinius in battle at Chrysopolis in 324.

✤ CONSTANTINE'S REFORMS ✤

As emperor of both East and West, Constantine reformed the structures of the empire. He afforded a new status to bishops, equal in rank to senators, making them almost like state officers. In theory, the church and the state were soon as one, although disunity and controversy were to persist both within the church and between the church and state. While Constantine now favored Christianity, he did not make it the official or "established" religion of the empire. He did, however, give presents, endowments, and property to Christian churches and built several basilicas, including St. Peter's in Rome, used Christian symbols on his coinage and Roman standards, and declared Sunday a rest day, replacing the weekly celebration of Mithras. He

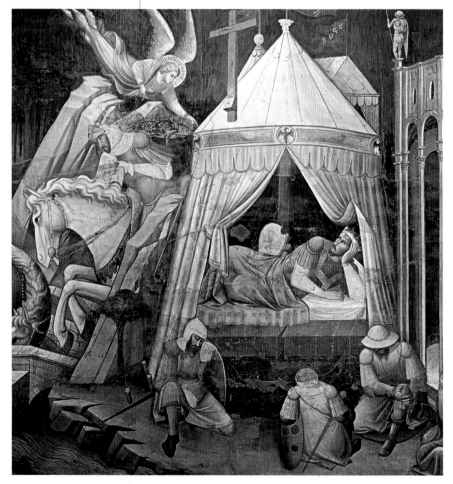

THE DREAM THAT LED TO CONSTANTINE'S CONVERSION
Maxentius's defeat at the Battle of the Milvian Bridge represented not only a political victory for Constantine but the beginning of the "church of Constantine." According to Eusebius (p. 61), Constantine had a vision of a cross of light emblazoned against the sun and saw the Latin words for "in this sign you will win." The Christian emblem he adopted is the Chi-Rho symbol (p. 41).

CONSTANTINOPLE
The meeting point of East and West, Constantinople (modern-day Istanbul) became one of the great world capitals. It was renowned for its political and religious power and wealth of art and architecture.

baptized on his deathbed. Yet Christians were grateful to Constantine. He gave them the opportunity to become respectable communities of faith protected by the state, publicly planting and nurturing churches that were centers for attracting Christian converts.

✤ IMPERIAL INFLUENCE ✤

The influence of the emperor over church affairs was now vast. Constantine attempted to unite the church, but after his death the feuding between his sons threatened to ruin the empire: one son adopted Arianism *(pp. 60–61)*, while the other remained orthodox in his beliefs. Julian the Apostate, who came to power in 361, also threatened to end Christian hopes by renewing the persecution of believers *(see also side column)*. However, his influence was short-lived when, after less than two years, he was killed in battle in Mesopotamia. His successor, Jovian (r. 363–64), removed Julian's recent ban on Christianity and instead patronized the Christian church, as did subsequent emperors in an empire that was once again divided.

✤ A STATE RELIGION ✤

In 379 Flavius Theodosius (r. 379–95) succeeded the emperor of the East, Valens, who was killed at Adrianople fighting the Visigoths. Theodosius was an Orthodox Christian opposed to any challenge to the Orthodox church, and in 380 he made Christianity the compulsory religion of the state. He subsequently closed down all the pagan temples in 391, forbidding any practice of pagan rites. "It is our will," he decreed, "that all the peoples we rule shall practice that religion that Peter the Apostle transmitted to the Romans."

Following Theodosius's example, many people converted to Christianity; as the fifth century dawned, Christians made up a majority of the population. Missionaries continued to set up churches and teach the Christian faith in Greek and Latin. Although Christianity was favored in the towns as the official religion of the empire, in the country it was slower to take root. Even today, ancient holy wells and place-names bear witness to a stubborn pagan past.

financed new copies of the Bible *(p. 61)* and expressed Christian ideals in the laws he introduced to protect children, slaves, peasants, and prisoners.

Constantine also tried to unite East and West under his rule and, in order to be at the center of his empire, moved east in 327 to a new capital, Roma Nova, later called Constantinople, which was built on the site of the ancient city of Byzantium on the Bosphorus. Though the empire ruled from Constantinople still thought of itself as Roman, it has since come to be known as the Byzantine Empire. As a result of Constantine's move, the bishop of Rome became the most prominent figure in the West.

Despite these policies, pagan practices and immoral behavior still persisted. Constantine himself had his wife and eldest son strangled on charges of conspiracy shortly before his death at Constantinople in 337 and, like many Christians of the day, was only

PAGAN LOYALTIES
Despite the Edict of Milan, pagan affinities remained deeply entrenched in the upper echelons of Roman society for decades.

> **❝** *It is a scandal that there is not a single Jew who is a beggar, and that the godless Galileans care not only for their own poor but for ours as well* **❞**
>
> **JULIAN THE APOSTATE**

JULIAN THE APOSTATE
Paganism enjoyed a brief revival under Emperor Julian (r. 361–63), whom Christians branded "the Apostate." A nephew of Constantine, Julian had been brought up as a Christian but renounced his faith in his twenties in favor of pagan deities. He was fascinated by classical literature and did his best to revive the traditional pagan religions. Once emperor, he banned Christian teachers from Roman schools and refused to allow Christian imagery to be displayed in public. Julian was not a popular emperor, however, and many Christian believers considered his death in battle to be divine punishment for his actions.

✤

CRISIS IN THE EMPIRE

AS CONSTANTINE STOOD before the church's first universal council, he spoke briefly: "Division in the church," he said, "is worse than war." This formal meeting, which the emperor convened in 325 to deal with a heretical crisis, was the first of what was to be a series of four councils that regulated discipline and defined theological doctrine in the Christian church.

✤ THE THREAT TO THE CHURCH ✤

In 319 a serious problem threatened the church. In Alexandria, Egypt, a Libyan presbyter, or priest, Arius (256–336), began teaching a new doctrine that contradicted orthodox beliefs about what was to become defined as the Trinity: the relationship between God,

Jesus, and the Holy Spirit (*p. 63*). Arius announced, "If the Father begat the Son, then he who was begotten had a beginning in existence, and from this it follows there was a time when the Son was not." In other words, Arius denied Christ's true divinity, arguing that God created Christ from nothing. The bishop of Alexandria tried to silence the priest, who was eventually forced into exile for his subversive teaching.

ATHANASIUS

THE most famous opponent of Arianism was Athanasius. He succeeded Alexander of Alexandria as bishop in 328, a time when the Arian controversy was dividing the Egyptian church. He was to face banishment from his diocese of Alexandria on five occasions because he refused to abandon his orthodox position, and he was subjected to hardship and harassment for most of his ecclesiastical career. During his periods of exile he went to Trier in northern Gaul, Rome, and from 365 to 66 he lived with monks in the Egyptian desert. His tenacity, despite opposition from all sides, including several emperors, earned Athanasius the sobriquet, "Athanasius against the world." He is also famous for his writings against Arian, pagan, and Jewish opposition, and for his *Life of St. Anthony*, which did much to promote monasticism.

Those who supported Arius's arguments and those who remained orthodox became fierce opponents; contemporary reports record that blood was frequently spilled. Christianity was sowing the seeds of violent division.

Constantine had already encountered Christian controversy in the form of a dispute that arose in North Africa in 311 over the election of a bishop of Carthage, Caecilian (*p. 55*). The Arian crisis, however, was much more serious. Arius was rapidly gaining followers, and the alarmed bishops in the East turned to their imperial protector for help.

✤ FURY AMONG THE BISHOPS ✤

Constantine eventually responded to the Arian crisis by convening the first general council. He wrote to 1,800 bishops across the Roman Empire and ordered them to meet at Nicea (modern-day Iznik in Turkey) in 325. It is thought that between 220 and 250 bishops actually attended. Most of these were from the East, where Arianism was most rife. The bishop of Cordoba, Hosius, was placed in charge of the proceedings together with

THE CONDEMNATION OF ARIUS
This sixteenth-century painting shows some of the bishops at Nicea, with Constantine sitting just to the right of the open Gospels, about to condemn Arius (pictured beneath their feet).

THE ORIGINS OF THE BIBLE

❖

THE word "bible" originates from the Greek *biblion*, "book," drived from *biblos*, "papyrus." Produced from the flattened stems of papyrus plants, scrolls were used for Hebrew writings in the ancient world, as revealed by biblical scrolls discovered in the Qumran Desert *(p. 19)* in the 1960s, which are dated at between 250 BC and 70 AD.

OLD & NEW TESTAMENTS
In the third to second centuries BC the Hebrew Bible was translated into a Greek version, the Septuagint, and Hebrew biblical writings were fixed into three divisions – Torah (the Law), the Prophets, and the Writings – in c. 164 BC. These two Old Testament versions were in circulation in Jesus' time. After Jesus' death, the documentations of his teachings and Paul's sermons – among others – soon constituted a large body of literature.

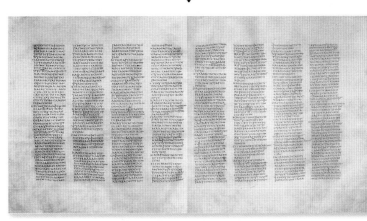

CODEX SINAITICUS
By the second century AD, vellum was increasingly replacing the use of papyrus. During Constantine's reign, more church buildings were constructed and as a result, more Bibles were needed. The emperor wrote to Eusebius of Caesarea, ordering "fifty volumes on prepared vellum, easy to read and conveniently portable, by professional scribes with an exact understanding of their craft." This codex, or manuscript (above), *looking much like a modern Bible, is the kind of volume that Constantine commissioned.*

They were collected, copied, and distributed, but it wasn't until about 150 that the heretic Marcion compiled a list of the writings and letters *(pp. 42-43)*. A number of church authorities reacted to this by trying to set their own list. In his 39th annual Easter Festal letter to the Egyptian church in 367, Athanasius compiled a definitive list of 27 writings to be included in the New Testament as trustworthy and inspired by God. Athanasius's list, which corresponds to the final canon, was confirmed by Pope Damasus at a council in Rome in 382 after taking advice from the scholar Jerome *(p. 62)*, and by a council at Carthage in 397. Both councils also defined the canon of the Old Testament to include the Old Testament Apocrypha *(p. 20)*. None of the early general councils of the Church felt it necessary to address the issue.

---

two ambassadors (priests) representing the absent bishop of Rome, Sylvester. Arius had also been invited to attend and, in the middle of his explanation of his beliefs, he broke into a chant of his teachings that was sung by his followers. It included the phrase, "The Son is not equal to the Father," causing consternation and fury among the bishops present.

The bishops condemned Arius and came up with what they thought was a solution to the problem. They drew up a statement of belief, known as the Creed of Nicea, to explain the relationship between God and Jesus, who was "of one substance with the Father." All except two of the bishops signed this creed, which further confessed faith "in one Lord Jesus Christ … true God of true God."

The Arians refused to accept defeat. Although they were declared heretics by the bishops, they re-

ORTHODOX CHRISTIANS FLEE THE ARIANS
Despite Constantine's efforts at unification, Christians and Arians continued to clash. For over a century Arianism fought for religious supremacy, spreading from North Africa across the empire as far as Germany where it became popular. The movement survived until the end of the fifth century, and Arius's ideas can still be traced in some groups today.

grouped to oppose the decisions of the council. Despite the unsatisfactory outcome of this first general church council, Constantine continued to endorse the teachings of Nicea while waiting for a compromise to be reached.

❖ DEFENDING DIVINITY ❖
Despite all the outbreaks of violence between orthodox Christians and Arians, progress had been made in theological thinking. The most formidable threat to Arius and his followers was the theologian Athanasius (c. 293–374), then a secretary to Alexander, bishop of Alexandria, and a great defender of orthodoxy. It was Athanasius *(see also box, opposite)* who labored to find a formula acceptable to all the bishops at the Council of Nicea, and who wrote a series of books between 336 and 366 in defense of Christ's true divinity.

EUSEBIUS
Bishop of Caesarea c. 315–40, Eusebius was caught up in the Arian controversy at the Council of Nicea. He was suspected of being an Arian sympathizer after he argued for moderation. Highly regarded by Constantine, he was commissioned to write the emperor's biography and a history of the church, a principal source for later Christian historians.

❖

THE HUMANITY OF JESUS
Whether Christ had a human nature, divine nature, or both, became a controversial debate in the church during the fifth century. Theologians such as Nestorius and other scholars from Antioch in Syria were accused of exaggerating the humanity of the man Jesus.

After Athanasius's death in 373, the orthodox position was sustained by the Cappadocian Fathers, Basil the Great, Gregory of Nyssa, and Gregory of Nazianzus *(see side column)*, who continued to clarify theological terminology. They made a distinction between the Greek words for "substance" and "person," recognizing the equality of the Father and the Son in one substance and their distinction in two persons.

❖ THE SECOND COUNCIL ❖

Although Arius died in 336, his teachings still had supporters. In 381, Emperor Theodosius summoned the bishops to his imperial residence at Constantinople. The council reaffirmed the Creed of Nicea, to which it added a statement about the Holy Spirit *(see caption, right)*. The reworked formula, still used in the Christian church today, was renamed the Nicene Creed. However, the council failed to completely resolve the Arian question. Arianism continued to survive among the Goths and other Germanic communities.

❖ TWO PERSONS IN ONE? ❖

Arianism was not the only heresy the church had to deal with during the fourth and fifth centuries. Many theologians, struggling to deepen their understanding of the mystery of God, veered away from orthodox views. During this time, different schools argued for two principal extremes regarding Christ, exaggerating either his humanity or his divinity.

Such heretical teaching prompted the Council of Ephesus to be convened in 431: a priest, Nestorius, appeared to argue that there were two persons in Christ, rather than the orthodox view that there was a single person, both God and man. Nestorius did not deny Christ's divinity, but he refused to attribute to a divine nature the human acts and sufferings of Jesus. He also argued that Mary, mother of Jesus, could not be titled "Mother of God" if she was mother of the man, Jesus. The council condemned Nestorius's doctrines, and he was exiled to Upper Egypt.

❖ THE FOURTH COUNCIL ❖

Twenty years later, in 451, Emperor Marcion informed Leo, bishop of Rome, that he had called a council at Chalcedon to deal with the priest Eutyches, who questioned the two natures of Christ by exaggerating his divinity. Leo sent a letter to the council that argued for two equal natures, human and divine; otherwise, it would be like the divine Jesus simply wearing a human mask – teaching that has become orthodox Christian doctrine. A contemporary report records that after the letter was read out loud, the bishops sprang to their feet saying, "Peter has spoken through Leo." However, Leo's sense of power was soon dispelled: the bishops voted to recognize Constantinople as second only to Rome. It was an ominous presage to stormy relations between the two powers and rival cities for centuries to come.

THE DIVINITY OF JESUS
Theologians from Alexandria and the priest Eutyches emphasized Christ's divine nature and lordship over heaven and earth.

AN ORTHODOX VIEW OF THE TRINITY

Much theological debate in the fourth and fifth centuries concerned the relationship between God, Jesus, and the Holy Spirit. The doctrine of this "Trinity" was embodied in creeds at the councils of Nicea and Constantinople. The Nicene Creed states: "We believe in one God … and in one Lord Jesus Christ, the Son of God, begotten of the Father, only-begotten, that is, from the substance of the Father, God from God … begotten not made." The Council of Constantinople added the statement: "We believe in the Holy Spirit, the Lord and Lifegiver, who proceeds from the Father, who with the Father and Son is worshiped and glorified."

THE CHURCH GAINS POWER

BASILICA PLAN

Typically an oblong building ending in a semicircular apse, basilicas were favored by Constantine's architects as they provided suitable spaces for people to gather to celebrate the liturgy. Clergy were seated in the apse, around the bishop, with the altar placed near where the apse met the nave. By the end of the fifth century, the apse was usually placed at the east end (a strict rule in the Byzantine Empire), so both people and priests could pray facing Jerusalem, the Holy City.

❖

CHRISTIAN COINS

Within three years after the Battle of the Milvian Bridge, Constantine had authorized the Chi-Rho symbol (p. 41) to adorn public buildings and had coins, such as the one above, stamped with the image invoking the protection of Christ.

❖

THE SIZE AND STATUS OF the church and its character were transformed in the fourth century. First, as the church grew rapidly in wealth and numbers, it began to construct splendid church buildings and magnificent liturgies (forms of church service) to celebrate in them. Then, its wealth and vast influence began to raise issues about abuse of money and power that have dogged it ever since. Perhaps worst of all, as the church became allied with the state, the state began to use force to promote orthodoxy and punish heresy, so beginning a bloody tradition that has repeatedly marred Christian history until recent times.

❖ THE NEW SPLENDOR ❖

Soon after the Edict of Milan in 313, Christians began to take advantage of their new-found wealth and freedom and started to build churches. Previously, the earliest Christian buildings had been shrines rather than churches. A few pagan temples, such as the Pantheon in Rome and the Parthenon in Athens, had been converted into churches, but Christian architects had avoided building to the plan of pagan temples as they abhorred the connection with those who had so recently persecuted them. Constantine's reign suddenly marked the beginning of specifically Christian architecture, and the emperor's architects chose to adopt the Roman basilica form for this new type of building.

The Roman basilicas were a cross between a place of public assembly, a law court, a meeting place for businessmen, and a king's judgment hall (the word comes from the Greek *basileus*, "king"). They were important buildings, situated at the heart of every Roman city.

The Christian architects adapted the pagan plan, installing an altar near the large, rounded recess, or apse, at one end of the edifice, where the king or judge sat; the bishop was now to take the place of the pagan dignitary. The congregation itself crowded into the body of the basilica. Whereas in pagan basilicas the entrance doors were at the side, in the Christian basilicas the doors were placed at the end opposite the apse. This basic structure has remained ever since as one of the most common styles of church building. In later centuries, Western churches were often elaborated into a cross shape, and Eastern churches into multidomed "cross and square" shapes. As church buildings changed, so too did the liturgy. The simple form of worship described by Justin Martyr (p. 40) was

> ❝ OUR WALLS GLITTER WITH GOLD ... YET CHRIST IS DYING AT OUR DOORS IN THE PERSON OF HIS POOR ❞
>
> **JEROME**

elaborated to become longer, grander, and more formal. This was partly to suit the new status of the church and the vast crowds that now attended services in huge buildings. It was also influenced by imperial splendor and a need to combat the popular appeal of Arianism by creating a dramatic spectacle, with splendid vestments and beautiful singing (by both congregation and choir). Arius himself had shown the way by setting his theology to catchy tunes; now writers such as Ambrose of Milan turned the tables on him by composing memorable hymns teaching orthodox theology.

The new forms of service were often very beautiful. The liturgies used in Eastern churches today are much the same as those developed in the East in the fourth and fifth centuries; the liturgies of the Catholic church are closely linked to those developed in the West.

AMBROSE OF MILAN
Ambrose had a high view of his office, saying, "Christ gave to his apostles the power of remitting sins, which has been transmitted by the apostles to the sacerdotal [priestly] office."

BASILICA OF SANTA SABINA, COMPLETED 432

The new services tended to increase the role and prestige of the clergy. By the end of the fourth century, the emphasis on the mystery and splendor of the Communion service had led to the altar being separated from the people in the main body, or nave, of the church by a curtain or screen (as shown above), further distancing the clergy and laity from each other.

RIGHTS AND PRIVILEGES

Since the time of Constantine, bishops have worn purple as their official color. Pure purple, which was a special dye, was worn only by the emperor himself. The bishops had all the rights and privileges of senators and, as senators wore a purple band to show their imperial dignity, so did bishops. Bishops also gained the senatorial right to travel using the imperial postal service, making it possible to hold many local synods as well as the four universal church councils. One pagan critic, Ammianus, said that they traveled so much, the system was bankrupted.

❖

❖ CLERICAL POWER ❖

The church's new wealth brought unforeseen problems. Having given Christian clergy privileges in 313, Constantine was, seven years later, already having to legislate to stop rich men from becoming clerics to avoid paying taxes.

With clerical power came violence: according to the pagan historian Ammianus Marcellinus, when Damasus defeated his rival Ursinus for the papacy in 366, "in the course of a single day, in the Christian basilica of Sicinius, one hundred and thirty-seven corpses were found." He added that the bishops of Rome "are free from money worries … dressing splendidly, feasting luxuriantly – their banquets are better than imperial ones. But they might be really happy if … they lived like provincial bishops, with harsh abstinence in eating and drinking, plain apparel, eyes cast to the ground – proclaiming themselves pure and reverent men."

❖ THE PRINCELY BISHOP ❖

Perhaps the most famous of all these provincial bishops was Ambrose of Milan. Originally the governor of the city, he was made bishop by popular acclaim in 374. He was a brilliant preacher, an able administrator, and a skilled evangelist – instrumental in Augustine's conversion. He invited monks to come from the East and establish monasteries in his diocese, helping the spread of monasticism in the West. Ambrose promoted the cult of relics, which grew hugely in importance throughout the fourth century. His views were very influential throughout the Middle Ages and beyond on everything from clerical poverty (unnecessary) to sex (he was against married bishops, fearing that clerical dynasties would be established), to different kinds of wealth (owning land is better than trade).

Ambrose publicly debated the leading pagan opponents of Christianity and won. He completed a great new basilica in Milan in 386 where he held daily mass, prayers several times a day, and special ceremonies to commemorate saints' days. This program would set the usual pattern for cathedrals throughout the Middle Ages.

Most remarkable of all, Ambrose forced the mighty emperor Theodosius to do public penance (*see side column*) in 390 after Theodosius had massacred thousands of civilians in Thessalonica. For an emperor to do this was unheard of. For the first time, the empire had bowed to the church.

PENANCE

Theodosius's penance came at a time when the practice of private confession was mostly replacing public penances. In the early church, penance appears to have been a largely public activity, following the biblical injunction to "confess your sins to one another" (James 5:16). By the mid-fifth century, private confession to a bishop or priest had become the norm. Later, manuals with lists of penances were developed for confessors to apply for particular sins, and priests were empowered to administer the sacrament of penance.

❖

MONASTICISM

F ROM THE MIDDLE of the third century onward, separate groups of men and women adopted a religious way of life that has been followed by hundreds of thousands of Christian believers through the centuries. Initially, the religious recluses living in the Egyptian desert devoted themselves to solitude and prayer, but after Anthony of Egypt introduced a rudimentary form of community life, religious fellowships flourished in the Byzantine Empire from the fourth century.

✤ PRAYING IN THE DESERT ✤

Wastelands and deserts had long exercised a powerful attraction for religious people. In the quiet of these barren lands men and women often searched for solitude, allowing them to concentrate on their search for God: Moses was in the desert near Mount Sinai when God spoke to him (Exodus 3); Jesus withdrew to the desert to pray before he began his public ministry. The hermits who settled in the deserts of the East usually lived near one another for practical reasons, such as safety. They prayed and meditated, fasted, and remained celibate, and met on Sundays for the Eucharist, sometimes meeting daily for common prayer. They were to become known as the Desert Fathers.

One such hermit was Anthony of Egypt (251–356). *The Life of Anthony*, a book attributed to Athanasius (*p. 60*), details Anthony's decision to retire to the desert. As a pious young man, he entered a church one day and heard an extract of the Gospel in which Jesus answered a rich ruler who asked how he might enter the kingdom of heaven: "There is one thing that you lack. Sell all you have and distribute the money among the poor, and you will have treasure in heaven. Then come, follow me" (Mark 10:21). Anthony

ANTHONY AND PAUL IN THE DESERT
This sixteenth-century painting depicts a meeting of the hermits Paul, the "greatest saint in the desert," and Anthony. Hermits lived an ascetic lifestyle; Anthony was described as "ever fasting.... He neither bathed his body with water ... nor did he ever wash his feet."

LEGACY OF SIMPLICITY
Still a monastery today, Monte Cassino was founded by Benedict of Nursia in 529 and became the principal monastery of the Benedictine order. Benedict and his sister, Scholastica, are buried in the crypt underneath the church.

was so struck by these words that he sold his belongings and gave the money to the poor. He lived in the desert, receiving spiritual direction from another hermit, and his reputation for holiness grew. His dedication to the gospel and the ordered discipline of his life inspired men and women to follow his way. He organized a community for these lay people to live together bound by simple vows of poverty and prayer, and they became the forerunners of monks.

❖ FROM HERMITS TO MONKS ❖

The move to found monasteries or settlements where religious people under vows – now known as monks – lived together was made by Pachomius (290–346). He encouraged members to share their work and meals and to celebrate the Eucharist and meditate on the message of the Bible together. He was also the first to write a rule to guide the members. The growth of this monastic lifestyle was rapid and extraordinary.

As well as organizing monasteries for men, Pachomius encouraged the foundation of similar settlements for women. Women were, at that time, still regarded as the property of their husbands, and those who did not marry seriously considered community life: such a life with other women offered them protection. The theologian Ambrose recommended this form of communal life to women, arguing that it would bring them freedom from a husband and allow them to devote themselves to prayer and good works. Jerome, for example, praised Paula, a Roman matron who became a nun, for her study of the Hebrew Scriptures.

There were still those who resisted communal life in an effort to take their ascetic life to an extreme. For instance, several monks chose to spend the rest of their lives on pillars. Simeon from Syria, for instance *(see side column)*, was venerated by the crowds who swarmed into the desert to ask his advice from the base of his pillar.

Another important figure in the development of monasticism was Basil of Cappadocia, one of the Cappadocian Fathers. Basil abandoned his career as a teacher in favor of a solitary life. Like Anthony, he was soon asked to share his wisdom with others. He wrote a rule, similar to that of Pachomius, urging monks to pray, to carry out good works for the sick and the poor, and to study the Bible. His rule is still observed in the East.

❖ MONASTICISM IN THE WEST ❖

The monasticism introduced by Martin of Tours *(see side column)* into the West was spread by St. Benedict of Nursia (480–547). As a young man, Benedict was drawn to prayer and meditation, and for three years he lived in a cave, attracting followers. He set up 12 monasteries before founding one at Monte Cassino, near Naples. Here he wrote a simple rule, guiding his monks in their day of prayer, manual work, study, and rest. He began his rule by explaining that he wished to establish a school of the Lord's service where nothing would be too difficult to discourage the fainthearted, nor anything too easy to leave the strong unchallenged. Benedict directed his followers to meet in church several times a day to pray the Psalms, listen to Bible readings, and meditate on them.

The Benedictine order has remained of enormous importance in the Catholic church to this day, especially in areas of prayer and study, and the Rule of Benedict is widely followed in the West. The rules of both Benedict and Basil were written not to limit or restrict the monks but rather, as Benedict once wrote, to be "a rule for beginners."

SIMEON STYLITES
Born in Sisan (in modern-day Turkey), Simeon moved into the Syrian desert in 423, where he erected a 6-ft (2-m) high stylite, or pillar. On top of this he placed a platform and lived on this for several years. The only time he descended was to move to an even higher pillar. The last pillar he lived on was 60 ft (18 m) high. He once received the emperor and gave kindly, if ascetic, advice on Christian living. He also inspired countless others to imitate him. After his death his pillar remained a pilgrimage destination, and a church was built on the site.

❖

BENEDICT PREACHES TO HIS DISCIPLES
Benedict's rule, composed in Latin, is simple and practical, with sensible admonitions and advice. Basil's rule was written in Greek and guided those who followed it to a different, more mystical development of monasticism.

AUGUSTINE: THE VICTORY OF GRACE

ONE OF THE MOST IMPORTANT figures in Christian history, St. Augustine, bishop of Hippo, was a prolific writer and theologian. For 1,000 years, Augustine was the most influential teacher in Christendom, and his writings are still valued today by many Christians. Born Augustine Aurelius in Tagaste (in modern-day Algeria), North Africa, in 354, he was the son of a pagan Roman

official and a devout Christian mother. North Africa was an important province of the Roman Empire in the middle of the fourth century, providing much of the empire's food supplies. The grip of Rome over its empire was slipping, however, and telltale signs of decay and stress were evident for all to see. Corruption in the government at Rome was common, and the empire was falling apart under waves of barbarian invasions. It was into this milieu that Augustine was propelled while still a boy, and during his life he had to deal with repeated pagan attacks against Christianity and the church.

❖ PROFLIGATE YOUTH ❖

As a boy, Augustine showed academic brilliance, and left home to study at Madaura and Carthage until his father's money ran out when he was about sixteen, whereupon he returned home. It was around this time that he began a relationship with a woman that would last for fifteen years. In his autobiography, *Confessions*, Augustine expressed some regret at the excesses of

> " OUR HEARTS ARE MADE FOR YOU, O LORD, AND ARE RESTLESS UNTIL THEY REST IN YOU "
>
> **AUGUSTINE**

his youth. Nonetheless, these formative years indicate a young man in search of meaning to his life.

When he was 19, Augustine began to explore the Persian philosophy Manichaeism in his search for philosophical truth. This school of thought combined Christian, Gnostic, and pagan elements, emphasizing the warring of light and dark, flesh and spirit. The teaching of Manes (c. 216–76) and his followers fascinated Augustine, and he chose to remain a disciple for nine years.

In 383, Augustine moved from Carthage to Rome, and, a year later, following the possibility of a teaching position in Milan, he went to live in the city. It was

SCHOLARLY BISHOP
This fresco of Augustine, from the Lateran Palace in Rome, may be the oldest-known picture of him. According to his biographer, Possidius, Augustine wrote more than 1,000 works in total, including 242 books. In this picture he is depicted as a scholar rather than a bishop, the scroll in his left hand and the opened Bible on the lectern in front of him reflecting his role as a theologian.

here that he again encountered his mother's religion. In *Confessions* he relates how one day he was sitting in a garden and overheard some children calling the Latin for take up and read. He absent-mindedly picked up a copy of Paul's letter to the Romans, which was nearby, and read the following verses: "Not in revelry and drunkenness, not in debauchery and licentiousness, not in quarrelling and jealousy, but put on the Lord Jesus Christ, and make no provision for the flesh to gratify its desires" (Romans 13:13–14). Deeply affected, he sought out the bishop of the city, Ambrose, and began to frequent the services at which the bishop preached. He decided to be baptized, and on the eve of Easter in the year 387 Ambrose baptized Augustine and his son Adeodatus.

In 391, Augustine was ordained a priest and returned to North Africa. Four years later he was elected bishop of Hippo (present-day Annaba in Algeria), where he remained until his death in 430.

OPTIMISTIC HERETIC
Pelagius, a British or perhaps Irish monk and theologian, denied the doctrine of original sin and maintained that the human will is capable of doing good without divine grace.

✤ BATTLING HERESIES ✤

Among the first difficulties Augustine had to combat as bishop were two heresies. North Africa was dominated by a group called the Donatists *(p. 55)*, who refused to accept as consecrated bishops any clergy who were suspected of compromise measures during the years of persecution in the empire. Augustine reacted to the crisis by writing that there could be no rival church and that the sacraments of Communion and baptism were effective through God's grace, not because of a priest's own righteousness. Augustine's teaching pre-vailed but the Donatist heresy lingered on.

The second heresy was as difficult to contain. Pelagius (died c. 420), a British monk, preached a doctrine of self-reliance that seemed to detach a person from the will of God, arguing that people could earn their way into heaven. Augustine countered by pointing out that all that Christians receive is from the goodness, or grace, of God. This grace was necessary in the face of so much evil in the world. Humans, Augustine main-tained, had a propensity to sin. Without God's grace, demonstrated in the life, death, and resurrection of Jesus, humans continue to do evil and fail to achieve the good of which they are capable.

✤ TEACHER OF GRACE ✤

As one who had once lived such a self-indulgent life, Augustine throughout his teaching under-lined the need for a conversion of heart, a fundamental message of the Gospels.

Augustine's teaching on grace was to influence church thought permanently, and it is no coinci-dence that Martin Luther, the first of the great reformers of the sixteenth century, was an Augustinian friar. Augustine became renowned for his clarity and doctrine. He employed scribes to take down his sermons while he preached in church, and these were copied and distributed to monasteries and other bishops.

Augustine's literary output was prolific, and he touched on a great variety of subjects. For instance, when faced with increasing threats of invasions in North Africa, he formulated a "just war" theory, arguing against traditional Christian pacifism by justifying the killing of an aggressor when there was no alternative to defend legitimate rights. Augustine's influential teachings are

"YOU HAVE PUT SALT IN OUR MOUTHS THAT WE MAY THIRST FOR YOU"

AUGUSTINE

a compelling combination of tender love for God, and a yearning desire to know him better – considered by Augustine to be the hallmark of an authentic faith. Little wonder then that people from all areas of Christian belief can identify with different aspects of his writings.

PUNISHMENT OF HERESY

In the 360s, Julian the Apostate criticized Christians' persecution of dissidents: "Many whole communities of so-called heretics were actually butchered, as at Samosata, and Cyzicus, Bithynia and Galatia, and among many other tribes … whereas in my time exile has been ended and property restored." Early in the next century, Augustine gave theological sanction to the punishment of heretics. The use of torture and death to destroy heresy remained rare, however, until the 1200s.

✤

CITY OF GOD

After the sack of Rome, Augustine set about composing a treatise, *The City of God*, arguing that such destruction came from the pagans' lack of faith. It was obvious to Augustine that while the city of man continued to decay, the city of God would continue into eternity. He believed that the church represented the city of God on earth and saw the periodic destruction of the city of man as a natural expression of the futility of humanity's efforts to achieve immortality without God.

✤

BARBARIANS IN THE WEST

THE BARBARIANS
The fifth-century invaders of the empire spoke in languages unintelligible to the Romans and were thus known as "barbarians," from the Greek for "foreign." They also scandalized the Romans because they wore trousers. The memory of these uncouth, destructive tribes lasted for centuries. When Pope Urban VIII (r. 1623–44) of the Barbarini family pillaged the bronze beams from the porch of the Pantheon in Rome to build the altar canopy in St. Peter's, one critic played on the association of words: "What the barbarians did not do, the Barbarini have done."

❖

CORRUPTING THE EMPIRE?
Like Augustine, a priest from Marseilles in southern Gaul, Salvian (c.400–80), tried to explain the corruption of the world. Unlike Augustine, he argued that the victorious barbarians were God's judgment on society and an incentive for Christians to lead purer lives. It was not unknown for Christian officials to exact unfair taxes from ordinary people. A number of Christians also abandoned law and administration because they did not wish to be defiled by the corruption they found all around them. This left the task of civil responsibility to others. All over the empire magistrates and officials who did not have Christian ideals were promoted.

❖

THE CLOSE OF the fourth century and the beginning of the fifth were fraught with difficulties for the Roman Empire and for Christians, who now made up the majority of the population. For some time, barbarian invaders had been mounting attacks along the borders of the increasingly unstable empire, which was once again divided between two emperors, in the East and the West. On the last day of December, 406, a Germanic tribe, the Goths, broke across the northeastern border and swept southward, terrorizing anyone who stood in the way of its ferocious soldiers. Such repeated and unrelentingly severe barbarian attacks succeeded in causing the downfall of the Roman Empire in the West and the eventual deposition of the last Western emperor.

❖ THE FALL OF ROME ❖

In 410, the unimaginable happened: Rome was captured and vandalized by the Goths. Although the city of Constantinople was now the seat of the Byzantine emperor, and so the main political capital of the empire, nonetheless Rome still occupied an important symbolic role and remained the spiritual focus of the church in the West. The assault on the city shocked the empire to its core. Many pagans blamed Christianity for the catastrophe, claiming that the gods were angry and were refusing to protect the empire as

> ❝ ROME, WHICH CAPTIVATED THE WHOLE WORLD, HAS HERSELF BEEN TAKEN CAPTIVE ❞
>
> **JEROME**

they had in the past. Several Christians also believed this was divine retribution for their transgression, despite Augustine's treatise, *The City of God*, which argued that far from blaming Christians, pagan critics should blame their own lack of faith (*p. 69*).

THE RUINS OF ROME
The fall of the Roman Empire gave many Christians a sense of foreboding that the end of the world was imminent. A number of pagan rulers, however, soon converted to Christianity and took an active interest in their adopted faith.

BARBARIAN INVASIONS
The barbarian conquests (as shown above) *were often brutal. Out in the far reaches of the empire, Gregory, bishop of Tours (c. 540–94), expressed the anxiety of Christians: "The churches have been attacked by heretics." Nothing was safe.*

It is difficult to imagine the horror and fear that seized people throughout the West in the face of the barbarian invaders. Already in 406, the Roman senate had conveyed a somber message to their outpost in Britain: If faced with invasion, they would be on their own, for there were no troops available to defend the populace. Hearing of the capture of Rome from his monastery in Bethlehem, Jerome wrote, "There is no created work which is not attacked by old age and consequently disappears. But Rome! Who would believe that Rome, built up by the conquest of the whole world, had collapsed, that the mother of nations had become also their tomb. … We cannot relieve these sufferers: all we can do is sympathize with them, and unite our tears with theirs."

❖ PAPAL POWER IN AN ❖ UNSTABLE WEST

The sack of Rome in 410 was followed by several significant victories for the barbarians. The Vandals conquered most of North Africa in 430 as Augustine lay dying in Hippo, and Carthage fell in 439. In 452 the Huns, an Asiatic tribe led by Attila, crossed over the Alps into Italy in an attempt to march on Rome, although the pope, Leo the Great *(see box)*, managed to persuade them to turn back. The fact that the pope

had successfully averted this disaster increased the political position of the papacy immeasurably. Leo took every opportunity to underline the supremacy of the bishop of Rome, especially after 451, when the bishops at the Council of Chalcedon had voted that the city of Constantinople be regarded as second only to Rome *(p. 62)*. "Due to the preeminence of the Apostolic See," wrote Leo, "made certain by the merits of the prince of the bishops, St. Peter, and by the prime position of the city of Rome, let nobody presume to attempt anything to the contrary. Thus will the peace of the churches be preserved if the whole body acknowledges its ruler."

Just a few years later, in 455, the Vandals pillaged Rome again. The Vandals' leader, Gaiseric, and his troops plundered the city for 14 days. Again, Leo was credited with initiating negotiations that left at least some of the buildings standing.

Successive popes made ever more explicit claims to their universal role as chief pastor of the church. The fact that the emperors continued to endow the papacy with funds, despite the threats to the empire, demonstrates the high esteem in which the papacy was held. Rome was fortunate in having several outstanding popes who upheld the special position of the papacy of Rome during these turbulent years.

LEO I

PRIOR to his becoming a priest, Pope Leo the Great (r. 440–61) distinguished himself in his civil career; his experience of the imperial system and his own qualities thus served the papacy well, and he strengthened the role of the pope in the Western church significantly with his preference for central government. He appropriated a title once used by the emperor: *"Pontifex Maximus."* He used this title, meaning supreme bridge-builder, to refer to the task of the bishop to mediate between God and humanity. Leo's greatest service was in dissuading Attila the Hun from attacking Rome *(below)*. Leo journeyed 200 miles (320 km) on horseback to meet Attila and probably used a large bribe to persuade the Huns to turn back.

RAVENNA
In 404, the imperial residence was established away from Rome at Ravenna, in northeast Italy. The city provided a safe citadel for the Western emperor during the sack of Rome and went on to grow in importance and wealth until it fell to the Goths in 493. It is unrivaled in its mosaics and early Christian art, such as that of the baptistery of San Apollinaris *(above)*.

❖

THE VANDALS
Characterized by their wanton destruction – hence the word "vandalism" – the Vandals were among the most successful of the tribes who swept northwestward into Europe, overrunning the western part of the Roman Empire *(see map, p. 72)*. The Vandals migrated in the fifth century through Europe to Africa. They invaded Gaul in 406, and Spain three years later, then founded a kingdom in North Africa, which lasted until the Muslim conquests. The Vandals built a navy that gained control over the western Mediterranean, and in 477 they also sacked Rome. The tribesmen, ferocious supporters of Arianism, were finally defeated by Justinian's general, Belisarius, in 534.

❖

71

Around the end of the fifth century a new means of ordering calendar years was introduced. Prior to this, years were calculated from the foundation of Rome in the eighth century BC. The new calendar that the monk Dionysius the Short invented dated history backwards (BC) or forwards (AD) from the birth of Christ, as the new age of salvation was seen to begin with this event. Though Dionysius's calculations were slightly off, as Jesus was born in the reign of Herod the Great, who we know died in 4 BC, this fifth-century method of dating history remains in use today throughout the world.

✣

During his reign, Constantine had organized the church along the lines of his civil administration, with territories divided up into areas called dioceses, each one supervised by a bishop. The bishop resided in a town, and the building – called a cathedral – where his "see," or official seat (Latin, *cathedra*, meaning "chair"), was located was a place not only of worship, but of bureaucratic power. With the breakdown of civil administration during the fifth century, people turned to the bishop and his court for help. The church was the only institution that would defend and sustain them.

✣ THE WEST COLLAPSES ✣

These bishops felt the impact of such disarray strongly, finding it difficult to deal with an emperor far away in Constantinople. The emperor in the East, however, appeared satisfied with this arrangement, occasionally sending dioceses money to help repair aqueducts (formerly in the care of the civil administration). In Rome, when Leo assumed the title *"Pontifex Maximus,"* he also assumed the duties of the emperor in the maintenance of public monuments. The claims of the bishops of Rome were increasingly unambiguous.

At the end of the fifth century, Pope Gelasius I (r. 492–96) was to claim that the pope was the ruler of the spiritual sphere, while the emperor was ruler of the temporal sphere: a clear statement that popes would not accept imperial directions on spiritual matters. Yet for the great majority of people it really did not matter now where the emperor lived or which emperor ruled over them. They were far more concerned that the aqueducts had broken down, the roads were full of brigands, and that civil services were no longer efficient. The old virtues of patriotism, military power, and economic stability were all under attack. It was from this political confusion that kings and tribal chiefs emerged, intent on establishing their control over territories abandoned by the Roman government.

In 476 the Gothic chief Odoacer deposed the last emperor of the West. This was the death blow to the Roman Empire in the West. Once in power, however, Odoacer sent an embassy to Constantinople to have his rule recognized: in reality, the barbarians did not want to destroy the Roman Empire. They were in awe of the culture in Rome and wanted to imitate it. They even adopted several Roman customs, substituting trousers for short tunics, for instance, and cutting their hair short and shaving their beards off.

> " GOD OUGHT TO BE PRAISED ... THAT SO MANY NATIONS WOULD BE RECEIVING, EVEN AT THE COST OF OUR OWN WEAKENING, A KNOWLEDGE OF THE TRUTH "
>
> OROSIUS,
> (A PRIEST OF THE ROMAN EMPIRE, ON BARBARIAN CONVERSIONS TO CHRISTIANITY)

In the midst of all this chaos, the church stood out as a beacon. Gradually it took up the task of missionary work among tribesmen, some of whom had initially converted to Arianism, or who were pagans. The barbarian kings were often glad to have the church as an ally, and some granted bishops, abbots, and abbesses large tracts of land. Land meant money, and from this period onward, the abbeys and dioceses throughout Western Europe developed extraordinary economic influence. These Christian leaders became important individuals themselves, wielding, in some cases, as much power as the local king.

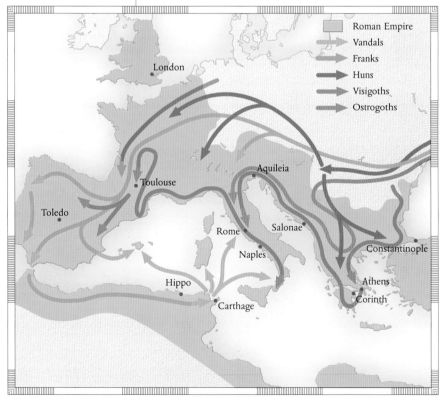

Roman Empire
Vandals
Franks
Huns
Visigoths
Ostrogoths

London
Toulouse
Toledo
Aquileia
Rome
Salonae
Naples
Hippo
Carthage
Constantinople
Athens
Corinth

BARBARIAN INVASIONS
In the fourth and fifth centuries barbarians broke through the frontiers of the Roman Empire and established their own kingdoms in countries such as Spain, Gaul, North Africa, Germany, and England.

MUSIC AND ART IN THE EARLY CHURCH

❖

THE first Christians were heirs to a rich and ancient tradition of Jewish music, which played a large part in Jewish liturgy, or public worship. The Bible contains vivid accounts of these liturgies, which were accompanied by instruments and voices. Unfortunately, we do not possess any written melodies within either the Jewish or Christian traditions before the fifth century, and although the music developed by early Christians was also undoubtedly influenced by Greek and Roman models, without written evidence it is almost impossible to identify the sources. However, we do know that the persecuted early Christians had no specially constructed buildings in which to worship, and so had to make do with meeting in one another's houses. As a result, they were unable to organize elaborate liturgies, and Christian music was restricted in its development. Added to this was the distaste early Christians felt towards pagan activities, such as dancing and its associated instrumental music.

It was the imperial favor granted to Christians in the fourth century by Emperor Constantine and his successors that was to play a pivotal part in the development of church music. Constantine established several churches, principally in Jerusalem, Rome, and Constantinople. These impressive buildings, built for worship, enabled the liturgy to flourish; the acoustics, for example, must have encouraged composers to experiment with elaborate arrangements. At the end of the fifth century, Pope Gregory I (r. 590–604) categorized all the music composed to date and encouraged a conformity in styles of worship across the empire (p. 93).

decorative techniques adopted from the Greeks and Romans. Pagan artists had already used mosaic for floor and wall art, but the Christian artists, and most especially the craftsmen of the Byzantine Empire, were to raise this technique to new and dazzling heights. Mosaic is a technique of making a picture with tiny tiles or *tesserae*. These tiles, about a third of an inch (a centimeter) square, are usually made from glass or marble. The glass used by these early church craftsmen often had gold leaf inlaid which, because of its richness, was frequently used to represent heaven. For example, the earliest known Christian mosaic, found in the 1940s underneath St. Peter's Basilica, uses gold mosaic in its represention of Christ as the sun-god, Helios.

Mosaics were not common because of the cost and so were generally confined to the wealthier churches of the Byzantine Empire. Far more common was the use of fresco in church decoration. Already popular in Greece and the Roman Empire, this decorative technique entailed preparing a wall with several thin layers of plaster. While the final layer was still wet, a combination of egg yolk and powdered colors, called a *tempora*, was laid over it. The artist had to work rapidly using this medium: as the plaster dried, the powdered colours sank into the plaster and became permanent, making any corrections almost impossible. The earliest surviving frescoes date from the Roman catacombs in the third century, but it was in Italy during the Renaissance that the greatest fresco decoration was to be undertaken.

IVORY PANEL OF CHRIST

This panel depicting Christ forms the cover of a lectionary and was carved at the height of the Byzantine era. Ivory panels were considered one of the most sophisticated forms of artistic decoration, particularly if the craftsman's work was expertly and delicately carved.

EARLY CHURCH ART

The increase in church building from 313 benefited not only music and liturgies but also art, which, until the end of the Middle Ages, was principally religious in its nature. Church art has served Christians in many ways, inspiring awe and wonder in the presence of God and helping believers to learn about, interpret, and meditate on God's work and message. Even in the catacombs in the third century, Christians decorated their places of worship, often with biblical scenes. Once purpose-built churches began to be erected in the fourth century, Christians began to decorate the interiors with frescoes and mosaics,

CHURCH ARTIFACTS

The ornamentation in early churches was not only restricted to decorations on the floors and walls. Church altars were often carved from marble and decorated with images of the Eucharist. Sumptuous gold and silver altar vessels and dishes, often inlaid with jewels, were crafted to be used during the celebration of the sacred liturgy. The basic shape of these vessels still survives to the present day. Many silver bowls and vessels were also inscribed with biblical verses. Carved ivory vessels and panels were also popular during the Byzantine period, the most elaborate usually having been carved by craftsmen from culture centers such as Antioch in Syria and Alexandria in Egypt.

THE CHURCH IN THE EAST

AT THE CLOSE of the fourth century, with the empire once again split and the last Western emperor deposed, the delicate unity of the church was undermined, and the differences separating East and West began to emerge. While the empire in the West disintegrated, the Eastern church experienced great tensions and witnessed some pernicious heresies that sowed seeds of confusion among the Christians. And while the church in the West effectively achieved independence from the imperial power in spiritual and moral matters, the ties between the emperor and the church in the East were not so easy to break: the Byzantine emperor was still considered both priest and king.

❖ GREAT PREACHER ❖ OF THE EAST

One example of this complex relationship of imperial and religious authority was the tragedy of the great theologian, John Chrysostom (c. 347–407). A native of Antioch, Chrysostom (Greek for golden mouth) first studied oratory and law and then theology. Yet he remained dissatisfied with his academic life and eventually decided to live as a monk in the mountains outside Antioch. In 381 he was ordained a deacon, and five years later he became a priest.

It was during this time that Chrysostom preached a series of homilies on Genesis and the books of the New Testament that established his reputation and proved his ability to convey both the spiritual meaning of the Greek Bible and its practical application. His popularity was such that people often pushed their way to the front of the church to hear him more clearly. Chrysostom said of his inspirational preaching: "When I begin to speak, weariness disappears; when I begin to teach, fatigue too

disappears. Thus neither sickness itself nor indeed any other obstacle is able to separate me from your love … for just as you are hungry to listen to me, so too am I hungry to preach to you."

Chrysostom's fame for sanctity and preaching came to the attention of the emperor in the East, Arcadius, who appointed him Patriarch of Constantinople against his will in 398. Although this was a position of tremendous importance within both the court and the church, Chrysostom alienated the empress Eudoxia with his preaching and demanded that the emperor conform to Christian morality.

Finally, he encountered the enmity of a rival, Theophilus, archbishop of Alexandria, who used his influence to encourage the emperor to condemn Chrysostom on trumped-up heretical charges at a church council. The emperor ordered Chrysostom to leave the church and the city, which caused his supporters to riot in the streets. Although exiled, he remains one of the great fathers of the Eastern church.

❖ CHRISTIAN ❖ REFORMS

In spite of all this imperial influence, the Eastern church continued to develop its rich and unique liturgical tradition, giving great importance to preaching. Theologians such as Basil the Great and Gregory of Nazianzus (p. 62) continued to define its doctrines. Monasticism also flourished and established itself as an important element of Eastern spirituality. Indeed, Basil the Great viewed monastic life as the climax of Christian achievement.

Imperial influence was not always malign. Emperor Theodosius II, who assumed the throne at Constantinople in 408, had strong Christian affiliations, although he was also considered a politically incompetent emperor. In 425 he

JOHN CHRYSOSTOM
Chrysostom himself said that he looked like a spider with his long limbs and short, thin body. He preached every Sunday and several times a week; about 800 of his sermons have survived.

founded the university of Constantinople and endowed it with a precious library of Christian texts. He also commissioned the Theodosian Code in 435, a list of all the general constitutions passed since Constantine I endorsed Christian beliefs.

✦ SCHISMS IN THE EAST ✦

However, the East was becoming increasingly vulnerable to the tensions and schisms within the church. Theodosius's most significant act as emperor was to summon the Council of Ephesus in 431, which had serious repercussions for the Eastern church. Theodosius convened this synod in an attempt to resolve the Nestorian controversy *(p. 62)*. When the council decreed that Nestorius's failure to affirm the fundamental unity of Christ (he seemed to be arguing that Christ was split into two persons) was heretical,

> **" WHEN YOU SEE THE CHURCH SCATTERED, SUFFERING THE MOST TERRIBLE TRIALS, CONSIDER ... THE REWARDS "**
>
> JOHN CHRYSOSTOM

few of the Syrian churchman's supporters actually accepted his excommunication. Those bishops who supported Nestorius against the orthodox position at the Council of Ephesus went on to organize themselves into a separate church, which came to be based in Persia. During the sixth and seventh centuries, the Nestorian church established Christian settlements in India, Arabia, and China, and at the end of the twentieth century it still survives, much diminished, in the Middle East.

The Council of Ephesus was not the only council to result in a major part of the church splitting away. Twenty years later, in 451, the Council of Chalcedon *(p. 62)* also caused a schism. In this case it was a group called the Monophysites who were excommunicated and condemned by the council for believing that Jesus had only one, divine, nature. As a result, the Monophysites also formed themselves into a distinct body separate from the main element of the church.

MEMORIAL TO MOSES IN THE DESERT
St. Catherine's monastery, founded c. 557 at Mount Sinai, is still a monastery today. It was built on this site to commemorate the place where it is believed that Moses saw the burning bush.

Eventually, by the sixth century, three distinct Monophysite churches had developed in different areas – the Syrian Jacobites, the Copts from Ethiopia and Egypt, and the Armenians.

✦ BLOODY AFTERMATH ✦

Although both of these controversies were over theological matters, the councils' rulings nevertheless manifested themselves in rioting on the streets and confusion among Christians. Popular religious feeling ran particularly high after the Council of Chalcedon. In Egypt and Syria there were bloody uprisings and fights between the orthodox believers and Monophysites: in Alexandria, a group of Monophysite monks were boiled alive in oil in front of the city cathedral, while in Syria a monastery was set alight and the monks died in the flames. The disputes over the nature, or natures, of Christ were to rage on for years. Whether or not ordinary people supported orthodox Christianity or Monophysitism, or remained bewildered by such controversies and schisms, the empire in the East was certainly weakened by these internal conflicts and would pay the price in the following centuries with the rise of Islam.

FIERCE CONTROVERSY
Theological debates could be extraordinarily heated. When Bishop Cyril of Alexandria died, his fellow bishop Theodoret of Cyprus declared, "The living are delighted. The dead, perhaps, are sorry, afraid that they may be burdened with his company. ... Let him take his new doctrines to hell, and preach to the damned all day and night." Bishop Proterius of Alexandria took the unpopular side at the Council of Chalcedon, and the mob tore him to pieces when he arrived home.

✤

BYZANTIUM IN ITS GLORY

THEODORA

Although, in religious matters, Justinian was orthodox, his wife, the empress Theodora, was a determined supporter of the heretical Monophysites (p. 75). After a serious riot erupted in Constantinople in 532, it was Theodora who gave Justinian the courage to stand his ground against the mob. After that, her influence was very great a fact that probably explains Justinian's subsequent conciliation toward the Monophysites.

❖

RECONQUEST OF THE EMPIRE

This gold medallion (dated 524) commemorates the reclamation of North Africa and Italy by the Roman Empire. On it the victorious emperor Justinian I is depicted as a warrior, with a spear in hand. In reality, Justinian left the business of battle to his generals.

❖

FROM THE FIFTH CENTURY onward the Roman Empire was in effect ruled from the East. The city of Constantinople was to remain the seat of the emperor and capital of the empire until it fell to the Turks in 1453.

By the sixth century, Constantinople had grown greatly in wealth and prestige, and visitors to the city were often overcome by its beauty. Its churches and palaces were encrusted with golden mosaics, and the great church of Hagia Sophia, meaning "Holy Wisdom," built in only six years and completed in 537, was established as the most beautiful church in the empire. An ambassador, sailing around Constantinople, was fulsome in his praise: "The city is full of churches, each as sails unfurled upon a ship, while the church of Holy Wisdom

JEWEL-ENCRUSTED CROSS

As Byzantium increased in power, its art became more elaborate and sophisticated. This cross was presented to the city of Rome c. 575.

outshines the temple of Solomon." This may not have been an exaggeration: the interior of Hagia Sophia sparkled with the light from thousands of lamps reflected in its mosaics. In the nearby palace the emperor held his court, surrounded by numerous courtiers. Yet one emperor of the East, Justinian I, was not content just to beautify the capital of the empire: as the leader of the Eastern church, he knew he had the power to rule over spiritual matters.

❖ JUSTINIAN'S REIGN ❖

A fearless champion of orthodoxy, Justinian I (r. 527–65) was convinced he had divine inspiration, and he was unwilling to bow to anybody. It was his decision as to which form of Christianity was to be observed in the empire, and the bishops in both the

East and the West were expected to observe his "divine" decrees. He opposed Pope Vigilius, for instance, and then publicly humiliated him, and on another occasion insisted that the Council of Constantinople, held in

"ONE EMPIRE, ONE LAW, ONE CHURCH"

JUSTINIAN I

553, damn the memory of three bishops who had stood against him. He clamped down on any deviations from orthodox Christianity, persecuted Jews, and forced pagans to convert. Yet Justinian was conscious that he was emperor by the grace of God: "The beginning, the middle and the end of our legislation," he wrote, "is God."

RISING TO THE HEAVENS
The historian Procopius (born c. 500) was ecstatic in his admiration of Hagia Sophia: "It rises to the very heavens as if surging up from amongst the other buildings. It stands aloft and looks down upon the rest of the city. … The church is full of light, so that you would declare that the place is lit, not by the sun without, but the light that is within."

❖ UNITING THE ❖ EMPIRE

For Justinian, as for other Byzantine emperors, the church was regarded not as an independent authority but as a department of State. Justinian commissioned a new code that systematized the law of the empire in order to reflect a Christian ethos. This Justinian code remains today as the basis of European law. While it may have exalted the powers of the emperor, it also confirmed the enormous influence of

THE EMPEROR AND HIS MEN
This sixth-century mosaic from the San Vitale Church in Ravenna depicts Justinian I with his retinue of officials, soldiers, and clergy. Justinian took an active interest in the life and morals of the clergy, encouraging them to be pure and avoid the theater or the races.

patriarchs and bishops throughout the empire. Indeed, under Justinian's absolute power the church was to reach its apogee of influence in the East.

Very much in the mold of Constantine, Justinian wished to restore the empire to its pristine glory, and together with his wife, the empress Theodora, he set about winning back North Africa, Italy, Sardinia, Sicily, and southern Spain. Like Constantine, he also attempted to unite the church across the empire. He ensured that the bishops of the five sees of Rome, Constantinople, Antioch, Alexandria, and Jerusalem were officially given the title of patriarch, and that each see had extensive privileges, including an annual income. These were not to last for long, however, for in the following century the great patriarchates of Antioch, Alexandria, and Jerusalem were eclipsed by the encroaching armies of the prophet Muhammad as Islam spread across the empire.

PATRON OF THE ARTS

Justinian I was arguably the greatest and most enlightened of all patrons of the arts. He secured Constantinople's reputation as the center for art and culture with a series of impressive buildings, both religious and secular, across the empire; mosaic decorations; and superbly crafted small artifacts made out of ivory, metal, marble, or limestone, sometimes inset with precious stones.

❖

AN ERA OF MISSIONS

SOME OF THE MOST remarkable missionary
expansion in Christian history occurred after the
conversion of Emperor Constantine in 312. In
the East, churches were planted as far apart as Georgia
and India. In the South, Christianity spread from Egypt
into Nubia (modern Sudan), while a shipwrecked slave
brought the Christian gospel to Ethiopia. In the West,
the heathen tribes flooding across the borders of the
empire proved a spur to evangelism. The Goths, among
the most warlike of these tribes, were converted by
a remarkable missionary, Ulfilas (c. 311–83), known
as "the apostle of the Goths."

❖ APOSTLES TO THE PAGANS ❖

Ulfilas's mother was a Christian Roman, his father
a pagan Goth, and thus Ulfilas was brought up a
Christian among the Goths of the Danube. While
on a visit to Constantinople in c.341, Bishop Eusebius
of Nicomedia made him a bishop and sent him back
to evangelize his own people, where he spent the rest
of his life. His greatest work was to convert the Gothic

language into writing and translate the Bible into it,
making this the first document of German literature.
Ulfilas, unfortunately, was an Arian (pp. 60-61) who
regarded Jesus as less than God, so the Goths later had
to be converted again to orthodox Christianity (p. 82).
Meanwhile, c. 333, the royal family of the kingdom
of Georgia was converted through the ministry of a
female slave from Cappadocia, Nina, "the equal of the
apostles." As had happened in Armenia (p. 49), the royal
family then made Christianity the national religion.

❖ CHRISTIANITY IN THE EAST ❖

Situated much farther east was one of the most isolated
groups of Christians in the ancient world, the "Thomas
Christians" of southwest India. According to its own
tradition, the church was founded by the apostle
Thomas – a story also found in the third-century Syrian
text, the *Acts of Thomas*. The first certain reference to
it is in the sixth century, when the geographer Cosmas
Indicopleustes referred to this Indian community as a
well-established one.

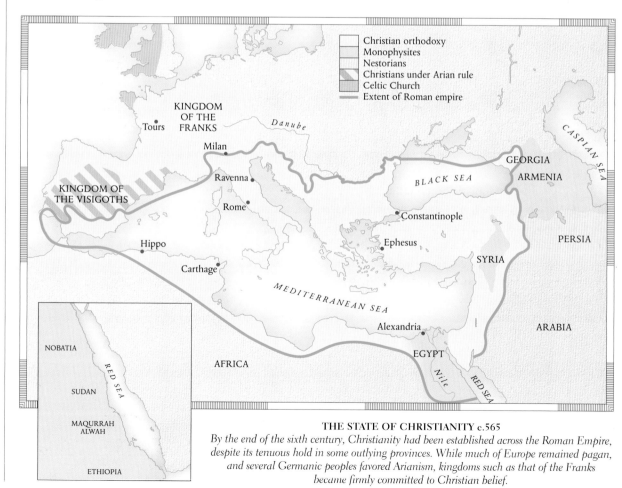

Christian orthodoxy
Monophysites
Nestorians
Christians under Arian rule
Celtic Church
Extent of Roman empire

THE STATE OF CHRISTIANITY c.565
*By the end of the sixth century, Christianity had been established across the Roman Empire,
despite its tenuous hold in some outlying provinces. While much of Europe remained pagan,
and several Germanic peoples favored Arianism, kingdoms such as that of the Franks
became firmly committed to Christian belief.*

place in western Europe besides Caledonia (modern Scotland) that had never been conquered by the Romans. It had therefore preserved its pagan gods, its particular law system, its own economy, and its own language. Patrick's mission there was not the first time Christians had worked to spread the gospel, but for 30 years he established local churches and monasteries as centers of the new Christian faith, which the Irish were swift to embrace. When barbarian invaders overran eastern Britain and extinguished the Roman churches there, the Celtic Christians – even though cut off from the rest of the Christian world – kept Christianity alive in the western part of Britain.

The largely Christian Gallo-Roman inhabitants of Gaul (modern-day France) suffered under the yoke of the pagan Germanic people, the Franks, until the conversion of the Frankish king, Clovis (r. 481–511), reunited the country in 496. The entire population of Gaul converted to Christianity after Clovis issued a decree: "Know that those who do not present themselves with me at the river tomorrow for baptism will incur my displeasure."

Thus in spite of the fall of the Roman Empire and numerous barbarian invasions, Christianity continued to spread across the world and leave its distinctive mark on the culture, art, philosophy, and daily lives of many thousands of individuals.

> **" I heard calling me the voices of those who dwelt beside the wood of Foclut which is nigh to the western sea, and thus they cried … 'We beseech thee, holy youth, to come and walk amongst us as before' "**
>
> **PATRICK, ON HIS MISSION TO IRELAND**

LALIBELA ROCK CHURCH, ETHIOPIA
After Christianity was first introduced to Ethiopia in the fourth century, churches such as the church carved out of rock at Lalibela (above) appeared. Frumentius established such strong ties between the Ethiopian and Egyptian churches that until 1959, the Egyptian church always provided the archbishop, or abuna, for the Ethiopian church.

The Ethiopians were converted through the work of one missionary, Frumentius, who was shipwrecked off the Red Sea coast, then made a slave in the court of the Ethiopian king at Axum, and subsequently won the favor of the king. After being given permission to preach freely, he won converts, and other Egyptian Christians came to support his work. In c. 341 Frumentius went to Alexandria to ask the bishop, Athanasius (p. 60), for his support. Athanasius promptly ordained him bishop, and Frumentius led the Ethiopian church until his death.

North of Ethiopia, the citizens of the three kingdoms of Nobatia, Maqurrah, and Alwah, in what is now Sudan, were converted between 543 and 575 through the work of the missionaries Julian and Longinus. The resulting Christian kingdoms endured for almost 1,000 years. Churches sprang up along the Nile, and ancient pagan temples were converted for Christian worship as enthusiasm for the new religion spread.

❖ NORTHERN EUROPE ❖

In the North, Celtic tribes were converted by a young "apostle to the Irish," St. Patrick (c. 390–460). Brought up a Christian, Patrick was captured by Irish pirates at the age of 16 and sold into slavery. Seeking ordination, he escaped Ireland to train in Britain, returning to Ireland as a bishop in about 432. Ireland was the only

THE CONVERSION OF CLOVIS
King Clovis's wife, Clotilde, had tried to convert Clovis to Christianity soon after they were married in c. 492 and failed. However, after being impressed by the powerful prayers of his wife the evening before a battle, Clovis returned victorious and converted to Christianity.

The Conversion of Europe

590–1054

I N THE EARLY MIDDLE Ages much of Europe underwent a steady conversion to Christianity, from England to Russia, and from Scandinavia to Hungary. By the eleventh century Christianity dominated almost the entire European continent, and the church had begun the slow process of civilizing the barbarian tribes. At the same time, a new Christian empire was established in the West under the leadership of the emperor Charlemagne.

In the East, Muslims (the followers of Muhammad) pushed westward, ending Christian dominance in North Africa and in Palestine, the birthplace of Christianity. Meanwhile, the emperors of the East were locked in a struggle for supremacy with the church. While Christianity gained more and more converts, the rift between East and West became increasingly untenable. In the first century of the second millennium, the church of the East and the West separated in a split that endures into the third millennium.

Infant baptism in medieval France

CIVILIZING THE BARBARIANS

A<small>T THE END OF THE SIXTH</small> century, the Christian church remained largely centered in the Mediterranean world of the old Roman Empire and the near East. Within it, the East remained politically, intellectually, and artistically far stronger than the West. However, all this was to change over the next few centuries: the southern and eastern Christian lands were overrun by Muslim armies, while many more of the northern barbarians were converted, leaving Christianity seeming a largely European religion.

At the same time, the Eastern and Western halves of Christendom were steadily to drift apart. In the year 600 Western Christians still saw themselves as part of the Roman Empire ruled from Byzantium. By 800, after Muslim and other invasions had greatly restricted contact between West and East, this was no longer so. Separated from the empire, the struggling Catholic church of the West was gradually to convert or absorb the pagan barbarians and the Arian and Celtic Christians around it, becoming very much central to society.

✣ CHRISTIANIZING AND CIVILIZING ✣

In the West, the church was the only source of education and of social services. A tithe was paid by each citizen to the bishop or his representative, who then administered the money. As pagan nations were converted, this system was extended to them also. In each diocese, church revenue was split between the bishop, the clergy, church maintenance, and the poor. Alms were paid regularly to widows, orphans, and others in need (a list was kept). Each diocese maintained at least one "hospital," which provided – as did monasteries – refuge for the poor, for travelers, and for the sick. Barbarian invasions had destroyed the old,

QUEEN THEODELINDA OF THE LOMBARDS
Married in 590 to the Lombard king, Agilulf, Theodelinda was a Catholic in an Arian world. She persuaded her husband to adopt a pro-Catholic policy and helped Catholicism spread through Arian lands. Here, gold is melted for her church at Monza.

BAPTIZING THE YOUNGER GENERATION

An indirect result of entire, usually barbarian, families embracing Christianity was that infant baptism became far more widespread.

Previously, each individual candidate had to undergo a period of spiritual preparation before entering the Christian church.

state-funded schools of the Roman Empire (except in Italy, where limited private education continued), and so education, too, was provided by the church. All subjects were taught in Latin. Each bishop ran a household school, largely to educate clerks, and all monasteries had schools to train their monks.

> **" LET US PRAY FOR THE MOST CHRISTIAN KINGS, THAT GOD MAY PUT ALL THE BARBARIAN PEOPLES UNDER THEIR POWER, SO THAT WE MAY HAVE LASTING PEACE "**

SEVENTH-CENTURY GALICIAN LITURGY

Boys began in these schools as young as seven. By 600 there were six grades, or "minor orders" of clergy below the presbyterate, or priesthood, and many church officials remained permanently in minor orders, never progressing to become priests. Those in minor orders wore the tonsure (partly shaved head) and enjoyed the legal benefits of clerks (p. 74) but were allowed to marry.

While the Sunday Eucharist remained the central event of Christian worship, it had, since the fourth century, become an occasion in which the congregation was largely passive. Gradually, other popular devotions developed in which the mostly illiterate society could play a more active role in worship. Processions, where the people chanted and sang songs to God, especially for intervention during a time of need, became widespread. The cult of the saints became more and more important, and by the fifth century Mary, the mother of Jesus, had become the subject of particular veneration.

As the church struggled to evangelize the barbarians, it deliberately altered some of its customs to accommodate them. A clear example of this principle is found in a letter sent by Pope Gregory the Great (p. 84) in 601, containing strict instructions for his missionaries in Britain: "The heathen temples of these people need not be destroyed, only the idols which are to be found in them. … If the temples are well built, it is a good idea to detach them from the service of the devil, and to adapt them for the worship of the true God. … The people must learn to slay their cattle not in honor of the devil, but in honor of God and for their own food. … If we allow them these outward joys, they are more likely to find their way to the true inner joy."

WANING IMPERIAL INFLUENCE

In 590 the emperor at Constantinople continued to exert his influence on the church in the West. The newly elected pope in Rome was obliged to seek the emperor's confirmation of his election. This imperial influence was soon to wane, however: the last emperor ever to visit Rome was Constans II (r. 641–68), who stripped the metal from its buildings and statues to make weapons, and the last pope to seek the emperor's approval of his election was Gregory III (r. 713–41).

❖

SAINTS' FEAST DAYS FROM A BOOK OF HOURS

From the second century onward, people who had lived extraordinary lives of holiness were venerated. Their tombs became places of pilgrimage, and the anniversary of their death was celebrated as a feast. Images of saints were increasingly found in churches, and "prayer" to saints was normal: believing that the saint's prayer would be more efficacious than their own, people used the saints as intermediaries to ask for God's help. "Books of Hours" contained the prayers and church services (usually seven daily) that were prescribed for different hours of the monastic day.

❖

MISSION & REFORM

IN THE CRUMBLING SOCIETY of the West the Christian clergy played a leading role in maintaining a degree of stability. The better-educated among them assumed key political and civic positions in society. At the end of the sixth century, a pope came to the papal throne who had a very clear idea of how to use this situation to further the cause of the Christian faith within the declining empire.

✤ GREGORY THE GREAT ✤

Gregory the Great (r. 590–604) was born to the noble Anicia family and was the nephew of Pope Felix (r. 526–30). Prior to his becoming a monk, he had been prefect of Rome, one of the highest civic offices. He had also been ordained a deacon and sent as legate to the court at Constantinople. On

"SERVANT OF THE SERVANTS OF GOD"
This was the title Gregory chose for himself as pope, and it has been retained by popes ever since.

the death of Pope Pelagius II in 590, Gregory was summoned from his monastery and elected pope by the people and clergy of Rome. The city had been laid waste by pestilence and plague during the fifth and sixth centuries, and contemporary accounts describe Gregory sailing through the city in a flood, bringing food and rescuing people stranded by the waters.

Just as Roman army officials established camps and legions in conquered territories to keep the peace, so Gregory knew that he had to convert the barbarians, who posed a constant threat to the church. Realizing that he could not count on any support from the emperor in the East, he believed it would be wise to make allies of the barbarians. As a monk and a former civil official of the Roman Empire, Gregory understood the importance of establishing monasteries and knew that monks could provide the missionaries needed to preach to the barbarians. Gregory did not favor the idea of monks locking themselves away to achieve their own sanctity. Rather, as the spiritual soldiers of the church, they could be ordered to go into barbarian lands, found monasteries, and convert and teach the pagan peoples.

✤ AUGUSTINE: ENVOY TO ENGLAND ✤

When Gregory became pope, he dispatched a monk, Augustine, to head a mission to the pagan Anglo-Saxons who had occupied the eastern half of England. There is a story that Gregory, while still abbot, was walking across the marketplace in Rome when he saw two tall, fair boys. Asking who they were, the reply came, *"Angli sunt"* – they were Anglo-Saxon, and furthermore, pagan. Gregory, punning on the word,

REMAINS OF SIXTH-CENTURY CELTIC CHRISTIANITY ON IONA
In c. 563 the Irish abbot and missionary Columba (521–97) established a monastery with 12 monks on the island of Iona, off the west coast of Scotland. Throughout the sixth and seventh centuries, the monastery served as a base for missionary activity in Scotland and northern England. The Celtic church thus played an important role in reviving Christianity in northern Britain.

replied, "*Non Angli, sed angeli sunt*" – they are not Angles but "angels." Gregory advised Augustine to accept those pagan practices he felt to be compatible with Christianity, quoting a text from Paul's letter to the Thessalonians: "Test everything, and hold on to what is good." It was best, he believed, to avoid giving the pagans needless offense, while offering the Christian message to them with respect.

Augustine succeeded in converting King Ethelbert of Kent, who was married to a Christian queen, and he established his cathedral at Canterbury. More monks were sent to help Augustine, and steadily they moved north. As they did so they found themselves in those territories where the Irish monks were already engaged in missionary work (*see p. 79*).

(*see p. 79*)

❖ RESOLVING DIFFERENCES ❖

The Celtic monks and the new missionaries from Italy were divided on a number of issues, such as fasting, penance, and discipline. The greatest source of conflict however, was the fact that the Celtic and Roman churches celebrated Easter on different days. In 664 the two sides agreed to meet at a synod in the town of Whitby in the north of England to thrash out their differences. After a tense debate, the British monks won the argument in favor of adapting to Roman customs. From this time onward, Easter was celebrated on the same day throughout western Europe. The harmonious fusion of the two traditions helped

THE VENERABLE BEDE

EDUCATED at the Benedictine monastery of Jarrow in Northumbria, England, Bede (c. 673–735) became a monk there. Using the immense library of manuscripts that had been amassed from all over the Roman Empire, Bede composed over 40 historical, scientific, and theological works. His most important was his *Ecclesiastical History of the English People*, which traced the history of Britain from the Roman conquest until the year of the work's completion in 731. Bede's method was exacting, reliable, and meticulous, and demonstrated an ability to distinguish fact from tradition and hearsay. Less than a century after his death he was given the title of "Venerable."

"DESTROY AS FEW PAGAN TEMPLES AS POSSIBLE; ONLY DESTROY THEIR IDOLS, SPRINKLE THEM WITH HOLY WATER, BUILD ALTARS AND PUT RELICS IN THE BUILDINGS"

ADVICE GIVEN TO ST. AUGUSTINE BY POPE GREGORY THE GREAT

the monks to consolidate their work. It also led to an interchange of ideas among those monks who left Ireland and Britain to work as missionaries in central Europe. Their missionary activity was to restore stability and some form of culture to Europe, long disorientated by the wars that had ravaged it.

Over the next decades, both Celtic and British monks continued southward into mainland Europe, establishing monasteries and Christian centers. The monks made an unparalleled contribution to the lives of the peasants, helping them restore and cultivate land that had been destroyed by the barbarians. The most famous of these monks were Willibrord, the "apostle of the Frisians," and Boniface, the English Benedictine monk revered as the "apostle of the Germans."

AUGUSTINE'S CHAIR, CANTERBURY CATHEDRAL

In 597 Augustine baptized King Ethelbert of Kent at Canterbury. For over 1,400 years this city has been the seat of the archbishops of Canterbury (the most senior bishops in England). The most famous archbishop was Thomas Becket, who was murdered in the cathedral in 1170. After his canonization three years later, it became one of the greatest shrines in Europe.

❖

A MISSIONARY STORY FROM BEDE

One of the best-known missionary stories of this era is quoted by Bede in his annals. It tells of bishop Paulinus's visit in the seventh century to the Northumbrian king Edwin and his court. The bishop was urging them to accept the new Christian teachings, when suddenly a bird flew through the hall and out into the darkness. On seeing this, a noble is said to have uttered the following words: "The life of a man is as if a sparrow should come to the house and very swiftly flit through. So the life of man here appeareth for a little season, but what followeth or what has gone before, that surely we know not. Wherefore if this new learning hath brought us any better tiding, surely methinks it is worthy to be followed" (Bede, *History* II:13).

❖

Willibrord rekindled Christianity in the Netherlands and in 698 was consecrated bishop of the Frisians by Pope Sergius I (r. 687–701). The king of the Franks, Pepin, gave Willibrord permission to build a cathedral in the Dutch town of Utrecht.

❖ BONIFACE AND PAGAN GERMANY ❖

In 717, Boniface set out in the footsteps of Willibrord. By this time, much of what Willibrord had accomplished had been destroyed by the pagan duke Radbod. Boniface came to Willibrord's aid and was successful in re-establishing Christianity in Frisia. A few years later, encouraged by Pope Gregory II, Boniface traveled throughout the pagan lands of Germany on a new mission. In 723 Gregory II consecrated him a bishop so that he could travel freely, ordaining priests and other bishops to establish new dioceses.

Boniface was soon to be famed for a courageous act he performed at Geismar in Hesse (in western Germany). The local community worshiped a great oak tree, believing it to be a sanctuary of the god Thor. They thought that showing disrespect to the tree would cause an angry Thor to punish them, but when Boniface felled the great tree, nothing happened. Those who witnessed this were convinced that Boniface could only be right in preaching that the Christian God was stronger than their own. According to the story, Boniface built a chapel with the wood from the tree and dedicated it to St. Peter. He continued to found monasteries in Germany, one of which, Fulda, has remained an important focus of Catholic Christianity in central Germany up to the present day.

Made archbishop of Germany, and papal legate, Boniface expanded his missionary activity and issued rules on what the converted people should be made to understand. The rite of baptism was to be in Latin, although German could be used for the Lord's Prayer, the creed, sermons, and for a few of the readings from the Gospels. Boniface and his fellow missionaries also attempted to teach a Christian way of life to the pagan people: the importance of differentiating right from wrong, the coming judgment, the need to fast, and the giving of money to the poor. Boniface's missionary work was cut short in 754, when he met a violent death at the hands of non-Christians while on a visit to the present-day Netherlands.

❖ CONVERTING THE VIKINGS ❖

For centuries, the Scandinavian invaders had caused terror and confusion with their violent raids southward. Quite understandably, therefore, the Christian missionaries were not very enthusiastic about a mission to Scandinavia, the lands of the "dreaded Norsemen." In 717, however, Willibrord traveled with a band of monks to preach the gospel in Denmark, the first attempt to Christianize the northern peoples.

He was followed by Anskar, a monk from Picardy, who was dispatched to Sweden in the 830s. In spite of an initial setback, Anskar met with some success when the Swedish king Björn gave the missionaries permission to build a church and preach in his country, but only a few converted to Christianity. With much patience and persistence, Anskar finally managed to enter Denmark, gain the confidence of the Danish king, and build his first church there. However, after Anskar's death in 865, much of what he had achieved was lost in the raids

BONIFACE – THE APOSTLE OF GERMANY
The above page, taken from an eleventh-century Mass book, shows Boniface's missionary work and martyrdom. According to his biographer, Boniface attempted to shield himself with his Gospel book.

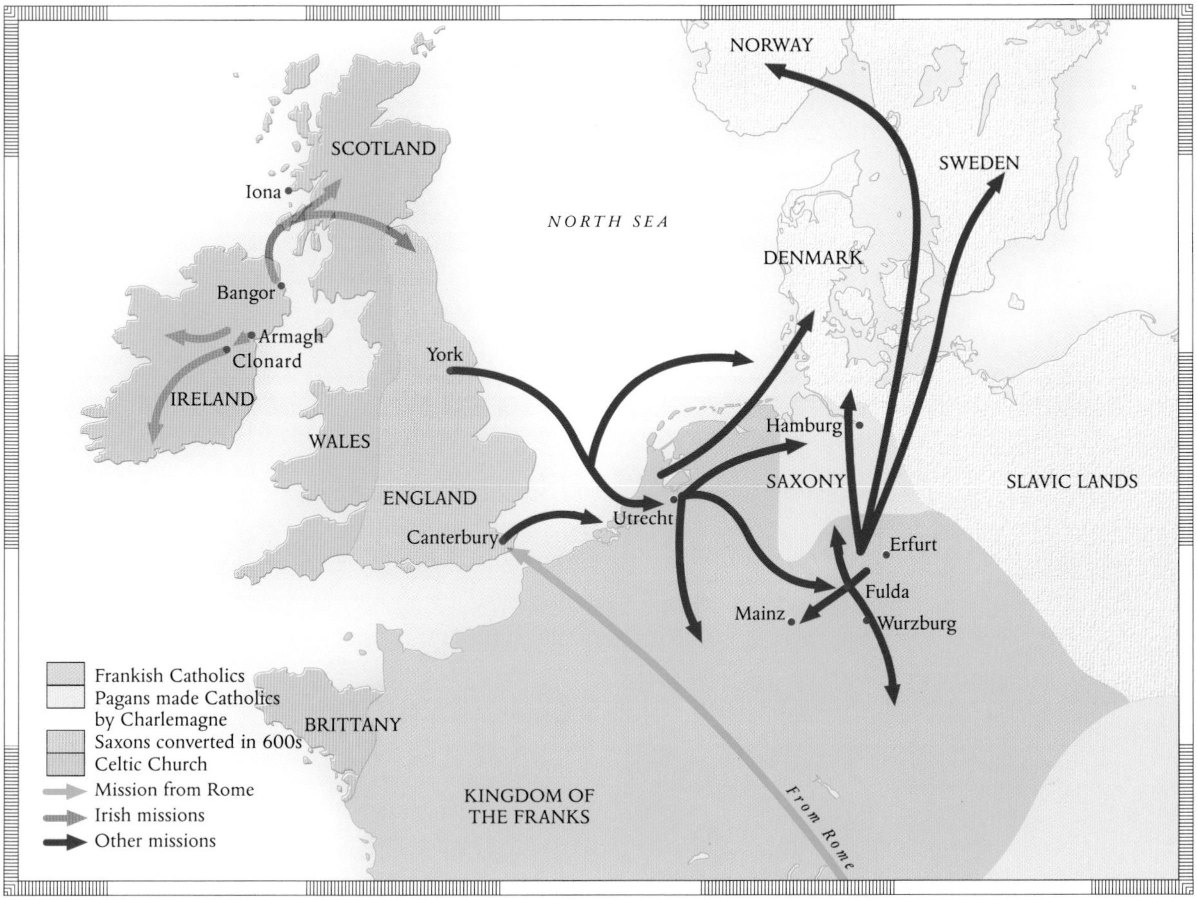
NORWAY
SCOTLAND
SWEDEN
Iona
NORTH SEA
DENMARK
Bangor
Armagh
Clonard
York
IRELAND
Hamburg
WALES
SAXONY
SLAVIC LANDS
ENGLAND
Utrecht
Canterbury
Erfurt
Fulda
Mainz
Wurzburg
Frankish Catholics
Pagans made Catholics by Charlemagne
Saxons converted in 600s
Celtic Church
Mission from Rome
Irish missions
Other missions
BRITTANY
KINGDOM OF THE FRANKS
From Rome

MISSIONARY ACTIVITY IN WESTERN EUROPE

Pope Gregory's policy of evangelization was one of the most significant factors in the conversion of western Europe during this period, beginning with the dispatch of Augustine to England. The map shows major missions from the sixth to the eleventh century.

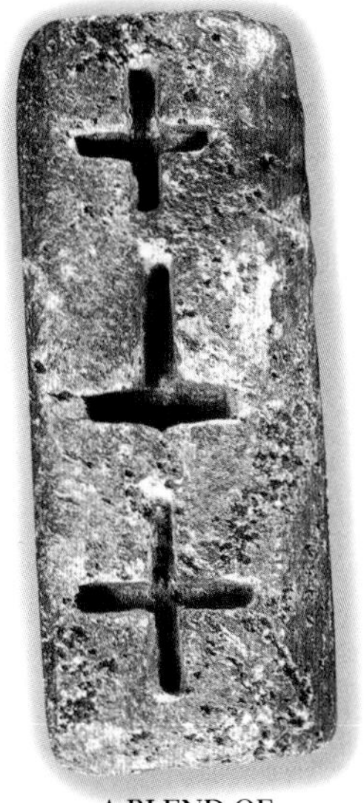

A BLEND OF CHRISTIAN AND PAGAN

Conversion to Christianity did not happen overnight, as this stone mold from Himmerland in Denmark shows. It is known as a Smith's mold and was used for casting both Christian crosses and Thor's hammers. Many "Christian" Vikings continued to remain loyal to the old Norse gods.

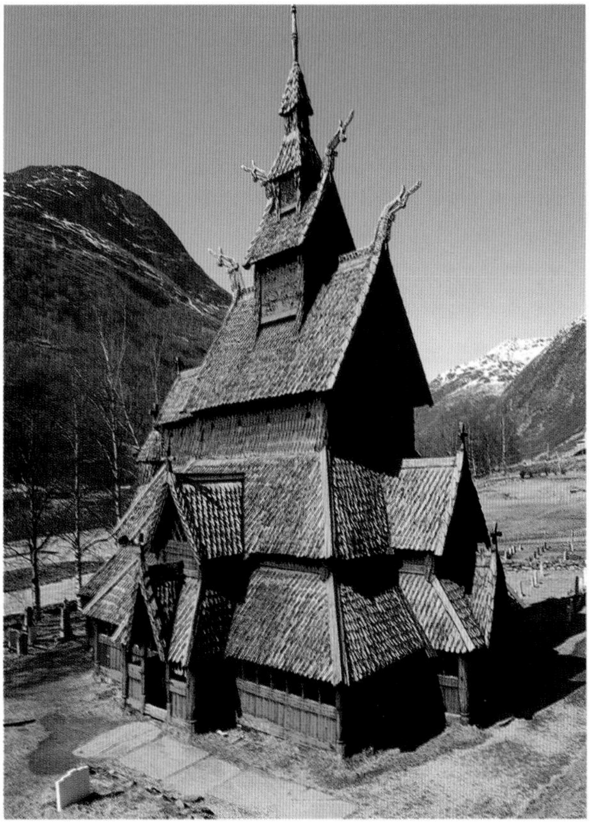

and destruction of the Viking attacks. It was not until over 100 years later, in the tenth century, that the Scandinavian countries were ready for conversion under the rule of the kings sympathetic to the Christian way of life. During the reign of King Canute (1018–35), Denmark became entirely Christian.

The way Christianity was introduced into Norway was unusual, insofar as it was preached not by a monk but a king. In 1016 Olaf I became king of Norway. He had been educated and converted to Christianity in England. Like many rulers before him, he forced the new faith on his subjects. After his death in 1030, he was canonized as Norway's patron saint.

Generally, however, Scandinavian society, with its own deep-seated pagan beliefs, proved very resistant to Christianity. Part of the reason the Christian church finally made headway was that the region's rulers wanted to strengthen their trade links with the rest of Europe, and this was a successful means to that end.

STAVE CHURCH, NORWAY

Christianity did not gain a permanent foothold in Norway until the eleventh century. This stave church dates back to 1150 and, like all such churches, is believed to have been modeled on pagan temples.

ICELAND AND GREENLAND

In the reign of Olaf Tryggvessön (969–1000), Icelanders democratically decided to become Christian. At the same time, Eric the Red's new colony in Greenland received its first priest and church thanks to his son Leif. By the beginning of the second millennium, the gospel really was being heard to the ends of the earth.

INVASIONS IN THE EAST

> **There is no God but Allah, and Muhammad is his prophet**
>
> QUR'AN

IN THE MID-SEVENTH century, the followers of Muhammad moved westward from Arabia with the intention of converting the world to the teachings of the prophet. They swept down through Palestine, Syria, and Egypt, lands sacred to the Christians and the Jews, determined to conquer the world and prepared to fight to achieve their aims. To this end,

they successfully overran the countries that had first responded to the Christian gospel. As they pushed farther into Africa, the monarchs of Europe looked on with dread at the approaching hordes, whom they viewed as no different from the barbarians. The Muslims pushed their way farther from Africa into Asia Minor and conquered much of it. However, despite besieging Constantinople, they were unsuccessful in their attempt to capture the city.

In 732 the Muslims pushed into France. At this time, Charles Martel (whose name means "the Hammerer"), the Christian king of the Franks, confronted the invaders at Poitiers, where, during a battle, the Muslim emir, or ruler, of Spain was killed.

A PERSIAN ILLUSTRATION OF THE PROPHET MUHAMMAD
Muhammad claimed that he had been inspired by God (in Arabic, Allah) to proclaim the true and final religion, and that this, Islam, was to be spread to all humanity throughout the world, using force if necessary. The image above shows the prophet ascending into heaven.

> **"HAVE FAITH IN ALLAH ... AND FIGHT FOR HIS CAUSE"**
>
> QUR'AN

The advance of the Muslims was thus checked for a while, and in 739, when they advanced as far as Lyons, Martel's army again routed them and drove them back into Spain. The threat of all of Europe being conquered was neutralized, the spread of Islamic power slowed down, and the rate of conversion to Islam became less dramatic. Whereas the barbarians were assimilated and became Christian, this was not to be the case with the Muslims, who resisted all attempts at conversion and had their own strong proselytizing mission.

❖ ISOLATING EAST AND WEST ❖

The overall effect of the Muslim invasions was the breaking of the link between East and West, isolating one from the other. The Christian church in the West was menaced by the invader, which effectively divided it from its contact with the emperor of the East. The

EIGHTH-CENTURY MOSQUE, DAMASCUS
Unlike the barbarians, the Muslim people could not be easily converted and assimilated into Christian culture. Their religion *and culture, as represented by this beautiful Islamic mosque in Damascus, still dominate many parts of the world today.*

popes were forced to look to European rulers for protection with the result that they became aligned with the barbarian West. The middle of the eighth century saw the last Greek pope to step onto the papal throne until the fifteenth century.

The Islamic expansion saw the loss to the Arabs of the patriarchates of Antioch, Alexandria, and Jerusalem, old rivals to the power of Rome and Constantinople. The struggle for supremacy was now between the bishops of the two imperial cities. Eastern Christendom became concentrated more than ever in Constantinople as many Christians left those regions ravaged by the Arabs to settle in and around the city. These refugees included monks and clergy who took with them the store of knowledge and the accumulated wealth of their monasteries and churches. Constantinople continued to grow in strength, and the balance of power tilted generously toward the East for the following three centuries. The East and the West had doctrine in common and a common enemy in Islam but culturally and politically drifted far apart.

❖ CHRISTIANITY'S SURVIVAL ❖ IN THE EAST

As the Muslims became more successful in their conquests, Western Europe became separated from much of Asia. However, in such areas as Persia, Palestine, and Egypt, the Islamic onslaught did not mean the end of the Christian church. For example, in Egypt Christianity continued in the form of the Coptic church (*see side column*), and in Persia the Nestorian form of Christianity survived (*pp. 63, 75*). Here, the Christians were protected and favored, with some even achieving positions of high status under the Muslim nobles.

More remarkable, however, was the arrival of Nestorian missions in China in the seventh century. At this time, China, under the T'ang Dynasty, was one of the wealthiest and most civilized countries in the world, and Nestorian monks were allowed to build monasteries and settle. For two centuries Christianity survived alongside other religious systems until a Taoist emperor in the ninth century brought about the dissolution of the monasteries, and Christianity subsequently dwindled away.

THE COPTIC CHURCH
During the turmoil of the Islamic invasion in the East, the Christian church in Egypt, the Coptic church, enjoyed freedom of worship. For centuries it had been in conflict with Byzantine authorities and saw the invasion of Egypt by the Muslims as a means of asserting its independence from Constantinople, as did its fellow Monophysite church in Syria.

❖

A NEW EMPIRE & A CHRISTIAN CULTURE

B Y THE MIDDLE OF THE eighth century, the papacy was finding it increasingly difficult to meet the burden of defending Rome from invasion by the Lombards. Pope Stephen II (r. 752–57) enlisted the help of the Frankish king, Pepin, in defending the city of Rome. Pepin and his two sons were consecrated by the pope and made protectors of the Romans. This papal-Frankish alliance proved most effective: Pepin routed the Lombards, forcing them to promise peace and to hand back treasures and important territories in northern Italy.

However, it was Charles, his son, who was to become one of the most important figures in the history of Europe. His reputation for culture and justice earned him the nickname of Charles the Great, or Charlemagne. A devout Christian, by the time of his death in 814, Charlemagne ruled over much of Western Europe, most of which had converted to the Christian faith.

Charles became king of the Franks after Pepin's death in 768. From this time onward Charles continued in his father's footsteps, pushing the Arabs back into northern Spain, extending his kingdom in the East, and converting the Saxons – a pagan tribe living in much of what is now Germany. In the autumn of the year 800, Charles settled a violent dispute between Pope Leo III (r. 795–816) and the aristocracy of Rome. And so it was that on Christmas Day of that year Charles was crowned emperor of the Holy Roman Empire by the pope. Not only did this restore the power of the papacy, but Charles's influence increased dramatically after his coronation. Thus by a quirk of fate, power was concentrated in the pontifical court, and a new empire in the West was established.

❖ CONVERTING THE EMPIRE ❖

Initially, the alliance between the popes and emperors was mutually favorable, but it became increasingly fraught with tension. Charlemagne resented the fact that he was beholden to the pope, and the pope in turn resented being treated by Charlemagne as a mere court official. In the East, the emperor and the citizens viewed the developments with dismay. The bishop of Rome was overstepping the mark, they thought, while the new, self-styled emperor was obviously setting himself up in opposition to the Byzantine emperor.

Charlemagne wanted all the people of the empire to worship in one language. Deeply affected by his Roman connection, in 781 he asked Pope Adrian to give him a *Sacramentary*, a book containing the text of all liturgical prayers, including the Eucharist, and ordered the Roman rites in Latin to be used throughout his lands. This was an important step in making Western Christians feel part of a united church. In fact,

THE CROWNING OF CHARLEMAGNE
On Christmas Day of the year 800, Charlemagne was crowned emperor of the Holy Roman Empire by Pope Leo III. The coronation took place in St. Peter's Basilica in Rome.

Charlemagne saw, much as Constantine had appreciated in the fourth century, how religion could be used as a unifying force. Conversion to Christianity for those who had not embraced the faith was often by force; Charlemagne commanded that any Saxon who refused baptism was to be put to death, and a similar fate awaited any pagans who plotted against the Christians. Like Clovis before him, he insisted on mass conversions – and mass slaughter in case of resistance.

Dedicated to improving his empire, Charlemagne engaged the services of the church, especially the monasteries. His chief advisor, Alcuin, was an English monk who supervised improvements in the liturgy and in sacred music, making them more in accordance with Roman usage.

✤ THE CAROLINGIAN RENAISSANCE ✤

For four hundred years, due to the barbarian invasions, little literature of any worth had been produced in Europe. Illiteracy became increasingly widespread as schools were destroyed, and learning became the preserve of the monasteries, which, under Charlemagne, became the center of a cultural renaissance. In the *scriptoria*, where the manuscripts were copied in Latin

A PAGE FROM THE GRANVAL BIBLE
As part of Charlemagne's cultural revival, a new script was developed known as the Caroline, or Carolingian, minuscule. The clear letters were written with a square-cut nib that produced strokes of even proportions. It became the dominant script in Western Europe.

ALCUIN OF YORK
Born in Yorkshire, England, Alcuin entered a monastery at York, where he soon became headmaster of the monastic school. His brilliant talents led to his appointment as head of the collegiate church of York. During a visit to Rome in 781, he met Charlemagne, who was so impressed that he invited Alcuin to transfer to his court at Aachen and take charge of his education program. Alcuin served as the emperor's advisor until 796, when he was appointed bishop of Tours. He played an important part in the fight against "Adoptionism" – a heresy that developed in Spain in the eighth century which taught that Jesus was simply a man "adopted" by God.

✤

THE CULT OF RELICS

✤

RELICS have long played an important part in the Christian tradition. The Latin word *reliquere*, meaning "to leave behind," indicates the origin of relics. After the death of a loved one, their personal belongings take on an important sentimental value. We know from the catacombs in Rome with what reverence the bodies of the deceased were regarded. As these became places of pilgrimage to honor the martyrs, visitors wished to have a small memento of their visit. Usually they rubbed a piece of linen against the tombs of the martyrs. These in turn were often brought home to relatives. In a superstitious era, such materials gained the power of a talisman. As early as the mid-fourth century, elaborate boxes were carved in ivory to house various souvenirs collected from visits to the Holy Land. In the Middle Ages, the cult of relics became indistinguishable from superstition. Churches vied with

TWELFTH-CENTURY RELIQUARY CASKET
Reliquaries were receptacles for holding the material relics of a saint, for example, their bones or objects associated with the saint or with Christ himself. Reliquaries were often carried in religious processions or became themselves objects of pilgrimage. They could be of any shape or size but were usually made of precious metals and richly decorated. The reliquary above depicts the murder of Thomas Becket in the twelfth century, and contains the martyr's bones.

each other, each boasting a superior collection of relics. Visitors to the cathedral of Cologne could venerate the bodies of the Three Wise Men, or baby Jesus' manger in a church in Rome. The heyday of relics came during the Crusades in the eleventh and twelfth centuries. When the crusaders returned to Europe, they brought booty in the form of relics. How many of these were genuine is impossible to say, although it is likely to have been only a tiny proportion. Such exaggerated devotion inevitably led to abuse. One of the principal objections of the Reformers of the sixteenth century was the proliferation of evident forgeries in the previous five centuries. Luther complained that with all the pieces of the true cross of Christ lying in various shrines, one could build a ship. Relics never became popular in the East, where icons (*p. 99*) were far more important.

because Greek was no longer commonly understood, pagan as well as Christian authors were transcribed. A new script was developed, and spelling was standardized by Alcuin and his students at the emperor's palace in Aachen.

Some of the finest illuminated manuscripts were produced during this period. Charlemagne recognized the importance of learning and, even before he was emperor, issued a capitulary, or collection of decrees, in 787 ordering that all monasteries and bishops' houses should become places of learning and study. Charlemagne's legacy to the West has been called the Carolingian Renaissance.

❖ THE EMERGENCE OF A ❖ CHRISTIAN CULTURE

By the end of Charlemagne's reign in 814, medieval Europe was thoroughly Christian. This was an age before television, cinema, magazines, videos, or computers, where the church offered a daily, and an annual, cycle of stimulation. Apart from the Sunday Eucharist, feast days, with their attendant devotions

> *" I am a poor old woman who knows nothing, who cannot read. But in the church I see Paradise painted, and Hell where the damned broil "*
>
> **WORDS OF MEDIEVAL FRENCH PEASANT WOMAN**

and processions, punctuated the often monotonous rhythm of the week. It was on these occasions, too, that the laity was allowed to partake in the Eucharist. (Usually only the priest took Communion since the Mass was celebrated *for* the people and not *with* the people.)

For such feast days, artists delighted in carving statues that were carried in colorful processions. These processions also provided the opportunity to embellish as much as possible, from richly embroidered vestments to elaborately wrought processional crosses, candlesticks, and thuribles. All was seen as glorifying God, and no effort was too great to that end. To serve and honor God – nothing could be considered more worthy.

The poor, whose lives were often marked by great difficulties, delighted in the distraction offered by such religious exercises. The decoration of the church was a communal effort, achieved through the cooperation of rich and poor alike. The execution of works of art offered many the opportunity of employment, in some degree relieving the burdens of poverty.

> **" PAINTINGS ARE THE BIBLE OF THE LAITY "**
>
> **GRATIAN, ITALIAN MONK, TWELFTH CENTURY**

❖ TEACHING THROUGH IMAGERY ❖

The stained-glass windows and the fresco-cycles of the medieval cathedrals of Europe are often referred to as the Bible of the Poor. In the Middle Ages, when literacy was quite rare, the great biblical scenes were narrated through the media of glass and pigment. Though beautiful to the eye, the stained glass and painted walls were primarily intended as instructive aids for teaching the illiterate poor the principles of their faith. Throughout the church services, preachers could refer to the luminous windows or point to the vaults, where scenes from the Bible were laid out above the gaze of the congregation.

Artists delighted in illustrating stories from the Old and New Testaments. The Tree of Jesse was a popular image, which depicted the family tree of Jesus as listed in the opening of Matthew's Gospel. The Nativity and Crucifixion were also favorite themes for artists.

ELEVENTH-CENTURY FACE OF CHRIST, FROM THE ABBEY OF WISSEMBOURG, ALSACE
This striking image is one of the earliest examples of stained glass. By the eleventh century, artists were able to convey great expressiveness in their stained-glass design, although the art of telling stories in glass was not perfected by craftsmen until the following century.

EARLY MEDIEVAL DEVELOPMENTS IN CHURCH MUSIC

❖

As the liturgy developed, so did church music. By the end of the sixth century, Pope Gregory I (r. 590–604) had not only reorganized the liturgy but had also codified all the music (*p. 73*) that had been composed to date. It is from the intervention of this pope that Gregorian chant takes its name. He organized a special *Schola Cantorum*, a school in which boys would be taught all the music necessary to accompany the pontifical liturgies. Gregory founded two choirs, one at the Lateran, the other at St. Peter's, to serve the liturgies performed in the basilicas. These choirs helped foster and promote the Gregorian chant. Over the next two centuries, this chant, also called plainsong, developed a rich repertoire and became the dominant form of music in church services in the West.

Monasteries also became focal points of musical development: monks composed melodies for their worship and laboriously copied out manuscripts, thus preserving and disseminating music.

CHARLEMAGNE'S LEGACY

The coronation of Charlemagne in 800 gave a new impetus to liturgical music. Anxious to have one style of music, to serve as a unifying factor in the liturgies celebrated throughout the Holy Roman Empire, the emperor set up schools to teach this style throughout his territories. Already, some years earlier, his father, Pepin the Short, had begun to copy the books of the Roman church ritual for dissemination throughout the Frankish kingdom. The energy with which Charlemagne approached the task ensured that plainsong became the music most commonly heard in church throughout the West until the Protestant Reformation in the sixteenth century.

SINGING IN PRAISE
Church music developed from a medium of facilitating the learning of Scripture in an age of illiteracy into an expression of praise in its own right.

EARLY ORGAN MUSIC
Not much is known about the use of the organ in early medieval times, but it may well have been used, like church bells, to call people to worship. For a long time the organ was regarded as an instrument that should have a voice of its own and was not to accompany congregational singing. The choir and the organ would therefore alternate verses.

Between the middle of the ninth century and the late eleventh century, however, there was a further development in church music in northern Europe. Experimenting with the human voice, composers began to add harmonies to the ancient melodies. From small monasteries to the great cathedrals, the chant was embellished and transformed.

In France in the late eleventh century, the organist began adding melodies above or below the main line, called the *cantus firmus* or the tenor. This was the origin of *polyphony* (literally, "many-sounding"), in which several strands of sound are interwoven to provide a delicate harmony.

MUSICAL NOTATION

In the early eleventh century, an Italian monk, Guido d'Arezzo, devised a method that enabled choirboys to sing music that they had never heard. He invented a system of notes on a written page, placed on four parallel lines. The notes and the spaces between them signified the different tones of the musical scale. When the pope heard of Guido's invention, he called the monk to see him. Guido wrote: "The pope was glad to see me. He leafed through my book and did not move until he had learned to sing a verse which he had not seen before." This system went on to form the basis of all modern musical notation.

In the same century, music was also written down for the first time in the East. In Russia, these chants, called *znamenny raspev*, or "chanting by signs," remained the music of the church until the seventeenth century, when trading brought Russia into closer contact with Europe and other forms of church music.

WESTERN EUROPE RETURNS TO CHAOS

WITHIN DECADES OF Charlemagne's death, his empire had disintegrated, his sons and grandsons neither capable of governing its territories nor of defending them against the aggressive attacks of the Muslims, Slavs, Magyars, and Vikings. Europe, with its vast array of riches, was alluring to the invading Vikings, who swept southward from Scandinavia. Norwegians, Swedes, and Danes all descended on the undefended people, destroying villages and looting monasteries. Small wonder the Irish monks included an invocation in their prayers to save them from the brutality of the Vikings, for brutal they most certainly were. Contemporary records are filled with horrific tales of the violent murder and pillaging which attended every invasion. By the time the worst of the incursions was over, Christian Europe had been reduced to a pale shadow of its former glory.

The ninth century was also to see a decline in the fortunes of the papacy, the cause of which was not exterior to the papacy but rather at its heart. Several of the incumbents of the papal office were not worthy

> **" FROM THE FURY OF THE NORSEMEN DELIVER US, O LORD "**
>
> **PRAYER OF NINTH-CENTURY CELTIC MONKS**

of their rank. From the ninth until the eleventh centuries, the papacy became the prize of influential Roman families. The papal throne was disputed among several candidates, each claiming to be legitimately elected by

THE ART OF MANUSCRIPT ILLUMINATION

❖

THE image we have of monks toiling away quietly illustrating books is, in fact, largely true. They were the only educated class in medieval society. With an almost total collapse of civil order and culture in the ninth and tenth centuries, it was the monasteries that preserved a sense of stability and allowed art and learning to continue developing.

Book production and manuscript illumination were not a cheap business. Pages were often made of vellum (sheets of fine-grained sheepskin or calfskin) carefully rubbed smooth and sewn together. Some of the later medieval books are of such fine quality that the pages feel like tissue paper.

Diverse materials were ground down in order to provide colors, with each monastery conserving carefully the secret ingredients of their colors. By far the most precious was lapis lazuli, a blue stone which was mined only in Afghanistan. Throughout the Middle Ages, this

ILLUMINATED LETTER FROM THE ARNSTEIN BIBLE
Initial letters offered many possibilities for illumination – a word that means "to light up," appropriate not only for the bright colors used but also for the delightful scenes that were often woven in and around individual letters. The letter above is the first of John's Gospel.

remained highly coveted and was reserved for illustrating the mantle of the Virgin Mary.

For manuscripts of particular value, gold was used, most often in the form of gold leaf. Thin sheets were laid on the surface to be decorated. A light glair or gum was pasted under the leaf, which was then burnished into a sheen. Only rarely was silver used, as it tended to oxidize when brought into contact with the air. Black ink was prepared from either carbon soot diluted with water, or from iron gall (sulfate of iron and oak apples).

The ink was mixed with gum, which allowed it to set on the parchment or manuscript. In liturgical books the sacred text was in black ink, with directions to the clergy and musicians in red ink. With such extensive barbarian invasions it is surprising that so many books have survived to the present day.

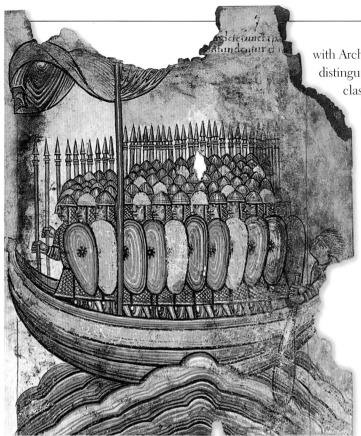

VIKING WARSHIP
Throughout the ninth century, Viking ships attacked towns and monasteries in Western Europe. Many Vikings made their homes in the conquered regions. One such group settled around the town of Rouen in France, the area subsequently becoming known as Normandy, "the Land of the Norsemen."

with Archbishop Hincmar of Rheims, the most distinguished of the Frankish bishops. Nicholas also clashed with King Lothaire of Lorraine for attempting to divorce his queen.

❖ MADNESS AND IMMORALITY ❖

In 882 the unbelievable happened: Pope John VIII was murdered, the first pope to be assassinated. He died at the hands of his disgruntled entourage, first being poisoned and then clubbed to death. Worse was to follow. In the autumn of 896, Pope Stephen VII had the body of his predecessor, Pope Formosus, disinterred from its grave and dressed in pontifical vestments. Charges were then read against the deceased pontiff before his blessing fingers were cut off and the body thrown into the Tiber. Stephen had been a jealous opponent of Formosus and certainly was unbalanced. Not surprisingly, Stephen himself was to meet a violent end, being thrown into prison and subsequently strangled by the Roman mob.

The century teetered on toward an unsteady end, and the tenth century opened with relative peace for the papacy and the church. When, in 915, Pope John X and King Berenger I of Italy united to finally defeat the Saracens, matters seemed to improve. Not for long, however, for in 928, John was exiled, and probably murdered.

the people and clergy of Rome, while in fact being imposed by family factions. Several popes were assassinated, poisoned, or deposed (*see below*). Effective popes were the exception rather than the rule.

❖ ROME UNDER ATTACK ❖

It was not an easy time for the papacy. In the face of opposition from powerful rulers, the popes needed to defend, in the stoutest terms, their independence. Yet in 824 the newly elected Eugene II agreed to take an oath of loyalty to the Western emperor. With the disintegration of the empire in 843, however, this became something of a formality. In any case, the popes were more concerned with the possibility of a Saracen attack (*see side column*). During the pontificate of Sergius II in the 840s, the Saracens swept into Rome, plundering the city, and even despoiling the tomb of St. Peter at the Vatican. The following pontificate of Leo IV was spent fortifying the Vatican and trying to repair Rome's shrines.

Nicholas I (r. 858–67) tried to reassert the papacy's independence against renewed interference from the emperor of the East, when he refused to recognize the appointment of Photius as patriarch of Constantinople (*p. 100*). He adopted a strict line against bishops whom he considered lax, which brought him into confrontation

EDUCATING THE CLERGY
Before seminaries for educating clergy were founded in the sixteenth century there was no system of theological education nor any firm control over who joined the clergy. It was even possible for powerful men to bypass the preparatory minor orders and obtain lucrative senior clerical positions for themselves. At the other end of the social scale were the humble parish priests, many with no education, little knowledge, and poor ability to teach the faith.

❖

> **❝** *For no power on earth may judge the Apostolic See* **❞**
>
> **SYNOD OF ROME, 800**

"POPE FORMOSUS AND STEPHEN VII" BY J.P. LAURENS
Clad in papal finery, the disinterred body of Pope Formosus attends his "trial" in Rome. The painting evokes the sense of madness that surrounded the papal court of the ninth century.

CHURCH, STATE, & MONKS

CLERICAL DRESS
Usually clergy dressed as lay people, but for ceremonies a chasuble, a cloak of sumptuous silks, was worn over a white ankle-length tunic. Some were jewel encrusted like the ceremonial robes worn at the imperial court.

CHURCH REFORM FINALLY began with the arrival of the German king Otto I, who was crowned emperor of the newly restored Holy Roman Empire in 936. Otto had developed a close relationship with the church in Germany, donating large areas of land to bishops and monasteries. He had elevated the status of church leaders and, by so doing, had won their support and loyalty. Once in Rome, Otto helped to rescue the popes from the depths to which they had sunk. Otto forced the papacy to agree that no new pope could be elected without his consent. He thus helped free the papacy from the destructive forces of Italian politics, while beginning a power struggle between popes and Western emperors that was to last for centuries.

THE CONSECRATION OF THE HIGH ALTAR AT CLUNY BY POPE URBAN II
Cluny was the first monastery to be free from the influence of local princes and bishops, answerable only to the pope in Rome. It played an important role in the reform of the medieval church, and advocated a return to the full teaching of the Benedictine rule.

✤ THE ABBEY OF CLUNY ✤

Help for the beleaguered papacy also came at the beginning of the tenth century from the Benedictine order. In c. 909 William, Duke of Aquitaine, founded a monastery for 12 monks at Cluny, in northern France. He endowed the order and made a special provision that it would be under the direct control of the papacy. In this way, the monks were able to avoid being unduly influenced by lay interference, or indeed by the meddling of neighboring bishops.

Over 20 years later, Pope John XI (r. 931–35) gave Cluny the right to form a confederation and accept any religious houses that wanted to belong to the Cluny family. Those wishing to do so had to become priories, directly subject to the abbot of Cluny. The right to freedom from lay control was attractive to many houses, and by the dawn of the new millennium more than 1,000 such monasteries looked to Cluny as their head. As one contemporary proudly observed, "There is one house for every year since the birth of our Holy Redeemer."

THE FEUDAL HIERARCHY AND THE CHURCH

❖

THE ordinary person in medieval Europe felt that he or she belonged to a divinely ordered society. The economic and political system of the period was strictly hierarchical and based on a pyramid model that was believed to be ordained by God. The vast majority of people endured near poverty, living from harvest to harvest on a small portion of land that was the property of another, more wealthy individual. They were serfs (near slaves), peasants, or worse, working for a pittance. Above this group, which included the majority of men, women, and children, was a lord, who owned the land. Usually, there was also a series of middlemen who controlled the lives of the workers, directing their activities. The lord was himself usually beholden to a prince or a king who, in exchange for a service

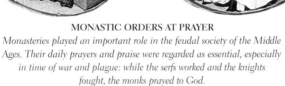

MONASTIC ORDERS AT PRAYER

Monasteries played an important role in the feudal society of the Middle Ages. Their daily prayers and praise were regarded as essential, especially in time of war and plague: while the serfs worked and the knights fought, the monks prayed to God.

or a tribute, protected the territories by means of a small army. Monasteries were also modeled on this feudal hierarchy. The abbot or bishop took the place of the lord and vassal, and he ruled over the land owned by the monastery.

The monasteries grew rapidly wealthy for a number of reasons. Usually efficiently run, they were often endowed by the families of the monks. When local landlords went to war, they entrusted their goods to the care of the monastery. If they failed to return, their treasures became the property of the monastery. Some monastic positions were soon to prove attractive to the younger sons of nobility, for, unlike noble titles, they were not hereditary titles. As monasteries gained more and more wealth and public protection from the monarchy, so their lifestyles often became increasingly comfortable.

Cluny was ruled by a succession of long-lived, wise, and holy abbots, one of whom, Odilo, elected abbot c. 994, worked hard to make Cluny a center of learning, liturgy, and ecclesiastical art. Shifting slightly away from the original Benedictine tradition of spending long hours in agricultural work, Odilo encouraged church music and the practice of singing the liturgy. Furthermore, Odilo "marvellously adorned the cloisters with columns and marble brought from the farthest parts of the province."

Aside from campaigning for the free election of abbots and priors, Cluny also pushed for a number of other far-reaching reforms: working in diocesan and provincial synods to promote local reforms (particularly the enforcement of celibacy among clergy in holy orders); promoting private peace by initiating a movement known as the "Truce of God," which aimed to protect clergy, women, children, and church buildings from any robberies or attacks; making Cluniac monks bishops of local dioceses. In addition, Cluny urged the popes to purge the church of various abuses, particularly the buying and selling of church offices, known as simony. Since Cluny had played such an important

role in the restoration of the papacy, several popes became ardent supporters of these reforms. For two centuries Cluny was to inspire hundreds of new foundations and to reform older abbeys. These communities valued their independence from lay rulers, and indeed from the interference of local bishops, but no ruler would wish to leave them unchecked, with their vast territorial holdings. Lay magnates constantly attempted to gain control of the land, wealth, and influence of the important abbeys in their domains, and indeed to control the bishops and other major clergy.

❖ MONASTERIES AND SAINTS ❖

Monasteries played an essential role in the daily and religious lives of the local community, and it was common for people to visit their local monastery in order to venerate the saints. Though living saints, such as Odo of Cluny, were considered the most effective of all protectors, local people came together to pray and to ask for help and protection from the holy relics and statues within the monastery. Many believed themselves greatly helped in their illnesses and general misfortunes.

CHURCH VESSELS

The principal vessels used in church were a paten, or dish, to hold the bread for the Eucharist, and a chalice, or cup, for the wine. These were made either of gold or of silver, often inlaid with jewels and precious stones. The above chalice is an eighth-century Byzantine vessel embossed with onyx.

❖

SPLENDOR & SCHISM

THE "FILIOQUE" QUESTION

An important theological difference between the Western and Byzantine churches concerned the Holy Spirit. In 589 the Council of Toledo made an addition to the Nicene Creed (pp. 61-63): "I believe in the Holy Spirit who proceeds from the Father *and the Son*" (*filioque*, in Latin). The ninth-century patriarch, Photius, objected to "*and the Son*" addition and condemned all who used it as heretics. He argued that the Council had no right to insert this clause and maintained that it did not reflect orthodox belief. It remains one of the dividing issues between Eastern and Western Christians to this day.

✤

IN THE 600S, AS THE WEST was sinking, the East was enjoying a remarkable renaissance. The emperor of the East was conscious that he was heir, in an unbroken line, to Constantine, and he lived in the first Christian emperor's city, Constantinople, rich in sumptuous buildings and successful in trade. Visitors to the imperial court were awed by the splendor that surrounded the person of the emperor. Dressed in costly silks and seated on a golden throne, he seemed like a god, while around him sweet incense perfumed the air, and fans of ostrich feathers cooled him. The beauty of his palace, decorated with gold mosaics, overwhelmed the ambassadors, scholars, and churchmen who were granted audiences. However, by the end of the tenth century the cultural, political, and religious gap with the West had widened so far that there were dangerous signs of an impending schism.

✤ THE ICONOCLASTS ✤

During the eighth century, one major division first surfaced as the emperor Leo III (r. 717–41) looked westward with displeasure from his imperial seat at Constantinople. Since the time of Gregory the Great, at the end of the sixth century, the bishops of Rome had improved the administration of their lands and indeed had become important landowners in their own right. Leo also saw the sweeping conquests made by the Turks and was aggravated by the fact that it was the unsophisticated Franks who succeeded in stopping their advance. He chose to lend his support to the iconoclasts, thereby winning support in the army and attacking the monks and other church leaders.

The iconoclasts were a group of religious people who vigorously opposed the veneration of icons, believing strongly that they were covered by the biblical ban found in the book of Exodus: "You shall not make for yourself an idol in the form of anything in heaven above or on the earth beneath or in the waters below. You shall not bow down to them or worship them" (Exodus 20:4). In 726 Leo ordered a great icon of Christ that hung over the gates of Constantinople to be smashed to the ground. He followed this with orders to destroy all the images of Christ and the saints in the churches, his actions winning the support and praise of the iconoclasts. The emperor then tried to extend his authority to the West, annexing land in Sicily and assuming authority in the south of Italy.

The controversy over the icons appeared to be resolved by the Second Council of Nicea in 787. The Council restored the use of the holy images but insisted that they should only be honored and not worshiped.

ICONOCLASTS WHITEWASHING OR SPEARING AN IMAGE OF CHRIST
This eleventh-century manuscript depicts the iconoclastic dispute of three centuries earlier. The destruction of religious icons and the persecution of icon worshipers (iconophiles) created a great divide in the Eastern church. Generally, monks and laity defended icons, while a number of emperors ruthlessly sought to destroy the images. Many icon worshipers were persecuted for defending the images they believed played a necessary role in their religious lives.

GREEK AND RUSSIAN ICONS – IMAGES OF FAITH

✤

AN ESSENTIAL part of Eastern theology, art, and devotion, icons (from the Greek *eikon*, meaning "image") are small painted wooden panels depicting Christ, Mary, and the saints. The earliest recorded icons are of Peter and Paul, and

> **❝** *What the written word is to those who know letters, the icon is to the unlettered; what speech is to the ear, the icon is to the eye* **❞**
>
> ST. JOHN OF DAMASCUS

are mentioned by Eusebius, bishop of Caesarea, before 340. These, like most early icons, no longer exist, having been destroyed in the Christian persecutions of the first centuries.

Throughout the eighth and ninth centuries a series of Eastern emperors banned the use of icons in public worship. The only forms permitted to represent Christ were the ancient Chi-Rho, or the Alpha and Omega symbols *(see p. 41)*. Jeweled crosses were also allowed. Feelings ran high, however, and the suppression of icons even led to the outbreak of war. Monks, the main venerators of icons, were persecuted, tortured, or martyred, and the period between 762 and 775 even became known as the "decade of blood." Once the decrees of the Second Council of Nicea (787) allowed the use of icons and the veneration of Mary and the saints again, a veritable explosion of icon production developed from the mid-ninth century until 1453, ending with the fall of Constantinople.

After the capture of the city by the Muslims, the centers of icon production shifted to Crete and Russia. From this period onward, icons

THE MOTHER OF GOD OF THE PASSION
The Eastern church places much importance on Mary's role as Theotokos, *"God-bearer" or "Mother of God."*

ICON OF GREGORY PALAMAS (1296–1359)
The fourteenth-century Greek theologian, Gregory Palamas, was canonized and named a father and doctor of the Orthodox church soon after his death.

changed very little in style due to the desire to remain faithful to ancient Eastern tradition, which had been so fiercely attacked and defended during the eighth and ninth centuries. In the West, however, the use of icons never developed in the same way – a major difference between Eastern and Western Christian worship.

Though icons represent historical figures, they are intended to be not realistic but spiritual portraits. They seek to communicate spiritual and theological truths. More important for the Orthodox, icons are "windows to heaven," a means through which believers communicate with God and receive grace. Through an icon, a saint becomes accessible and visible. In the past, Eastern Christians often had a small icon of a saint at home, and carried icons with them on journeys. Troops going into battle were blessed with these images.

In Eastern Orthodox churches, a large screen called the *iconostasis* shields the sanctuary from public view and is heavily decorated with icons. During religious ceremonies, the images are perfumed with incense and kissed as a sign of reverence and respect for the saint. To this day the faithful visit their churches and kiss each image, praying to the saint whom the icon makes visible to the eye of the beholder.

The domed interior swallows up the day.
There, where to light a candle is to pray,
The candle flame shows
up the almond eyes
Of local saints who view with no surprise
Their martyrdom's depicted upon walls
On which the filtered daylight faintly falls
The flame shows up the cracked paint –
sea-green blue
And red and gold – with grained wood
showing through
Of much-kissed icons, dating from, perhaps,
The fourteenth century. …

Extract from "Greek Orthodox" by Sir John Betjeman

CYRIL AND METHODIUS

Born in the second quarter of the ninth century, these two Greek brothers were ordained priests and in 862 traveled to convert the people of Greater Moravia. They translated the New Testament and the liturgy into the language of the people (to do so they had first to create an alphabet for the previously unwritten Slavonic language), a move that gained papal approval in 868. Cyril died in Rome the following year, while his brother Methodius was appointed archbishop of Moravia, where he remained until his death in 884.

❖

However, in 813 the issue flared up again when the emperor once more ordered the destruction of the icons. In 843 the dispute was finally settled when empress Theodora II convened the Council of Orthodoxy, where the veneration of icons was restored. This episode shows just how dependent the Eastern church had become on the will of the emperor. Such was the significance of the end of the iconoclastic controversy that, today, the Orthodox churches commemorate it with an annual feast.

❖ THE PHOTIUS DISPUTE ❖

In 858 Ignatius, patriarch of Constantinople, was deposed in favor of Photius. Ignatius had opposed the iconoclasts and refused to readmit the clergy who had fought against the use of icons. The people regarded him as something of a hero, because the suppression of the icons had involved much bloodshed. Three years later, when the appointment of Photius was confirmed at the Synod of Constantinople, Ignatius turned to Rome for help and found support from the pope. The newly appointed Photius sprang to the counterattack, accusing the pope of meddling in the affairs of Constantinople.

Eventually, in 867, Photius summoned another synod at Constantinople, where he managed to persuade the participants to excommunicate the pope. After Ignatius died ten years later, there was the possibility of patching up the differences, and Rome

and Constantinople agreed once more to reestablish relations. However, the damage was done, and from then until the total break in 1054, there were effectively two separate churches.

❖ THE SLAVIC MISSION ❖

Meanwhile, the gospel message was making its way eastward. The first missionaries to Moravia (part of the modern Czech Republic) came from Germany. However, their efforts at conversion were hampered by the fact that they could neither speak nor write the native language.

In 862 two brothers from Thessalonica in northern Greece, Cyril and Methodius, set out with the goodwill of the emperor, Michael III, with the intention of preaching the gospel to the people of Moravia. They translated the sacred Scriptures into Moravian and began celebrating the Eucharist in the language of the people. Their missionary work was crowned with success, and a great number of people were converted to Christianity. The brothers were not unopposed, however, and, as was so often the case in Christian history, it was their own who were to betray them. German bishops petitioned the pope to forbid the celebration of the sacraments in the vernacular, but Pope Adrian II gave the brothers permission to use the language of the people. Some years later, however, Pope Stephen V placed a ban on the use of the Slavic language for the liturgy, and the followers of the two

THE JUDGMENT OF PATRIARCH PHOTIUS

Photius (third from the left) is depicted here with his palms raised upward before his accusers after enemies from the Byzantine court had brought false charges against him in 886. An outspoken and radical man, Photius denounced the Latin missions in Bulgaria, rejected the filioque (p. 98) in the Creed, and accused Pope Nicholas of being "a heretic who ravages the vineyard of the Lord." Photius was patriarch twice, deposed once, and eventually resigned in 886.

ORTHODOX MISSIONS IN THE EAST
The boundaries of the Eastern church were greatly widened in the ninth, tenth, and eleventh centuries by missionary activity extending out from Constantinople. The Eastern churches allowed the people to celebrate the liturgy in their native language.

brothers were forced into exile, fleeing to Bulgaria. In 864 the Bulgarian czar had been baptized, and his people, along with those of Romania and Serbia, gradually followed him into the Eastern church. Moravia, however, was firmly within the Western church by the end of the 800s. Bohemia (part of the modern Czech Republic) followed in the tenth century, under Prince Boleslav II (r. 967–99). Meanwhile, to the north of Moravia, Poland converted to the Latin form of Christianity: the country's ruler was baptized in c. 967, and under his son Boleslav Chrobry (r. 992–1025) the Christianization of the people was energetically begun.

❖ RUSSIA ADOPTS EASTERN ❖ CHRISTIANITY

Farther east lay the vast territories of Russia. For some years missionaries from both East and West had made efforts to bring the gospel to Russia, with little success. Towards the end of the tenth century, Vladimir, emperor of Kiev, decided to adopt Christianity as the official religion of his territories. He was aware of the divisions in Christianity and wanted to embrace the purest form possible. Accordingly, he sent out ambassadors to scout around and investigate what would be most suited to the Russian temperament. The ambassadors were stunned by the sumptuousness of Constantinople, especially when they visited the church of Hagia Sophia, founded by the emperor Justinian in the sixth century (*p. 76*), and witnessed

the lavish liturgy celebrated there. They reported back to the emperor, unable to put into words the beauty of what they had seen.

Thus it was that Vladimir chose the Byzantine form of the faith, and in 988 he gave orders for all his subjects to be baptized with him. He let it be known that those who did not do so would face the emperor's displeasure:

> ❝WE KNEW NOT WHETHER WE WERE IN HEAVEN OR ON EARTH. FOR ON EARTH THERE IS NO SUCH SPLENDOUR OR SUCH BEAUTY AND WE ARE AT A LOSS TO DESCRIBE IT❞

EMISSARIES SENT OUT BY VLADIMIR DESCRIBING HAGIA SOPHIA IN CONSTANTINOPLE

ALLIANCE WITH ROME

While the Greek missions entered the Slavic lands and were successful in their conversions, Western Christianity also gained ground there. To the Western church came the Croatians, Bohemians, Slovaks, Moravians, and Poles. Further, the Magyars, who settled in Hungary, joined the Western church when their king, Stephen I (r. 997–1038), was converted and led the evangelization of his country. The process of conversion was often aided by the installing of bishops by the pope, political alliances, and the influence of devout rulers.

❖

VLADIMIR'S BAPTISM INTO EASTERN CHRISTIANITY
Learning that Islam did not accept his messengers, and believing that Judaism was not right for his people and that Western Christianity was too simple, Vladimir converted to Greek Christianity. The image above is from The Chronicle of Nestor, *the oldest surviving account of Vladimir's life.*

"Whoever he be, who will not come to the river tomorrow to be baptized, be he rich or poor, will fall into disgrace with me." However, Vladimir's decision to adopt this form was probably based largely on political motives, as the following year he married the sister of the emperor at Constantinople, thus consolidating his union with the seemingly impregnable empire of the East.

❖ GROWING FISSURES ❖

By the beginning of the eleventh century the cultural and religious differences between the East and the West were set to cause problems. The East had allowed the Hellenistic tradition to continue little altered for 1,000 years, and many could no longer speak Latin. In the West few were able to understand Greek. The East had also begun to look upon the West as uneducated and uncultured barbarians. In the East, levels of education were high among the laity as well as the clergy, whereas in the West education was confined solely to the church.

While Rome succumbed at various times to barbarian invasions, the emperors at Constantinople continued to adorn the capital of the empire. East and West had grown politically far apart; the West saw the East as the source of all heresies, while the East looked upon the West as a mere shadow of its former glory. In reality, both East and West faced a common enemy, Islam (*see also pp. 88-89*), which ought to have brought them together in a common cause.

Another source of friction between East and West came when the Normans began to invade the southern regions of Italy, which politically was governed by the East but belonged, in fact, to the West. The Byzantine emperor needed aid from the West to conquer the Normans, but the pope was unwilling to help because he wished to claim back jurisdiction over southern Italy from the patriarch of Constantinople.

Pope Leo IX (r. 1049–1054) sparked a clash with Byzantium by asserting his spiritual authority, holding a synod to reform the Sicilian church and appointing

❝ BETWEEN US AND THE FRANKS [THE WEST] IS SET THE WIDEST GULF. WE HAVE NOT A THOUGHT IN COMMON ❞

TWELFTH-CENTURY BYZANTINE HISTORIAN

BYZANTINE PLATE FOR HOLDING COMMUNION BREAD
When the split finally came between the Orthodox and the Catholic churches, it was no surprise. This unusual sixth-century paten appears to show Christ giving the sacrament of Communion simultaneously to two groups of apostles as if in anticipation of the split to come. Even at this early stage the two factions, East and West, were developing their own Christian traditions. Cultural differences may have been more important than theological issues in their parting.

a new archbishop of Sicily. He was met with furious opposition by the patriarch of Constantinople, Michael Cerularius, who was perhaps encouraged by the emperor of the East. Cerularius, in retaliation for Pope Leo's refusal to cooperate, ordered the closure of the Western

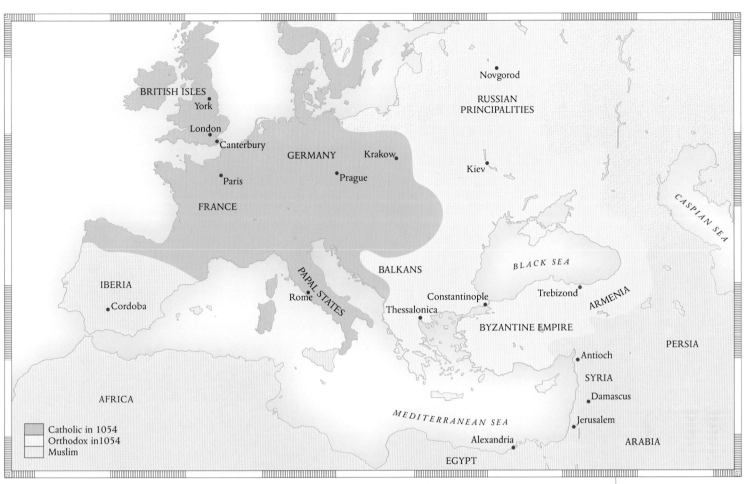

THE STATE OF THE CHRISTIAN WORLD AFTER 1054
The above map shows the boundaries of Catholic and Orthodox Christianity after 1054 and how far Islam had extended its influence by this stage. The Muslim area embraced many Orthodox, Monophysite, and Nestorian Christians living under Islamic rule.

Map legend:
- Catholic in 1054
- Orthodox in 1054
- Muslim

churches in Constantinople, and expelled the clergy. The pope dispatched his legate, Cardinal Humbert de Silva Candida, to meet with the patriarch. Negotiations, if they were ever begun, were broken off when the papal legate excommunicated Michael and his court.

❖ THE FINAL BREAK ❖

On July 16 1054, Humbert strode into the church of Hagia Sophia and slammed the bull of excommunication on the high altar. (This was in spite of the fact that the pope, the author of the bull, had died the previous April.) The patriarch responded in kind, and in this the Greek church supported him. Rows between Rome and Constantinople had occurred before and generally were settled after a certain cooling-off period. It was not to happen in this case.

In 1136 a bishop from the East wrote to a bishop in the West, succinctly summing up the root of the problem: "How may we accept the decrees which have been made without consultation with us, and without our knowledge? If the Roman pontiff desires, from the raised throne of his glory, to hurl his mandates at us from on high; if he desires to judge us and even rule over our churches, without asking our advice but at his own pleasure, what kind of fraternity could that be, what kind of parent would he be?"

The sack of Constantinople in 1204, at the hands of the Venetians and the Crusaders, ended whatever hope there had been of reconciliation. The central orthodox Christian tradition had suffered a schism that still has not been repaired. The Eastern part of the church was to become known as the Orthodox church, or churches, the Western part as the Catholic church. The two communions remained very close in terms of doctrine and practice – both hold firm to the Bible; to the ancient structure of the church, headed by bishops and priests; to the seven sacraments; to the saints' days and other festivals; to veneration for Mary. Yet culturally they grew progressively farther apart, and there remains a fierce division over the issue of papal supremacy. The Orthodox churches have historically accorded the papacy a "primacy of honor" and a "presidency of love" but never acknowledged that the papacy has power of jurisdiction over them.

THE ORTHODOX CALENDAR
The Julian calendar, authorized by Julius Caesar and widely used throughout Europe in the Middle Ages, is still followed by many Orthodox churches today. Since the Julian calendar runs 13 days behind the West's Gregorian calendar (Pope Gregory XIII's 1582 revision of the Julian calendar), the Orthodox church celebrates its holy days almost two weeks after the West.

❖

Crusades *to* Renaissance

1054–1517

T HE LATE MIDDLE AGES, from the eleventh century onward, were a high point in Christian influence throughout Western and Eastern Europe. Church authorities organized charity and education, while Christian doctrines influenced not only theology but also philosophy and law. During this period, however, the personal faith of individuals varied widely. Movements to encourage nominal Christians to experience a deeper faith alternated with waves of decline in piety and morals.

Missionary activity was largely blocked by a hostile Islam to the south and east – some attempts were made to convert the Muslims, but these were generally unsuccessful, except in Spain. Only in the north was progress made – around the Baltic Sea, where the last remaining pagan nations in Europe received the gospel.

Meanwhile, as Europe recovered from centuries of war and invasion, Christianity inspired a flourishing of art and learning that led to the Renaissance.

A view of Lincoln Cathedral, England

THE GREGORIAN REFORMERS

CARDINALS

Cardinals were originally those clergy from the churches in and around Rome who assisted the pope. The name means "hinge," expressing their useful place in church administration. In 1059, Pope Nicholas II decreed that they were to be the exclusive electors of the pope, as they still are, and began to recruit cardinals from many countries, no longer just from Rome. By so doing, he hoped to end the influence of the noble Roman families who had fought each other to make the papacy their private possession in the two preceding centuries.

❖

THE CHURCH IN THE WEST was at a low point in the 1040s. Its head, the papacy, was paralyzed by corruption, there was no one to check the abuses that were rife across Europe, and in the absence of strong church leadership, lay rulers had taken a huge degree of control over the church.

The founders of churches and monasteries, and their descendants, had traditionally had the right to nominate clergy to run these institutions. In the tenth century they frequently treated these church offices, and the lands attached to them, as their own private property, often selling them to the highest bidder. Anxious to control the church's vast lands and wealth, kings and emperors took it upon themselves to "invest" bishops and abbots with the ring and staff that symbolized their office and make them swear loyalty. These leaders of the church were thus compromised, corrupted, and under pressure to obey the rulers who had invested them, rather than God. The reformed monks who followed the lead of Cluny were able to resist this corruption because their only patron was the pope, but they were powerless to call the rest of the church back to a holier life.

❖ THE INVESTITURE CONFLICT ❖

Ironically, the campaign against lay dominance began with the actions of a pious layman. In 1046 Emperor Henry III, confronted by the sight of three rival popes squabbling in Rome, deposed all three and installed a saintly German bishop in their stead. Pope Leo IX (r. 1049–54) traveled throughout Italy, France, and Germany to abolish abuses and curb lay interference, with the support of the influential cardinals Peter Damian and Humbert of Moyenmoutier. His successors, especially Stephen X (r. 1057–58), Nicholas II (r. 1058–61), and Alexander III (r. 1061–73) pursued an ambitious agenda of reforms.

Primarily, they wished to end the buying and selling of church offices and to see bishops and abbots elected by their clergy or monks, not appointed by lay lords. At the same time, they wanted clergy to be outside the jurisdiction of the secular courts so that the lay lords who often controlled those courts could not use them to coerce clergy. They also tried to enforce clerical celibacy, which was still widely being flouted, with married clergy sometimes treating their offices as hereditary possessions.

All of these campaigns reached a peak when Cardinal Hildebrand took the papal throne as Gregory VII in 1073. He brought papal claims to a new level, declaring that no one on earth had jurisdiction over the papacy, while popes could depose even emperors. Emperor Henry IV had no time for such claims. In 1076 he deposed the archbishop of Milan and invested his own candidate. Gregory excommunicated Henry, and when a number of Henry's own barons then

THE EMPEROR KNEELS TO THE POPE AT CANOSSA
Henry IV's humiliation (above) when he had to kneel before Gregory VII and Gregory's host, Matilda of Tuscany, was so famous that 800 years later Germany's Iron Chancellor, Bismarck, rallied support for a campaign against the Catholic church with the words, "We will not go to Canossa."

HOUSE OF HOLINESS
The legendary monastery at
Grande Chartreuse, in the later Middle Ages.
We can glimpse the Carthusians' reputation for holiness in a story
about Henry II, the loose-living king of England. Despairing of
life in a storm at sea, he sighed, "If that little Carthusian of mine,
Hugh, were now pouring forth his prayers … God would not have
forgotten me for so long." He asked God to have mercy on him for
the sake of Hugh's prayers, and, we are told, the tempest ceased.

threatened to rebel, the emperor was forced to journey in the freezing weather of January 1077 to find Gregory at Canossa in the Apennines and kneel in the snow for four days before the pope would grant him pardon. This was just the beginning. Gregory died in exile in 1085 after Henry IV had captured Rome to enthrone his own antipope, and the struggle went on.

" THESE MEN … ARE HARDER THAN THE ROCKS THEMSELVES "

A CLERK OF GRENOBLE, TRYING TO DISSUADE HUGH OF LINCOLN FROM JOINING THE CARTHUSIANS

It was finally ended by compromise at the Concordat of Worms in 1122, at which it was agreed that bishops were to be elected properly by their clergy but in the emperor's presence, and that he was not to invest them but they were to do homage to him. By that time, half a century of reforming popes had left churchmen in many countries looking to Rome for a lead and to resolve church disputes in a way that would have

been unknown a century before. The Gregorian Reformers left the church in a far stronger position than they found it, more independent of the powerful and with many abuses severely curbed.

❖ SPIRITUAL REVIVAL ❖

As popes and emperors struggled for supremacy, a great spiritual revival was growing. In an age when many of the devout dedicated themselves to a life of prayer by becoming monks or nuns, an increase in devotion in the church was naturally led by, and reflected in, an increase in monastic numbers and zeal.

In the eleventh century, Benedictine monasticism was dominant in the West; a rule designed for a single house, it had become almost universal. Cluny (*pp. 96-97*) had reformed many monastic houses, but now, in the great splendor of its worship and the wealth of many of its monasteries, it seemed to have lost its original apostolic simplicity. The zealous wished to go further, to deny the flesh more fiercely that the soul might focus, undistracted, on Christ alone. By 1200, eight new monastic orders had been formed.

The first was that of the Carthusians. The ultra-strict monastery of the Grande Chartreuse was founded near Grenoble in France in 1084, and gradually Carthusian houses, called "Charterhouses," spread throughout Europe. Their rule was so severe, however, that their popularity was limited. Carthusians lived almost as hermits within their monasteries, meeting only for church services and the occasional meal.

The most popular of the new orders, the Cistercians, began in 1098 when a small group of monks founded a monastery at Cîteaux in Burgundy, eastern France. The new foundation initially struggled until joined by a young noble called Bernard, known to history as St. Bernard of Clairvaux (*pp. 110-11*), after which time it mushroomed across Europe.

> " *I have loved righteousness and hated iniquity – therefore I die in exile* "
>
> **POPE GREGORY VII ON HIS DEATHBED**

CISTERCIAN ORDERS
Unlike Benedictines, who dyed their wool habits black, Cistercian monks and nuns left theirs white and untreated (*above*). They avoided ornament, often ate only one vegetarian meal a day, and founded their monasteries in the wilderness, considering austerity and hard manual labor to be useful disciplines. By the 1100s monks were often also priests and were recruited from the higher classes; a very popular Cistercian innovation was to allow peasants to become lay brothers, sharing the manual work of the community and saying simple prayers.

❖

THE CRUSADES

O N NOVEMBER 27, 1095, Pope Urban II climbed a wooden platform in the shadow of the walls of Clermont-Ferrand. The elderly pontiff had traveled to the French city to participate in a council that was taking place there. Addressing the assembled bishops and layfolk, the pope gave them a call to a holy war.

The pope had received an urgent request from the Byzantine emperor Alexius I Comnenus, begging his help in the face of the hostile Seljuk Turks. These had invaded Asia Minor, Syria, and Palestine, defeating Greeks and Arabs alike and attacking Christian pilgrims to the holy places. In response Urban urged the nobles of Europe to mount an armed crusade, united under the banner of the Cross, and march to Jerusalem. Their agreement was immediate. Up went the cry from the crowds, *Deus Vult* – "God wills it".

❖ FRUITLESS CONQUEST ❖

The call to crusade spread throughout Europe. By the following autumn, several armies of mainly French and Italian Crusaders were ready to leave. On July 15, 1099, they captured Jerusalem. Every inhabitant was put to the sword. Flushed by the success of their mission, the invaders installed a Christian king in Jerusalem and founded three other small states: the counties of Edessa and Tripoli and the

MONUMENT TO CONFLICTS PAST

The vast castles the Crusaders left behind them, such as Krak des Chevaliers, "the Rock of the Knights," in Syria *(above)*, serve as a grim reminder of past conflict. The word "crusade" comes from the Spanish for "to take up the Cross," and the Crusaders created a new link between the Cross and the sword – Christians had never before claimed a war to be holy. They also left a legacy of bitterness in the Middle East that endures to this day: European and American troops in the Persian Gulf in 1991 were referred to by their opponents as "the new Crusaders," in an attempt to reignite the old hostility.

❖

❝ *In the temple and the porch of Solomon, men rode in blood up to their knees and bridle reins ... the city was filled with corpses and blood* ❞

RAYMOND OF ARGILES ON THE CAPTURE OF JERUSALEM

THE CONQUEST OF JERUSALEM
The climax of the First Crusade was marred by a bloody massacre of the inhabitants of Jerusalem. This now seems a strange way to honor the Prince of Peace, but none of the Crusaders found it odd.

principality of Antioch. Their subjects, however, whether Muslims, Jews, or Eastern Christians, were unimpressed by their new rulers. The vast majority of the population continued to regard the Crusaders as alien conquerors, and as soon as Muslim power recovered, the Crusaders were in trouble. The city of Edessa was taken in 1144, which led Pope Eugene III, together with St. Bernard of Clairvaux *(pp. 110-11)*, to call for another crusade. Conrad, the Holy Roman emperor, and Louis VII, king of France, led their hopes and their armies to disaster in Syria between 1146 and 1148.

After Jerusalem was captured in 1187, Emperor Frederick Barbarossa, King Philip Augustus II of France, and King Richard I of England led the Third Crusade. They failed to liberate Jerusalem itself, although they did manage to capture Cyprus, plus Acre and a number of other cities, restoring a pale shadow of the Crusader states. The Fourth Crusade managed its own bishop in 1123. Pagan customs and ideals, however, lingered on for centuries. Across the Baltic were the last pagan lands in Europe (*see map, below*). From the 1190s, the popes supported attempts to conquer and convert them. Danish crusaders and the Brothers of the Sword, a military order of German settlers founded by the bishop of Riga to convert the native pagan tribes, conquered and baptized Livonia. Another German order of warrior monks, the Teutonic Knights, had taken all of Prussia by 1329, encouraging settlers and founding their own state. Conquered Prussians who became Christians kept their land and rights; those who did not were treated less kindly.

The other great crusade was the *Reconquista*, the reconquest of Spain from the Muslims. In 1000 all but the far north was ruled by the emirs of Cordoba. A steady series of attacks by the Christian kingdoms of Castile, Aragon, and Portugal culminated in a decisive victory at the battle of Las Navas de Tolosa in 1212, after which all Spain was reconquered, save only the kingdom of Granada in the far south. As the knights conquered, the church baptized, persuading Jews and Muslims, by fair means or foul, to become Christians.

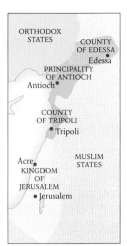

CRUSADER LANDS
The leaders of the First Crusade founded four small states. The County of Edessa fell in 1144, and Saladin swept most of the rest away in the 1180s. Antioch, Tripoli, and a few other towns along the coast were maintained for a further century. The last was lost in 1291.

❖

THE ILL-FATED PEASANTS' CRUSADE
While the knights and princes of Europe were readying their armies, an impatient raggle-taggle horde of peasants set off for the Holy Land, inspired by the preaching of Peter the Hermit and disregarding their own lack of military training and equipment. In August 1096, shortly after they had crossed over to Turkey, the Turks massacred them in a single battle.

only to sack Constantinople (*p. 122*), while the Fifth, Sixth, Seventh, and Eighth could achieve nothing at all. Only the crusades in Europe achieved lasting results.

❖ THE BALTIC AND THE RECONQUISTA ❖

Perhaps the least known of all the European crusades were those to Finland by the Swedes between 1155 and 1249, leading to the enforced baptism of the Finns. In Sweden itself paganism had only just been routed by King Sverker (r. 1130–55) with the aid of Cistercians from southern Europe. With the baptism of the Finns, the nominal conversion of Scandinavia was complete – even faraway Greenland had received

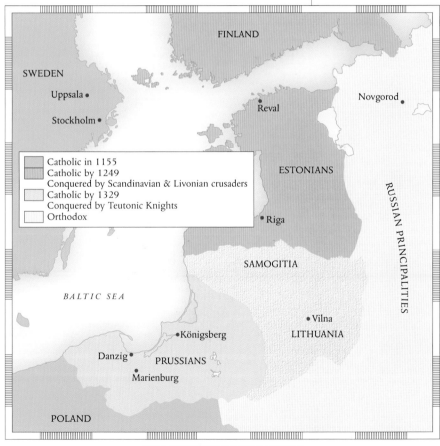

Catholic in 1155
Catholic by 1249
Conquered by Scandinavian & Livonian crusaders
Catholic by 1329
Conquered by Teutonic Knights
Orthodox

THE CRUSADES IN THE NORTH
After 1150, the last pagan lands in Europe were Finland, Prussia (mostly in modern Poland), Lithuania, and Livonia (roughly speaking, modern Latvia and Estonia). By 1329, Crusaders had conquered all but Lithuania, which remained outside the fold until 1386 (p. 120). After conquest and forced conversion, missionary bishops encouraged the gradual growth of genuine faith.

REVIVAL IN FAITH, ART, & LEARNING

ANTI-SEMITISM

The twelfth and thirteenth centuries saw a great increase in anti-Semitism in Europe. This was partly due to the Crusades, which bred an atmosphere of intolerance. Having previously been more or less accepted, the Jews suffered increasing restrictions and various persecutions, including being expelled from England in 1290 and from France in 1394. Popes and other church leaders sometimes tried to restrain the prejudice, but their efforts were largely ineffectual.

❖

THE TWELFTH CENTURY saw incredible economic, civil, and political progress in the West, allied with rapid development in the arts and sciences and the continuing revival of spirituality and discipline in many parts of the church. The centuries of invasion were over: Vikings, Magyars, and Saracens had been defeated or converted and civilized. Towns and cities grew quickly and improvements in agriculture (spread by monastic farmers) and increased trade created new wealth, which helped to fund an explosion in learning and the arts and led to the glories of the thirteenth century.

Supported by the reforming papacy, zealous Christians across the West took heart, inspired by the enormously influential Bernard of Clairvaux (*see box*). Reform spread from the monasteries to the rest of the clergy. Many took to living communally under a monastic-like rule, so as to encourage each other in holiness and to make celibacy easier. Such clergy came to be known as "Austin canons" because they followed a version of a rule of life (similar to a monastic rule) first written by Augustine of Hippo (*pp. 68-69*). Although, like monks, they lived in austerity, their work remained focused on preaching, teaching, and hearing confessions, not on the enclosed life of prayer.

❖ PAPAL POWER ❖
AT ITS ZENITH

The power of the church had never been greater, and in the hands of Pope Innocent III (r. 1198–1216), this new power found its ablest and fairest exponent. In order to reform the church, he supported the new orders of friars (*pp. 114-15*), that they might teach and care for the poor, and rebuked kings

BERNARD OF CLAIRVAUX

THE holiness and forceful personality of Bernard of Clairvaux (1090–1153) influenced and inspired the West. Although only a humble Cistercian abbot, he chastised kings and princes; acted as a spiritual guide to bishops, abbots, and even the pope; transformed the Cistercians from a single struggling monastery to a major order; and inspired the Second Crusade by his preaching. Utterly devoted to Christ and fearless in his service, the power of Bernard's preaching and of his personal charm can scarcely ever have been equalled. It was said that each time he preached, some of those who heard would hear the call and become monks themselves, so that "mothers hid their sons from him, wives their husbands, and companions their friends." Some of the hymns he and his followers wrote are still sung, most notably that which begins: "Jesus, the very thought of thee with sweetness fills the breast, but sweeter far thy face to see and in thy presence rest."

and emperors, particularly when they tried to interfere with the right of clergy to elect their own bishops and abbots. Where clerical elections were disputed, Innocent claimed the power to install his own candidates. He strengthened the power of the papacy over church appointments in other ways, claiming the right to move bishops from diocese to diocese and to redistribute the church offices of pluralists (those who held more than one ecclesiastical office at a time).

Innocent's authority drew over 400 bishops and 800 abbots from all over the West to a great council at Rome in 1215. The council directed bishops to provide good preachers in their dioceses (since the food of the Word of God was deemed necessary to salvation). To provide capable clergy, bishops were directed to make sure their cathedral schools had good teachers, and archbishops to employ a master theologian to teach the clergy. All forms of profiteering by clergy, such as selling relics or displaying them for money, were condemned; bishops were enjoined to be vigilant against heresy. It was the greatest reform program of the Middle Ages, but even Innocent could not make all the clergy educated and able teachers, nor all the laity devout.

TWELFTH-CENTURY INTELLECTUAL CURIOSITY
The study of all forms of knowledge became more popular, including medicine, which remained still rather impractical, as the "representations of medicinal plants" in this English herbal (c. 1200) show. Salerno in Italy was the greatest center for medical study, as it had been since the tenth century.

❖ SEEDS OF DECLINE ❖

The growth in papal patronage and power sowed the seeds of new problems, as the machinery of papal administration grew and grew. Already in 1145, Bernard of Clairvaux was a critic. In a treatise that he wrote to guide his friend Pope Eugenius III he claimed: "The ambitious, the grasping, the simoniacal, the sacrilegious, the adulterous, the incestuous, and all such like monsters of humanity flock to Rome, in order either to obtain or to keep ecclesiastical honors." To pay for all this machinery, popes began to tax national churches heavily, which created increasing resentment. In addition, popes began to impose their staff on far-off dioceses as nominal bishops who remained at Rome to work for the pope while claiming the revenues of the see, a tactic which left those dioceses without guidance.

In his efforts to save the papacy from being bullied by princes and kings, Innocent built up the papal states in central Italy, which strengthened the political power of the popes at the cost of embroiling them in endless wars and alliances to keep their lands free.

THE GLORIES OF GOTHIC ARCHITECTURE

❖

NORTHERN France in the twelfth century saw the birth of a style of architecture that was to dominate European architecture until the Renaissance. In 1140 an unknown master mason was commissioned to rebuild the choir of the royal abbey of St. Denis. He used external flying buttresses to carry much of the building's weight, ribbed vaulting for the ceilings, and pointed arches that required less support than the round arches of the previously dominant Romanesque style, so that fewer internal pillars were needed and windows could be much larger. The result, four years later, was a building that inspired a continent. It seemed to soar to heaven, filled with light and space, its stone framework far lighter than that of any church before it.

FAITH WRIT LARGE IN STONE

The new style spread rapidly across Europe. Its blossoming coincided with growing prosperity in the West, and, in a reflection of that society's values, this increase in wealth was used to build churches. In the four centuries after 1100, over 500 cathedrals and countless churches, monasteries, and convents were built.

Whereas the skylines of modern cities are dominated by commercial buildings, in medieval Europe cathedrals and churches were the biggest, most important buildings. The cathedral was a symbol of the city. Gothic cathedrals are the greatest representation of their age and its faith. Most of those who labored on them are unknown. They worked for God's glory and not for their own.

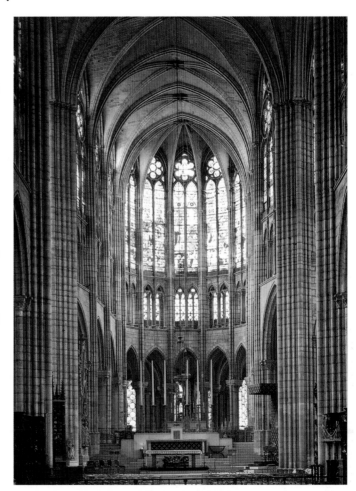

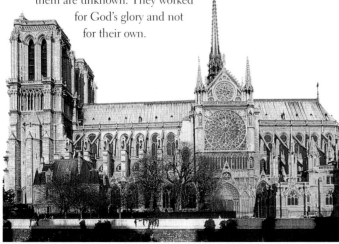

THE FIRST GOTHIC CHURCH
Nothing like the choir of St. Denis (above) had ever been seen before. Only the choir (the part of the church behind the altar) was rebuilt in the new style, before the money ran out. This was a common fate for medieval churches and is why they could take centuries to build: Cologne cathedral was built over a 700-year period.

THE CATHEDRAL OF OUR LADY – DEDICATED TO THE VIRGIN MARY
Notre-Dame cathedral in Paris, built 1163–c. 1250, is one of the great Gothic cathedrals. Its doors, like those of other Gothic cathedrals, are surrounded by carved biblical scenes to teach the illiterate (p. 92). Ever more intricate carved decoration, largely of biblical scenes, was one of the major characteristics of Gothic architecture. Stained-glass windows, too, were devoted to biblical scenes, making churches into visual libraries.

THE ALBIGENSIANS

The Albigensians, or Cathars, were dualists who held that matter was evil and only spirit was good, and so rejected the Incarnation and sacraments, including marriage. This heresy became very popular in southern France, c. 1200. St. Dominic and his new order attempted to convert them by preaching. That failed and in 1209 a crusade was called against them. Finally in the 1230s the Inquisition (see also p. 118) was founded to root them out. In 1252 it was licensed to use torture, and the heresy dwindled.

The Papal States were an endless source of controversy. They absorbed vast amounts of energy that might have been better focused on other things, and they provided ammunition for critics of papal worldliness.

✧ THE EXPANSION OF LEARNING ✧

The clergy led incredible developments in education, which was firmly based on Christian belief. Before the twelfth century, the only education in the West had been provided in monastic and cathedral schools (p. 83), and was usually very limited. After 1100 the cathedral schools rapidly expanded, often splitting into a lower school, called a "grammar school," where young boys learned grammar and other core subjects, and a higher school for advanced learning. By the year 1200, a number of these higher schools had developed into universities, first in Bologna in northern Italy (which was to be preeminent in law), then at Paris (most famous for theology) and Oxford. Other universities of lasting fame developed rapidly in the next century. Education remained, except in Italy, the preserve of clerks, whose numbers multiplied. Many of the new "scholar clerks" went to work for kings and nobles, carrying out their increasingly complex administration rather than being ordained as priests. Most parish priests were not graduates, and the standard of their education remained low. A few rich layfolk had their sons educated, and very occasionally daughters, but the ruling classes remained illiterate.

The new learning led to new codes of both secular law, where old Roman law mixed with ancient national custom, and religious law (known as canon law). In 1148 the great lawyer Gratian, a scholar of Bologna, compiled a definitive collection of the decrees (or canons) of popes and general church councils, which between them provided the rules by which the church was governed. All subsequent codes of canon law were based on his collection. Codification of the canons added to the power of the papacy, which was their arbiter, and tended to replace church government by the whim of the powerful with the rule of law.

✧ THE RISE OF SCHOLASTICISM ✧

Medieval thinkers sought to make a synthesis of all knowledge, both natural and divinely revealed. If God, they argued, was the author of truth, he could be found in all manner of knowledge. For them there was no split between the sacred and the secular, so the intellectual systems they created, together known as "Scholasticism," merged theology and philosophy and are based on biblical as well as philosophical assumptions, because they accepted the Bible as authoritative on all questions.

Among the movement's forerunners were the Italian Anselm (c. 1033–1109), famous for his saying, "I believe in order to understand," and the French maverick genius Abelard (1079–1142). The movement was brought to maturity by the great German philosopher Albertus Magnus (c. 1206–80), who taught at Paris, and his pupil Thomas Aquinas (c. 1225–74).

The Scholastics' greatest challenge was the work of Aristotle, much of which was rediscovered in the West in the twelfth and thirteenth centuries. This gave the Scholastics the philosophical tools they needed while at the same time raising a new range of questions. How could the new knowledge be reconciled with the biblical revelation? Thomas Aquinas answered this question, adopting much of Aristotle's philosophy while dropping those parts that conflicted with the Bible. For

THOMAS AQUINAS AND HIS ADMIRERS
Dubbed "the Angelic Doctor" in tribute to his philosophy, Aquinas went on to be named the official philosopher of the Catholic Church, as he remains – every Catholic ordinand must study his works. This seventeenth-century Spanish painting shows the respect in which he is held.

ST. THOMAS AQUINAS

BORN into an aristocratic family in Aquino, southern Italy, Thomas' family originally planned for him to enter the ancient and respectable Benedictine order. Horrified to hear that he intended to join the new, unknown Dominicans (pp. 114-15), they locked him up to make him change his mind. He defied them and went to study at Paris, where he was so silent that his fellow students nicknamed him "the Dumb Ox." His teacher, the great Albertus Magnus, silenced the critics, saying, "One day that Dumb Ox will bellow so loudly that he will shake the world." Aquinas's subsequent career proved him right.

example, Aristotle asserted that the universe had neither beginning nor end, whereas the Bible relates that God created it. Aquinas observed that reason alone could not decide but that faith led him to accept the Bible rather than the philosopher (Aristotle).

✤ A LUMINOUS PHILOSOPHY ✤

Aquinas's own thought eloquently translates Christian concepts into a philosophical system. He believed that the way human beings are made is oriented toward happiness with God, that "God … wills for the creature that eternal good which is himself." Our sinfulness, however, twists us away from the good for which we were made and prevents us from actualizing the incredible potential with which God created us. We retain our appetite for happiness although we now seek it in the wrong places: "No one can live without delight, and that is why a man deprived of spiritual joy goes over to fleshly pleasures." We need God, "moving us inwardly through grace," to rescue us from our sin. For all the complexity of Aquinas's thought, God's joy and love are at its heart, as in his dictum "Sheer joy is God's, and this demands companionship."

Aquinas argued that the existence of God is not self-evident, although good evidence for it can be found in the world, on the basis of which he constructed five "proofs" that God exists. His trust in philosophy was great, but he also recognized its limits, observing that "our view of the most sublime things is limited and

weak" and that we cannot know what God is except by analogy with Creation – we call God "Father," "Lord," and "King," but he transcends these concepts – so that for all the knowledge of him we have by divine revelation, God remains a mystery.

Aquinas also wrote on many specifically theological issues, such as the "Real Presence." Because of Jesus' words at the Last Supper – "This is my body. … This is my blood" – theologians since the Apostolic Fathers (p. 41) had agreed that, in a mystical way, Jesus really was present in the bread and wine at Communion. But how? It must be a unique kind of presence, so a new word had to be coined to describe it: "transubstantiation." Aquinas gave philosophical depth to the word, arguing that the bread and wine were genuinely changed into the body and blood of the Lord but not in a way that the senses could detect. The belief behind the doctrine can be gauged from a hymn the philosopher himself wrote: "By his word the Word almighty makes of bread his flesh indeed. … Faith God's living Word must heed! Faith alone may safely guide us where the senses cannot lead!" Aquinas's output was prodigious, including

" IN HIS WILL IS OUR PEACE "

DANTE ALIGHIERI, WRITING ABOUT GOD

many biblical commentaries, as well as commentaries on Aristotle, a huge manual of apologetics, and the *Summa Theologica*. This work set out to be a comprehensive guide to theological and philosophical knowledge, but it was left unfinished when, just before his death, he had a mystical experience after which he said, "All I have written is as straw beside the things that have been revealed to me." He wrote no more.

✤ LATER SCHOLASTICISM ✤

After Aquinas, thinkers such as the Scotsman Duns Scotus (c. 1265–1308), the Englishman William of Ockham (c. 1285–1347), and the German Gabriel Biel (c. 1415–95) attempted to delve to the roots of questions of being. These scholars are little regarded today, but the work of the Scholastics, taken together, constitutes a remarkable attempt to understand everything in the light of the Christian revelation.

CHRISTIAN EDUCATION

The structure of medieval education meant that all educated people were trained to think in Christian terms and to see the world with a Christian worldview. Students typically went to university between the ages of 13 and 16. They began with the study of theology (focusing on Scripture) and the seven liberal arts – logic, rhetoric (public speaking), et al – and might then proceed to a doctorate in law, medicine, or theology. Having reached that stage, which took at least 14 years, all theologians focused first on the study of Scripture. Theology was seen as the "Queen of the Sciences," the central, most important discipline.

❖

THE DIVINE VISION

The Italian Dante Alighieri (1265–1321) was inspired by the work of Aquinas to write the *Divine Comedy*, a tour of hell, purgatory, and heaven in which the medieval view of theology and the universe is put into poetic form. Dante (*pictured above, in a scene from his poem*) had a petty side and enjoyed placing his enemies in hell, but his epic work is structured around the belief that the love of God is the supreme power in the universe, so that he could even say that it is "love that moves the sun and the other stars." The *Divine Comedy* was the first great poem written in Italian, breaking the tradition of writing in Latin and setting a precedent for new vernacular literatures.

❖

FRIARS & FAITH

ST. FRANCIS'S CHRISTMAS

According to legend, it was Francis of Assisi who began the tradition of setting up a crib at Christmas. Before Midnight Mass one Christmas Eve, Francis went in procession with the villagers of Assisi to a small grotto, singing hymns. There he placed a statue of the infant Jesus, joining those of Mary, Joseph, a midwife, shepherds, as well as three wise men. This tradition spread from the Umbrian hill town throughout the world.

❖

BY THE EARLY THIRTEENTH century, intellectual advance and institutional reform had transformed the church. These developments had had little effect, however, on the faith of the peasants. The fast-growing towns and cities, in particular, posed a huge problem. The parish system had been created for rural areas, and parish priests were unable to serve the throngs of the poor in the towns.

Into this world came the friars, followers of two remarkable men who changed the face of medieval Christianity. The first of these was Spanish-born St. Dominic Guzman (1170–1221) who, c. 1204, went to convert the Albigensian heretics of the south of France *(p. 112)* by preaching and debate. In 1215, convinced that uneducated clergy left their flock open to heresy, he founded the Order of Preachers, known as the Dominicans, to specialize in preaching and teaching. A parallel order of Dominican nuns was founded, and both the Dominican sisters and the friars became very important as educators and scholars.

❖ THE JESTERS OF GOD ❖

Of equal importance was another great order of friars, founded at almost the same time, the Order of Friars Minor, known as the Franciscans, which grew from the work and witness of St. Francis of Assisi. Born Francesco di Bernadone (c. 1182–1226), Francis was the only child of a rich merchant in the hill town of Assisi in Tuscany, Italy. As a young man, he was wounded during a battle with a neighboring town and returned home to recuperate. During that time he decided to reject his family inheritance in order to dedicate himself to service of the poor, taking literally the Gospel texts on leaving all to follow Christ. It is said that he sang as he walked out into the snow of a Tuscan winter. Francis dedicated himself to a life of prayer and service near his hometown, and a band of followers gathered around him, attracted by his remarkable charisma and sanctity.

Sharing all they had, they devoted themselves to preaching the gospel in simple language and caring for the poor. So that they could really empathize with the very poor, Francis insisted that they should possess nothing and gain their food only by begging. They nursed the sick, especially lepers (whom others shunned – it was the most feared of illnesses), held their own church services, prayed through the night, slept in the open or in rough shelters, and, following the example of their leader, were so joyful and

LOVE FOR ALL CREATION: FRANCIS PREACHING TO THE BIRDS

Francis's overwhelming love was such that, according to early accounts of his life, he even preached to the birds. His famous poem, The Canticle of the Sun, *praises "Brother" sun, "Sister" moon, and all God's creation for reflecting their Creator.*

ST. FRANCIS OF ASSISI

OFTEN called "the most perfect Christian since Christ," Francis, "the little poor man" of Assisi, is perhaps the most loved. He was utterly selfless, joyful, impractical, and whole-hearted in his love for his Lord, with whom he identified so totally that he is reported to have received Christ's wounds, the "stigmata," in his own body late in his life (*above*). He wrote some of the greatest of all prayers, which express an ardent desire to live for Christ: "Most high, glorious God, enlighten the darkness of my heart, and give me a right faith, a sure hope, a perfect charity."

cheerful that they were called "God's jesters." In the spring of 1209, Francis traveled to Rome with 11 friends, where his new order received the approval of Pope Innocent III. Three years later a friend of Francis, a wealthy young woman of Assisi called Clare, founded a similar order for women.

Unlike the men, the sisters were an "enclosed order," unable to travel outside their convents, as were all women's orders at the time. In 1221 Francis formed a "Third Order" for lay people who wished to follow his way of life and to dedicate themselves to the needs of the poor, while remaining "in the world." (The Dominicans founded a similar Third Order.) After Francis's death in 1226, a rift appeared between those who wished to keep to his rule of absolute poverty and those who felt the order should own houses and books with which to shelter its members and train the young. As the number of friars exploded, and training and organization were needed, the latter group dominated.

✧ THE FRIARS' INFLUENCE ✧

These two religious orders marked a shift from the traditional monastic orders, which fled from the world and prayed for it. The disciples of Dominic and Francis, rather, ministered to the townsfolk and traveled the highways and the byways preaching and teaching the gospel. They served and evangelized the poor of the towns, setting up churches where the parish system was failing.

Their zeal, at least initially, was magnetic. People flocked to join the new orders. Pope Gregory IX (r. 1227–41) canonized Francis in 1228 and Dominic in 1234. Soon popes were to come from these orders,

Innocent V (r. 1276) being the first Dominican and Nicholas IV (r. 1288–92) the first Franciscan. Monks were eclipsed by friars as exemplars of holiness. Having already lost their primacy in education, the monastic orders became both less popular and less important. Monks had come to seem somewhat upper class: peasant recruits were now liable to become only lay brothers (*p. 107*). The friars, in contrast, took in recruits from all parts of society and trained them very well. Most of the great names in medieval theology were friars (*pp. 112-13*): Albertus Magnus and Thomas Aquinas were Dominicans; William of Ockham, Bonaventure, and Duns Scotus were Franciscans.

✧ MISSIONARY FERVOR ✧

Dominic spent his life endeavoring to bring heretics to the true faith, and Francis traveled to Egypt to preach to its Muslim rulers. Their followers continued their example and were the leading missionaries of the later Middle Ages. Dominicans made endless efforts to preach in Spain and North Africa, while Franciscans traveled as far as China to witness for Christ. In Central Asia they saw many individuals convert to Christianity, including a number of Mongol leaders, but

"LORD, MAKE ME AN INSTRUMENT OF YOUR PEACE"

PRAYER OF FRANCIS OF ASSISI

could never establish viable churches, with the result that Christianity soon died out again. John of Monte Corvino labored in China from 1294 until his death in 1328 to establish the Catholic church. The pope made John archbishop of Beijing in 1308 – there was a rival Nestorian archbishop in the city also (*p. 122*) – and the mission survived until the 1360s, when the Mongol dynasty fell, and the Christians, who had become associated with it, were expelled. Efforts to evangelize Muslims proved similarly fruitless, leaving Christianity largely restricted to Europe.

"In beautiful things Francis saw Beauty itself, and through Beauty's traces imprinted on creation he followed his beloved everywhere, making everything a ladder by which he could climb up and embrace the One who is utterly desirable"

ST. BONAVENTURE (1221–74), ITALIAN FRANCISCAN THEOLOGIAN

PRACTICAL MYSTICS
Many early friars seemed very close in spirit to Christ (hence pictures such as the above). At the same time, they were intensely practical and produced detailed preachers' guides to help others to teach. These books of sermon outlines and useful anecdotes included the *Liber Exemplorum*, the "Book of Examples," which contained skeleton sermons on the life of Christ and an A to Z of other subjects (for example, "Charity; Clerics, evil; Carnal thoughts; Confusion"). Another such book was titled the *Dormi Secure*, "Sleep Soundly" (because your sermon is prepared within).

✧

THE LAST RITES

The sacraments were seen as vital to spiritual health in the Middle Ages, as they always have been in the Catholic and Orthodox churches. Baptism and Communion were central to church life. Confession and penance were used to encourage Christians to greater devotion (the Franciscans were great confessors). The last sacrament, extreme unction (*above*), prepared the soul to meet God.

✤

✤ THE PIETY OF THE PEOPLE ✤

In an illiterate society it is hard to know the shape of an ordinary Christian's faith. Almost everyone went to church, and Christianity played a part in every stage of a person's life, from the baptism of babies to the last rites administered to the dying. The marriage service was usually an exchange of vows at the church door followed by a nuptial Mass and a bridal feast.

The rhythms of the church's year commemorated Christ's life. Christmas could hardly avoid mention of the Incarnation; the invention of the crib, attributed to Francis (*p. 114*), provided an easy visual aid to show God become a baby. Each Easter, Passion plays were put on, which meant that everyone saw the story of Christ's suffering, death, and resurrection enacted many times throughout their lives.

The increasing number of festivals provided opportunities for teaching: there were perhaps 20 or 30 feast days celebrated each year, with an entire eight days of celebration at Christmas and Easter. These feasts commemorated the events in the life and death of Jesus as well as the greatest saints. There would have been processions for all of them, and for many lesser saints' days: some parishes may have seen 100 processions a year. Thanks partly to these events, devotion to Mary and the other saints grew and grew (hence the great veneration for the relics of saints),

as did devotion to the Eucharist and to the Passion of Christ – groups called confraternities used Masses and sermons to deepen devotion to the suffering Christ. By the 1300s copies of the Gospels and the Psalms for laypeople's use were increasing in number. More common than either of these were Books of Hours containing the Psalms and prayers from the services for the different hours of the monastic day, usually in Latin, which people used for their daily prayers. Copies of the whole Bible were expensive, and therefore rare,

> ❝ THE WISE LADY WHO LOVES HER CHILDREN ... WILL ENSURE THAT THEY WILL LEARN FIRST OF ALL TO SERVE GOD AND TO READ AND WRITE, AND ... LEARN THEIR PRAYERS WELL ❞
>
> FOURTEENTH-CENTURY FRENCH WRITER CHRISTINE DE PISAN, IN "THE TREASURY OF THE CITY OF LADIES"

PILGRIMAGES

✤

ABRAHAM was a pilgrim to the Promised Land, and Christians have been traveling to see the places where Christ walked the earth since at least the second century when Miletus of Sardo made a pilgrimage (c. 170). The most famous visitor of the early centuries was the empress Helena, mother of the emperor Constantine. She spent two years in Palestine between 326 and 328, and built shrines at Bethlehem, the Mount of Olives, and Jerusalem. Other distinguished early pilgrims included the Spanish abbess, Egeria (or Etheria), who has left us vivid memories of her tour through France, Italy, Egypt, Palestine, and Asia Minor. In the eleventh century, as people began

to travel more after centuries of chaos, the number of pilgrims began to increase and continued to do so until the Reformation. The many sites housing relics of famous Christians became places of pilgrimage; the most important were Jerusalem, Rome, Santiago de Compostella in Spain, and Canterbury in England. Pilgrimages have remained important to Catholic and Orthodox Christians, and while Protestants do not see visiting relics as beneficial, they travel to the Holy Land to walk and wonder at the scenes of Christ's life on earth. For them as for earlier Christians, the physical journey is made to help the spiritual journey toward God, surrendering time to learn from the past.

THE MOST FAMOUS PILGRIMS: THE PROTAGONISTS OF CHAUCER'S "CANTERBURY TALES"

The English poet Geoffrey Chaucer (c. 1343–1400) painted the pilgrims of his Canterbury Tales as a mix of saints and sinners, from the devout Knight to the crooked Pardoner. The Friar was harshly satirized, indicating that the friars' reputation for holiness had dimmed by the late 1300s. The humble Parson fared rather better.

MEDIEVAL WORSHIP

❖

ALL were expected to attend Mass on Sundays and holy days. Although only priests, monks, and nuns actually took Communion frequently, everyone was required to receive it at Easter, having first confessed. Mass was always in Latin, although in some places the Scripture readings were read in the local language after being read in Latin, and the sermon and some of the prayers were always in the vernacular. Every church would have a choir, with music in Latin. In cathedrals, for example, the choir sang most of the Mass. The people "assisted" at Mass merely by being present, and there was little real participation, although the Franciscans managed to improve this situation slightly: as clergy or choir chanted invocations to God, the congregation replied with a simple rhythmical refrain such as "*Laudate Dominum*," "Praise the Lord." It was the duty of the parish priest to preach each Sunday, but preaching was often poor, except where the friars were

A MONASTIC VIGIL
Many feasts involved prayer vigils or processions, involving layfolk or nuns and monks (as above).

involved. The church found other ways to teach. Each church building was a visual library: scenes from the Bible were carved on the walls and built into the windows in stained glass; crucifixes told of the passion of Christ, the altar of Communion, the font of baptism; images of the saints were used to inspire their weaker brothers and sisters in the congregation to emulate them. During the service, the congregation stood; the moments at which they were called to kneel to pray were marked by the ringing of bells. All ages attended, so it cannot have been very quiet. At times people conducted business and gossip during services, as these were often the best opportunities in the week to meet one's neighbors. Each person would have felt completely at home, for the parish church was open all the time and was used for many kinds of meetings during the week: as a market, a school, a church law court, for business, for feasts, and for socializing.

until the invention of printing. In the home, parents were expected to teach their children at least the Lord's Prayer, the Nicene Creed, the Hail Mary, the Ten Commandments, and the Seven Deadly Sins.

❖ UNIVERSAL SOCIAL SERVICE ❖

In addition to its specifically spiritual role, the social, medical, and educational work of the church reached each part of society. Every cathedral city had a grammar school and at least one hospital, usually at least three or four, more in large centers: London had 17 hospitals in the fourteenth century. These hospitals originally cared for the poor and travelers as well as the sick, but after the Black Death (1347–50) they came to focus on the ill. There were even specialist hospitals for lepers (leprosy had become very common after the Crusades) and for the insane – in 1300 England alone had at least 200 leper hospitals. All of these were run by priests, monks, friars, and nuns, who were far greater in number than in any modern society.

As for the humble parish priest, his duties ranged from saying Mass daily to reconciling quarreling parishioners, collecting the compulsory church tithe, visiting the sick, and blessing the parish crops (with processions through the fields). By the 1300s a number of parishes had little parish schools, run either by the priest or his clerk, both of whom were usually very poor. At the other end of the social scale, the richer bishops and abbots had the wealth of princes.

PRIVATE WORSHIP
One indication of the level of private devotion is that most large houses and castles of the later Middle Ages were built with their own private chapels, a visible, expensive symbol of faith, where the family of the house could attend Mass daily (right).

DEVOTION & DIVISION

SACRAMENTS, FAITH, AND THE BLACK DEATH

The Black Death completely disrupted the pattern of church services and church-blessed events that gave a rhythm to people's lives. So many priests died or fled that in many places there were none to perform the sacraments; so there could be neither Communion nor baptism nor marriage.

Some bishops took emergency measures. One, advising his flock on what to do if "the comfort of a priest is denied the people," wrote: "Persuade all men ... that, if they are on the point of death and cannot secure the services of a priest, then they should make confession to each other ... whether to a layman or ... even to a woman." If there were no priest to administer the sacrament of extreme unction (*p. 116*) "then, as in other matters, faith must suffice."

❖

WHEN THE CARDINALS MET to choose a pope in August 1294, they felt drawn to a hermit of renowned holiness whom they persuaded to take the papal throne as Celestine V. In December he resigned, proving that holiness was no longer enough to be supreme pontiff: papal government now demanded a firm leader and strong administrator. Celestine was succeeded by Boniface VIII (r. 1295–1303), of the powerful Caetani family. The future must have seemed set fair to Boniface: the institutions of the church had been reformed, and the friars had preached to the hearts of the common folk.

❖ THE FRENCH CAPTIVITY ❖

Boniface felt moved to issue the strongest statement of papal power ever made. In his papal bull (solemn letter) *Unam Sanctam*, he called on all to submit to the pope's authority. At this point, the pope collided

THE INQUISITION – A POTENT PAPAL WEAPON
The Inquisition (p. 112) was empowered by the papacy to find heretics and to reform or punish them. It was rarely used in the 1300s but remained a threat to those whose orthodoxy wavered.

with the new force in European politics, the powerful nation states, led by France and England, which were henceforth to pose great challenges to the papacy. In 1303, having disagreed with King Philip the Fair of France over the taxation of the French clergy, the elderly pontiff withdrew to his family palace at Anagni. He was pursued by the agent of the king of France, Nogart, who confined him at his palace. Returning to Rome some days later, the pope died unexpectedly.

The cardinals then assembled at Perugia to choose a successor to the See of Peter. After almost a year of arguing among themselves, their choice fell on the archbishop of Bordeaux, Bertrand de Got, who chose the name Clement V (r. 1305–14). Though neither a member of the College of Cardinals, nor indeed even present at the conclave, he was a friend of the king of France, and so thought to be able to achieve the normalization of relations between France and the Holy See. The archbishop was summoned to Rome for his coronation but chose instead to be crowned at Lyons. His desire not to go to Rome found him delaying in France, where finally, at the suggestion of Philip the Fair, he settled in the town of Avignon, near the southern coast of France. Here, on French soil, the pope was effectively a vassal of the French king.

> ❝ A SOUL CANNOT LIVE WITHOUT LOVING ... FOR IT WAS CREATED TO LOVE ❞
>
> **ST. CATHERINE OF SIENA**

The next six popes would be French, and each decided to remain in Avignon. Their residence there was referred to by contemporaries as "the Babylonian captivity of the church" (a comparison to Israel's captivity in Babylon). It scandalized Christendom and made the French popes seem more like secular princes than the rightful rulers of the Christian world. It also increased papal expenses, leading the Avignon popes to tax the churches of Europe more than any popes before them. They transferred revenue from local bishops to themselves, created new taxes, and levied taxes that were nominally for crusades but were in

PLAGUE – RECURRING BANE OF MEDIEVAL LIFE

The bubonic plague which ravaged Europe in the late 1340s, known as the Black Death, was only one of many epidemics in the Middle Ages. Local plagues, such as that at Tournai in 1095 (above), *had always been a threat. The Black Death, however, affected everyone and returned at intervals, leaving a heightened awareness of the fragility and brevity of life.*

reality for general administration. In addition, they packed the curia (the pope's court and administrative center) with their fellow Frenchmen, causing great resentment. When the Black Death struck in the late 1340s and one-third of the population of Europe died, many saw it as a judgment on the sins of the age, not least those of the popes. Finally, with papal prestige lower than it had been for centuries, Gregory XI (r. 1371–78) returned to Rome in 1377, persuaded to do so by the Italian mystic Catherine of Siena, whose fervent faith gave her spiritual authority of a kind that the papacy sorely lacked. Gregory was not to know that this action would lead the papacy to even lower depths.

❖ THE GREAT SCHISM OF THE WEST ❖

In 1378, the cardinals united in conclave to elect Gregory's successor. The Roman populace had made it clear that they wanted an Italian, not French, pope, and so the cardinals chose the archbishop of Bari, Bartolomeo Prignano. The archbishop, the last non-cardinal to be elected pope, was duly brought to Rome

and proclaimed Urban VI (r. 1378–89). His autocratic manner, however, soon disconcerted the French cardinals who had elected him (at one point he had six cardinals under torture, five of whom were simply to disappear), and the cardinals therefore left Rome for the town of Anagni, claiming that Urban's election had been invalid as they had been in fear of their lives from the Roman mob. They then moved to Frondi, where they elected a new pope, Robert of Geneva, as Clement VII (r. 1378–94). Thus began the Great Schism of the West.

Clement took up residence in Avignon. The church was faced with a dilemma. To whom should loyalty be given? The theologians claimed that only a church council could decide who was the legitimate pope. It was a legalistic nightmare, with the unity of the Western church hanging in the balance. A council was called to meet at Pisa to decide the fate of the two contending bishops, Urban in Rome, Clement in Avignon. Before the convocation of the council, however, both pope and antipope died, and they were

THE WORKING WORLD

Saint Eligius (*above*), a seventh-century goldsmith and evangelist, became the patron saint of smiths and metal-workers. Each trade had its guild, which trained its craftsmen, regulated their work, and helped those in need; and each guild had its patron saint. Guilds played their part in church processions and charity – there was no division between the spiritual and the workplace.

❖

Far to the north of the warring popes, the king of Lithuania finally accepted Christianity in 1386 so that he could marry the heiress to the throne of Poland. As part of the wedding agreement, the Lithuanian nobility agreed to be baptized, and Polish clergy were brought to Lithuania to teach and baptize the people. Thus, the last pagan kingdom in Europe accepted the Christian gospel. Meanwhile, far to the south in Africa, another outpost of Christendom was dying. Between 1300 and 1500, repeated Arab attacks on the Christian kingdoms of the Sudan finally succeeded in destroying them. Muslim Arab settlers flooded in. Soon, the only traces left of nearly a millennium of Christianity were ruined churches in the desert sands.

❖

succeeded by Boniface IX and Benedict XIII, respectively. The council that eventually met in Pisa in 1409 complicated the matter by electing the Greek cardinal Pietro Philarghi as Pope Alexander V (r. 1409–10), calling on the others to resign. Not surprisingly, they declined the suggestion. There were now three popes, or rather one legitimate, and two illegitimate. The situation was hardly simplified by the sudden death of Alexander in Bologna a year after his election, and his succession by the antipope John XXIII (r. 1410–15), who had once been a pirate. At this point, Emperor Sigismund intervened to summon another council, at Constance in Switzerland, which met in 1414 and continued for four years. The Council of Constance called on all the contenders to resign for the sake of the unity of the church. Thus the legitimate pope, Gregory XII, who had been elected pope in 1406 in succession to Innocent VII (r. 1404–6), chose to abdicate with the two antipopes, the most recent pope in history to do so, and with the election of Martin V the Great Schism of the West came to an end.

THE PALACE OF THE POPES, AVIGNON
Pope Benedict XII spent a fortune building this fortresslike palace between 1334 and 1342, showing that he had abandoned any idea of moving back to Rome. Later, during the Great Schism of the West, it became the residence of the antipopes Clement VII and Benedict XIII.

❖ THE COST OF THE HIERARCHY ❖

During its captivity and schism, the papacy was in no condition to reform the church; in fact its money-raising measures were often corrupting. Some clergy were forced to pay a tax to the pope when they entered a new benefice (a clerical office that had an income attached to it); they recouped the money from their flocks. Many traveled to Avignon to seek preferment. The critics of the papacy multiplied. John Wycliffe in

JOHN WYCLIFFE: "THE MORNING STAR OF THE REFORMATION"
John Wycliffe (c. 1330–84), a theologian from Oxford University in England, was a fierce critic of the Avignon papacy, the church's wealth, and aspects of its theology. The bishops had failed to translate the Bible into English, so he and his followers did, "for the government of the people."

> ## " I BELIEVE THAT IN THE END TRUTH WILL CONQUER "

JOHN WYCLIFFE

England inspired a lay movement, the Lollards, that was bitterly hostile to the entire church hierarchy. The popes' expenses multiplied – on one estimate, two-thirds of all their revenue while at Avignon went to pay for wars to protect their lands in Italy – and they funded their staff by appointing cardinals and others to bishoprics and other prominent offices in distant lands, which they seldom or never visited, so that those offices were effectively left vacant. The fault was compounded when popes appointed favorites to more than one benefice at a time, a practice known as "pluralism." Kings and lay magnates did the same, giving their senior civil servants plum clerical jobs. These civil servants had no time to attend to their benefices.

The popes also took for themselves the money that had previously paid bishops' expenses when they visited their dioceses, so many ceased to inspect their clergy – with dire results for clerical discipline. Monastic houses, too, had insufficient direction and many lost their self-sacrificing spirituality. The prestige of the papacy sank so low that papal attempts at disciplining the church were largely ignored.

❖ THE CRY FOR CHANGE ❖

There were significant attempts at reform. In Germany and the Netherlands the largely lay movement called "the Brethren of the Common Life," inspired by the great mission preacher Gerhard Groot (d. 1384), did important evangelistic and pastoral work, and ran excellent schools, whose most famous product was Thomas à Kempis (c. 1380–1471), author of the devotional classic *The Imitation of Christ*. They were supported by the German and Dutch bishops, and synods ordered clergy "to preach on Sundays and on holy days the holy Scripture of the Old and New Testament, plainly and intelligibly." In Bohemia and Moravia (now the Czech Republic), however, the reformer Jan Hus (c. 1369–1415) clashed with the church hierarchy. Much influenced by John Wycliffe, Hus declared that the church had departed from the Bible. He was burned at the stake, but his followers remained supreme in the Czech lands, defeating several crusades against them (*see also p. 142*).

The Christian laity were perhaps more educated and articulate than ever before. In contrast, the long traumas of the popes, combined with nonresidence and pluralism, had left the clergy in a disordered, undisciplined state and the monasteries even worse. The situation cried out for reform lest the tension between the spiritual energy of the laity and the lack of leadership at the center should reach breaking point.

(*see also p. 142*)

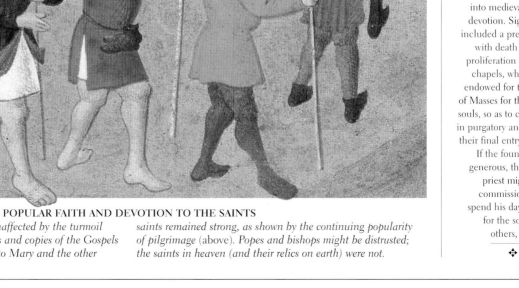

POPULAR FAITH AND DEVOTION TO THE SAINTS

Popular faith appears to have been unaffected by the turmoil that afflicted the papacy. Prayer books and copies of the Gospels were increasingly common. Devotion to Mary and the other saints remained strong, as shown by the continuing popularity of pilgrimage (above). Popes and bishops might be distrusted; the saints in heaven (and their relics on earth) were not.

ABSENTEE BISHOPS

Many fourteenth-century church leaders rarely went near their flocks. One not untypical bishop, Sandale of Winchester, held over 20 separate church offices, including 10 different rectorships (a rector being the priest in charge of a parish church). A non-resident bishop or priest was meant to appoint a deputy, called a "vicar," but these were often not fully qualified. The most talented clerical leadership was concentrated in the centers of power, often in administrative jobs, with too few gifted clergy left to carry out pastoral and preaching work in the parishes.

❖

❝ *Jesus now has many lovers of his heavenly kingdom, but few bearers of his cross* **❞**

THOMAS À KEMPIS

DARKNESS OF SOUL?

After the Black Death, a strain of morbidity crept into medieval art and devotion. Signs of this included a preoccupation with death and the proliferation of chantry chapels, which were endowed for the singing of Masses for the founders' souls, so as to cleanse souls in purgatory and thus speed their final entry to heaven. If the founder was generous, the chantry priest might be commissioned to spend his days praying for the souls of others, too.

❖

THE EASTERN CHURCHES

WELL-EDUCATED BYZANTINES

Throughout the medieval period, the standard of education was far higher in Constantinople (*above*) than in the West. Most of the Western ruling classes were illiterate until at least the fourteenth century, whereas noble Byzantines were brought up on the Greek classics. As a result, there was far more lay involvement in theological matters in the East.

❖

IN THE TWELFTH century, the newly Christian kingdom of Kiev (*pp. 101-02*) enjoyed a golden age, while its mother church in Byzantium, although always threatened by the advances of the Seljuk Turks, enjoyed an era of great artistic and intellectual achievement.

A century of peace in Kiev saw Christianity permeate every level of society, creating perhaps the best system of care for the poor anywhere in Christendom at that time. The devout Prince Vladimir Monomachos (r. 1113–25) even abolished the death penalty. His advice to his sons shows how seriously the rulers of Kiev took their faith, and it was taken as a model for all future rulers: "Above all things forget not the poor, and support them to the extent of your means. Give to the orphan, protect the widow, and permit the mighty to destroy no man." Under such enlightened rule, the spirituality and civilization of their realm blossomed.

THE MONGOLS
The Mongol mounted archers (left) *were the most formidable military force in the medieval world. In the early 1200s they carved out an empire that stretched from China to the borders of Europe.*

❖ **TIME OF DISASTER** ❖
In 1200 the fortunes of both Constantinople and Kiev were at a peak. By 1250 both had been reduced to servitude.

The kingdom of Kiev was brought to a sudden end by the most dreaded force of the Middle Ages, the Mongols. In 1237 they swept across from Central Asia and devastated the kingdom. The *Chronicle of Novgorod* recorded: "For our sins, unknown tribes came, none know who they are or whence they came." All the Russian kingdoms had to pay tribute, and that of Kiev never recovered. In 1325 its patriarch transferred his seat to Moscow (from the 1400s, each city had its own patriarch), and by 1380 the Grand Dukes of Moscow had become the political leaders of Russia.

These centuries produced some of the greatest saints and finest art in all of Orthodox history. Missionary bishops and monks preached both to the Mongols and to the pagan tribes of the vast forests in the east and north of modern Russia, translating the Bible and the liturgy into the local languages as they went. The most famous was St. Stephen, bishop of Perm (c. 1340–96), who ministered to the pagan Zyrians. St. Sergius of Radonezh (c. 1314–92), the most revered of all Russian saints, not only evangelized but also founded the greatest of Russia's monasteries, the Monastery of the Holy Trinity, in the forests north of Moscow. Inspired by such saints, religious art flourished. St. Andrey Rublev (c. 1370–1430) painted perhaps the finest of all icons for Sergius's monastery.

The Christians who benefited most from the Mongol scourge were the Nestorians (*p. 75*), based in Iraq and Iran. The Mongols swept in to defeat their Muslim rulers and, once the initial devastation was over, proved tolerant rulers, who allowed their Christian subjects freedom to evangelize throughout their central Asian kingdoms. The fourteenth century saw Nestorian churches and bishops in most of the major cities from Iraq to China, but as Mongol power declined, most of these churches dwindled away.

THE OUTRAGE THAT DIVIDED EAST AND WEST
The Fourth Crusade of 1204 (p. 109) was meant to liberate Jerusalem; instead, it looted Constantinople. The three days and nights of pillaging by Western Crusaders have never been forgotten, and what little hope there was of reunion vanished in the smoke above the burning city. Ever since, Orthodox Christians have fiercely resisted all attempts to renew unity on papal terms.

❖ THE FALL OF BYZANTIUM ❖

Byzantium was devastated by its fellow Christians of the West. In 1204 the Fourth Crusade *(p. 109)* was diverted from its path to Jerusalem by Venetian machinations, and the Crusaders ended by sacking the city and setting up a Latin kingdom in Constantinople. The Orthodox spent half a century under Western rule, and by the time a Greek emperor was restored in 1261, their hatred for the West was fervent and ferocious.

The strength of this hatred was shown by the popular reaction to the (unwilling) attempts by two Byzantine emperors to reunite their church with Rome. Desperate for help against the steady advance of the Ottoman Turks, who were gradually swallowing up their dominions, they were ready to compromise on doctrine in the hope of military support. In 1274, Emperor Michael VIII agreed upon a formula of reunion at a church council at Lyons, which was then rejected by his people and repudiated by his successors with such anger that when he died he was buried in unconsecrated ground as an apostate. His own sister is reported to have said, "Better that my brother's empire should perish than the purity of the Orthodox faith."

The Turks resolutely advanced toward their goal, Constantinople, and in 1438 Emperor John VIII led a delegation of bishops to Italy, where they delivered an appeal for help, ready to agree to whatever deal was needed to buy Western aid. The Greek legates then signed an agreement which would, in theory, unite the Greek church under the bishop of Rome.

> ❝ I WOULD RATHER SEE THE MUSLIM TURBAN IN THE MIDST OF THE CITY THAN THE LATIN MITRE ❞

GRAND DUKE LUCAS NOTARAS, REPUDIATING THE UNION OF FLORENCE, 1438

This treaty met the same wholesale rejection as that of 1274, and in 1453 the unthinkable happened: the Turks breached the walls of Constantinople. The last emperor fell in battle, and the city founded by Constantine the Great more than a thousand years earlier was reduced to a township of the Turkish Empire. Its patriarch joined the other ancient patriarchs of the East in submission to the Ottoman sultans. Henceforth, the sultans appointed the

THE NEW POWER IN THE ORTHODOX WORLD
Until Constantinople fell, the Russian patriarchs deferred to its fellow patriarchs. Afterwards they regarded themselves as the spiritual heirs of Byzantium and leaders of the Orthodox world. St. Basil's Cathedral in Moscow (above) expressed that new confidence.

patriarchs, as the Byzantine emperors had done. They held them responsible for all the Christians in the empire. This system preserved the identity of the Greek church, while leaving it very nationalistic, but it was also highly corrupting, since the Turks made the patriarchs and other church leaders pay for their offices, forcing them to collect the money from their flocks to finance their promotions. In addition, the sultans frequently deposed patriarchs to raise money from new candidates, reminding the Orthodox of the cost of being a captive church.

HOMELESS SCHOLARSHIP

For 1,000 years Constantinople had been the home of the finest Greek scholars. After 1453 there was an exodus to Italy and Moscow. Theological education in Greece and the other lands ruled by the Ottomans suffered so badly that many prospective Orthodox scholars had to go to the West, to Kiev, or to Russia for their training.

❖

THE RENAISSANCE

THE EARLY FIFTEENTH century in Italy was marked by an explosion of creative and intellectual activity, sparked by the rediscovery of much of the learning, art, and values of ancient Greece and Rome. During this period, known to modern generations as the Renaissance, extraordinary progress was made in several spheres, most notably in science and the arts. Around 1420, the ancient theory of perspective was rediscovered by Italian painters, and in the mid-1430s, Donatello of Florence cast the first bronze sculpture since antiquity. The discovery of gunpowder revolutionized warfare. Increased wealth, improved scholarship, and new challenges to church authority and Christian belief all demanded a strong response from the leaders of Christendom. First, Pope Martin V (r. 1417–31) and his successor, Eugenius IV (r. 1431–47), reasserted papal authority after the Great Schism of the West (pp. 119-20).

For Eugenius this meant a long struggle with the council of Basel, which met intermittently between 1431 and 1449. In this, the last of the three councils provoked by the Great Western Schism, the conciliar movement reached its peak. The scholars and church leaders who led this movement wished to transfer supreme authority in the church from the papacy to general councils, but divisions between the nations represented at the council enabled the pope to thwart that plan. At the same time, any hope of general church reform vanished in the conflict.

❖ THE RENAISSANCE PAPACY ❖

The next pope, Nicholas V (r. 1447–55), was a humanist, a scholar of great depth, and the first true Renaissance pope. An advocate of church reform, Nicholas reasoned: "To create solid and stable convictions in the minds of the uncultured masses, there must be something that appeals to the eye: a popular faith, sustained only on doctrines, will never be anything but feeble and vacillating. But if the authority of the Holy See were visibly displayed in majestic buildings, imperishable memorials … belief would grow and strengthen." To this end, he set about restoring Rome – a task begun by Martin V – repairing the city's ancient monuments, adding imposing new ones of his own, and founding the Vatican Library.

Nicholas's successors continued as leading patrons of the Renaissance, as well as making abortive efforts to mount crusades against the Turks. Their achievements were considerable. They rebuilt Rome, promoted scholarship, commissioned some of the greatest art and architecture in history, and made Rome the focus of the Renaissance, but they did not reform the church.

In fact, the only country in Europe that did see real reform was Spain, which did so after the pope had transferred effective authority over the Spanish church to the king and queen. Before renewal, it experienced terror. In 1478 the pope allowed Ferdinand and

THE WHEEL OF FORTUNE, CONTROLLING HUMAN LIVES
Renaissance leaders sought to revive the culture of ancient Greece and Rome, lauding such classical ideas as the dominance of Fortune (above). The poet Petrarch claimed that the Greek and Roman classics held "all wisdom and rules of right conduct" and that a man should aim for undying fame.

Isabella to take over the old papal Inquisition in their domains (throughout the century, the papal Inquisition was largely inactive). Under the leadership of Grand Inquisitor Thomas de Torquemada, from 1483 to 1498, the Spanish Inquisition burned perhaps 2,000 people, terrorizing any whose orthodoxy was suspect. Almost as much a political as a religious organization, it was firmly under the control of the king and queen, who wished to unify their country and saw enforced religious unity as a means to that end. More positively, they appointed the reforming Cardinal Ximenes archbishop of Toledo in 1495. He improved the morals and education of the clergy and of his own order, the Franciscans, so much that Spain had a ready supply of missionaries when her ships discovered a new world in the Americas, and its citizens did not echo the complaints against church corruption that were so common elsewhere.

✤ THE DEPTHS OF EXCESS ✤

The clamor for papal reform was growing louder. At this critical juncture, disaster overtook the papacy, with the election of Roderigo Borgia, father of ten illegitimate children, as Pope Alexander VI (r. 1492–1503). Under his rule, the papacy descended to one of the lowest points in its fluctuating history. He acquired a

PRINTING THE BIBLE

The invention of printing made it possible to produce far more Bibles. Between the printing of the first Bible in the 1450s and the production of Luther's translation in 1522, there were 14 German editions of the Bible, 4 in Dutch, and numbers in other languages. In England, however, Bible translations were banned pending an officially approved version, which failed to appear.

✤

FAITH AND ART IN THE RENAISSANCE AND CATHOLIC REFORMATION

✤

IN the baptistery of St. Peter's Basilica in Rome, an elaborate bronze lid surmounts a porphyry basin. The basin, which now serves as a baptismal font, was once the lid of the sarcophagus of the Roman emperor Hadrian, whose mausoleum is the present-day Castel Sant' Angelo. In May 1527, the city of Rome was sacked by the troops of Emperor Charles V, whose soldiers looted the sarcophagus in the hopes of finding some treasure. The tomb was desecrated. Some years later, the artist Antonio Sangallo brought the lid of the sarcophagus to the Basilica and used it as the new baptismal font. Thus, that which was once the lid for the coffin of death became the basin for the waters of eternal life. The symbolism of this simple yet eloquent design suggests that the artist understood the mysteries of faith.

ARTISTS AND BELIEVERS

In the context of Christian history, mention of the great art of this era is incomplete without considering the ardent faith of many of its creators, and the effects their work has had on the spiritual and emotional lives of countless Christians since. To take one example, few can view the paintings of Fra Angelico, such as that below, without feeling the artist's faith and sanctity in the genius with which he depicted the holy, the heavenly, and the angelic. At a time of vast corruption in church leadership, it was often artists who showed bishops how a Christian should live. Even in Counter-Reformation Rome, so much stricter in faith and morals, artists might still stand out for self-sacrifice. Michelangelo began work on St. Peter's Basilica in 1547, at the age of 72 and continued for the remaining 17 years of his life, refusing any payment since he wished his work to be an offering to God and to St. Peter. His work, and that of other artists of faith, still inspires awe and wonder. Believers find in it a reflection of the majesty of God, shown in his creation and in his redeeming work in history; it serves to teach, to mediate, and to help interpret God's message. The many masks which art wears allow for an understanding of spiritual and emotional things very different from that which comes from words.

FRA ANGELICO'S IMAGE OF THE DAY OF JUDGMENT

Fra Angelico (c. 1395–1455) joined the Dominican friars as a young man. His famous frescoes at the priory of San Marco in Florence so impressed Pope Nicholas V that he called the friar to Rome to decorate his chapel at the Vatican. Born Guido de Piero, his remarkable skill at depicting angels earned him the nickname by which he is known.

NEW WORLDS

In 1492 Christopher Columbus *(above)*, an Italian sailor in the employ of the king and queen of Spain, led the first European expedition to set foot in the Americas. Then a Portuguese ship successfully navigated the sea route from Europe to India, around Africa, in 1497. These discoveries brought immense wealth to Europe, particularly to Spain and Portugal. They also renewed Western Christians' awareness of mission, as hundreds of priests and friars sailed to evangelize the newly encountered peoples, and to try to protect them from the rapacious colonizers. In Congo, for example, an early mission saw one of the local princes depart to Rome to be trained as a bishop, only for his mission to be destroyed by slave traders *(pp. 150-51)*.

❖

reputation for murderous corruption that few have ever matched. He was thunderously denounced by the devout, widely respected friar, Savonarola, a brilliant preacher who dominated Florence for four years from 1494, persuading the city's sophisticated citizens to repent of their pride and greed and to burn many of their treasures on public "bonfires of the vanities." For four years the Florentines followed him, but the pope excommunicated him in 1497, and, tired of his puritan leadership, they burned Savonarola at the stake the next year. A number of Catholic leaders, however, although loyal to the church, venerated Savonarola's memory. The pope, having accomplished his critic's downfall, continued as before. Where other popes had called for a crusade to recapture Constantinople, Alexander asked the Ottoman sultan to pay him to prevent the possibility.

❖ **POPE IN ARMS** ❖

Alexander's successor, Julius II (r. 1503–13), determined to strengthen the Papal States, began his papacy leading his troops into battle in silver armor. When Christians looked to him for spiritual leadership, he

CREATION OF THE RENAISSANCE POPES
The old St. Peter's cathedral, decrepit and unsafe, was demolished in 1506. Pope Julius II laid the foundation stone of its replacement (above), which was to take over a century to build, requiring vast sums of money.

seemed a secular prince, in full armor, leading the papal army through the breached walls of conquered cities, or commissioning leading artists to beautify his palace. Even when, in May of 1512, Julius finally capitulated to pressure and opened a church council, it failed to tackle seriously the roots of reform.

Like his predecessors, he continued the endless quest for money. To fund wars and building, these popes invented hundreds of new offices, all of them for sale, thereby creating a vast bureaucracy with no interest in spiritual revival. In the 1450s, Pope Nicholas V's legate had preached against the sale of indulgences; now Julius II began a huge campaign to sell them to fund the new St. Peter's *(see image, above)*.

Worse was still to come, however. The new pope, Leo X (r. 1513–21), son of Lorenzo the Magnificent, the Medici ruler of Florence, indulged in the ephemeral delights of processions and ceremonies, and spent much of his time hunting, ignoring important

> **" SINCE GOD HAS GIVEN US THE PAPACY, LET US ENJOY IT "**

REMARK ATTRIBUTED TO POPE LEO X

business of the church – most notably the pressing need for reform. As his predecessor had done, he promoted the selling of indulgences. Leo was unconcerned to hear, in 1517, that the preaching of these indulgences was being challenged by an obscure German professor of theology named Martin Luther.

RAPHAEL'S "THE SCHOOL OF ATHENS"
Julius II commissioned Raphael to decorate his private apartments. One of the resulting pictures (above), showing the greatest philosophers of classical Greece and Rome, illustrates the Renaissance ideology that strove to ally Christianity with classical art and literature in a new "Humanism."

MICHELANGELO'S VISION: THE CEILING OF THE SISTINE CHAPEL, VATICAN PALACE, ROME

Even the fiercest critics of the Renaissance popes must admit that they had good taste. Pope Sixtus IV rebuilt the papal chapel at the Vatican, henceforward called the Sistine Chapel. It was decorated by the foremost artists of the day – most notably Michelangelo, whose work there, fired by his own deep faith, spans history from Creation to Judgment and remains one of the greatest artistic achievements. Such costly patronage was, however, a continuing drain on the papal treasury.

The Reformation

1517–1648

THE GLORIES OF THE Renaissance led to deplorable excesses in the Western church, such as the sale of indulgences to raise money for dubious causes. Martin Luther, a German theologian, publicly refuted such practices and thus precipitated the Reformation. Other reformers were encouraged to follow his example and join the effort for reform. The Catholic church refused to listen to any of these proposals, and the unity of Christianity became fractured once more. The Reformation soon ceased to be a matter only for individual consciences: political rulers sensed the advantage of breaking the church's political and territorial power and took sides.

The Catholic church was slow to respond, and by the mid-seventeenth century the religious map of Europe had been completely redrawn. These Christian divisions led to bloody wars as Catholic and Protestant nations battled against one another. Meanwhile, Catholic missionaries travelled to distant countries and continents where the gospel had yet to take root – Latin America, Africa, India, China, and Japan.

Martin Luther makes his protestations public

EUROPE AT THE TIME OF THE REFORMATION

BY ALL APPEARANCES, the church in the West at the dawn of the sixteenth century had successfully weathered many of the storms that had besieged it during the Middle Ages. Although Islam continued to spread in Africa and Asia, Western Christendom remained loyal to papal authority, which had been reinforced as successive church councils failed to usurp the pope's authority (p. 124). The age of exploration had begun, and soon Catholic missionaries would be sent around the globe. However, many real and perilous challenges still existed.

❖ THE STATE OF THE CHURCH ❖

Local parishes everywhere had long suffered from symptoms of neglect, indifference, and uneducated and untrained clergy who, in an age of rising literacy, no longer met the expectations of many Christians. The need for the church to refill its coffers with ready money led to a prevalence of the immoral customs of selling church offices and attempting to buy divine favor in the afterlife by purchasing indulgences (p. 132). These practices were met with anger and, in some cases, fierce resistance by the peasant class, so by the sixteenth century some Christians determined to bring about reform. The Dutch Christian humanist Desiderius Erasmus (c. 1466–1536) was one such example.

Erasmus was a noted theological scholar and the articulate author of many books that became popular for their witty and satirical attacks on the poor state of the church. He also sought a better knowledge of the original Hebrew and Greek texts of the Bible, hoping to rethink theological opinion with these accurate sources. He abhorred violence and wanted only to nudge the church into common sense, but Europe seemed eager for more reform, and instead his work helped pave the way for the Reformation. The subsequent controversy over Erasmus's

THE SALE OF INDULGENCES
Professional "pardoners" sold documents known as indulgences to individuals who wished to be released – or to release one of the deceased – from a certain amount of time in purgatory. A total indulgence, also called a plenary indulgence, could release a person from purgatory at once. Martin Luther would later call this practice "the pious defrauding of the faithful."

work and the resulting violence were to break apart the church in the West. As the popular sixteenth-century saying stated, "Erasmus laid the egg and Luther hatched it."

❖ RESISTING ROME'S AUTHORITY ❖

Combined with the popular spiritual unrest that was felt across Europe was the desire of many monarchs to control their national churches and church lands. These rulers presented a growing challenge to the authorities in Rome as nation-states became ever stronger. While the intentions of the rulers had little to do with church reform, their actions enabled the Reformation to succeed as the pope's power grew weaker.

> **" I WISH THAT THE SCRIPTURES MIGHT BE TRANSLATED INTO ALL LANGUAGES.... I LONG THAT THE FARM LABORER MIGHT SING THEM AS HE FOLLOWS HIS PLOUGH, THE WEAVER HUM THEM TO THE TUNE OF HIS SHUTTLE, THE TRAVELER BEGUILE THE WEARINESS OF HIS JOURNEY WITH THEIR STORIES "**

ERASMUS

In France Charles VIII (r. 1483–98) consolidated his power and made (ultimately unsuccessful) plans for France to be the head of the Holy Roman Empire. His intentions became clear when he invaded Italy in 1494 and was crowned king of Naples the following year. By 1516 French power was so strong that Pope Leo X was forced to draft the Concordat of Bologna with the then French king, Francis I, which essentially made Francis

INSPIRATIONAL SCHOLAR
Erasmus became the most famous scholar in Europe during his lifetime. He published an enormous amount of literature, including a new scholarly edition of the Greek New Testament in 1516.

the independent head of the church in France. Spain had successfully ended centuries of Muslim rule when Granada was reconquered in 1492 and the Moorish rulers were driven out. A Spanish monarchy was born from the marriage of Ferdinand of Aragon to Isabella of Castile – "the Catholic Monarchs," as they became known. Together, they brought the church under the authority of the monarchy rather than the papacy, and launched the Spanish Inquisition in an effort to consolidate their empire. The Inquisition resulted in thousands suspected of heresy being imprisoned, tortured, and sometimes even executed (*p. 126*).

Although the Hapsburg Holy Roman Emperors Maximilian (r. 1493–1519) and Charles V (r. 1519–56) remained firmly Catholic, anti-papal sentiment was rife in the lands of their empire – in Germany, across much of central Europe, and in the Netherlands. Central Europe was eager for reform, with some nobles in Poland, Bohemia (in the modern Czech Republic), and Hungary keen to curb papal powers in their land. Inspired by the talk of reform elsewhere in Europe, the Netherlands moved to the brink of a long and bitter struggle to free itself both from the Catholic Church and the Spanish monarchy. In Scandinavia, too, discontent with Rome was rising, leaving the way open for reform to take root in Sweden, Norway, and Denmark. Yet the fires of religious and political resentment against papal corruption and authority burned brightest in Germany, Switzerland, France, and England, where the key reformers and rulers of these lands were to change the complexion of Christianity for good.

THE REFORMATION IN GERMANY

AT THE TIME OF THE Protestant Reformation, Germany was divided into nearly 300 independent states, all loosely under the headship of the Holy Roman emperor. Although the pope exercised ostensible control over the German churches, the strong nationalistic nature of the German people and their anti-papal sentiment was an open invitation to a reform-minded individual to seize ecclesiastical authority over the country.

❖ INDULGENCES ❖

The catalyst for a breach with Rome was the despised practice of selling indulgences. The theology behind the granting of indulgences was the notion that the church had a "treasury" of good works built up by the Apostles and saints, along with the sinless life of Christ. Merit from this treasury could be granted to any church member to reduce or eliminate time they would spend in purgatory being purged of their sins before going to heaven. Indulgences could be purchased through a financial donation or, as in previous centuries, by per-

AT THE DOOR OF THE CHURCH AT WITTENBERG
After Luther nailed up his theses on the church door, Pope Leo X tried to "quench a monk … and thus smother the fire before it should become a conflagration". He failed.

forming a service such as fighting in the Crusades. By the early sixteenth century, indulgences were aggressively being sold. In Germany a Dominican, Johann Tetzel, marketed indulgences with the promise that "as the coin into the coffer rings, the soul from

purgatory springs!" Those who gave money were told that it would be used to rebuild St. Peter's Basilica in Rome. Actually, only half of the donated money went to this purpose. The rest was used to pay off the debts of men such as Prince Albert of Brandenburg. Albert had paid large fees and bribes to be named the archbishop of Mainz. To gather the necessary money he secured a loan from the Fugger bankers (*p. 137*), promising that he would authorize Tetzel to sell indulgences in his realm.

When a parish priest and professor named Martin Luther (1483–1546) – who had already preached against the sale of indulgences – became aware of the secret arrangement between Tetzel and Albert, he decided to bring his views into the sphere of public debate. On October 31, 1517, he nailed his *Ninety-Five Theses* to the door of the castle church at Wittenberg and, in the process, sent a thunderbolt to the heart of papal authority and launched a reformation.

✧ LUTHER'S WORK ✧

From his translation work as a professor, Luther had developed the theology of *sola scriptura* – that the Bible is the final authority for Christians – and *sola fide* – that salvation comes by faith alone and not by good works. He was also convinced that the Bible should be available to all people, not just to clergy and scholars, and that every Christian is a member of the priesthood

of believers. While these propositions ran contrary to more than a thousand years of church tradition, he believed he was doing nothing more than righting a ship that had strayed from its rightful course. This dialogue might never have extended beyond the walls of academia but for the fact that Luther was also a parish priest, experiencing at first hand some of the political and spiritual unrest at that time, and so he chose to speak out publicly against what he saw as abuses, deficiencies, and misunderstandings in the church. It wasn't long before his ideas took root and his fame spread through Germany and beyond.

In 1518 the papal inquisitor Silvester Prierias ordered Luther to come to Rome and face charges of heresy. Luther refused the summons, stating that only the Bible, not the pope, was infallible and that he answered to Christ's authority alone. Fearing for the priest's life, Prince Frederick of Saxony changed the venue to

PREACHING FROM THE PULPIT
Luther (pictured right) *declared that peace with God can be found only by those who believe in Christ and realize that Jesus canceled all human sin when he died on the cross (hence the symbolic image here). Thus Christ is the only source of salvation and freedom.*

MARTIN LUTHER

A**S is so often the case with people destined for greatness, there was little in Luther's background to suggest that he would become a key figure in church history. The eldest child of a wealthy miner who wanted him to study law, Luther felt called to pursue the monastic life after a series of spiritual crises. Yet his search for inner peace proved futile, and he found little comfort in the good works, confession of sins, and self-denial he thought would save him. He became deeply depressed in 1507 when he performed his first Mass and realized his sinful nature and unworthiness before God. Hoping that a trip to Rome in 1510 might renew his sense of purpose, he found himself shocked by the cynical attitudes and worldly lifestyles of the Catholic leaders he encountered. By 1517 he had discovered a new assurance of forgiveness in the Bible, which was to greatly influence the rest of his life and work. Although

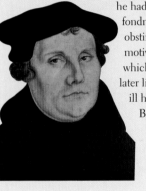

he had a quick temper, a fondness for beer, and was obstinate, Luther was motivated by a great faith, which sustained him in later life when he suffered ill health and depression. Believing that priests should be free to marry, he wed a former nun in 1525 and had six children.

INITIATING DEBATE
Luther's act of nailing his declarations, or theses, to the door of the castle church at Wittenberg (*above*) was at the time a common practice for initiating dialogue and debate among scholars on controversial subjects. While Luther's theses covered a variety of issues, they focused on three church policies that Luther strongly disagreed with: the selling of indulgences; the pope's authority to forgive sins; and the true treasure of the church, which Luther believed was the gospel message of salvation and not the good works of Christ and the saints. Although the theses were written in Latin, they were quickly translated into German. Not only did Tetzel's sales of indulgences drop, but he had to go into hiding from angry mobs. The Reformation in Germany had begun in earnest.

✧

THE NINETY-FIVE THESES
A sampling of the key tenets from the theses includes:
6) The pope has no power to remit any guilt, except declaring and warranting it to have been remitted by God;
21) Thus those preachers of indulgences are in error who say that by the indulgences of the pope a man is freed and saved from all punishment;
62) The true treasure of the church is the holy gospel of the glory and grace of God.

✧

THE COUNCIL OF WORMS
In April 1521 Luther was brought before the emperor to defend his beliefs and actions. In reply, the emperor said: "A single friar who goes counter to all Christianity for a thousand years must be wrong. I have decided to mobilize everything against Luther: my kingdoms and dominions, my friends, my body, my blood, and my soul."

THE GREAT POPULARIZER

Luther wrote several popular tracts that expressed his convictions. They were written in an accessible format and in understandable language and were spread among a wide audience. In his *Babylonian Captivity of the Church*, Luther condemned the Catholic traditions regarding the sacraments. In *To the Christian Nobility of the German Nation* Luther addressed German princes and magistrates, insisting it was their duty to reform the Church. *The Freedom of the Christian Man* boldly asserted that a Christian is subject to no one but Christ and that justification is by faith alone.

❖

Augsburg, where Luther was confronted by Cardinal Cajetan. Luther refused to recant his position and, in defiance of the pope's authority, asked that a general council be appointed to decide the matter.

Pope Leo X did not want to alienate Frederick, hoping that the prince, who did not have the political strength of other candidates, would become the new Holy Roman emperor after Maximilian's death in 1519. Yet Luther refused to compromise, and the battle lines were drawn between those who supported him and those who defended the papacy. Although Luther had never anticipated breaking with Rome, his ideas, distributed via a series of tracts he wrote about his convictions *(see side column)*, soon aroused German nationalism. Pope Leo responded to Luther's pamphlets with a treatise of his own, titled *Exsurge Domine*. Calling the priest a "wild boar [who] has invaded [the] vineyard of the Lord," he condemned Luther and ordered him to submit within 60 days or be excommunicated. On December 10, 1520, Luther burned the treatise in front of the citizens of Wittenberg. Hearing this news, the pope made good his threat to excommunicate Luther.

❖ LUTHER'S STAND ❖

Charles V, who had been elected emperor of the Holy Roman Empire in 1519, resisted the pope's demand that Luther be burned as a heretic. He called a hearing at the Diet (Council) of Worms on April 18, 1521.

Moderate Catholics, who feared that a schism might destroy the church if Luther was condemned, urged Luther to rethink his position. Instead, he uttered his famous statement, "Here I stand. I cannot do otherwise. God help me." Charles V reluctantly outlawed Luther's writings and condemned him and anyone who supported him. Prince Frederick secretly hid Luther in Wartburg Castle near Eisenach for his protection. In Luther's absence, other reformers such as Philip Melanchthon and Andreas Carlstadt temporarily assumed leadership roles in the burgeoning reform movement in Germany. In many cases, however, their actions were either too radical or too conciliatory.

Luther originally had no intention of founding a new church. He hoped that by returning to the gospel, as he saw it, the Catholic church would reform. When that did not happen, he rejected any doctrine – such as the cult of saints, indulgences, and sacraments – not

> ❝ FAITH IS THE 'YES' OF THE HEART, A CONVICTION ON WHICH ONE STAKES ONE'S LIFE ❞
>
> **MARTIN LUTHER**

explicitly referred to in the Bible. Lutheran churches became national churches, varying from one state to another. Despite being outlawed, Luther returned to Wittenberg. His death sentence was never carried out, as the emperor was preoccupied with other matters, and Luther lived in relative peace for another 25 years.

❖ THE PEASANTS' REVOLT ❖

The German Reformation did not arise without bloodshed. The peasant class had long suffered enforced oppression at the hands of their rulers. Many peasants embraced Luther's convictions as religious justification for their desire to be free from lives of servitude. They demanded the right to choose their own clergy and be paid by their rulers for extra services performed. They also claimed certain rights to land ownership.

Although Luther initially supported the peasants in their cause, he turned against them when one of their leaders, Thomas Müntzer, a radical reformer, massacred the inhabitants of Weinsberg and burned castles and churches. In an ill-conceived tract, Luther gave license to the German princes to use whatever means necessary to put down the revolt, telling them to "wash your hands in their blood." The nobility united their armies and killed an estimated 100,000 peasants in 1524. Luther's response was swift: he condemned the nobility as "devils," but the damage had been done. The ultimate result was that Luther lost the trust of those he had initially sought to help with his reforms.

A majority of German princes remained sympathetic to Luther. In 1526 they were granted the right to support either Catholicism or Protestantism in their realms as they saw fit. In 1530, at the Diet of Augsburg, Melanchthon was commissioned to draft the Augsburg Confession, the official statement of Lutheranism. Disagreements among the reform leaders about the document's content continued for many years.

War soon broke out between the Protestants and Catholics in Germany and continued until 1555, when a peace treaty was signed in Augsburg. Its defining theme was the principle "whose region, his religion." In other words, each prince was allowed to make his territory Lutheran or Catholic. With the Peace of Augsburg, Lutheranism had attained legal status in the Holy Roman Empire just nine years after Luther's death.

❖ LUTHER'S IMPACT ❖

The Lutheran faith soon spread to other countries. Hans Tausen, a professor of religion in Copenhagen, brought Lutheranism to Denmark, and it then took hold in Norway and Sweden as part of political reforms sweeping those countries in the sixteenth and seventeenth centuries. Encouraged by Luther's writings, the Bohemian reformers, the Hussites, initiated reform in Poland (p. 142). Elsewhere in central Europe, Lutherans and Calvinists united against Catholic authorities. Luther was also instrumental in inspiring reformers in England, Italy, and Spain.

LUTHERAN BIBLE
While in hiding, Luther translated Erasmus's Greek New Testament into German, translating the text at a rate of over 1,500 words per day and completing the task within a matter of weeks.
❖

LUTHERAN CHURCH
Although Luther tolerated religious images and ornamentation in churches, some of his followers did not. Later Lutheran churches were often simple buildings stripped of all unessential detail. Luther, in contrast to the Catholic Mass at that time, offered both bread and wine to lay people at communion.

CALVIN'S WRITINGS

Calvin (1509–64) had one
of the most analytical and
brilliant minds in church
history. His *Institutes of the
Christian Religion*, written
in 1536 in Latin, is a
classic statement of
Protestant Reformed
theology (Reformed and
Lutheran theology are the
two main branches of
Reformation thought). He
later translated the text into
French. Other scholars
followed his example and
began to write in French
as well as in Latin. He
also wrote four books
defending Protestant
Reformed theology.

❖

GENEVA'S BLUE LAWS

Calvin was concerned that
every aspect of daily life
should be lived in
obedience to God. To
further this, he helped
convince city leaders to set
out a practical moral code
for Geneva known as the
"Blue Laws." Examples
include conduct in inns:
"If anyone blasphemes the
name of God or says, 'By
the body, 'sblood, zounds'
or anything like, or who
gives himself to the devil
or uses similar execrable
imprecations, he shall be
punished"; "The host shall
be obliged to keep in a
public place a French
Bible, in which anyone
who wishes may read";
"[He] shall not allow any
dissoluteness like dancing,
dice or cards, nor receive
anyone suspected of
being a debauch."

❖

THE REFORMATION IN SWITZERLAND

AS LUTHERANISM spread across the European continent, another form of Protestantism developed in Switzerland with the next generation of reformers. Known as the Reformed Church, its prime movers were Ulrich Zwingli and John Calvin.

❖ ULRICH ZWINGLI ❖

Born in Switzerland, Zwingli (1484–1531) was greatly influenced by Erasmus *(p. 130)*. His skill as a preacher led to his appointment as priest at the Great Minster church in Zurich in 1518. Having studied the New Testament, Zwingli was convinced that justification was by faith alone and that biblical authority superseded human interpretation. His attacks on such Catholic practices as Lenten fasts and celibacy of the clergy soon stirred the bishop of Constance to act in 1522 – demanding that Zwingli desist from any further attacks on Catholic traditions. Yet the city council in Zurich endorsed Zwingli's position on the supremacy of the Bible for all civil rule. During the next two years a series of public debates on church authority took place in Zurich. At the first, in 1523, Zwingli presented his *Sixty-seven Articles*, which declared that the veneration of saints, monastic orders, primacy of the pope, absolution, indulgences, and the merit of good works were all human inventions and had no basis in the Bible. At a debate later that year, he called for the removal of crucifixes, relics, tapestries, and statues, for the abolition of the Mass, and for the cessation of organ playing, chanting, and bell ringing. The city council repeatedly supported Zwingli, and in 1525 the first evangelical communion service was conducted in the Great Minster church.

While his reform movement spread to other cities, differences between Luther and Zwingli emerged over the Lord's Supper: Luther believed that Christ was actually present in the consecrated elements, Zwingli

THE RISE OF CALVINISM
This Flemish engraving (dated 1566) shows Calvinists destroying statues in Catholic churches. Calvin's ideas spread quickly, and his biblical pamphlets and commentaries were read and studied widely. Geneva became not only a refuge for Calvinists but the center of the new movement. Elsewhere in Europe, Calvinism found supporters in England, Scotland, Germany, and Holland.

THE POWER OF MONEY

❖

FOUNDED by Johannes Fugger in the fourteenth century, the Fugger banking dynasty controlled the destiny of monarchs and popes alike throughout the late medieval period with their lending practices. It was, in fact, an ecclesiastical debt owed by Albert of Brandenberg (*p. 133*) to the house of Fugger for the purchase of the archbishopric of Mainz that sparked the Reformation. Johann Tetzel's sale of indulgences to pay off this loan met with the condemnation of Martin Luther.

THE EUROPEAN ECONOMY

Albert's situation was in many ways a result of the shifting economic landscape in Europe at that time. Wealth was no longer simply a result of titled land ownership, and the barter system was becoming an antiquated form of payment, used primarily by the peasants. The advent of expanded trade had created new fortunes, and gold and silver were now the standard means for gaining tools and services. Jakob Fugger (1459–1525), or Jakob the Rich as he was

FUGGER WITH HIS BOOKKEEPER
This illustration of 1518 depicts Fugger with his bookkeeper, Matthaus Schwartz. It is thought that Schwartz himself was the artist of this picture.

called, was a prototype for the modern business executive. Based in Augsburg, he had branch offices in Rome, Lisbon, and Budapest. He expanded his father's empire to include copper and silver mining, industry, real estate, and farming. Although he was born a commoner, Fugger was able to secure the title of count and live in a castle that befitted his station.

FINANCIAL POWER

Along with his bookkeeper, Matthaus Schwartz, Fugger operated an efficient financial empire that produced typical annual profits of 50 percent between 1511 and 1527. Other powerful banking families of this era included the Herwarts, Hochstetters, Paumgartners, and Grossembrots – each striving to monopolize the market. Yet it was the Fuggers who dominated, and their power was such that when Jakob demanded repayment of a loan to the Holy Roman emperor, Charles V humbly complied. Such hidden forces, as well as spiritual matters, helped to shape the history of the Reformation.

that the rite was simply a memorial. Zwingli also came into conflict with Anabaptist groups (*pp. 138-39*) over the issue of infant baptism, in which they did not believe. After his death, Zwingli and his movement were soon overshadowed by the enduring influence of the man who has been called the greatest Reformer after Luther – the Frenchman, John Calvin (1509–64).

❖ JOHN CALVIN ❖

Calvin's outstanding mind has earned him the mantle of the greatest of Reformation theologians and organizers. His influence remains to this day through his innovations in church government and "Reformed" theology.

Sometime after 1532, Calvin had a spiritual reawakening. Initially he had no desire to leave the Catholic church, although he associated freely with a group of Protestants active in Paris. In 1534 he severed his ties to the church of Rome, and when Francis I, king of France, ordered the persecution of all Protestant believers, Calvin moved to Strasbourg and then to Basel, where he wrote the first edition of *Institutes of the Christian Religion*. After spending some time in Ferrara in Italy to promote the Reformation, Calvin went to Geneva, and it was here that he initiated many

of his ideas for congregational worship, including regular observance of the Lord's Supper, a governing church board, and psalm-singing as a form of praise.

Calvin was eventually driven from Geneva over disputes with the city council regarding his practice of the Eucharist. He settled in Strasbourg and from 1538 to 1541 pastored a congregation of Protestants who had fled persecution in France, continuing to refine his theology and convictions concerning church government and corporate worship.

Meanwhile, in Geneva, Cardinal Jacopo Sadoleto was working to return the city to Catholicism. However, when Calvin wrote his masterful apologetic for the Protestant Reformation, *Reply to Sadoleto*, his words had such impact that in 1541 he was asked by the city to return. Calvin inspired Geneva magistrates to restructure all facets of religious and social life in Geneva in line with his belief that church and state should together be under the dominion of Christ. His vision of a utopian Christian society made Geneva the "Rome of Protestantism." Many foreigners studied theology at the Academy of Geneva, which was founded in 1559, and went on to spread Calvinism abroad as leaders of the Reformed Presbyterian and Puritan movements (*pp. 140-43*).

PREDESTINATION

Although Calvin's doctrine was similar to Luther's, and equally Bible based, it was much more systematic. It placed a particular emphasis on God's sovereign power and the lack of human free will, because Calvin wanted people's salvation to rest, not on their fickle good works, but on God's unwavering will. This led Calvinists to a doctrine of election by which God chose some people for salvation, not others. This is often considered the most defining feature of Calvinism.

❖

THE RADICAL REFORMATION

WHILE THE REFORMERS Luther, Calvin, and others, were passionate about their cause – often sacrificing personal safety and comfort – they were, for the most part, unwilling to completely abandon the tenets of the Catholic church they and their forebears had served. Others, however, were far less conciliatory. Known as radical reformers, these Protestant believers firmly rejected the Lutheran position that only those Catholic practices that actually seemed to contradict the Bible should be abolished.

❖ EXTREME BELIEFS ❖

The radical reformers – called Anabaptists (from the Greek, meaning "to baptize again"), as they believed that anyone baptized as an infant had to be "recleansed" as an adult – abandoned any doctrine, worship practice, or ecclesiastical act that was not clearly sanctioned in the Bible. For them this included refusing to support such national causes as bearing arms in warfare and swearing allegiance to rulers. Even Calvinists, who had similar belief in the authority of the Bible, saw no need to break with these practices. Thus, many Anabaptists were persecuted and killed by governing authorities, the Catholic Inquisition – even by other Protestant groups.

❖ ANABAPTIST LEADERS ❖

Although loosely allied under the tenets of the "Brotherly Union" adopted at the Schleitheim Synod in 1527, the Anabaptists are best defined by the convictions of those who organized the various groups. Perhaps the two best-known Anabaptists were Menno Simons and Jakob Ammann. Born in Holland, Simons (1496–1561) was ordained a Catholic priest in 1524, but his study of the

> **❝ WE ARE NOT REGENERATED BECAUSE WE ARE BAPTIZED.... WE ARE BAPTIZED BECAUSE WE ARE REGENERATED ❞**
>
> **MENNO SIMONS**

New Testament led him to doubt the validity of transubstantiation (p. 113). In 1536 he converted to Anabaptism and began serving a congregation in Groningen. While his ministry was marked by moderation, especially when compared to the apocalyptic visions of some other Anabaptist leaders, he was an extreme literalist when interpreting the Bible. For instance, he refused to accept the term "Trinity" since it does not appear in the Bible. Simons believed in a clear separation of church and state, so government officials could not be members of his church, and he held that the dual nature of Christ as defined at the Council of Chalcedon (p. 62) was inaccurate – that Christ's nature was solely divine and he was born "through" and not "by" Mary. The Mennonite church, which bears his name, survived in large part because of his vigorous church-planting activities and the numerous books he wrote.

COUNTRY LIFE

As reformers and Catholics quarreled and monarchs and emperors clashed, the daily life of the typical peasant during the years of the Reformation remained pretty much the same. Peasants not only had to provide sustenance for their families, they also had to pay regular tithes to the church and heavy taxes in the form of goods and services to the ruler or lord of their realm. They also had to be wary of marauding bands of mercenaries who would sack and burn a village that was not prepared to defend itself. It is little wonder, then, that peasants sometimes revolted in bloody uprisings. It is also clear why they used any excuse, from a wedding to a saint's holiday, to engage in boisterous and drunken revelry – activities that the ecclesiastical hierarchy condemned and that made the local authorities understandably nervous.

THE ADULT BAPTISM OF BELIEVERS
The Anabaptists comprised various groups (whose different leaders are illustrated above) which all endorsed only adult baptism of those whose Christian faith was clearly apparent.

AMISH GIRLS – HEIRS TO THE RADICAL REFORMERS

Like many persecuted groups, the Anabaptists survived by migrating to new lands where they could practice their beliefs in relative peace; large numbers settled in North America. The Amish Mennonites are now mostly settled in Pennsylvania. They remain to this day firm in their conviction that much of modern technology tends to undermine the simple life Christ called them to live. As a result, they refuse to use many modern inventions, and they live in tight communities to sustain their values.

Ammann (c. 1644–c. 1711) was a Mennonite elder who lived and worked in Alsace and Switzerland. His zealous attitude towards separation from the rest of the world, as defined in the *18 Articles of Confession of Faith* adopted by the Mennonites in 1632, led him in 1693 to sever relations with other Mennonite churches and, with more than 4,000 followers, to found the Amish Mennonites.

✥ APOCALYPTIC ANABAPTISTS ✥

Thomas Müntzer, who had once been Luther's ally and was granted a clerical position in Zwickau with the aid of the great reformer, came under the influence of the apocalyptic Zwickau Prophets and began demanding social and political upheaval. When he moved to Mulhausen in 1524 and set up a theocracy, Catholics and Protestants joined forces to bring an end to his call for civil war. He was soon captured and executed.

In 1526, while serving as a minister in Stockholm, Melchior Hoffman (c. 1500–c. 543) became obsessed with the end of the world, predicting Christ's return in 1533. After joining the Anabaptists in Strasbourg,

he was sent to preach in various places, then returned to Strasbourg to await the end of the world. Here he was arrested and imprisoned for life by the authorities. However, he did attract converts, and the Melchiorites survived him as a distinct party among the Anabaptists. One of Hoffman's converts, Jan Mathys, believed that the city of Münster would be the New Jerusalem, and in 1533 he stormed it with an army of Anabaptists, believing he could take over the world. Such actions partly explain why authorities distrusted the Anabaptists; after his attempt, Mathys and his supporters were imprisoned, tortured, and killed.

Other radical reform leaders, including Felix Manz, and Balthasar Hubmaier of the Swiss Brethren, suffered similar fates as they were hunted down and sentenced to death. Even peaceful and well-respected Anabaptists such as Jakob Hutter were brought before local courts. Although the Hutterites were pacifists and their skills as craftspeople and farmers were much admired, Hutter was eventually killed as part of the sweeping genocidal purges of Anabaptists ordered by King Ferdinand I.

FOXE'S BOOK OF MARTYRS

Written to preserve the memory of Protestant martyrs and inspire the author's fellow Englishmen to embrace the Reformation, *Foxe's Book of Martyrs* is one of the great works of Protestant literature. Foxe (1516–87), a Protestant clergyman, fled to the Continent when Mary I of England restored Catholicism. After settling in Basel, Foxe began work on his book, which was eventually published in England during the reign of Elizabeth I. It was widely read during Foxe's lifetime and went through four editions before his death. Horrific in many places, and almost numbing in its sheer scope and detail, the book has survived as a testament to the courage and dedication of those who sacrificed their lives rather than renounce their convictions.

✥

THE SPREAD OF THE REFORMATION

> **" The most perfect school of Christ that ever was on earth since the days of the Apostles "**
>
> **JOHN KNOX ON CALVIN'S PROTESTANT CENTER, GENEVA**

AS WITH LUTHER AND the Lutheran church, the death of John Calvin did nothing to impede the theological movement he began. In fact, Reformed churches began to proliferate in the sixteenth and seventeenth centuries. That they were able to thrive (in spite of severe persecution in some places) was in large part due to Calvin's legacy of establishing organized representative forms of local church government.

✦ THE DUTCH REFORMED CHURCH ✦

During the early decades of the Reformation, the Netherlands had been fertile ground for the birth and dissemination of Protestant movements. Along with lesser-known sects, the area that is today Belgium and Holland embraced Lutheranism, the Brethren of the Common Life, the Waldensians, and the Mennonite church. This was due, in part, to the fact that the Netherlands, although under Spanish rule, enjoyed a certain degree of religious freedom under the rule of Emperor Charles V. However, when Charles's son Philip II assumed the Spanish throne in 1556, the Netherlands became a stage for the horrors of the Spanish Inquisition. War broke out and a former Catholic, William of Orange, led the resistance against Spain. William was killed in 1584, but wars continued until 1648, when the Netherlands gained its freedom and was recognized as the United Provinces.

During this time the Dutch Reformed church was formed and rose to prominence. Noted for its tolerance of other religious groups, including Catholics, it adhered to a Presbyterian form of government and accepted the tenets of the Belgic, or Walloon, *Confessions* of 1561 and the *Heidelberg Catechism* of 1563. These Protestant confessions of faith brought consensus to the Reformed churches on issues such as the sacraments, the authority of the Bible, the role of the church as a singular institution of Christian discipline, the importance of good works, and the predestination of the soul.

✦ THE HUGUENOTS ✦

In France, Calvinist Protestant ministers – known as Huguenots – who had studied in Geneva, took advantage of Francis I's temporary cessation of the persecution of Protestants as he concentrated his efforts on war with Spain. The number of Reformed churches in France grew from fewer than 50 in 1559 to over 2,000 in 1561.

This rise to prominence could not be ignored by the government or Rome, and in 1562 a war broke out between Protestants and Catholics. The first of the French Wars of Religion, it reached a climax in 1572 at what was to be called the St. Bartholomew's Day Massacre. The scene of this infamous event was the wedding of Henry of Navarre, a Protestant, to Marguerite, the Catholic daughter of Catherine de Medici. Catherine used this occasion as a bait to lure the Huguenots and order their mass execution. This bloody incident only served to fuel the conflict, and the war continued until Henry was crowned King Henry IV of France in 1594. Although he had converted to Catholicism, Henry swore to protect the Huguenots from further oppression, a promise that was drafted into the Edict of Nantes in 1598. The edict was later rescinded, however, under Louis XIV in 1685, and thousands of Huguenots fled to other parts of Europe and America. It wasn't until over a century later, in 1802, that the Huguenots were granted permanent legal protection in France.

THE DUTCH WARS OF INDEPENDENCE
Spain, the most devoutly Catholic and powerful nation in Europe, ruled the Netherlands during the later sixteenth century. After a series of wars lasting into the seventeenth century, the Netherlands became a Protestant republic. Here, Velasquez commemorates the Treaty of Breda of 1625.

REFORMED CHURCH BUILDING

Preaching was held in high regard by Calvinists, so the structure of Reformed church buildings such as this one, built in 1655 in the Hague, included a central pulpit. Initially, few churches were built, which was partly due to a lack of funds. In the Netherlands, some congregations worshiped in open fields: in 1566, for example, a congregation of 15,000 met in a field outside Antwerp.

✤ SCOTTISH PRESBYTERIANISM ✤

Scotland lays claim to one of the great Reformation leaders, John Knox (c. 1513–72), although he is not as historically prominent as Luther or Calvin. Ordained a Catholic priest in 1536, and a papal notary in 1540, Knox's subsequent Protestant conversion is shrouded in mystery. After early involvement in the Scottish Reformation as a preacher and teacher, the death of Edward VI in 1553 and the coronation of Mary I, a devout Catholic, forced Knox to flee Britain for Europe – traveling first to France and later to Geneva, where he studied under Calvin.

✤ AN INFLUENTIAL REFORMER, ✤ AND AN ENEMY OF THE STATE

When Mary was succeeded by Elizabeth I, many Protestants returned to England, including most of Knox's congregation in Geneva. Knox had made an enemy of Elizabeth, however, after attacking her in one of his tracts. Thus in 1559 Knox sailed for Scotland, where he became minister of St. Giles church in Edinburgh. Protestants were still in the minority in Scotland, and the next few years were marked by religious strife and bloodshed as civil war between Protestants and Catholics erupted – the two sides aided by England and France, respectively. Conflict also arose between Protestant leaders and Mary, Queen of Scots, who was a Catholic.

When Mary was executed in 1587 for plotting to overthrow Elizabeth, her son, James VI, assumed the throne. When James succeeded Elizabeth to become James I, king of England, Knox's dreams for the independence of both his church and his country were finally realized: after a century of political and ecclesiastical struggles, Presbyterianism was at last established as the national faith in Scotland.

MARY, QUEEN OF SCOTS
Although subjects were required to adopt their ruler's religion, Knox believed that Protestants should forcibly resist Catholic monarchical pressure to conform. He clashed repeatedly with Mary, Queen of Scots and was convinced that she had "a proud mind, a crafty wit, and an indurate heart against God and his truth."

✤

Tyndale (c. 1494–1536)
was a Greek and Hebrew
scholar who dedicated his
life to creating an English
translation of the New
Testament that even "a boy
that driveth the plough"
could understand. After
settling in Germany where
he could write in relative
safety, Tyndale worked
on his translation and
completed it in 1525. Over
the next five years more
than 15,000 copies were
smuggled into England.
Although the religious
authorities burned every
copy they could find, they
were unable to stop these
secret shipments of Bibles.
Tyndale was arrested and
killed before he could
complete his translation
of the Old Testament.

❖

CONDENSED WORSHIP

The *Book of Common
Prayer* simplified and
condensed the Latin service
books of the medieval
church into one volume.
Written in English, this
official service book was
intended for both the
priest and the congregation
to use. The book was
first issued in 1549, and,
after a revision in 1662,
it remained almost un-
changed for centuries.
Even today, Anglicans
around the world still
use prayer books based
on Thomas Cranmer's
original work.

❖

The Protestant Reformation was changing the political
and religious landscape of Europe. A Lutheran creed
was adopted in Denmark in 1530 with the enthusiastic
consent of the Danish king, Frederick I. Sweden, which
had recently secured independence from Denmark,
broke off relations with Rome in 1524, although it did
not formally endorse Lutheran doctrine until as late as
1593. The Lutheran church was also established as the
state church in Finland, which was under the domain
of Sweden; in Norway, through the efforts of Frederick I;
and in Iceland, controlled by Norway. Lutheranism also
spread to the eastern Baltic region, including Latvia,
Estonia, and Lithuania. In Bohemia the Hussites,
followers of the Bohemian reformer Jan Hus (*p. 121*),
continued to oppose the papacy.

❖ ENGLISH REFORM ❖

England also experienced a Protestant upheaval –
although the causes began with politics, in the
form of Henry VIII (r. 1509–47). When
Henry ascended the English throne
in 1509, he married his brother's
Spanish widow, Catherine of
Aragon, for purely political
reasons. However, he later
fell in love with an English
woman, Anne Boleyn, and
when Catherine failed to
provide him with the son he
wanted, he threatened
divorce. Although
ostensibly a Catholic
and honored with the
title "Defender of the
Faith" by Leo X after
writing a tract con-
demning Lutheranism,
Henry nevertheless peti-
tioned Rome for a divorce.
His efforts were in vain; not even
Cardinal Wolsey (c. 1474–1530), was
able to advance his petition. Henry dismissed
Wolsey and instead made Thomas Cranmer
(1489–1556) archbishop of Canterbury. After
Cranmer secured an annulment for Henry, all
financial, administrative, and judicial ties with
Rome were broken. An act of Parliament named

HENRY VIII AND CARDINAL WOLSEY
*As Henry's unpopular chief minister, Thomas Wolsey exerted
power over England as the representative of both king and
pope from 1518, before falling from grace in 1529.*

the king Supreme Head on earth of the Church of
England, and Henry married Anne in 1533. Although
he condemned the Lutheran Reformation, Henry
continued to burn Anabaptists and Bible translators alike
at the stake, and for a time maintained Catholic rites
and doctrine in the Church of England.

❖ THE BIRTH OF ANGLICANISM ❖

Yet many of those who served Henry in ecclesiastical
affairs moved the nation closer to Protestantism. As vicar
general of the church in England, Thomas Cromwell
(c. 1485–1540) had Bibles placed in churches for public
reading and closed most monasteries. Cranmer began to
define his distinctly English application of Protestant
theology: *Ten Articles* of 1536 maintained Catholic
doctrines such as transubstantiation; asserted that justification is by faith, confession, and good works; but
identified only three sacraments –
baptism, the Lord's
Supper, and
penance.

PROTESTANT MARTYR
Like many other influential English Protestant leaders, Cranmer was eventually burned at the stake on the orders of Queen Mary I.

Cranmer also served as an adviser to Henry's successor, Edward VI (r. 1547–53), encouraging him to embrace Protestantism. In 1549 a group led by Cranmer, under the Act of Uniformity, prepared the *Book of Common Prayer (see side column)*. In 1553 Cranmer drafted *Forty-two Articles of Religion* – later reduced to 39 – which defined the beliefs of the Church of England. Edward's premature death brought Mary I (r. 1553–58), Henry's eldest daughter, to the throne. A devout Catholic who revered her mother, Catherine of Aragon, Mary undertook a vengeful campaign to erase all vestiges of Protestantism and had hundreds of Protestant leaders executed. At her death, her vision for a Catholic rebirth withered under a weight of reaction toward Protestantism and the desire for a self-governing national Church.

As Elizabeth I (r. 1558–1603), daughter of Henry and Anne Boleyn, assumed leadership of England, the nation was spiritually fragmented between Protestant and Catholic extremists. She sought a compromise between the two faiths and thus became the real founder of Anglicanism. As a doctrine, Anglicanism was close to Calvinism while maintaining traditional elements such as the office of bishops and vestments.

❖ SAILING FOR THE NEW WORLD ❖

After Elizabeth's death, Puritans became angry with James I's (r. 1603–25) attitude toward their observance of the Sabbath and freedom of their clergy from government interference. Archbishop William Laud (1571–1645), tried to quell the growing Separatist and Puritan

THE BAPTISTS

One of the largest Protestant groups today, the Baptists originated from a group of Separatists, led by John Smyth (c. 1554–1612), who fled from England into exile in Holland in 1608. The Separatists were an offshoot from Anglican Calvinism, and under Smyth's direction this group established the first modern Baptist Church. Baptists returned to England in 1612, where they attracted many followers. The denomination later became popular in the US, and then in the rest of Europe. The distinctive Baptist doctrine advocates the baptism of adult believers only by total immersion in water.

❖

ROYALTY AND RELIGION

❖

THE faith of individual rulers had enormous influence over the religious life of a country, and not just within the Holy Roman Empire. Where monarchs remained Catholic, or converted to the Protestant faith, so did the majority of their subjects.

REGAL RELIGION

In Spain and Italy, which were both ruled over by fiercely Catholic regimes, any flickering of Protestant Reformation was snuffed out instantly. In France, royal opposition ensured that Protestantism would remain a minority religion. Even the powerful Henry of Navarre had to convert to Catholicism when he became king so that the city of Paris would acknowledge his rule, enabling him to end the French Wars of Religion. More concerned with power than with faith, his own attitude toward religion may be reflected in a remark he is alleged to have made before converting: "Paris is well worth a Mass."

SUSPICIOUS MOTIVES
One monarch who exploited her political authority was Queen Catherine de Medici, who ordered the massacre of hundreds of Protestant Huguenots in Paris (above) as her Catholic daughter married Henry of Navarre (p. 140).

One unintended consequence of the Reformation was that the state gained more power over the church, accelerating a process that had already begun before the Reformation in Spain and France *(pp. 130-31)*. Henry VIII's rejection of papal authority paved the way for the English Reformation, which left the monarch as the head of the church of England. For a number of German princes, the Reformation gave them a chance to control the church in their own countries. Luther invited German princes to reform their churches, who then used this belief in alliance with "the godly prince" to assert control over their national churches.

Thus, in the wake of the Reformation across most of Europe, the church was at a low ebb in its struggle for independence from secular rulers: the king appointed bishops and so controlled the church. Only where Reformers had overthrown the state, in Scotland and the Netherlands, or where the pope was strong, as in Italy, did the church maintain a distance from the state.

LANDING IN THE NEW WORLD

Painted in the seventeenth century, this idealized scene shows a group of Puritans arriving at the first European settlement in Jamestown, in the modern state of Virginia. The painting belies the tough conditions these travelers faced.

churches by enforcing uniformity and suppressing any public gatherings. Laud became a symbol of all those ecclesiastical rules and trappings that the Separatists and Puritans stood against. The result was a migration of believers from England to countries where they could practice their religion as they saw fit. Though a group of Separatists fled to Holland in 1608, the New World seemed to hold the most promise for religious freedom.

In 1620, a group of Separatists and Puritans – the latter commonly known as "the Pilgrims" – set sail for Virginia, although they actually landed at Plymouth, Massachusetts. In December of that year, 41 of the 102 Pilgrims drafted the Mayflower Compact, the first written constitution in American history, to ensure majority rule and prevent any dissenters from seizing control.

❖ PURITAN IDEALS ❖

Despite harsh conditions, sickness, and a shortage of food and supplies, the settlers eventually thrived. In 1630 John Winthrop led c. 1,500 English Puritans to the Massachusetts colony; c. 20,000 more followed in the next decade as the reign of Charles I (r. 1629–40) bolstered Laud's strength in England. Ironically, the Puritans in the New World were nearly as intolerant of other expressions of faith and worship as those from whom they had fled. Yet like most persecutions, suppression in the New World only served to organize and strengthen the

oppressed: Roger Williams (c. 1603–c.83) founded a new colony in Rhode Island in 1636 so that other Protestants could practice their faith freely; while George Calvert (c. 1580–1632) inspired the formation of the colony of Maryland as a haven for Catholics. As a result of their exuberant worship practices, the Quakers – a Protestant denomination founded in England c. 1650 – faced similar persecutions in the U.S., and so from the 1670s a Quaker, William Penn (1644–1718), began to acquire territories for Quakers, Mennonites, and Lutherans in what would become Pennsylvania and Delaware.

❖ TURMOIL IN ENGLAND ❖

In England itself, the Reformation continued. Laud's undoing came when he attempted to force the Scottish people to abandon Presbyterianism for Anglicanism. Outraged Scots invaded northern England in 1640, and civil war broke out in 1642. Oliver Cromwell (1599–1658), a member of the English Parliament, led English and Scottish soldiers to victory against the king of England, Charles I, in 1646, and in 1649 he assumed the title of "Lord Protector" of the English realm. He took a lenient view on most forms of Christianity – with the notable exception of Catholicism. Although the Puritans were a regular source of aggravation to him, Cromwell still supported them and so brought stability to the country. From 1660 England experienced more turbulence, with Charles II (r. 1660–85) secretly allied to, and James II (r. 1685–88) publicly devoted to, Catholicism. After James II was overthrown, Parliament passed an Act of Toleration in 1689 allowing religious freedom to all Protestants – a privilege not granted to Catholics until as recently as the nineteenth century.

Thus, while England came relatively late to the religious fray, and endured many religious conflicts, the effects of the Reformation – particularly the many dissenters who fled to the U.S. to form a government founded on the principles of religious freedom – owes as much to England and its reformers as to Germany.

THE GROWTH OF PROTESTANT DENOMINATIONS IN THE U.S.

THIS simplified diagram charts the development of some of the main Protestant churches that broke with Catholicism in the Reformation, many of which divided into splinter denominations and separate churches when immigrants arrived in the United States.

CATHOLIC CHURCH

ANABAPTIST CHURCHES

European National Groups

North American Baptist (German)
Baptist General Conference (Swedish)
Advent Christian
Seventh Day Adventist

Mennonite

Amish
Conservative Mennonites
General Conference Mennonite
(Old) Mennonite Church

Brethren

Brethren in Christ
Hutterite Brethren
Independent Brethren
Mennonite Brethren

LUTHERAN CHURCH

Scandinavian

Lutheran Brethren
Evangelical Covenant
Evangelical Free

Danish/General Synod

Evangelical Lutheran
Church in America

German

Missouri Synod Lutheran
Wisconsin Synod Lutheran

Moravian

Moravian Church

REFORMED CHURCHES

Presbyterian (Scottish)

Presbyterian Church in USA
Presbyterian Church in America
Orthodox Presbyterian
Reformed Presbyterian

Dutch

Reformed Church in America
Christian Reformed

Irish

Churches of Christ
Disciples of Christ
Christian Churches

ANGLICAN CHURCH

Puritans

United Church
of Christ
(Congregational)

Separatists

Baptists

Free Will Baptist
Conservative Baptist
Progressive National Baptist
American Baptist

Episcopal

Plymouth Brethren

Independent
Bible Churches

Friends

Friends United
Friends General
Conference

Methodists

United Methodist
African Methodist
Episcopal
Nazarene
Wesleyan
Free Methodist
Assemblies of God
Pentecostal
Church of God

THE CATHOLIC REFORMATION

INEVITABLY, AS THE RESULT of some nations adopting Protestantism, the Catholic church in the West increased its crusading fervor. Yet there was a sense in which it also encouraged its own form of reformation (sometimes known as the Counter-Reformation) to remedy the fact that for centuries some areas of the Catholic church had lacked well-educated, well-trained, and moral priests and bishops. The first signs of this desire for renewal were the new religious orders of the 1520s – the Capuchins, Theatines, Barnabites, and the Jesuit order, founded in 1534 by St. Ignatius Loyola. The internal reforms that took place during this time encouraged reformers to seek papal support for this renewal of discipline and spiritual life, which resulted in 1545 in the Council of Trent.

✤ REFORM AT ✤ GRASSROOTS LEVEL

By the early 1500s, it was clear that some aspects of the church, and in particular the papacy, suffered from a certain lack of piety, discipline, and order, and needed to shed medieval corruptions *(pp. 124-27)*. In addition, the close association of the church with the monarchy in many Catholic countries meant that there was little chance to promote constructive change that might endanger these monarchies. Thus the first attempts at any Catholic reform were made by individual church members such as

IGNATIUS OF LOYOLA
Before founding the Jesuit order, Loyola tried to concentrate his mind on obedience to Christ and conquer his self-will. He rose at midnight, prayed for seven hours each day, grew his nails and hair long, begged for bread, and flagellated himself.

BORROMEO OF MILAN
Charles Borromeo (1538–84) was a leading figure of the Catholic Reformation and had extensive influence. He patronized the Jesuits, initiated reform in his own diocese, and took part in the Council of Trent.

the archbishop of Milan, Charles Borromeo, and by various religious orders. In 1524 St. Gaetano of Thiene and Gian Pietro Caraffa (later Pope Paul IV) founded the Theatines, in Rome. The order's name was taken from the bishop of Theate, and it was aimed at improving and injecting new vigor into the clergy. Members adhered to a strict vow of poverty and conformed to a severe rule.

The order flourished, spreading through Italy and into Spain, France, Portugal, and elsewhere. The Theatines also undertook the earliest papal missions to countries such as Peru, Borneo, and Sumatra, and the order, though small, still exists today.

At around the same time, the Barnabite order was founded to promote educational, parochial, and missionary work. It also sought to deepen Catholic understanding of the Eucharist, a sacrament that had been under attack since the beginning of the Protestant Reformation *(pp. 136-37)*. Thus the Catholic Reformation was to be marked by a popular devotion to the Eucharist, or Lord's Supper, as a result of which magnificent tabernacles to house the Host became central features of Catholic churches, and eucharistic processions and public devotions became increasingly popular.

✤ THE JESUITS ✤

Of all of the new orders, it was the Jesuit order, first called the Society of Jesus and founded in 1534 by the Spaniard Ignatius of Loyola (c. 1491– 1556) and six companions, that made the greatest impact. Before founding the order, Loyola had lived an austere lifestyle of self-denial, yet, like Luther *(p. 133)*, he was unable to find inner peace. Instead, he chose to obey the leaders of the church and thus, in addition to taking the usual three vows of chastity, obedience, and poverty, Jesuits also vowed obedience to the pope and to carry out whatever task the pope might deem necessary. If Luther's faith had led him to rebellion, then, in contrast, Loyola's faith led him to obedience.

Ignatius and his friends were enthusiastic to live their Christian faith more fully and at first devoted themselves to education. Certain members of the Jesuit order were to become some of the foremost theologians at the Council of Trent, as well as great thinkers in the seventeenth century. By 1640, the Jesuits had established 500 schools and several seminaries and universities. Such schools helped to convert many nobles who held power in central Europe, and also enabled the Jesuits to institute reform and halt the spread of Protestantism. After establishing themselves in Poland in 1565, for

> ## " WHOEVER WISHES TO ENTER OUR SOCIETY MUST ... WORK FOR THE ADVANCEMENT OF SOULS IN LIFE AND CHRISTIAN DOCTRINE, AND FOR THE PROPAGATION OF THE FAITH "

THE FUNDAMENTAL RULE OF THE JESUITS (1540)

example, the Jesuits encouraged a reluctant church to reform, even though some of the officials, such as the papal representative, attempted to resist any change.

After the reforms of the Council of Trent, which fired their missionary zeal, the Jesuits were active abroad (*pp. 150-51*), traveling to the East and to South America, particularly Paraguay: Francis Xavier led missions to India and Japan, while Matteo Ricci traveled to China. Sometimes the missions proved hazardous: in Canada, a group of Jesuits were brutally murdered by Native Americans.

❖ THE OLD ORDERS ❖

While new orders were beginning to flourish, some of the old orders managed to successfully reform themselves. In 1524 Pope Clement VIII gave permission to a branch of the Franciscan order to establish separate

SAINT FRANÇOIS XAVIER
Patron de l'Œuvre de la Propagation de la Foi

ARISTOCRATIC MISSIONARY
Many new orders were founded specifically to care for the poor and the sick, to educate, and to evangelize. Born into an aristocratic Spanish-Basque family, Francis Xavier (1506–52), one of the original Jesuits, devoted himself to evangelism. He traveled to India, Sri Lanka, and Japan, and by the time he died, on his way to China, he had helped to convert tens of thousands of people.

reformed houses. The Capuchins, so named from the type of pointed hood they wore, adhered to strict austerity and poverty. They are still known and recognized around the world today as evangelists, preachers, and confessors.

In Catholic Spain, where new wealth from the recently discovered Americas enabled it to become a leading nation, church and state were united in their religious fervor. Any forms of Protestantism were soon quashed by the Spanish Inquisition (*pp. 124-25*). Despite this climate of repression, the deep spirituality of figures such as St. Teresa of Avila (1515–82) and St. John of the Cross (1542–91) flourished.

John of the Cross and Teresa of Avila, both born in the town of Avila, in central Spain, became two of the most famous mystics in Catholic history. As mystics, they sought a contemplative life of total

SPIRITUAL EXERCISES
Loyola's most important work, *Spiritual Exercises*, is a series of exercises in prayer. Loyola believed that by subjecting each believer to certain disciplines, he or she would master their own will, as Loyola himself had done. He recommended that the exercises be undertaken while living in solitary confinement for a month in order to realize the "terrible consequences of self-will." *Exercises* has contributed to the training not only of Jesuits, but also many other Christians, both Protestant and Catholic.

❖

MISSION TO CHINA
Born in 1552 to a wealthy Italian family, Matteo Ricci joined Loyola's order in 1571. In 1582 he was sent to Macao in South China, and later to Chaoching, where he spent several years learning Chinese and adopting local customs, including dressing like a Buddhist monk. His understanding of Chinese culture and history served him well when he traveled to Beijing in 1601 to work for the government as a cartographer and clock maker. He won favor with the royal court and was given permission to evangelize, which he did, using Confucian thought as a starting point to explain the gospel. His efforts, and the conversions he achieved, laid a solid foundation for the Jesuit missionaries who followed him to China after his death in 1610.

❖

TERESA OF AVILA
In her writings, Teresa of Avila described having mystical visions of Christ, angels, and saints in her search for the profound love of God. She was also said to fall into a trance while praying.

❖

absorption and surrender to God that involved personal emotional ecstasy and passion, something the Catholic church was keen to endorse at a time of dry theological debate. As well as detailing their mystical experiences in poems and books, they devoted themselves to reform,

> ❝ IF WE ARE GUIDED BY DIVINE SCRIPTURE, WE SHALL NOT ERR, FOR HE WHO SPEAKS IN IT IS THE HOLY SPIRIT ❞
>
> JOHN OF THE CROSS

improving lax conditions in Carmelite monasteries. In 1562 Teresa founded a convent in Avila for Carmelite nuns, restoring the stricter "primitive rule" instead of the "mitigated rule," which other Carmelites followed. Despite suspicion and opposition from the Spanish Inquisition, Teresa and John went on to jointly found 16 more monasteries for Carmelites. The high standards of this so-called "Teresian Reform" were subsequently adopted in many other monasteries.

❖ **BELATED DECREES** ❖

Although the Catholic Reformation soon rectified many abuses in the church, guided by such inspirational figures as Ignatius Loyola and Teresa of Avila, reformers still agitated for more improvements. A new spiritual energy was coursing through the heart of the Catholic church – an important element to harness if it was to survive. For almost two decades after the Catholic Reformation began, the church grappled for a solution to its problems. Pope Paul III (r. 1534–49) was enthusiastic for reform and implemented many positive changes, such as appointing reformers to the College of Cardinals and setting up a papal reform commission. Ironically, the report produced by the commission laid the blame for the malaise in the church squarely on the popes' lack of spirituality.

❖ **THE COUNCIL OF TRENT** ❖

Perhaps Paul III's most important act in trying to resolve the issue that confronted him was in calling a general council in 1542, which opened, belatedly, in 1545 in the northern Italian town of Trent.

The first session of the council, adjourned in 1549, dealt with questions of justification and the obligation of bishops to reside in their own dioceses. It also reaffirmed the Nicene Creed (*p. 62*) as the basis of faith and defined the theology of the seven sacraments.

Although the council reassembled briefly in 1551, it was disbanded after only one year – having repudiated Lutheran, Calvinist, and Zwinglian doctrines – and ten years elapsed before the final session met to issue new decrees on disciplinary reforms and further clarify Catholic teaching.

At the last session, begun in 1562, the council re-endorsed much medieval doctrine and practice, such as celibate clergy and the existence of purgatory. It also defended belief in free will against Luther's doctrine of the bondage of the will, and rejected his doctrine of faith alone, insisting that love and hope are also necessary for salvation, and issued decrees that ended pluralism and the buying and selling of church offices.

THE FIRST SESSION OF THE COUNCIL OF TRENT (1545–49)
Only 30 or so Catholic bishops and some Lutheran theologians attended the council's first session; at the last, one of the meetings attracted an audience of 255. Although it did not heal the rift between the Catholic church and the reformers, the Council of Trent formulated several codes of practice that remained in force within the Catholic church until the 1960s.

WORSHIP AND THE REFORMATION

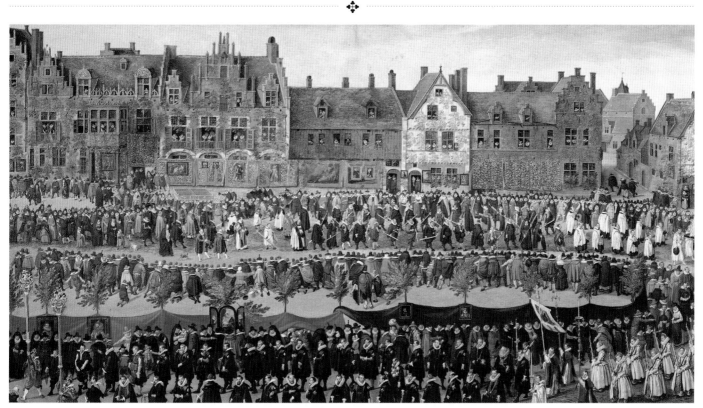

VENERATION OF THE VIRGIN MARY, BRUSSELS, SIXTEENTH CENTURY

ACROSS Europe, reformers transformed church services. In the Protestant churches, liturgies became simpler, with the focus on the sermon rather than on communion. Colorful vestments were abandoned, along with the Latin language, to be replaced by the use of vernacular languages and, often, black ministerial robes (like those academics wore). Church buildings, too, were radically transformed. The reformers felt that images of God and the saints were idolatrous and that visual splendor was distracting and unhelpful and liable to give Christians a false picture of spiritual realities to which no artist could do justice. Accordingly, images and statues were destroyed and elaborate decorations were whitewashed. As for music, Lutherans and Anglicans looked to the Psalms as evidence that God intended music of all kinds to be used in worship and so promoted congregational singing; Calvin allowed only the Psalms themselves to be sung without accompaniment. As Protestants placed more emphasis on preaching, so the pulpit, not the altar, became the focus of each church. Protes-

tants such as Zwingli, who did not believe in the real presence of Christ in the bread and wine at communion, downgraded the altar to a mere table, around which believers could share a commemorative meal.

ELABORATE EXPRESSION

The Catholic church, meanwhile, underwent a more elaborate change. Baroque art – a more extravagant form of Renaissance art accentuating the effects of light and darkness – expressed the aims and served the goals of the Catholic Reformation, with its powerful, dramatic richness. Catholic churches, with their impressive ornamentation and splendid size, were built to overwhelm, and an even greater emphasis was placed on Mary and the saints. Believers were encouraged to take communion and make confessions more frequently, and processions and devotions were popular and frequent. The Orthodox churches, in contrast, remained relatively unchanged by the tumults of the West, and their doctrine and worship continued unchallenged.

When the Council of Trent finally came to a close in 1563, the bishops present asked the pope to proclaim its decrees and canons, a gesture that emphasized the significance of Rome as the center of the Catholic church and the focus of Catholics. As a result of these decrees, seminaries were founded to train the clergy, a catechism was printed (originally for the use of parish priests), popular devotions were revived, and bishops

undertook to reform their dioceses. The course of the Catholic church was charted for the next 400 years; not until the 1960s, at the Second Vatican Council, would another major reexamination take place. Yet it wasn't until the end of the Thirty Years' War, in 1648, that the final outworking of the decisions reached 85 years earlier at the Council of Trent could be achieved, and the Catholic Reformation was at last complete.

EARLY WORLD MISSIONS

**CONQUEST
OF THE INCAS**

The Spanish conquistador
Francisco Pizarro
(c. 1478–1541) arrived
in Peru in 1531, motivated
by the desire "to take away
from [the Incas] their
gold." This woodcut
depicts the famous incident
when Pizarro (*kneeling left,
above*), accompanied by a
friar, was received shortly
after his arrival in the
country by the emperor
Atahuallpa. Here, the friar
proffers a cross and a copy
of the Bible, which the
emperor rejects.
Pizarro went on to defeat
the Incas and conquer their
empire, establishing a new
capital at Lima.

⚜

IN 1493 POPE Alexander VI divided
the world with an imaginary line
drawn from north to south just west
of the Azores, and declared that any
lands east of the line (later adjusted
to include Brazil) could be claimed as
Portuguese; everything west of the line
would fall under Spanish control. He
granted Spain and Portugal the right
to rule their conquered lands, providing
those lands were not already Christian.
Dominican, Franciscan, Augustinian,
and later, Jesuit friars accompanied the
conquistadors as they sailed to conquer
new territories and search for gold, thus
spreading Christianity across the globe.

The Portuguese ships traveled to West
Africa, the Congo, Angola, Mozam-
bique, India, Sri Lanka, Brazil, China,

**SIXTEENTH-CENTURY
CHURCH, MEXICO**
*The Catholic church had
tremendous success in its religious
conquest of the Americas. Indian
converts were settled in villages,
churches and schools were built,
and mass baptisms were conducted.*

and Japan; the Spanish to Mexico, Peru,
the West Indies, Colombia, Panama,
and Chile. Their conquests in Central
and South America were particularly
swift and successful, and although the
conquistadors enslaved and abused the
Native Americans, they converted for
a number of reasons. Some converted
out of fear, others because the friars
generally respected them and
defended their rights, others still
because they developed a deep faith.
A Mexican laborer, for instance,
claimed in 1531 that Mary, mother of
Jesus, had appeared to him. Believing
in this appearance, others also converted, so that by the end of the
decade over eight million people in
Mexico had become Christians. Yet

WORLD MISSIONS
*The missionary activity
that was begun during the
Reformation (right) was
continuous and prolonged
in the West, particularly in
Latin America, but only
made a brief impact in the
Far East in countries
such as Japan and China.*

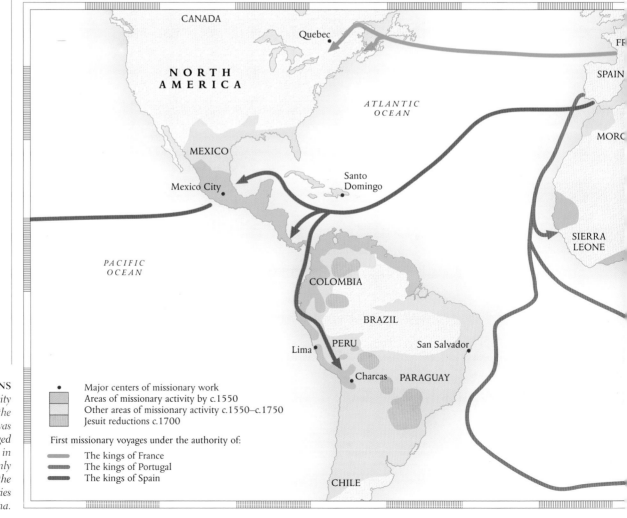

CANADA

Quebec

FR

SPAIN

NORTH
AMERICA

ATLANTIC
OCEAN

MORO

MEXICO

Santo
Domingo

Mexico City

SIERRA
LEONE

PACIFIC
OCEAN

COLOMBIA

BRAZIL

Lima • PERU

San Salvador

• Charcas PARAGUAY

CHILE

•   Major centers of missionary work
    Areas of missionary activity by c.1550
    Other areas of missionary activity c.1550–c.1750
    Jesuit reductions c.1700

First missionary voyages under the authority of:
— The kings of France
— The kings of Portugal
— The kings of Spain

despite such high numbers of converts, many people remained half-Christian, half-pagan in their beliefs, and often they rebelled against their cruel conditions – sometimes killing the missionaries in the process.

❖ THE EAST ❖

The missionaries also traveled to Asia and the Far East, where their success was less complete. The French Jesuit Alexander de Rhodes, who worked in south-east Asia between 1623 and 1645, is regarded as "the apostle of Vietnam": by the mid-seventeenth century there were about 30,000 Vietnamese Christians. From 1565 Jesuits (*pp. 146-47*), Dominicans, and Augustinians all worked in the Philippines, which proved so responsive to Catholicism that the nation became pre-dominantly Christian. A small Christian community

SUSPECTED OF SPYING
This missionary in Nagasaki, accused of spying and subjected to water torture, was one of many: thousands of Japanese Christians were tortured and killed.

was also established in the Portuguese colony in Goa, India, but the most amazing initial success in the East was in Japan. Missionaries such as Francis Xavier (*p. 147*) introduced Christianity into the culture so skillfully that by 1600, over 30,000 Japanese had converted. Eventually, Japanese fears that the Catholics were a prelude to European invasion became so great that from 1597 Japanese authorities persecuted Christians and expelled missionaries; within 30 years, almost all trace of Christianity had disappeared.

China, too, also proved to be only briefly a fertile mission ground: until 1704 Mass was celebrated in Chinese, but when the pope decided that Mass had to be celebrated in Latin, the emperor was offended, expelling all missionaries and outlawing Christianity.

> ❝ *I and the brother who was with me baptized in this province of Mexico upwards of 200,000 persons – so many in fact that I cannot give an accurate estimate of the number. Often we baptized in a single day 14,000 people, sometimes 10,000, sometimes 8,000* ❞

PETER OF GHENT, FRANCISCAN MISSIONARY, 1529

LAS CASAS

Bartholomew de Las Casas (1484–1566) arrived in the New World in 1502 as a newly ordained Spanish Dominican friar. At first he lived much as the other colonists did, but in 1514 he became convinced that "everything done to the Indians thus far was wrong and tyrannical." He spent the next 50 years as a voice of Christian conscience, campaigning for native rights. His efforts bore fruit when the Spanish king abolished slavery in 1542.

❖

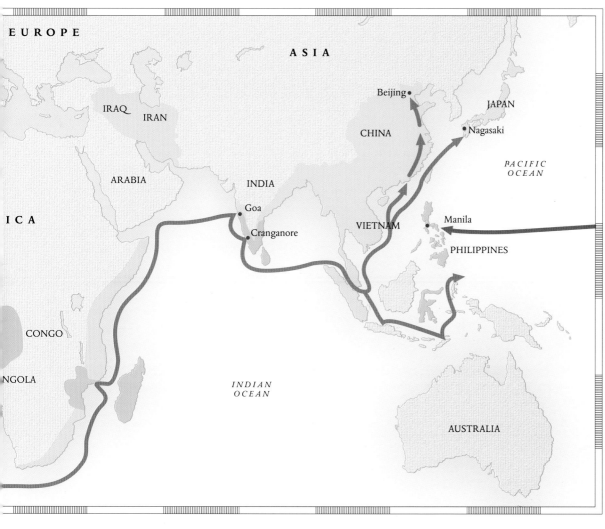

EUROPE

ASIA

IRAQ
IRAN

Beijing

JAPAN

CHINA

Nagasaki

PACIFIC OCEAN

ARABIA

INDIA

ICA

Goa

Cranganore

VIETNAM

Manila

PHILIPPINES

CONGO

NGOLA

INDIAN OCEAN

AUSTRALIA

THE CLOSE OF THE REFORMATION

HUGO GROTIUS

A Dutch theologian and statesman, Grotius (1583–1645) became involved in the conflicts between the Calvinists and Arminians *(p. 160)*. His support for the Arminian cause resulted in his imprisonment after he was condemned at the Council of Dort in 1619. He escaped and later produced a collection of works that advocated unity between the Protestants and Catholics. He proposed that God is revealed as much in natural law as in miraculous revelation, and proclaimed that totalitarianism is one of the world's greatest evils.

❖

THE PATH OF HUMAN HISTORY is marked by internal conflicts and national disputes, which are often only resolved after years of warfare and bloodshed. Such was the case in the closing decades of the Reformation, when the turbulence and upheaval of the Protestant and Catholic Reformations resulted in religious wars across much of Europe. Religious divisions, persecution, and allegations of heresy fueled these wars, yet at the same time they were fought only partly for religious reasons: the Netherlands, for instance, fought for its independence; Spain sought to suppress insubordinate subjects. By the end of these wars, a new political and religious map of Europe was drawn up, and the absolute grip of the Catholic church over religion in many countries was lost for ever.

❖ OPEN HOSTILITY ❖

The last three decades of the Reformation, known as the Thirty Years' War, was a particularly bloody period. The success of the Catholic Reformation had given the

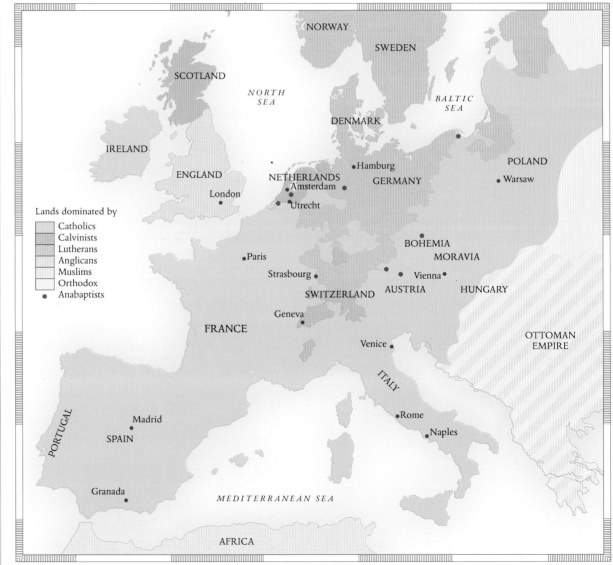

Lands dominated by
- Catholics
- Calvinists
- Lutherans
- Anglicans
- Muslims
- Orthodox
- • Anabaptists

EUROPE AT THE CLOSE OF THE REFORMATION
England, Scandinavia, Holland, most of Scotland, and parts of Switzerland and Germany were Protestant, with Anabaptists scattered across Europe (the blue dots on the map mark concentrations of Anabaptists). Most of the rest of Western Europe remained Catholic, with Protestant minorities in France, Hungary, and Poland. Ferdinand II had re-Catholicized Bohemia and Moravia by force.

THIRTY YEARS OF WAR
At the Siege of Magdeburg in 1631 (above), Catholics overcame a Protestant garrison and killed thousands of the city's inhabitants. The battles were all fought in central Europe, reflecting the continuing spiritual unrest of the churches there.

Catholic church, particularly the Jesuits, renewed vigor to reclaim land that had been lost to Protestants and armed conflicts erupted between the Lutherans and Catholics. Calvinists were also discontented, since they had been virtually outlawed. An uneasy peace, brought about by the Peace of Augsburg in 1555, finally came to an end some 60 years later in 1618, when open hostility erupted after Bohemian noblemen threw two of Emperor Ferdinand II's regents from a window in Prague. With the support of Philip III of Spain, Ferdinand declared war on Frederick V, the Protestant king of Bohemia. In 1620, Ferdinand seized Protestant lands and closed Lutheran and Reformed churches and schools in Bohemia, Austria, and Moravia.

✦ CHANGING TIMES ✦

Between 1623 and 1629, a new phase of the Thirty Years' War spread across Europe as Lutheran princes in northern Germany – joined by Christian IV of Denmark in 1625, as well as forces from England and Holland – attempted to reclaim the lost territories. Again, imperial and Catholic armies won decisive victories. In 1629 Emperor Ferdinand issued an edict to restore all those Catholic properties claimed by Protestants since 1552.

The last phase of the war, between 1635 and 1648, was the most extensive and bloody. It was also a period of confusing alliances, with Catholic France and Protestant Sweden joining forces, and several Protestant states siding with the emperor. The veil had finally been lifted, and it became apparent that the wars were due more to nationalistic causes than religious disputes. Germany, especially, suffered during this period, with invading armies and foreign mercenaries pillaging villages and killing innocent peasants.

Finally, in 1648, the Peace of Westphalia was signed, which once again gave each prince in the empire permission to determine the religion of his particular state. Calvinism was also legalized, along with Lutheranism and Catholicism. Of most importance to the future political landscape of the empire, Switzerland and Holland won independence while France, Sweden, and Brandenburg-Prussia expanded their territories.

✦ THE COST OF FREEDOM ✦

Essentially, the Reformation was a time of purifying the Western church and of fighting for human and national rights and religious convictions. None of these achievements came without tremendous human cost, however. It is ironic, then, that after so many people had sacrificed their lives to attain religious freedom, this privilege would result in the next generation questioning the very validity of religion itself during the Age of Enlightenment that was to follow.

HEIRS TO THE REFORMATION
A literary revolution was created through the rise of Protestantism, with its change of emphasis from the liturgy to the written word, together with printing and the increase in book production. John Bunyan (1628–88) was one product of this change. When he was imprisoned for preaching without authorization from his local Anglican parish, Bunyan remained in prison for more than 12 years and used this time to write what are now classics of Puritan literature. His allegorical tale, *Pilgrim's Progress*, describes the spiritual journey of a character named Christian who travels from his hometown, the City of Destruction, to the Heavenly City. The book was a best seller for centuries.

✦

GEOGRAPHICAL SPLIT
By the end of the Reformation, Christians in northern and southern Europe would have been shocked at the difference between their places of worship, as illustrated here by St. Peter's Basilica, Rome (above right) and a Dutch Reformed church (above).

Enlightenment & Revival

1648–1776

THE FIERCE RELIGIOUS WARS of the Reformation period inspired a strong reaction against Christianity. By decentralizing the authority of the Church, the Reformers left the way open for seventeenth- and eighteenth-century philosophers and scientists to begin to explain the world and human affairs in purely secular terms.

However, this period also produced some of the greatest and most sweeping Christian revivals in history. At one end of the spectrum were such figures as Voltaire and Rousseau, two of the principal architects of the Enlightenment; at the other end were Wesley and Whitefield, two of the giants of revivalism. In the oft-quoted words of Charles Dickens, this period was truly "the epoch of belief [and] the epoch of incredulity" and, for the churches, "It was the best of times, it was the worst of times." Amid these titanic struggles in the West, enthusiasm for foreign missions was at a low ebb.

John Wesley preaches from his father's tomb in London

THE IMPACT OF THE ENLIGHTENMENT

THE INTENT OF THE reformers, both Protestant and Catholic, was to rescue the church from whatever malaise they perceived had plagued it. Their ultimate goal, regardless of their theological persuasion, was to draw people closer to God. Few would have anticipated, therefore, that their sincere efforts on behalf of the kingdom of God would inspire the great thinkers of succeeding generations to turn from religion to other, more humanistic, forms of faith.

The signing of the Peace of Westphalia in 1648, ending the Thirty Years' War, essentially brought the more serious religious and political conflicts surrounding the Reformation to a close. The period that followed was characterized by a critical reevaluation of existing thoughts and beliefs and is known as the Enlightenment or the Age of Reason. Although the scientific and social revolution that resulted from the Enlightenment spread most dramatically in the eighteenth century, its foundation had been laid earlier with the advent of secular systems of thought. Previously, Christian doctrine had been a vital part of the bedrock of ideas on which medieval and Reformation philosophy was built. The most influential thinkers of the Enlightenment, however, did not rely on Christian doctrine in their philosophies, and many did not believe it.

❖ NEW PHILOSOPHIES AND ❖ THE CHURCHES

Two new schools of philosophy came to dominate European thought. In Britain the Empiricists tried to explain everything on the basis of the information we receive from our senses, while in France and Germany the Rationalists attempted to treat philosophy as a kind of mathematics, working out everything by reason alone from first principles. The leading Empiricists were John Locke (1632–1704), George Berkeley (1685–1753), and David Hume (1711–76). Hume proved that the logical end of empiricism is scepticism, a view that was

> **❝** I believe in God, not the God of the mystics and the theologians, but the God of nature, the great geometrician, the architect of the universe, the prime mover, unalterable, transcendental, everlasting **❞**
>
> **VOLTAIRE**

SIR ISAAC NEWTON – SCIENTIST AND CHRISTIAN DEIST

As a physicist and mathematician, Newton is best remembered for his scientific achievements. However, he was also a deeply religious man, if not orthodox in his Christian beliefs. Among his many scientific and religious works, Newton speculated on the millennium in Observations upon the Prophecies of Daniel and the Apocalypse of St. John, *published in 1733.*

to be immensely influential and encourage many intellectuals to doubt the supernatural aspects of Christianity.

Rationalism began with René Descartes (1596–1650), was developed by Baruch Spinoza (1632–77) and Gottfried Leibniz (1646–1716), and then reached a kind of perfection in the work of Immanuel Kant (1724–1804), who created a system that reconciled empiricism and rationalism. (In so doing he created an intellectual consensus for the view that the existence of God is unprovable.) Both schools of philosophy had been begun by Christians – Descartes, Locke, and Berkeley were all believers, but others developed their theories in ways inimical to Christianity. In Locke's case his unorthodox beliefs were open to such development (*see below*). Where empiricism had eroded belief in the supernatural elements of Christianity, rationalism split morality, faith, and doctrine from their roots in the historical events of the biblical revelation.

✦ DEISM ✦

Empiricist and Rationalist thought first entered the church in the form of Deism, the belief that a supreme, intelligent being (commonly referred to as God) set the universe and its natural laws in motion but that he assumes no control over its daily activities, including the affairs of humankind. In contrast to Christians, Deists viewed God as distant from humanity, so that their chief

> **" A LITTLE PHILOSOPHY INCLINETH MAN'S MIND TO ATHEISM, BUT DEPTH IN PHILOSOPHY BRINGETH MEN'S MIND ... TO RELIGION "**
>
> **FRANCIS BACON**

interest lay, not in the study of God, but in identifying and defining the exact laws God had applied to his creation for its independent operation.

The man historians recognize as the father of the English Enlightenment, John Locke, was a Christian with strong Deist leanings who tried to synthesize the essence of his faith into two basic truths: that Jesus was the Messiah, and that Christians must live in harmony with his teachings. His religious convictions were spelled out in two works, *An Essay on Religious Toleration* (1667) and *The Reasonableness of Christianity* (1695).

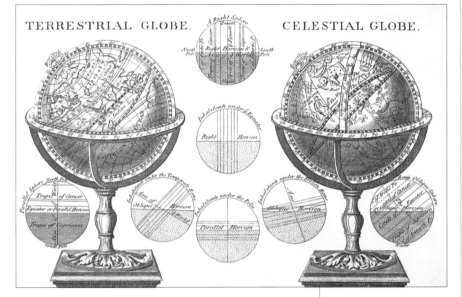

TERRESTRIAL AND CELESTIAL GLOBES
Enlightened philosophical thought created a view of the universe as a well-ordered machine, with God very much in the background.

Together these two publications reveal Locke's determination that liberty should extend to the practice of one's religious beliefs and his conviction that revelation enhances, and never contradicts, what reason imparts. Although he tried to defend Christian beliefs, his theology did more to inspire Deists than Christians.

The work of Isaac Newton (1642–1727), famous for his tremendous contribution to the understanding of science and mathematics, did much to promote Deism. Although Newton, a member of the church of England, believed that Jesus was the redeemer sent by God for humanity's salvation, he did not believe in Christ's divinity. For Newton, observation and experience were the only paths to true knowledge. His views on natural law were a great influence on the Deistic philosophers who followed him.

One of the great adversaries of Christianity, Voltaire (1694–1778) became influenced by the Deistic works of Locke and Newton while exiled in England for three years. The son of Jansenists (*p. 158*), Voltaire was a prolific writer who expressed his views freely, particularly his enmity towards the Catholic church. In hugely popular works such as *Candide*, he denounced all forms of orthodox Christianity and denied the existence of a good and all-powerful God.

The impact of Voltaire's contemporary, Jean-Jacques Rousseau (1712–78), was more immediately dramatic but has been largely forgotten over time. Rousseau was raised a Calvinist but eventually settled on a unique blend of Deism and reverence for nature. His political theories did much to shape the bloody revolutions that were to shake France and America.

NEW POLITICAL THOUGHT

Much Enlightenment philosophy firmly placed politics above religion. In his book *Leviathan*, Thomas Hobbes (1588–1679) argued that God is virtually unknowable and that religious disagreement ignites chaos and warfare; therefore a strong ruler should decide absolutely what form religion should take in his realm, determining what is and isn't truth. Later, Rousseau taught that society has a collective will of its own not subject to any divine revelation, against which individuals have no rights – a doctrine which later provided a charter for Communist and Nazi governments. In contrast, John Locke, working from a basically Christian world-view, taught that government exists to protect people's individual rights and is subject to them.

❖

CATHOLIC MOVEMENTS

> *" Apart from Christ we know neither what our life nor our death is, we do not know what God is nor what we ourselves are "*
>
> **BLAISE PASCAL**

ONE OF THE MOST SIGNIFICANT and lasting effects of the Enlightenment, particularly among Catholics, was a shift in focus away from the church as a corporate body toward the individual. New questions regarding the individual's salvation and personal relationship with God began to occupy the minds of those conditioned through centuries of tradition to accept the doctrines and liturgical practices of the church for their spiritual comfort and assurance.

✧ THE RISE OF JANSENISM ✧

It was in this atmosphere that the Augustinian theology of grace was revived through the posthumous writings of Cornelius Otto Jansen. Jansen, a Flemish Catholic theologian born in 1585, was the director, professor of exegesis, and rector of the Saint Pulcherie Seminary in Louvain. He died from the plague in 1638 while serving as Bishop of Ypres (in what is now Belgium).

After his death a number of Jansen's lectures were published; it was his study of St. Augustine *(pp. 68-69)*, however, that drew the widest attention. Published in 1640 as a vast three-part work entitled *Augustinus*, Jansen provided a thorough analysis of Augustine's views on the doctrine of predestination, the utter sinfulness of humanity, and God's redeeming grace through Jesus Christ.

Since Jansen attacked the theological basis for the ethics of the Jesuits, *Augustinus* was consigned to the Index for Prohibited Books by Pope Urban VIII in 1643. Jansenists condemned the Jesuits because of their optimistic teaching on man and because of the ease with which they gave out absolutions to those who confessed their sins. The Jansenists felt strongly that absolution should be given only to those who could truly prove their repentance, and that communion should be approached with great fear and awe.

In 1653, in his bull *Cum Occasione*, Pope Innocent X condemned certain propositions derived from

Jansen, particularly concerning predestination, as heretical. In 1713 Pope Clement XI also condemned the work of the Jansenists, and throughout much of the eighteenth century they suffered great persecution in France. Yet, despite such opposition, the Jansenist movement survived under the leadership of such key figures as Antoine Arnauld and Jean Du Vergier. Perhaps its greatest champion was the mathematician, philosopher, and scientist Blaise Pascal (1623–62), whose classic work *Pensées* ("Thoughts"), posthumously published in 1670, brilliantly expressed his conviction that while the proof of Christianity's validity is evident by the weight of revelation and history, it can be truly known only by a personal relationship with God.

❖ DEVOTION AND SERVICE ❖

Even in France, not all was controversy. The nation was the center for another of the major movements of the age, Quietism, which downplayed doctrine in favor of a personal experience of God *(see side column)*. At the same time, the great Cardinal Bossuet (1627–1704) led a preaching and Bible-reading movement which attempted to reach the worldly leaders of the nation.

PORT-ROYAL MONASTERY, PARIS
The Convent of Port-Royal became a Jansenist center in the seventeenth century, and many nobles, parliamentarians, and intellectuals made their spiritual retreat here. In 1709 Louis XIV had the monastery closed, and the following year it was razed to the ground.

BLAISE PASCAL

PASCAL was born in 1623 in Claremont, France. His father, a lawyer, moved his family to Paris to provide better educational opportunities for his children. In 1654 Pascal nearly died after an accident and dedicated the remainder of his life to attaining a deeply personal relationship with Christ. Pascal held a Christian world-view that was decidedly more pious and orthodox than his contemporary scientific peers. He also recognized the limits of reason in the face of a rationalist age that almost deified it, saying, "Reason's last step is the recognition that there are an infinite number of things that go beyond it," and "The heart has its reasons, which reason knows not."

The Lazarist order, founded by St. Vincent de Paul (c. 1580–1660), tried to evangelize the poor and train their priests, while the Sisters of Charity worked to alleviate the terrible poverty of the peasants – groundbreaking work when female orders had previously been largely enclosed in nunneries.

❖ LITERATE LAITY ❖

One important impact of the Enlightenment was an increasingly literate and educated populace. New translations of the Bible appeared, devotional literature became more readily available, and parish schools flourished, allowing all classes of society to be educated. While Rome initially discouraged the laity from reading the Bible and clung to the Latin Vulgate, fearing that unrestricted access to Scripture would provoke further schisms within the church, in 1752 new translations were permitted on the condition that they be accompanied by authorized commentary. By the end of the eighteenth century there were more than 70 Catholic vernacular Bibles, including translations in German, Italian, Spanish, French, and Polish.

INNER PEACE
Inspired by the teaching of a Spanish priest named Miguel de Molinos (1628–96), Quietism is the belief that true Christianity lies in losing oneself entirely in the presence of God through prayer and meditation rather than in adherence to creeds or the performance of good works. In some ways, the success of the Quietist movement can be attributed to a bad marriage. Its most ardent and visible supporter was the French mystic Jeanne Guyon (1648–1717), better known as Madame Guyon. Because of the many problems she had with her husband and mother-in-law, Madame Guyon dedicated herself to the inner life and a mystical unity with the mind of God.

❖

❝ *It is impossible to love God without loving the Cross; and a heart that delights in the Cross finds the most bitter things sweet* ❞

MADAME JEANNE GUYON, FRENCH QUIETIST

ARMINIANISM & PIETISM

THE PIOUS DESIRES OF PHILIP JACOB SPENER

In 1675 Spener published *Pia Desideria* ("Pious Desires"), which detailed his convictions for reforming the church in general and Lutheran congregations specifically. These proposals included, among other things, small group Bible studies and a greater attention to theological training. He also wished to see Protestant ministers return to preaching a traditional gospel message. He was able to put these desires into practice in the Pietist movement.

❖

IN THE LATE 1600S OBSCURE debates concerning the finer points of theology raged in the halls of academia, and traditional Protestantism seemed to have waned in its enthusiasm, only a century after its birth. New spiritual movements were taking shape, however, among those Christians who cared only about their personal and eternal relationship with God. In what was increasingly perceived as a cold and lonely universe, pastors and teachers who offered a gospel of hope and compassion found a ready audience for their message.

❖ ARMINIANISM AND CALVINISM ❖

One of the most influential of these renewal movements, throughout the seventeenth and eighteenth centuries, was Arminianism, which had begun soon after the initial Reformation. Arminianism arose as a reaction to the harsh and inflexible application of Calvinism practiced by the Dutch Reformed church and in particular to the belief that God predetermined the eternal fate of each person before the Creation. Those who rejected the specifically Calvinist emphasis on predestination, human wickedness, and the irresistible nature of God's grace were known as Remonstrants, or Arminians, after the Dutch Reformed theologian Jacobus Arminius (1560–1609). Arminius softened Calvinist teaching, arguing instead that God wishes to save all, not only the elect, although not all choose to accept his salvation. In order to argue his point he weakened Calvinist teaching on the irresistible effectiveness of Christ's redeeming work, thus causing his opponents to claim that his teaching diminished God's power and authority.

After his death, his followers' advocacy of his views led to a national crisis in the Netherlands, which ended at the Synod of Dort (1618–19), at which the Arminians repeatedly tried to defend their position but were eventually condemned. Their thought, however, was to play a significant role in the Protestant churches, since they provided a more optimistic message than either Luther or Calvin had done, asserting the freedom of man's will for good and evil.

FAITH AND DAILY LIFE IN THE SEVENTEENTH AND EIGHTEENTH CENTURIES

❖

THE introspective nature of the great thinkers of the seventeenth and eighteenth centuries and the spiritual revivals they encouraged, inspired a reevaluation of the family and how it fitted into society. Children, especially, were treated with greater affection, and family prayers and devotions became part of everyday life for the pious. And, since women were accepted as writers and missionaries by many of the Pietist and revivalist leaders, attitudes slowly began to change toward their abilities and their role in society.

Attitudes to work and family were very different in the seventeenth century. Whereas today a person's status is often determined by their career and achievements, then, in far more stable and less fluid societies, it was more a product of their family, and of the state in life into which they were born. Society was (by today's

A GLIMPSE INTO SIMPLE DUTCH LIFE
This late seventeenth-century painting illustrates the rise in family piety and individual spirituality at that time.

standards) very stratified and restrictive, although this may have been less apparent in an age in which it was generally believed that God has given each of us a place in life, in which it is right for us to be – an attitude reflected in Luther's famous dictum that a tree serves God best by being a tree.

Some of the most well-known spiritual guides of the age devoted themselves to leading humble people to prayer in the midst of work. One of the most famous, the French bishop François de Sales (1567–1622), wrote the renowned *Introduction to the Devout Life*, in which he instructed his flock to "belong to God even in the thick of the disturbance … of human affairs" and to do the little things of life "with great love." Another highly influential figure was a French Carmelite lay brother, known only as Brother Lawrence (1611–91), who wrote that "the time of business does not differ from the time of prayer."

Das Hällische Waysenhaus

UNIVERSITY OF HALLE, GERMANY

Halle became the Pietists' study center after Francke took up his post as professor. He established a thriving network of enterprises based on Pietist ideals, including a seminary, a bookshop, a boarding school for poor students, a medical center, and other support services. One of the fundamental concerns of Pietists was looking after the physical as well as the spiritual welfare of their neighbors.

> **" We must accustom the people to believe that mere knowledge is by no means sufficient for true Christianity – which is much more a matter of behavior "**
>
> PHILIP JACOB SPENER

❖ THE WARMTH OF PIETISM ❖

Another very influential Protestant renewal movement was formulated in Germany, the first home of the Reformation. Known as Pietism, it was a response to the mechanistic rituals and rote formalism that had come to mark the worship services of the now fully established Lutheran church. Ironically, much as Martin Luther had committed his energies to renewing the Catholic church a century before, so efforts were now earnestly made to revive the hearts and minds of Christians who had been spiritually dulled by the church that bore his name.

Philip Jacob Spener (1635–1705) is considered the intellectual founder of Pietism. After serving a Lutheran congregation in Strasbourg, he became a preacher and teacher in Frankfurt. Impressed by a community of Christians known as the Labadists, he experienced a burning desire to revive the Lutheran church. Spener began preaching a message that called for self-discipline, the need for a personal relationship with Christ, and the importance of daily prayer and reflection on the Scriptures. Although he adhered to the Lutheran form of church government, he also believed in the priesthood of all believers and held twice-weekly Bible studies in his home. As these groups became more popular and spread to other churches, they came to be known as *Collegia Pietatis* – from which the name Pietism was derived. However, the animosity Spener received from his peers was such that he was forced to resign his position in Frankfurt and move to Dresden.

In 1687 Spener was joined in Dresden by his close associate August Francke, a brilliant student of biblical languages. In 1684 Francke took up a position at the University of Leipzig, where he began holding Bible studies with the students and the faculty. These meetings led to a revival on the campus which, along with his strong opinions on social reform, caused many of the administration's more conservative members to become alarmed, and so he was forced to resign.

❖ THE EFFECTS OF PIETISM ❖

In 1692 Francke accepted a position at the University of Halle. Here, he had much greater success in gaining favor among the populace, and soon he had established a thriving network of enterprises based on Pietistic ideals *(see caption, above)*. Although Pietism was not a denomination in and of itself and was not part of a national identity movement like the Anglican church in England or the Lutheran church in Germany, it was a transforming agent within other established Christian traditions – including the Catholic church. And, while its tenets did not translate intact to the evangelical revivals of the eighteenth century, it did have a dramatic impact on the lives of the men and women who led those movements of the spirit.

ZINZENDORF AND THE MORAVIAN BRETHREN

One of Halle's leading pupils, Count von Zinzendorf (1700–60), was a wealthy aristocrat with a post in the government of Saxony in Germany. He allowed Hussite refugees, who were being persecuted in Bohemia and Moravia, to build a settlement on his Berthelsdorf estate in 1722. The refugees soon created a community and religious center known as *Herrnhut* or the "Lord's Watch."

Zinzendorf was so impressed with their efforts that he left his court position and became the spiritual leader of the thriving group. Eventually the Moravian Brethren, as they came to be known, joined with the Halle Pietists, and together they launched the modern Protestant mission movement.

❖

CHURCHES UNDER ATTACK

AS NEW TRENDS IN philosophical thought were taken up by the wealthy and fashionable classes in the mid-eighteenth century, Christianity increasingly came under attack. For many European leaders the Enlightenment thinking created a far more secular and therefore attractive climate for winning more power from the churches, both Protestant and Catholic. The most powerful and influential leader of the age was the Prussian emperor Frederick the Great (1712–86), who cared very little about religion and who had much respect for the philosophical thought of his time – indeed, he even invited Voltaire as a guest to his court. As far as Christianity was concerned, Frederick was a tolerant man but only because he believed that all religions were absurd.

Meanwhile, critical reactions to Deism were coming from both ends of the religious spectrum. Christians such as Joseph Butler, an Anglican bishop, attempted to defend Christian doctrine. They were very much on the defensive, however, against secular philosophers,

the most important of whom were Voltaire, Rousseau, and Immanuel Kant *(pp. 156-57)*. Kant espoused a subjectivist world-view that fostered the conviction that all knowledge of religion or philosophy is confined to pure reason and is completely separate from the knowledge we derive from experience and history, so that a person's conscience is the only true standard of morality.

❖ ABSOLUTE POWER ABUSED ❖

This was the era of absolute monarchs who wished to rule every aspect of their nation's lives. In Russia Peter the Great (r. 1682–1725) placed himself at the head of the Russian church *(p. 170)*. In Catholic Europe the rulers of Spain, France, and the Holy Roman Empire allowed the popes no authority in their domains, taking it upon themselves to regulate the church in their lands. The pious Emperor Joseph II of Austria (r. 1765–90) issued over 6,000 decrees directing the religious life of his subjects and, together with his fellow Catholic monarchs, kept strict control over the

A FLOURISHING OF CHURCH MUSIC – PSALMS, ANTHEMS, AND ORATORIOS

❖

ONE of the Reformers' criticisms was the unintelligibility of some Catholic church music. With the development of elaborate harmonies for the liturgy, the clarity of the words sometimes suffered. A further problem was that several composers from Flanders, Germany, France, Spain, and Italy chose to base their sacred music on love songs or military tunes. The Council of Trent *(pp. 148-49)* forbade the use of secular tunes within sacred settings and demanded that the words be intelligible and uplifting, initiating a renaissance in Catholic church music.

The late seventeenth century saw church music flourishing. Hymns, motets, and psalm-settings, sometimes accompanied by lavish orchestral arrangements, became immensely popular, as composers sought to stir people to ever greater heights of devotion. Cities vied with each other to have their churches furnished with excellent choirs

**THE PERFORMANCE OF HANDEL'S "MESSIAH,"
WESTMINSTER ABBEY, 1785**
*Handel was a devout Lutheran and composed several
settings inspired by the Bible.*

and orchestras. At St. Mark's in Venice in the seventeenth century, the congregation could listen to the music of Monteverdi or the Gabrieli brothers as well as many lesser-known composers. Pious concerts with music based on biblical texts were often played in church *"oratories,"* or prayer chapels (hence the name "oratorio").

These musical splendors were not confined to one denomination or culture. The Reformed tradition produced great names such as the Bach family and the greatest composer of the oratorio, the German composer G.F. Handel (1685–1759), as well as a host of lesser-known musicians. Protestant composers, such as J.S. Bach (1685–1750), happily imported southern Catholic music into their worship. Great Catholic composers, most notably W.A. Mozart (1756–91), produced music of equal quality. The musical achievements of the age, whether Catholic or Protestant, have become a part of the heritage of all Christians.

appointment of bishops, abbots, and other church leaders. A devout ruler such as Joseph might appoint able men, but more often than not royal connections and noble birth counted for far more than spiritual leadership qualities. On the eve of the French Revolution, all but one of France's 130 bishops were aristocrats. The last prime minister of France, although an atheist, was made archbishop of Toulouse and a cardinal. There were limits, however: King Louis XVI refused to make him archbishop of Paris, saying that the head of the French church "must at least believe in God." Earlier

> ## " ALL RELIGIONS MUST BE TOLERATED. EVERY MAN MUST GET TO HEAVEN IN HIS OWN WAY "
>
> **FREDERICK THE GREAT OF PRUSSIA**

in the century another atheist prime minister, Dubois, had been made both archbishop and cardinal even though it was said that "all the vices ... struggled within him for mastery."

In earlier centuries papal corruption had paralyzed reform in the Catholic world. In the Age of Reason even the best of popes could do nothing, since virtually all major church appointments outside Italy were out of their hands. When they did object, as Pope Innocent XI did over Louis XIV's persecution of French Protestants, they were ignored.

The low point of the papacy was reached in 1773, when the sovereigns of Europe forced Pope Clement XIV to dissolve the Jesuit order, the most loyal and

SILENT STUDY AND PRAYER
As more of the laity learned to read, Protestant spirituality came to emphasize private Bible study more and more. Protestants also studied lectionaries (above) *and other devotional aids.*

powerful bulwark of the papacy since the Reformation. One result was the destruction of the peaceful communities the Jesuits had set up for the Guarani people of what is now Paraguay *(pp. 150-51)*. Deprived of their protectors, the Guarani were soon enslaved.

The situation was just as bad in the Protestant churches. The bishops of the Church of England, appointed by the monarch, were mostly well-connected, though rarely spiritual, men. In Lutheran Germany the church was even more a department of state than in the Catholic countries. Religious leaders were monitored not for their loyalty to the gospel but for their support of the government.

❖ THE UNAFFECTED MAJORITY ❖
For the majority, however, religious life changed very little. Most ordinary Protestants and Catholics were unaffected by the philosophical debates among intellectuals. Catholicism continued to be largely a religion of ceremony, public worship, and private prayer, while by the eighteenth century, Protestant piety had become lay oriented, very biblical, and focused much more in the home than in the church.

> " *Christianity is now railed at and ridiculed with very little reserve, and its teachers without any at all* "
>
> **THOMAS SECKER, ARCHBISHOP OF CANTERBURY**

REVIVAL FIRES

MUCH AS PIETISM SOUGHT TO rescue the Lutheran church from its spiritual formalism, the Methodist movement tried to transform the stagnancy that had become pervasive in the Church of England.

❖ THE WESLEY BROTHERS ❖

The most prominent names in the formation of Methodism were the Wesley brothers, John (1703–91) and Charles (1707–88). John was his parents' fourteenth child and second surviving son. When aged six, he was rescued from a fire that consumed his family's home – an event that would leave a lasting impression on his life and his calling (he referred to himself as a "brand plucked from the burning").

After studying at Oxford from 1720 to 1724, John returned there to join his brother, Charles, who had formed a group of undergraduates for Bible study, prayer, and mutual encouragement. As a result of their piety and zealous devotion to holy living, the group was derisively referred to by classmates as the "Holy Club." Its members were later called "Methodists" for their methodical adherence to rules and personal order. They performed good works in and around London's orphanages, jails, and schools, but they were so driven that even William Law, the morally uncompromising author of *A Serious Call to a Devout and Holy Life* (1728), told John and Charles to practice a faith that was less burdened by rules and more devoted to joyfully loving others.

❖ MORAVIAN CONFIDENCE ❖

In 1735 the Wesley brothers embarked on a voyage to America. It was a journey that made a strong impression on both of them. John suffered from depression over his spiritual state. Despite his work among the poor, his daily Bible reading, and weekly fasts, he felt nothing but dissatisfaction with the direction his life was taking and with his Christian walk. His despair only deepened on the voyage to the New World when a violent storm, endured with cheerful and confident stoicism by a group of Moravians on board, sent him into a panic. John's initial experience in America was even worse. Invited by the governor of Georgia, James Oglethorpe, to minister among the colonists and Native Americans, his sour demeanor and gloomy outlook made him an unpopular presence among the flock he had been called to serve. The one fortunate relationship he made was with the Moravian pastor Augustus Spangenberg, who encouraged him, in evangelical fashion, to look to Jesus as the personal Savior who desired an indwelling presence in the lives of his believers. His friend's encouragement was not enough, however, to subdue John's inner turmoil.

JOHN WESLEY – FOUNDER OF THE METHODIST MOVEMENT
With his extensive proselytizing missions, his prolific writings, tens of thousands of sermons (probably over 40,000), and his genius for organization, Wesley helped Methodism survive while other sects died away. Today the Methodist church is the second-largest Protestant denomination in the United States and the largest independent Protestant group in the United Kingdom.

SONGS OF PRAISE FOR ORDINARY PEOPLE

❖

THE saying "Why should the devil have all the best tunes?" is attributed to Martin Luther, the founding father of the Protestant Reformation. Anxious to help uneducated people understand the Bible, he began a tradition of composing uncomplicated tunes, which could be sung by the whole congregation. The eighteenth century was a great age of hymn-writing; perhaps best known is the hymn "Amazing Grace," composed by a former slave trader and leader of the evangelical revival, John Newton (1725–1807). "Amazing Grace" remains one of the world's most popular pieces of music because of its simple expression of God's love and forgiveness.

"THE VILLAGE CHOIR" BY THOMAS WEBSTER
For the majority, singing hymns occupied an important place in Christian worship. The Wesley brothers in particular helped to popularize congregational hymn-singing from the eighteenth century onward.

Another great hymn-writer was Charles Wesley, who began composing hymns after health problems forced him to stop traveling in 1756. A prolific writer with more than 6,000 known works to his name, Wesley is the author of such well-loved standards as "O for a Thousand Tongues to Sing," and the Christmas carol "Hark, the Herald Angels Sing." Hymns continued to gain in popularity as a means of inviting the congregations of the Reformed churches to worship. However, there were those who continued to reject the singing of hymns. For example, some Quakers believed that prayer and all forms of praise should be conducted in silence.

When he finally returned to England in 1738, he felt a great sense of frustration and failure as a minister. That same year, the brothers were to find the peace they had so desperately been seeking. On Whit Sunday Charles experienced what he called a true conversion and finally found the inner confidence he had seen in the faces of the Moravian settlers during their stormy voyage. Three days later, on May 24th, John reluctantly attended a Moravian service where he too experienced a deep and lasting conversion *(see side column)*.

❖ THE METHODIST REVIVAL ❖

A few days after his conversion experience, John boldly preached at Oxford the sermon that would become his singular message throughout the rest of his life: "By Grace Ye Are Saved Through Faith."

After spending a short time in Germany with the Pietist Count von Zinzendorf, John returned to England and, together with Charles, began preaching in local churches, on the streets, and at public gatherings, so launching the Methodist revival that would transform English society. Claiming that "the world is my parish," John ignored the Anglican establishment, which criticized his stress on a personal experience of salvation through faith alone. Although John was a competent speaker, his true talent lay in

administrating the growing Methodist movement. He organized his converts into what he called "societies." Each society was further divided into "classes," with "class leaders" attending to individual members' spiritual needs and "stewards" handling each class's

> ❝ THERE ARE TWO THINGS TO DO ABOUT THE GOSPEL — BELIEVE IT AND BEHAVE IT ❞
>
> **SUSANNAH WESLEY,**
> **MOTHER OF JOHN AND CHARLES**

financial concerns. Seeing the need to hold annual conferences to address issues and the governance of each society, he called the first such gathering in London in 1744. The rapid growth of Methodism necessitated further innovations, including sending traveling evangelists on "circuits" around the countryside and ordaining ministers to serve the burgeoning congregations.

> ❝ *Amazing Grace! how sweet the sound That saved a wretch like me! I once was lost, but now am found! Was blind but now I see* ❞
>
> **JOHN NEWTON**

Wesley was Arminian (*p. 160*) in theology, believing that Calvinism and its positions on election and predestination was one step removed from the heresy of Antinomianism – the belief that Christ's redeeming work on the cross frees the elect from any moral responsibility. His Arminianism led him in 1740 to a split with the other great leader of the evangelical revival, George Whitefield (1714–70). Whitefield was an even more brilliant preacher and an old friend from the Holy Club. Although they publicly supported one another's ministries, the two men were never reconciled theologically. Whitefield remained a staunch defender of Reformed theology and stayed within the Church of England, rather than join the Methodist movement.

❖ WESLEY'S LEGACY ❖

Wesley eventually experienced similar reversals in his relationships with many of his closest associates and co-workers. His brother strongly disagreed with his practice of ordaining lay ministers – many of whom were uneducated and ill-trained for their responsibilities. Wesley himself became frustrated with the Arminians who had originally been his greatest inspiration. Considering them to be too passive in their teaching about applying one's salvation in the care and ministry of

"IF THY HEART BE AS MY HEART, GIVE ME THY HAND"

JOHN WESLEY

others, Methodists and Arminians mutually agreed to part company. Wesley publicly stated that men like Zinzendorf and Law, who had instilled a sense of passion in him when he was a dour young man, had views that were too mystical and open to false conclusions.

Wesley's own teachings on holiness in the church were extremely controversial, although they have had an enduring influence. He had his supporters, notably John William Fletcher, or De la Flecheire, the most prominent early Methodist theologian and apologist.

Desirous of perpetuating the Methodist movement, Wesley took steps to ensure that it would carry on after his death. In 1743 he drafted rules for the societies; in 1763 he created standards for Methodist preachers; in 1784 he secured the legal rights of the societies and ordained two of America's most active early Methodist bishops, Thomas Coke and Francis Asbury.

❖ REVIVALS IN SCOTLAND AND WALES ❖

In 1741 Whitefield was invited to Scotland by a group known as the Seceders to address the heresies being taught in the Scottish churches. While some religious leaders embraced a form of Deism, others, known as Moderatists, preached a humanistic message of simple morality. The Seceders, organized by Ebenezer Erskine (1680–1754), had set up an independent presbytery in protest at these developments, but in 1740 the Church of Scotland expelled the reform-minded leadership from the national body.

Never one to be boxed in by sectarian quarrels, Whitefield began his work among the Seceders but soon initiated revivals in the Church of Scotland itself. Those who assisted Whitefield, such as William McCullough, were ostracized and called zealots by many in the established church. Their efforts eventually began to have an impact, however, as the fires of revival gradually spread from the laity to open-minded and newly inspired members of the church leadership.

In Wales the Society for Promoting Christian Knowledge (SPCK) had been promoting the causes of social reform and religious revival since the early eighteenth century – along with enterprising individuals such as Griffith Jones, the founder of the Welsh circulating schools. In 1735 a schoolteacher named Howell Harris was converted at a communion service and immediately began working as a lay minister. His inspired preaching, together with the efforts of men like Daniel Rowlands, brought revival to Wales. In 1752 Harris gained the support of the Countess of Huntingdon (*see side column*), who provided the resources for him to establish a religious community at Trevecca to train others in evangelism and ministry. Harris was also instrumental in creating the Welsh Calvinistic Methodist church.

❖ THE FIRST GREAT ❖ AWAKENING IN AMERICA

While Pietism was flourishing in Germany and Methodism was bringing revival to the churches in England, what has come to be called the First Great Awakening was sweeping the colonies in America. The seeds for revival were initially planted among

"GEORGE WHITEFIELD PREACHING" BY JOHN COLLETT

In 1740 George Whitefield preached to packed American congregations in New England, New York, Philadelphia, Charleston, and Savannah. A Calvinist Anglican, he preached with enormous passion and based his theological message on original sin, justification by faith, and regeneration. One local farmer compared Whitefield's preaching to that of "one of the old apostles," with "many thousands flocking after him to hear ye gospel and great numbers were converted to Christ."

JONATHAN EDWARDS

THE American Jonathan Edwards (1703–58) was a brilliant scholar and theologian who had studied Latin at the age of six, was fluent in Hebrew and Greek by 13, had graduated from Yale University with highest honors by the age of 17, and was a Congregational minister from the age of 24.

In 1734 he preached a series of Calvinistic messages on justification by faith alone that gripped the small town of Northampton, Massachusetts, so much that within a year nearly its entire adult population had professed repentance and conversion. He died of smallpox in 1758.

> " ... *the work of conversion was carried on in a most astonishing manner, and increased more and more; souls did, as it were, come by flocks to Jesus Christ* "
>
> JONATHAN EDWARDS

Dutch Reformed church in America in 1737. The most significant events of the First Great Awakening were the result of the efforts of a young Congregational minister in Massachusetts named Jonathan Edwards *(see box)*. His sermons, including the famous "Sinners in the Hands of an Angry God," brought parishioners to their knees, and his books inspired other evangelists and preachers to spread the gospel message. His theological works were of such profundity that he became the most influential theologian North America has ever produced.

> " GRACE IS BUT GLORY BEGUN, AND GLORY IS BUT GRACE PERFECTED "
>
> JONATHAN EDWARDS

the Anabaptist *(p. 138)* and Moravian groups that had settled in Pennsylvania. However, it wasn't until a German Pietist named Theodore J. Frelinghuysen began preaching the need for inner transformation rather than merely observing ecclesiastical rites that true revival took hold. As Frelinghuysen's popularity spread, so did criticism of his methods and his message. Despite this he was successful in laying the spiritual foundation for others, and his efforts resulted in the creation of the

THE UNIQUE STYLE OF DANCE PRACTICED BY THE SHAKERS

A fringe charismatic Christian group originating from the English Quaker revival of 1747, the Shakers earned their nickname because they shook vigorously when under the influence of spiritual exaltation. They firmly believed in abstaining from alcohol and advocated a strictly celibate lifestyle. Ann Lee, known as Mother Ann, took a small band of Shakers to North America in 1774, where they benefited from the revival movements of the time. They had their own style of dance, song, and folk art.

By 1742 the First Great Awakening had swept through New England. Men such as Samuel Davies helped build Presbyterian churches in Virginia, while others, including Daniel Marshall, worked among the Baptist congregations in the Carolinas. Gilbert Tennent of New Brunswick was an eloquent scholar who founded the "Log College" in Pennsylvania to train new ministers and worked extensively among the English and Scottish Presbyterians. Whitefield made a number of voyages to America during this time and inspired thousands with his dramatic style of preaching and his ability to cross denominational lines.

The American religious scene provided the ideal climate for diverse Christian groups to grow and develop. By the end of the eighteenth century, the framers of the American constitution had passed laws *(p. 175)* forbidding the prohibition of religious worship in any form.

❖ NATIVE AMERICANS ❖

While most of the activity in the American colonies was undertaken by Protestants who had escaped religious persecution in Europe, missions among the Indian tribes of Canada were attempted primarily by French Jesuits. Although their efforts were heroic, they met with limited success and many were martyred.

One of the successful missionaries among the Native Americans was John Eliot (1604–90), an English Presbyterian minister who became known as the "apostle to the Indians." He established the first church for the Native Americans of Massachusetts and was also the first to translate the Bible into their native language *(see right)*. By 1675 almost 4,000 Pequot Indians had become Christians.

In the eighteenth century David Brainerd (1718–47), a strong-willed preacher who was thrown out of Yale University for criticizing a tutor, found much success among the tribespeople of New York, New Jersey, and Pennsylvania. His work ethic and heroism resulted in the conversion and baptism of many Native Americans. He was a close friend of Jonathan Edwards, who preached at his funeral and later published his journal, which motivated many others to become missionaries.

In Central and South America Spanish clergy worked more or less diligently to convert the indigenous peoples. Priests and bishops tried to make their message meaningful by learning local languages such as Nahuatl or Quechuan, and by filling their sermons with imagery familiar to the natives. Unfortunately, they were very slow to train indigenous people – Indian priests were not ordained until 1794 – leaving Christianity still largely a foreign religion.

❖ SOCIAL EFFECTS OF THE ❖ RELIGIOUS REVIVALS

The religious revivals that took place in the eighteenth century had a dramatic influence on the social and political structures of the following decades. Many of the revivalists were highly educated, and their efforts resulted in the founding of numerous Bible colleges and universities.

In America, particularly, the First Great Awakening produced many great schools, including Rutgers and Dartmouth colleges and what would later become Princeton, Brown, and Columbia universities. Important social programs were created by Christians

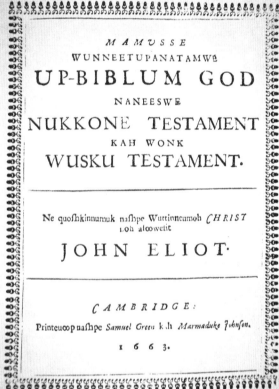

TITLE PAGE OF THE MASSACHUSETTS INDIAN BIBLE
John Eliot mastered the language of the Pequot Indians, into which he translated the Bible for the first time. It was published in Cambridge, Massachusetts, in 1663.

who wanted to live out their faith by helping others, and both Enlightenment thinkers and Christian reformers had a dramatic impact through their promotion of democratic ideals.

In England innumerable mission and charitable organizations were formed to spread the message of hope and salvation at home and abroad. These ministries, and stalwart individuals who dedicated their lives to serving others, together helped bring relief and aid to poor children, widows, the homeless, the unemployed, prisoners, and those suffering from alcohol and gambling addictions.

MISSION AND CULTURE
In 1659 the central Catholic authority for mission in Rome issued enlightened guidelines on missionary attitudes: "Do not … bring any pressure to bear on the peoples, to change their manners, customs, and uses, unless they are evidently contrary to religion and sound morals." This and other warnings not to transport European culture abroad were frequently ignored. The seventeenth-century carving above, created by Guarani Indians (from what is now Paraguay), reveals an obviously European influence.

❖

THE AFRICAN MISSIONS
Missionary efforts in Africa were begun in the fifteenth century by Portuguese Catholics, who first achieved success in the Congo, and later in Angola. In the seventeenth century, French missionaries evangelized among the people of the Ivory Coast, Senegal, and Madagascar. Yet national interests typically took precedence over saving souls: when, in 1665, King Antonio I of the Congo refused to allow Portugal to open mines in his land, he was captured and beheaded. The practice of trafficking in African slaves also undercut the efforts of the missionaries.

❖

THE ORTHODOX CHURCH IN THE AGE OF REASON

HOLY RUSSIA

Over the centuries, a distinctive church architecture developed in Russian churches. Typically, they were made of wood (*above*), often with onion-shaped domes (*p. 123*). Nor was it just Russian buildings that were distinctive. Russian spirituality was so fervent that by 1650 Muscovy, the state ruled by the Russian czar, was known as "Holy Russia." Both clergy and laity were expected to fast regularly and to devote much time to prayer each day. The czar and the entire court also stood through services lasting seven hours or more.

❖

ORTHODOX MISSIONS

In the early 1700s missionaries from the Russian Orthodox church became active in the harsh region of Siberia. Orthodox communities were formed in Kamchatka and Yakutsk, and efforts were even extended into Alaska in 1794. Orthodox clergymen established churches all the way down to San Francisco.

❖

IN THE SEVENTEENTH CENTURY, most Orthodox Christians had to endure the oppressive rule of the Ottoman Turks (*p. 123*). Under their Muslim masters Christians were heavily taxed, their children could be taken to serve in the army, religious processions were banned, new churches could not be built, and evangelization of Muslims was forbidden on penalty of death. In addition, many religious schools were closed, resulting in a dearth of educated clergy, and corruption was rampant as patriarchal offices were sold by the Turkish authorities. The Russian church, which was not under alien rule, became the center of Orthodox Christianity.

❖ DIVISION IN THE RUSSIAN CHURCH ❖

In the middle of the seventeenth century, Patriarch Nikon of Moscow (1605–81) instituted liturgical modifications that caused a split in the Russian Orthodox church. Nikon was an authoritarian and a great admirer of all things Greek. He insisted that the sign of the cross should be made as the Greeks made it, using three fingers instead of two. However, many Russians felt little reverence for Greek Orthodoxy. Why should they be forced to make such a change when *their* way of making the sign of the cross was the most ancient? The "Old Believers" even broke away from the main body of the church over this issue. It caused so much controversy because the Orthodox religion placed, and still places, great emphasis on its ritual practices and symbolic gestures. In spite of Nikon's persistence in the proposed reforms, and his persecution of those who opposed them, he was eventually deposed and exiled.

❖ RELIGIOUS REFORMS ❖

In 1682 Peter the Great (1672–1725) was proclaimed czar of Russia. A ruthless dictator, he kept his nation in a perpetual state of war, and even had his son executed for treason. He was also a great reformer, however, in the political sphere, and introduced many changes in Russian society, including revising the Christian calendar, simplifying the alphabet, and moving the capital to St. Petersburg.

In 1721 Peter issued the *Spiritual Regulation*, which abolished the Moscow patriarchate and placed the church and its priests under the control of a spiritual college or Holy Synod, comprising 12 clergy, that answered, ultimately, to secular agencies. As part of Peter's plan to Westernize Russia, the synod was not based on Orthodox canon law but rather followed the practices of the Protestant church constitutions in Germany. The emperor had the final say in church matters, having the power to nominate and dismiss the Holy Synod members at will.

In many ways the patriarch of Constantinople, who labored under Islamic rule, had fewer restrictions upon his authority than those faced by the synod of the Russian church. Yet during this era Russia remained steadfastly Orthodox at virtually all levels of society and could still produce great leaders and preachers such as St. Tikhon of Zadonsk (1724–83), bishop of Voronezh.

CZAR PETER THE GREAT
Peter the Great's church reforms remained in place until the Revolution of 1917, when the Bolsheviks seized power.

The czar, determined also to reduce the influence of the monasteries in the state, decreed that new monasteries could no longer be founded without the state's permission, that all monks were forbidden to live as hermits, and that no women under 50 were allowed to enter a convent and take their vows. Peter's successors, Elizabeth (r. 1741–62) and Catherine II

> ## " THE KING OF HEAVEN HAS SENT A LETTER TO YOU ... WHENEVER YOU READ THE GOSPEL, CHRIST HIMSELF IS SPEAKING TO YOU "
>
> **TIKHON OF ZADONSK**

(r. 1762–96), were even more vehement in their attempts to reduce the power of the monasteries: by the end of the eighteenth century, more than half of the monasteries had been suppressed, and those that remained open had strict limitations placed on the number of monks allowed. The impact of these changes was greatest in remote areas where the monasteries were the only centers of culture, education, and charitable works.

❖ MOUNT ATHOS ❖

Meanwhile, the Orthodox Christians under Turkish rule managed not only to maintain their faith, but even to hold important synods such as the Council of Jerusalem in 1672, which reaffirmed Orthodox beliefs in the face of questions raised by the Protestant and Catholic Reformations. One of the keys to the survival of Orthodoxy was "the Holy Mountain," Mount Athos,

THE MONASTERY OF ST. PAUL ON MOUNT ATHOS
Independent of the political upheavals of the time, the monks of Mount Athos continued to be the religious heart of the Orthodox church. Men came not only from Greece, but from all over the Orthodox world to join the monastic community. Then, as now, no women, animals, or beardless youths were allowed to set foot upon the peninsula.

a peninsula that juts into the Aegean Sea (*see side column*). The monastic community produced spiritual leaders such as St. Kosmas the Aetolian (1714–79), who inspired a religious and cultural revival in eighteenth-century Greece. "The Greek John Wesley," he traveled tirelessly, preaching the gospel and teaching huge crowds before becoming one of the many martyrs executed by the Ottomans.

A HOLY SITE

The first monastery was built in 972, and Mount Athos was officially designated a holy site in 1045. Since the Byzantine era, the mountain has been a monastic center for Orthodox churches of every nationality. There are 20 "ruling" monasteries on the peninsula, and there have reputedly been up to 40,000 monks residing there at one time.

❖

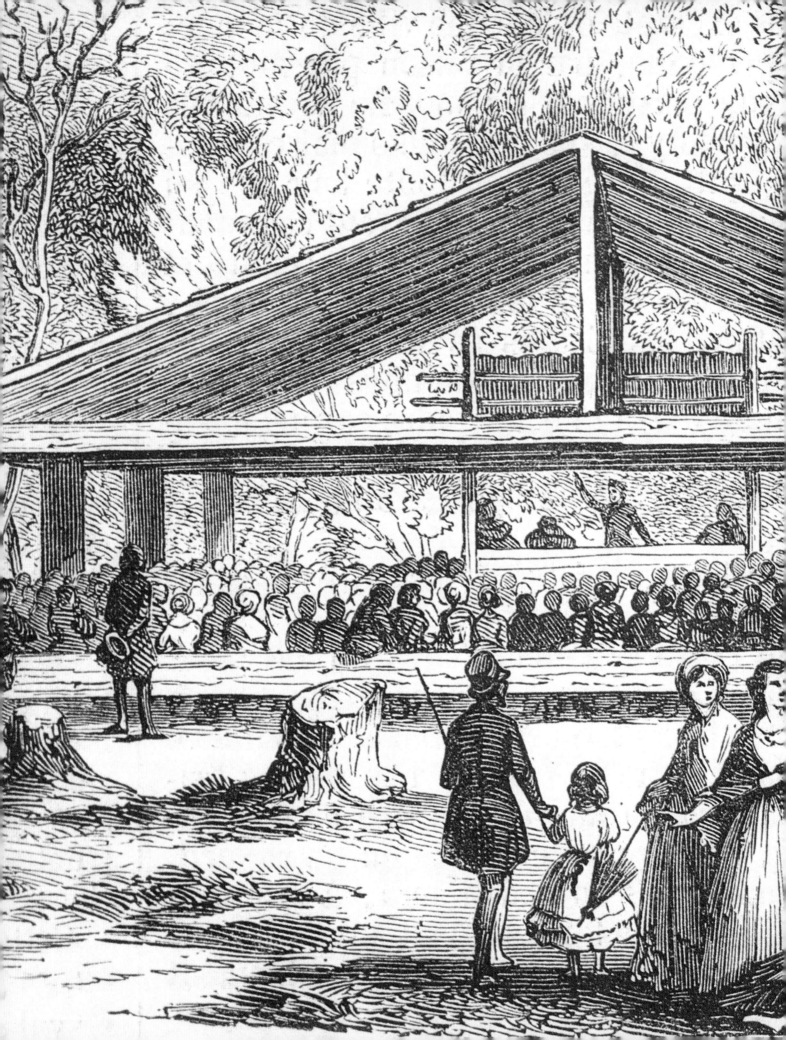

Mission & Revolution
1776–1914

THE SOCIAL and religious impact of the Reformers and the Enlightenment thinkers carried on into the late eighteenth and the nineteenth centuries. The explosion of populist movements sparked by the Reformation continued through the subsequent two centuries and culminated in a bloody revolution against England by American patriots, and an even bloodier uprising in France. As governments toppled, so did the authority of the church in countries where its primacy had gone virtually unchallenged just a few generations before. Such assaults came from Liberal theologians and opportunistic political firebrands alike, who attacked the basic doctrines and convictions of the church.

Yet the limits of the church were expanded on all levels. Missionaries such as William Carey took the gospel to lands where the people had not heard it before, preachers such as Charles Finney and Charles Spurgeon reinforced the vitality of Christianity with massive revivals, and social reformers such as William Booth used their moral authority to forcefully challenge such evils as slavery and the exploitation of workers.

Camp meeting in Tennessee, 1850s

NEW WORLD OF FREEDOM

> " *There is a time to preach and a time to pray, but there is also a time to fight, and that time has now come* "

JOHN PETER GABRIEL MUHLENBERG, A LUTHERAN MINISTER WHO BECAME A REVOLUTIONARY GENERAL

BY 1770, THE RELIGIOUS FERVOR of the First Great Awakening was waning in the 13 North American colonies that were to form the United States, and church attendance declined over the next quarter century. Christianity was still enormously influential, however. During the American Revolutionary War (1776–83), for instance, the Continental Congress issued annual thanksgiving and fast-day proclamations that regularly invoked the name of Jesus Christ and asked for his blessing on the war effort.

✧ THE REVOLUTIONARY MIND ✧

By 1776, an important "revolution" had already taken place in the minds of many American colonists: they wished their churches to be free of the state – a concept then foreign to any European country. Most of the colonists were Protestants of one form or another, and they believed that government had no role in the spiritual life of the individual. Not only did they believe that each person was answerable first to God and not to a secular monarch or divinely appointed pope, they also maintained the English attitude toward liberty and a representative form of government, believing that the freedom to govern oneself and to practice one's religion were inviolable rights. The colonists' resolve was all the stronger because a number of their forebears had fled persecution – the Puritans, for example. It was seconded by the influential Deists who played a leading role in the revolution, and it was to be enshrined in the Constitution of the United States in 1787 (*see feature, right*).

A number of the leaders of the revolutionary era were devout Christians, including Patrick Henry, John Jay, and Alexander Hamilton. George Washington appears to have had a genuine faith (he kept a prayer

SIGNERS OF A DEIST DECLARATION, OR THE CHARTER FOR A CHRISTIAN NATION?
The Declaration of Independence was adopted by delegates representing each of the 13 American colonies on July 4th, 1776 (above). Although its author, Thomas Jefferson, was a Deist, he used language that embodied the revival spirit of the First Great Awakening (pp. 166-69). He carefully chose language and concepts acceptable to both Christians and Deists, referring to the deity as "Nature's God," the "Creator," the "Supreme Judge of the World," and "Divine Providence."

CHRISTIANITY AND THE CONSTITUTION OF THE UNITED STATES

✛

THE new constitution of the United States of America recreated the relationship between church and state. Previously, the two had always been viewed as a unity. Wherever Christianity had become the dominant religion, it had in some way or other been linked with rulers and nations by law, lending its authority to government and receiving government protection. Church and state were seen as totally intertwined, whether by popes who tried to direct rulers and states; or by eighteenth-century absolute monarchs who tried to make the church a department of state. In the new United States the two were to be completely separated. (The Constitution does not even mention God.) Churches were to be free of state control, and the state to be free of church interference. This established a culture in the sphere of religion that was analogous to the "free market" in the sphere of economics – all religions were allowed to thrive or die by their own efforts, without the support or enmity of the state. It was increasingly to become the model for the

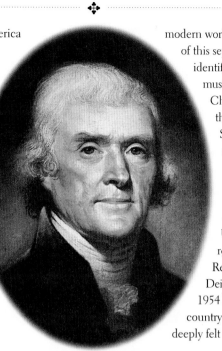

DEIST INSPIRATION
Deist influence on the American Constitution came especially from Thomas Jefferson. Although he was out of the country while it was drafted, his ideas were a major influence.

modern world. In the U.S. and elsewhere, the result of this separation has been to make it harder to identify a country as "a Christian nation" – its laws must be grounded in something other than the Christian revelation, even where Christianity is the religion of the majority, as in the United States. The churches are left in an ambiguous position vis-a-vis government, free but barred from influencing the conduct of the State. This has sometimes led to Christianity being marginalized, and to conflict between church and state over education. In the United States Christianity has often been replaced in the public arena by "Civil Religion" – a less defined faith, mingling Deism and patriotism. To give one example, in 1954 President Eisenhower told Americans: "Our country makes no sense unless it is founded on a deeply felt religious faith – and I don't care what that is." Such a nebulous faith, including belief in a "manifest destiny" guiding America to a glorious future, is often invoked to support government, rarely to challenge it.

"WE SHALL NOT FIGHT ... ALONE. THERE IS A JUST GOD"

PATRICK HENRY

diary and wrote that God would accept him because of "the merits of thy Son Jesus Christ"), although he was not a regular churchgoer. Even the Deist leaders of the era, Benjamin Franklin, Thomas Jefferson, John Adams, and James Madison, had great respect for Christianity and its founder, if not for his church.

For the most part, the various sects and denominations that existed in America supported the revolutionary cause. Congregational pulpits became

sounding boards for the revolution as Puritan ministers promoted insurrection in sermons and pamphlets. John Witherspoon, a Presbyterian minister, signed the Declaration of Independence. The Lutheran church sent many to the battlefield. Only the churches that preached the gospel of pacifism attempted to stay out of the fray. Groups such as the Amish, Mennonites, Quakers, and Moravians refused to take up arms and in return were, at best, harassed and ridiculed and, at worst, persecuted for their stand.

✛ THE NEW CHURCH LANDSCAPE ✛

Staunch support for the revolution from Baptist churches helped that church grow in membership greatly, during and after the war. After 1783, the Methodist church, too, grew very rapidly. The major loser among the denominations was the Church of England in America, which was reestablished in 1789 as the Protestant Episcopal church, a shadow of its former self. The new religious landscape of the United States was unlike any other – a profusion of denominations, none of them dominant – and the freedom and energy of the American churches were a wonder to European eyes.

RELUCTANT WITNESS
It is a measure of the strength of Christianity in the United States that even one of its most bitter critics, Thomas Paine (1737–1809), appealed to the Bible to justify the rebel cause. In his best-selling pamphlet *Common Sense*, he declared that "monarchical government" was condemned in the Bible and "impiously invades the prerogative of heaven."

✛

CHRISTIANITY ATTACKED, DIVIDED, & FLOURISHING

THE CLOSE OF THE EIGHTEENTH century saw a startling attempt to destroy Christianity in France. The assault began after France fell into political revolution in 1789.

At first the new revolutionary government attacked church corruption and the wealth of the bishops and abbots who ruled the church – causes with which many Christians could identify. Clerical privileges were abolished, and church property was nationalized. Soon, however, the new regime began to interfere in the internal life of the church, declaring that priests and bishops should be elected by the laity, and further restricting the pope's authority over the French church – decrees which brought papal condemnation. Worse was to follow: when the country went to war in 1792, moderate leaders were ousted and a radical government was formed. The government set up a "constitutional church," which it kept firmly under its thumb, and the Catholic church was repressed.

❖ THE CHURCH OUTLAWED ❖

The next two years, known as the Reign of Terror, were far more brutal than anything foisted on the populace by any king. The guillotine would become the symbol of the era as royalty, nobility, clergy, and anyone else accused of being a counter-revolutionary lost their head to its blade. Christianity was banned and 30,000 clergy were forced into exile, while hundreds were killed. In an effort to completely eradicate vestiges of the past, and to quell threats from other countries that accused it of being a godless and immoral regime, the French government formed a new, official "religion of reason" on June 7th, 1794. Deistic in nature, its basic doctrine held that there was a Supreme Being but that this entity was not the God of Christianity. Images of the Goddess of Reason were placed in churches, the clergy were no longer paid and were forbidden to teach in schools, and holy days were replaced with festivals honoring secular ideals.

Christianity survived, however. This secularization was deeply unpopular and was abandoned in 1795 when the radicals were overthrown, and a degree of religious freedom restored. Then, in 1799, a young military genius named Napoleon Bonaparte made himself dictator of France. Although not favorably inclined towards Christianity, Napoleon believed that absolute rule was easier in a nation with an established religion. Pope Pius VI (r. 1775–99) would brook no compromise, so he was taken into custody in France, where he died. Napoleon then negotiated a concordat with his successor, Pius VII (r. 1800–23), in 1801, which formally recognized the revolution and gave the First Consul virtual control over the Catholic church in France. At the same time, the agreement allowed the pope much greater influence over the French

BEFORE THE REVOLUTION: POPE PIUS VI VISITS VENICE IN 1782
No one could have imagined in 1782 that both church and monarchy would be overthrown in France only a decade later, or that Pope Pius VI would die a prisoner in 1799. Nor could anyone have foreseen the dramatic rise in papal influence that was to follow his sufferings.

church, because the bishops would only agree to Napoleon's plans when the pope agreed. By 1808, however, relations between Pius and Napoleon had degenerated so far that Napoleon imprisoned the pope.

✣ TRIUMPH AND DIVISION ✣

After the defeat of France in 1814, Pius returned to Rome triumphant to find that Napoleon had strengthened the papacy, without ever intending to. Wherever Napoleon led his armies, he abolished monastic orders, ended religious education, and seized church lands. Where previously there had been proud national churches, which happily ignored the pope, he left chastened and crushed hierarchies looking to Rome for a lead. Moreover, whereas the eighteenth-century popes had seemed pampered princelings, the sufferings of Pius VI and Pius VII restored the aura of sanctity to the Vatican, giving the papacy a renewed moral authority.

There followed a great revival of faith in a number of Catholic countries, including France, Belgium, and southern Germany, reflected in increased church attendance, missionary activity, and church influence. France was to the fore, perhaps because its revolution had destroyed so much church corruption there.

The maltreatment of the church by the French revolutionaries, however, left Christians divided over politics. Many enthusiastic Christians, in all the churches, felt that the churches should support political liberalism and the extension of democracy, seeing these as simple struggles for justice. Conservatives, however, both Protestant and Catholic, felt that the French experience proved that all radical programs of social change would lead to bloody revolution and attacks on Christianity.

This division was strongest in the Catholic church. The popes had been left with such a fear of revolution that they remained aligned with the established rulers of Europe for nearly a century. Worse still, Pius VII and his successors were convinced that they must retain control of the Papal States or be at the mercy of violent despots. So they resisted all democratic attempts to reunify Italy. Those Catholics who supported political liberalism found themselves at odds with the church hierarchy, which was determined to maintain the alliance of "throne and altar." When half of Europe was engulfed by revolution in 1848 (see caption, below), the church stood firmly on the side of repression, alienating many.

A VISION OF HEAVEN ON EARTH: CHRISTIAN OR SECULAR?

This picture, painted in 1848, shows the peoples of Europe marching in solidarity past a statue of the Rights of Man, with Christ watching from the sky. Some Christians viewed support for political liberalism and even for revolution as simply a struggle for justice; others saw it as a futile attempt to create an illusory secular heaven on earth, distracting Christians from eternal issues.

NEW MOVEMENTS IN PROTESTANTISM

ROMANTICISM AND FAITH

The German composer Felix Mendelssohn (1809–47) was one of a number of artists who combined their Christian faith with an emphasis on emotion, intuition, and imagination, and on the beauty of nature, each a characteristic of the Romantic movement. Other such Romantics included his fellow Germans Caspar-David Friedrich (1774–1840), a painter, and the philosopher Friedrich von Schlegel (1772–1829), as well as the English poet Samuel Taylor Coleridge (1772–1834).

❖

NEW CRITICISM

After Schleiermacher's death, the most influential Liberal theologians of the century were Ferdinand Baur and Albrecht Ritschl. Baur was the first to bring to biblical studies the assumption that anything miraculous must be untrue, a belief which led him to attempt to unravel the New Testament into component strands. Ritschl rejected Schleiermacher's focus on religious experience and all metaphysical knowledge of God. He and his many followers focused instead on ethics and social action.

❖

T HE FIRST HALF OF THE nineteenth century was an immensely creative time for the Protestant churches. Germany led the way, both in the development of Christian Romanticism and of Liberal theology. In England, for the first time since the Reformation, an influential group of Protestants tried to align themselves with Catholicism and Orthodoxy. In Denmark the lone genius Søren Kierkegaard wrote the books that created Christian existentialism. Meanwhile, evangelicalism flourished, and commitment to world missions grew (pp. 182-83), particularly in England, Norway, Protestant Switzerland, and Germany (where a major Lutheran revival reached a peak in the 1850s).

❖ A NEW THEOLOGY ❖

Friedrich Schleiermacher (1768–1834), the founder of Liberal theology, tried to make the Christian faith palatable to those who had been educated and influenced by Enlightenment thinkers. The tradition of theology he founded, which is still very important today, is called "Liberal" because of its emphasis on the individual's right to define the terms of his or her own faith without being dictated to by any authority. This was an idea which it shared with the Romantic movement – Schleiermacher was much influenced by German Romanticism. His theology opened the door for secular Enlightenment thinking to enter the theological sphere.

While he did not believe that the Bible was the inspired Word of God, nor that one could be certain of anything beyond personal experience, he firmly held that each person has a God-consciousness that instills a sense of dependence on some-thing beyond the self, and that since man is totally dependent on God, sin results whenever a person

strives for independence. For Schleiermacher, the Jesus found in the New Testament and exalted in the creeds has been misinterpreted as God, as opposed to a man who achieved pure God-consciousness.

A contemporary of Schleiermacher, the hugely influential German philosopher G.W.F. Hegel (1770–1831) taught that knowledge progresses toward

> ❝ RELIGION IS … CONSCIOUSNESS OF THE DEITY AS HE IS FOUND IN OURSELVES AND IN THE WORLD ❞
>
> FRIEDRICH SCHLEIERMACHER

perfection by a process of synthesis, implying that early Christianity was a primitive form of belief in need of further refinement. His work encouraged the idea that Christian doctrine needs to be changed and perfected over time, a belief that was to be very important in Liberal theology.

Schleiermacher's work was developed by theologians such as Ferdinand Baur (1792–1860) and Albrecht Ritschl (1822–89) into a number of different schools of thought, almost all of which shared certain central tenets. These include a focus on the individual above the church (and with it a rejection of the authority of Scripture or church over the individual) and a focus on reason, leading to the refusal to accept a number of the mysteries of Christianity which baffle reason, such as the Incarnation, the Trinity, and miracles. Along with this skepticism about the

THE FATHER OF LIBERAL THEOLOGY
Schleiermacher could not reconcile orthodox Christianity with the Enlightenment beliefs of his age, so he altered, or reinterpreted, Christian doctrine to remove the contradiction between the two.

AN ART BOTH CHRISTIAN AND ROMANTIC

Caspar-David Friedrich (1774–1840) painted The Wanderer over the Sea of
Clouds *(above) in 1818. Friedrich was one of the artists who managed to use
Romanticism to express a firm Christian faith. He and other Christian Romantic
artists and writers used the beauty of nature as an echo of the divine beauty, and
the sense of transcendence, sublimity, and reverence which nature can give as a
signpost to the ultimate transcendence and sublimity which belong only to God.*

included reforming laws that affected those with mental illnesses, housing conditions for the poor, the exploitation of children in such jobs as mining and chimney sweeping, and the mistreatment of workers.

The struggle for social reform was also supported by the members of the Oxford Movement, begun in 1833 by John Keble and Edward Pusey, which sought to bring back Catholic traditions into the Church of England. This movement had a lasting influence, although 250 of its clerical members left to join the Catholic church between 1845 and 1862, including John Henry Newman, its most brilliant thinker.

❖ LONE GENIUS ❖

Considered the father of Christian existentialism, the Danish philosopher Søren Aabye Kierkegaard (1813–55) was a reclusive and sickly person who suffered from feelings of inadequacy and guilt. He believed that the shared experience of reciting creeds and partaking of the sacraments had little to do with truly experiencing the fullness of Christianity. God is "Wholly Other," wrote Kierkegaard, and to commune

WILLIAM WILBERFORCE
Wilberforce led the influential evangelical pressure group called the Clapham Sect, campaigning for social reforms that brought Christianity to the workplace – ending the slave trade and child labor.

SEARCHING FOR JESUS
The materialist presuppositions of Liberal theology inspired a series of attempts to strip away the miraculous and the supernatural from the New Testament and uncover an ordinary human Jesus behind them. David Friedrich Strauss (1808–74), a pupil of Ferdinand Baur, published his *Life of Jesus* in 1835. It portrayed Christ as an ethical preacher thrust onto the stage of history by the messianic expectations of his time. The French philosopher Joseph Ernest Renan (1823–92) wrote a book of the same title in 1863 which made Jesus an amiable provincial preacher. In 1906, in *The Quest for the Historical Jesus*, Albert Schweitzer surveyed these and other such attempts. His title provided the name by which they are collectively known. He pointed out that searchers for "the historical Jesus" had usually found someone very like themselves.

❖

supernatural went the idea that Jesus had been misunderstood by the early church, and ever since, so that "the Jesus of history" was separate from "the Christ of faith." Liberal theologians also introduced psychology into systematic theology, emphasizing the experience of the divine, and repeatedly attempted to reinterpret Christianity to accommodate secular philosophy. Their ideas swiftly spread beyond Germany and soon led a number of Christians in every church to abandon significant parts of traditional Christian belief for various revised systems.

❖ BRITISH REFORMERS ❖

In England an evangelical Christian, William Wilberforce (1759–1833), led the campaign against the slave trade, which was finally banned in 1807, and against slavery itself, which, from his deathbed, he saw abolished throughout the British Empire in 1833. After his death another evangelical, the Earl of Shaftesbury (*pp. 192-93*), led this campaign of charity, whose efforts

THE CHALLENGE FOR THE CHURCHES
This drawing caricatures life in the slums during the Industrial Revolution (pp. 192–95). The quality of life for the inhabitants was appalling, offering little hope and scant contact with the Christian Church or gospel, although many Christians wished to help.

with him it is essential to make a personal "leap of faith" that has nothing to do with objective truth or religious dogma. For him, there were three spheres of existence: the aesthetic, where a person lives for the moment while suffering from feelings of unfulfilment; the ethical, in which the individual tries to live a moral life but experiences frustration and guilt after discovering his or her inadequacy; and the religious, the highest attainment of mankind, where the individual recognizes that he or she will not be complete without first submitting to the perfect will of God.

" FAITH ... URGES THE BELIEVER ONWARDS SO THAT HE CANNOT SETTLE AT EASE IN THE WORLD "

SØREN KIERKEGAARD

JOHN HENRY NEWMAN

JOHN Henry Newman (1801–90) helped to found the Oxford Movement, then became a Catholic in 1845, and was eventually made a cardinal in 1879. Famous for his scholarship, he wrote extensively and brilliantly, particularly about the nature of and grounds for religious belief, and the development of Christian doctrine. Newman's insights probed the relationship between reason, imagination, emotion, and faith, aware of the limits of human knowledge, yet defending reason brilliantly. His influence has been immense; the Second Vatican Council *(pp. 220-21)* has been called "the Council of Newman" because his ideas greatly influenced it. A man of great piety, he wrote, "True religion is a hidden life in the heart."

" *The sin of what is called an educated age … is, of resting in things seen and forgetting unseen things and our ignorance about them* "

JOHN HENRY NEWMAN

LIFELINE FOR WORKING CHILDREN

In the early nineteenth century many children had to work up to 16 hours a day for a pittance, six days a week, with no chance of an education. To give them the chance of a better life, the Christian Sunday school movement was formed. It ran schools to teach poor children reading, writing, and arithmetic on Sundays. These schools also taught the children from the Bible (the book these children learned to read from) and included a church service. The first such school was started in c. 1780 in England. They were popularized by Robert Raikes (1735–1811), and by 1851 over two million English children attended them. Sunday Schools rapidly spread to continental Europe, Ireland, Scotland, and the United States.

❖

A NEW ERA FOR MISSIONS

The journals of the American pioneer evangelist David Brainerd *(p. 169)* were a great inspiration to early missionaries. Equally influential was a book written by Jonathan Edwards *(p. 168)* in 1747 called *A Humble Attempt to Promote Explicit Agreement and Visible Union of God's People in Extraordinary Prayer for the Revival of Religion and the Advancement of Christ's Kingdom on Earth, Pursuant to Scripture Promises, and Prophecies Concerning the Last Time*. This was reprinted repeatedly for over 50 years.

❖

AT THE CLOSE OF THE EIGHTEENTH century, European interest in foreign missions began to increase rapidly. As the nineteenth century progressed, numbers of missionaries multiplied, and literally dozens of mission societies were formed to support them in North America and in almost every European country. Support for missions was particularly strong in Britain, France, Germany, and Belgium.

❖ LEADERS AND PIONEERS ❖

One of the great leaders and inspirers of Protestant missions was William Carey (1761–1834), born into a poor family in Northamptonshire, England. Although he became a shoemaker at the age of 14, his private study was so intense that he could speak six languages while still a teenager. An eager advocate of mission work, he helped organize the English Baptist Missionary Society and was one of its first missionaries to India. There, Carey's exhaustive efforts and those of his associates included building numerous churches and over 120 schools, translating the Bible into more than 40 languages, creating a medical center, founding

WILLIAM CAREY, PIONEER MISSIONARY
Called "the father of modern [Protestant] missions," the self-taught English Baptist William Carey, tireless in service, inspired countless others to follow him into missionary work.

THE HAYSTACK GROUP

One of the more unusual events in the history of missions occurred in 1806, when a group of students from Williamstown, Massachusetts, gathered under a hay shelter during a rainstorm and prayed for a global missionary movement. They formed the Society of the Brethren in 1808 but were more commonly referred to as "The Haystack Group," reflecting the circumstances of their impromptu meeting. In 1810 they formed the American Board of Commissioners for Foreign Missions – the first society in America created specifically for world-wide missions.

❖

THE EVANGELIST JOHN CAMPBELL NEGOTIATES WITH SOUTH AFRICAN TRIBES IN 1812
The collective missionary effort added greatly to the sum of the world's learning – in many cases creating written forms of languages which previously were only spoken, in order to translate the Bible, thus making it possible to preserve the oral heritage of many remote cultures. In the early 1800s Bible translation was largely a Protestant occupation; it was later shared by Catholics.

THE AGE OF EUROPEAN EXPANSION

THERE were a number of reasons for the remarkable increase in European missionary interest. By the end of the eighteenth century, European navigators had traversed every ocean, plotted the outlines of most of the continents, and colonized much of the new world. Explorers such as the English Captain James Cook, who voyaged across the Southern Ocean, proving that the mythical great southern continent did not in fact exist, had become heroes in Europe. As Europeans read of distant lands, the Christians among them thought of the far-off peoples who had never heard of Jesus Christ.

MEANS TO TRAVEL

At the same time, the spread of European trade and empire meant that ships regularly traveled to every continent. There was a considerable revival in spiritual enthusiasm in Europe (*pp. 177-78, 196*), especially in Britain, France, and Germany, which provided many willing would-be missionaries. While the increase in European power made missionary activities easier, however, it also compromised them. In the eyes of the

COOK'S SHIP, "THE ENDEAVOUR"

colonized, Christianity became inextricably linked to commerce and European civilization. It was often seen as the religion of the oppressor, even though many missionaries resisted the traders and slavers who sought to exploit colonized peoples.

INSPIRATION AND IMITATION

As foreign missions developed, stories of heroic missionary efforts began to filter back to Europe and North America, encouraging Christians to emulate such faith and bravery in the service of the gospel of Christ by going out to "the mission field." One famous example is that of seven English missionaries who starved to death in 1850 in the bitter winter cold of Tierra del Fuego at the southern tip of South America, almost at the end of the world. One of them, Allen Gardiner, left behind a diary in which he had written, before dying, "Poor and weak as we are … we feel and know that God is here. Asleep or awake, I am, beyond the power of expression, happy." Such self-sacrifice fired many young hearts.

---

a seminary, and successfully advocating social reform – including the traditionally harsh treatment of women. Carey inspired countless others to follow him to the mission field, including the gifted linguist Henry Martyn (1781–1812). Before his early death, he completed a translation of the Bible into Urdu that

" EXPECT GREAT THINGS FROM GOD; ATTEMPT GREAT THINGS FOR GOD "

WILLIAM CAREY'S MOTTO

is still the basis for modern translations, and worked extensively on Persian and Arabic translations.

Other English missions, including the London Missionary Society and the Church Missionary Society (founded in 1795 and 1799, respectively), sent out missionaries to Oceania, China, India, and parts of Africa, Asia, and the Middle and Far East. Their most common pattern of action was to establish "mission stations" as Christian centers, consisting of a church and a school, and in later years a hospital.

Catholic missionary efforts received a renewed impetus during the pontificate of Gregory XVI (r. 1831–46). The kings of Spain and Portugal then still claimed the right to control all missionary enterprises outside Europe, but Gregory circumvented them by appointing apostolic vicars (bishops without specific territories, answerable directly to the pope) for missionary lands. He appointed 195 missionary bishops, condemned slavery and the slave trade, pushed for the ordination of more native clergy (with little success), and fought the new governments of Latin America – most of that continent having achieved independence in the early nineteenth century – for the right to appoint its bishops.

BRINGING THE WORD TO THE WORLD

Bible and tract societies proliferated during the 1800s. The American Bible Society was founded in 1816 to provide Bibles for immigrants, Native Americans, and others who could not afford or did not have access to the Scriptures. The British and Foreign Bible Society, formed in 1804, launched a wave of similar Protestant and Catholic organizations around the world, including societies in Scotland, Ireland, Australia, New Zealand, Russia, Germany, Holland, Norway, Sweden, Denmark, and Canada. These groups' collective work continues to the present day, bringing the Scriptures to all people in their native language.

AMERICAN CHRISTIANITY

WHILE SUPPORT AMONG the mainstream denominations for the American Revolution was strong, the immediate impact of the war was detrimental to the church. Not only had church buildings been leveled and burned, but hundreds of ministers and key parishioners had died in battle, leaving a leadership vacuum that would not quickly be filled.

❖ THE SECOND GREAT AWAKENING ❖

This unfortunate situation, coupled with the growing popularity of secular European philosophies such as Empiricism and Rationalism, decimated membership within the churches and left a population that was overwhelmingly indifferent toward religion. Near the end of the eighteenth century, however, a revival began sweeping through the United States. Known as the Second Great Awakening, it started in 1795 with camp meetings (also known as tent meetings) held in the frontier towns of Kentucky and Tennessee by such fervent evangelists as James McGready and Barton W. Stone. Tens of thousands of rural pioneers attended these emotionally charged gatherings, most staying for days to listen to fiery preaching, sing countless hymns, be baptized in local streams and rivers, and zealously pray for the salvation of friends and family.

As the camp meetings grew in popularity and the revival spread westward, the established churches began to regard the movement with suspicion and disdain. The sudden and emotional conversions,

> ❝ *The power of God seemed to shake the whole assembly* ❞
>
> **JAMES MCGREADY, REVIVALIST PREACHER**

together with the active work of self-appointed clergy who had received little if any education, alarmed the conservative hierarchies within the denominations. The result was the rise of new sects that broke from the established churches, among them the Disciples of Christ and the Cumberland Presbyterian church. Together these groups set their own loosely defined congregational governments and successfully propagated the revival fire along the widening frontier.

The next phase of the Second Great Awakening, beginning about 1810, took root in New England. Influenced in large part by Timothy Dwight, president of Yale University and grandson of Jonathan Edwards (*p. 168*), this revival was more conservative and nationalistic in tone than its earlier counterpart. Among its leaders was Lyman Beecher, the great Boston orator and Presbyterian minister who proclaimed that the destiny of the nation lay in moral, spiritual, and educational reform and advancement.

GIANT OF REVIVAL
By combining the emotional appeal of the camp meeting preachers with the cool logic of a theologian, Charles Grandison Finney (1792–1875) set the standard, in both style and intellectual content, for the evangelists who have since followed him.

❖ CHARLES FINNEY ❖

The final phase of the Second Great Awakening started in 1825 and centered on the work and ministry of Charles G. Finney. An attorney who had abandoned his law practice after his conversion to become a Presbyterian evangelist, Finney began preaching in western New York State, employing many of the rhetorical skills he had used in the courtroom.

Although religious leaders at first distrusted Finney's easy success, including Lyman Beecher, who demanded that he stay out of Boston, he was eventually accepted, and preached in a number of churches throughout the Northeast before moving to

THE POWER OF PRAYER
This picture of a prayer tent at a camp meeting in Eastham, Massachusetts, evokes the atmosphere of fervent devotion and expectancy that characterized the Second Great Awakening. Such revivals had tangible results: after Finney's 1830–31 missions in Rochester, New York, the crime rate dropped by two-thirds. One area of New York State was even dubbed the "Burned-over District" because it had felt the flames of revival so many times.

> ## "A REVIVAL IS NOTHING ELSE THAN A NEW BEGINNING OF OBEDIENCE TO GOD"
>
> **CHARLES FINNEY, IN "LECTURES ON RELIGION"**

LASTING RESULTS
The Second Great Awakening led many Christians into anti-slavery campaigns and spawned a vast network of volunteer Christian organizations to improve society, collectively known as "the Benevolent Empire." These included the American Bible Society, the Sunday School Union, and the Temperance Society.

❖

THE THIRD GREAT AWAKENING
The Second Great Awakening waned after 1840, but revival broke out again in 1857 and lasted two years. There were vast prayer meetings across the nation. About 10,000 people met daily to pray in New York alone, and mass conversions were reported in many parts of the U.S. – making national news and inspiring many Americans to volunteer for service in foreign missions. In 1858 this revival leaped the Atlantic: British churches also saw a wave of mass prayer, many conversions, and a new concern for holiness and missions.

❖

New York to become pastor of the Second Free Presbyterian Church and later of the Congregational Broadway Tabernacle. In 1835 he moved to Ohio, where he served as professor of theology at Oberlin College and later as the school's president from 1851 to 1866. He continued to hold revival meetings until his death in 1875: some estimate that his revivals were responsible for over half a million converts, and he vigorously supported such social causes as women's rights and the abolition of slavery.

❖ SLAVERY AND THE CIVIL WAR ❖

Slavery, the sorriest and most shameful chapter in American history, caused the Civil War of 1861–65, the bloodiest war the US has experienced. The spark that ignited it was the election of Abraham Lincoln as president in 1860, at which time there were more than four million slaves in the United States.

Although Lincoln was not an abolitionist, he deplored slavery and opposed its expansion beyond the South. Immediately following his election, the southern states of the U.S., in which slavery was legal, left the Union, forming a would-be independent confederacy. Initially they won a series of victories,

but the tide really began to turn after Confederate General Robert E. Lee's disastrous defeat at Gettysburg in 1863. Two years later, on April 9, 1865, he had to surrender to the commander-in-chief of the Union army, Ulysses S. Grant, at Appomattox. After the war the Thirteenth Amendment to the constitution abolished slavery entirely. Tragically, an assassin's bullet prevented Lincoln from overseeing the effort to reconcile black and white, north and south, in his divided nation.

❖ ABOLITION AND SCHISM ❖

The early part of the nineteenth century saw a massive growth in slavery and an increasingly bitter national debate over its abolition. The churches played a significant role on both sides of the slavery issue before, during, and after the war, and the efforts of Christian abolitionists were instrumental in creating a moral climate where slavery was viewed as an evil that should be stamped out at any cost.

Among the first activists were leading Christians such as Frederick Douglass, a former slave and editor of the abolitionist journal *North Star*, Theodore Dwight Weld, a forceful evangelist who spoke against slavery in pulpits in the north, and James G. Birney, an aboli-

---

SLAVES, CONSTITUTION, PRESIDENT, AND CHURCH

❖

I N the 1700s, most Christians in the southern states acknowledged that slavery was wrong, but called it a necessary evil. In the nineteenth century, however, they began to defend it. Sermons and religious tracts interpreted Scripture to justify the practice, and those clergy who stood up to the majority were generally censured by their denominations. There was a move to abolish slavery at the time the constitution was drawn up, but it foundered on the objections of southern delegates that their economies would collapse if slavery were to be abolished. Greed won the day, and the constitution of the United States registered a slave as three-fifths of a human being for the purpose of calculating electoral college votes, which decide presidential elections.

THE HOUR AND THE MAN

It fell not to the churches' official leaders but to their ordinary members to campaign against slavery, and to a Christian politician to remedy the constitution's fault. Abraham

LINCOLN ON THE EMANCIPATION PROCLAMATION
On January 1, 1863, this presidential proclamation made the abolition of slavery one of the Union's war aims. Lincoln himself was given the nickname "The Great Emancipator."

Lincoln (1809–65) came from a humble background to become the sixteenth president of the United States. A leader of great spiritual depth, whose speeches and actions reflect his religious convictions, it was his hatred of slavery that sparked the Civil War. Growing up on the Indiana frontier, Lincoln attended Hardshell Baptist Church and, as they were among the few books available to him, read *Pilgrim's Progress* and the Bible repeatedly. Typically for his time, Lincoln was not vocal about his beliefs, but he did express his faith in Christ on several occasions and quoted the Bible often in speeches – once writing to a friend, "Take all of this book upon reason that you can, and the balance on faith, and you will live and die a better man." He once said, "We cannot be free men if this is, by our national choice, to be a land of slavery. Those who deny freedom to others, deserve it not for themselves." Unfortunately, he did not live to lead the attempt to end the divisions and inequities slavery left behind it.

A PRAYER MEETING OF FUGITIVE SLAVES
After the Civil War, newly freed slaves formed their own churches, many loosely connected to Baptist or Methodist denominations. Racism within the church left it largely segregated. A number of movements attempted to tackle this, notably the early Pentecostals (p. 201), but even their congregations soon split into black and white, and much segregation remained in the 1890s.

tionist who ran for president. Harriet Beecher Stowe also contributed to the anti-slavery cause with her novel *Uncle Tom's Cabin*, which detailed the injustice and indignities of slavery. It made such an impact that Lincoln, on meeting her, said, "So you're the little woman who wrote the book that made this great war."

In the south, pastors and other Christian leaders, representing all the major denominations, supported slavery. Many denominations split over the issue, including the Baptists, Methodists, and the Presbyterians. After the war, hostilities abated, although the breach between northern and southern churches remained within most denominations. The overall effect of the Civil War on the churches was to initiate a new splintering that continued throughout the nineteenth and early twentieth centuries, leaving the United States the home of literally hundreds of denominations, many very tiny.

MR MOODY'S SUNDAY SCHOOL
D.L. Moody was especially interested in revival ministries among the urban poor. In 1860 he quit his job, began working with the local YMCA (p. 193) as an evangelist, and started a Sunday school ministry that cared for over 1,500 children.

❖ THE GREAT EVANGELIST ❖

Into this fragmented religious landscape strode one of the unlikely giants of American religion. Dwight L. Moody (1837–99), born into poverty in East Northfield, Massachusetts, left home at 17 to become a shoe salesman. His education was extremely limited, and he was not, by contemporary reports, a dramatic speaker. Yet he preached to an estimated 100 million people, helping countless thousands to convert, founded two schools and a Bible college, and inspired the creation of two Christian publishing companies. He was at the heart of an enormously influential evangelical movement that sent out thousands of young missionaries. His work, and that of other evangelists, revived the energy of the American churches once more, making them perhaps the most dynamic force in world Christianity at the end of the nineteenth century.

THE EASTERN CHURCHES

> **"** *When the Spirit of God comes down to a man and overshadows him with the fullness of his presence, then that man's soul overflows with unspeakable joy, for the Holy Spirit fills with joy whatever he touches* **"**
>
> SERAPHIM OF SAROV

THE NINETEENTH CENTURY was a great era for the Orthodox churches in both Russia and eastern Europe. In Russia there was a great flowering of Orthodox spirituality and literature, while the defeat of the Ottoman Empire unshackled the churches of Greece and the Balkans.

❖ NATIONAL CHURCHES ❖

The frontiers of the Ottoman Empire were gradually rolled back during the nineteenth century. As this happened, the newly liberated nations freed their own national churches from the jurisdiction of the patriarch of Constantinople, as had the Russian church after 1453. The patriarchs of Constantinople retained the title of ecumenical patriarch and nominal seniority, but after a bitter struggle they were forced to relinquish power over the churches of eastern Europe. The Church of Greece was established in 1833 and that of Romania in 1864. The Church of Bulgaria and the Church of Serbia, both of which had claimed independence centuries before, reestablished their autonomy in 1871 and 1879, respectively.

Neither the doctrines nor the practices of the churches changed at all, only their relationship with the patriarch of Constantinople. The Orthodox churches remained one in faith, if not in structure. This reorganization reflected the increasing identification of church and nation in the Orthodox world, which sometimes led the churches into supporting crude nationalism and the persecution of minorities.

❖ GLORY AND TYRANNY IN RUSSIA ❖

The link between nation and church was at its strongest in Russia. Christianity affected every part of national life, but the church was controlled by the state in all matters relating to politics. It gave its

A RELIGIOUS PROCESSION IN THE PROVINCE OF KURSK, RUSSIA

The deep faith of the ordinary peasants of Russia constantly amazed Western observers during the nineteenth century. The church's strength lay in the countless villages dotted across the Russian vastness, in which the rhythms of life had been measured for a millennium by the festivals and sacraments of the church. Here the Orthodox church and its doctrines and practices reigned without real challenge, in a way unknown to any church in the West since the Reformation.

FYODOR DOSTOEVSKY

FYODOR Michael Dostoevsky (1821–81) was one of the finest novelists in the rich history of Russian fiction. His works reflect the evils human systems have foisted upon society, and portray redemption from life's miseries through the suffering of Christ. He once prophesied, "The preachers of materialism and atheism who proclaim man's self-sufficiency are preparing indescribable darkness and horror for mankind under the guise of renovation and resurrection." Despite hardships including exile and imprisonment, poverty, epilepsy, and the loss of family members, Dostoevsky wrote such masterpieces as *Crime and Punishment*, *Notes from the Underground*, *The Idiot*, and *The Brothers Karamazov*, novels which underscore the need for God and the inadequacies of human relationships and institutions.

Siberia before being dragged from retirement in a monastery to be made metropolitan (senior archbishop) of Moscow at the age of 70. In this position he attempted to convince every member of the church to evangelize. Russian missionaries founded churches from the inaccessible Altai mountains of Central Asia to China and Japan. Meanwhile, however, the hierarchy of the church remained wedded to the state. Church corruption and wealth alienated idealistic intellectuals such as Tolstoy, many of whom abandoned Christianity.

> " LOVE ALL GOD'S CREATION, THE WHOLE OF IT AND EVERY GRAIN OF SAND IN IT. LOVE EVERY LEAF, EVERY RAY OF GOD'S LIGHT. ... IF YOU LOVE EVERYTHING, YOU WILL PERCEIVE THE DIVINE MYSTERY IN THINGS "

FYODOR DOSTOEVSKY

blessing to the State's every action – even where this involved the severe persecution of Jews, Catholics, and other minorities. The name of Christianity thus became linked to injustice and xenophobia in Russia.

The strength of the Russian church in this period did not come from its center but from its roots, from the deep faith of countless peasants, from the timeless beauty of its liturgy, and from the *startsy* (or "elders") – hermits providing spiritual guidance to others. The most famous of these *startsy*, exercising influence across the whole country, were firstly St. Seraphim of Sarov *(see side column)*, and then a succession of hermits linked to the monastery of Optino: Leonid (1768–1841), Macarius (1788–1860), and Ambrose (1812–91).

People came from all parts of Russia to consult these hermits, who had a direct influence on intellectuals and writers, including Dostoevsky and Tolstoy. Nor were they isolated examples of spiritual zeal: a monastic revival, begun by St. Paissy Velichkovsky (1722–94), a Ukrainian monk trained at Mount Athos *(p. 171)*, saw the number of monasteries in Russia increase from 452 in 1810 to 1,025 in 1914.

❖ MISSIONS TO FARAWAY LANDS ❖

At the same time, the inner renewal of Orthodoxy bore fruit in a new vision for missions, largely inspired by John Veniaminov (1797–1879), who ministered for more than 40 years in the Aleutian islands and eastern

THE LIFE OF A HERMIT

The most famous of the hermits of nineteenth-century Russia was St. Seraphim of Sarov (1759–1833). He entered the monastery of Sarov at 19, and at 35 he retired into seclusion. Having trained himself in such austerities as spending 1,000 consecutive nights in prayer, at the age of 56 he chose to make himself available to counsel all comers. It was not unknown for hundreds to come and see him in a single day; it was said that he healed the sick and answered questions before they were asked.

❖

THE CZAR AND THE CZARINA LEAVING CHURCH
While several of the czars were personally devout, including Nicholas, the last czar (r. 1881–1917; seen above with his wife, Alexandra), none were inspired to reform the social order in their realms. The Russian Orthodox church acquiesced in this situation, and even used its nationalistic power to suppress and persecute other Christian groups, including Baptists and Lutherans.

CHRISTIANITY IN INDUSTRIAL SOCIETY

THE SECOND HALF of the nineteenth century saw the church in the West facing a new world of massive, fast-growing cities, oppressive urban poverty, and constant change *(see feature, opposite)*. Some Christians sought to change the structures of society in order to alleviate the suffering of the poor. Others formed nondenominational societies, such as the Salvation Army, which were free to focus their ministries in the most flexible ways. Still others focused on galvanizing their denominations to spiritual and social ministries for the masses of the new cities.

❖ REORGANIZING THE CHURCHES ❖

The older churches were handicapped by their rigid structures, such as the parish system, which made it hard to respond quickly as urban populations mushroomed. Organizations such as the Church of England's Pastoral Aid Society (formed in 1836) worked to ordain and support more clergy; large parishes were divided, and new churches were formed; and wealthier dioceses helped support those who were unable to financially support their own parishes.

The Methodists and Baptists were able to respond more quickly than the Catholics and the Anglicans to the spiritual needs of the burgeoning middle and lower classes. Informal meeting places, local preachers who shared the same needs and concerns as their congregations, and a willingness on the part of church leaders to join workers in their labor disputes all helped these denominations to spread the gospel message to the masses. To address the needs of the poorest members of society, mission churches, called chapels, were formed by evangelical leaders who recognized that they faced a new mission field. Providing everything from soup kitchens and clothing centers to orphanages and schools, the chapels attempted to meet both the spiritual and the physical needs of those they served.

❖ THE HOME MISSION FIELD ❖

One of the largest and most influential mission chapels was the Metropolitan Tabernacle in London – a church renowned for its pastor, the great orator Charles Haddon Spurgeon. Spurgeon (1834–92), the son of a Congregational minister, joined the Baptist church after his conversion in 1850. While still in his early twenties, he demonstrated such powerful skills as a preacher that the small chapels he spoke in were unable to contain the crowds that came to hear him.

In the 1850s, while a vast new church was being built for him, he preached to audiences of 10,000 people each week at the Surrey Music Hall. His new church, the Metropolitan Tabernacle, was built and opened in 1861. Capable of holding 6,000 individuals, this multifunctional building was Spurgeon's church home until his death. His many accomplishments included the creation of a monthly magazine, *The Sword and the Trowel*; the publication of more than 2,000 sermons, and such books as *Lectures to My Students* and *Commenting and Commentaries*; the establishment of the Stockwell Orphanage, which housed 500 children; the creation of the Colportage Society, which distributed Bibles and tracts; and the formation of a pastor's college. His influence in Britain was roughly parallel to that of the great evangelist D.L. Moody in the United States *(p. 187)*; both have remained evangelical heroes.

C.H. SPURGEON PREACHING AT THE CRYSTAL PALACE IN 1857
Spurgeon regularly preached to vast congregations: this was the largest – 23,654 people gathered for a day of fasting and prayer. He advised preachers, "Some are dead; you must rouse them. Some are troubled; you must comfort them. Some are burdened; you must point them to the burden-bearer."

CHRISTIAN RESPONSES TO TECHNOLOGICAL REVOLUTION

✥

CELEBRATION OF THE NEW INDUSTRIAL WORLD
London's Great Exhibition of 1851 was a showcase for the Industrial Revolution that was then gathering pace. Centered in a "crystal palace" erected in Hyde Park (above), the exhibition lasted nearly five months, with more than six million people attending. It brought together new technology from around the world and introduced Westerners to the arts, sciences, and religions of exotic cultures from China, Russia, India, Australia, and Africa.

THE Industrial Revolution posed many questions for Christians. The advances in technology aroused great hopes among the prosperous classes that humanity was on the way to a new utopia where all problems would be resolved. This confidence was bolstered by the evolutionary tone of the leading philosophies of the period which, under the influence of Hegel *(p. 178)*, the visible advance of invention, and a relatively peaceful century in Europe from 1815 to 1914, tended to assume that human society and knowledge were progressing toward perfection. The Great Exhibition was seen by contemporaries as tangible evidence that the problems of the past would all be solved by technological advances. Much Liberal theology was affected by this optimism and predicted ever more rosy futures for humanity, until World War I shattered all such optimism.

HELL ON EARTH FOR OTHERS
Where a few basked in wealth and luxury, however, millions were slaves to poverty and disease. Factories ran around the clock, and workers, many of them children, toiled in dangerous conditions and were viewed by their employers as little more than expendable, interchangeable parts. In such conditions those who looked at the dark side of society questioned its very foundations. Christians were split between those who felt society was on its way to perfection, those who wished to reform its laws and institutions through established channels, including the evangelical reformers and (eventually) the papacy *(p. 199)*, and those who felt that only revolutionary change could achieve justice. Members of the last group were often greatly influenced by Karl Marx.

KARL MARX AND CHRISTIAN SOCIALISM
Marx was an atheist who famously dismissed religion as "the opium of the people," a false and destructive human invention. A number of Christian theologians, while repudiating Marx's atheism, were attracted to aspects of his philosophy. In England several Christian leaders, including J.F.D. Maurice, Thomas Hughes, and Charles Kingsley, founded the Christian Socialist Movement. In the United States opposition to socialism was nearly unanimous among all clergy. The most famous of the few exceptions was Walter Rauschenbusch, pastor of a Baptist church in the Hell's Kitchen slums in New York, who preached "the Social Gospel": that the kingdom of God is earthly, realized through economic and political justice.

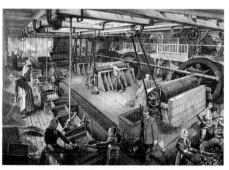

SUFFERING THAT MADE INDUSTRIAL WEALTH
Very many people, including these mine workers in France, labored for a pittance for up to 16 hours a day, six days a week, with few holidays or none.

PRACTICAL CARER

The English nurse Florence Nightingale (1820–1910) transformed her profession. Motivated by her deep Christian faith, she overcame her privileged family's disapproval to train as a nurse, then took a team of 38 nurses to the Crimean War (1854–56). Before her arrival 42 percent of the British wounded died in hospitals; she cut that rate to three percent. Florence became famous as the "Lady of the Lamp" because of the lamp she carried on night rounds.

❖

❖ SOCIAL REFORMERS ❖

A number of towering individuals led the attempts to change the laws of their lands to reflect gospel values more closely. In England, Anthony Ashley Cooper, Earl of Shaftesbury (1801–85), took over from William Wilberforce (*p. 180*) as the leader of the evangelical campaign which sought to bring Christian charity to the outcasts of British society.

His many efforts included reforming laws that affected those with mental illnesses, housing conditions for the poor, the exploitation of children in such dangerous occupations as mining and chimney sweeping, and the mistreatment of workers. He served as president of a number of evangelical missions and charitable organizations, including the British and Foreign Bible Society and the Society for the Prevention of Cruelty to Children. One of his greatest

Christian allies was William Gladstone (1809–98), four times prime minister. Over a period of more than half a century these evangelical campaigns greatly softened those British laws that affected the poor.

In Germany the Catholic Bishop Ketteler (1811–77) led campaigns to improve the lot of the masses, as did his fellow Catholics Lucien Harmel, an industrialist, and Count Albert de Mun in France. Harmel introduced model housing, saving schemes, health and welfare benefits, and workers' councils, which had a role in directing the business. He even took 10,000 of his workers with him on a pilgrimage to Rome in 1889, encouraging Pope Leo XIII to speak out on social issues (*p. 199*). From 1884, Catholic thinkers from France, Germany, Austria, Italy, Belgium, and Switzerland met each year at Fribourg to discuss social issues. Meanwhile, in the United States, Catholics

"SALVATION ARMY PREACHER" BY JEAN FRANCOIS RAFFAELLI

The Salvation Army employed such unique methods as holding services in theaters and factories and attracting crowds with lively band music. By these means, and its compassionate service of the poor, it became a thriving organization, successfully reaching the deprived and unchurched. Salvation Army officers were predominantly working class, and women were accepted as officers, preachers, and evangelists on the same terms as men – both very unusual features by the standards of the day.

PLACES OF DARKNESS AND DESPAIR
The dark side to industrial and technological progress showed itself in the slums (above), where poverty and disease flourished. The poor lived in squalid tenements that bred drunkenness and misery. Crime was rampant. Few outsiders entered such pits of despair.

" WHERE THERE REMAINS ONE DARK SOUL WITHOUT THE LIGHT OF GOD – I'LL FIGHT! "

WILLIAM BOOTH

were beginning to organize unions, as English Methodists had already done. In continental Europe, too, Catholic trade unions began to appear to protect working people against unscrupulous employers.

❖ BEYOND DENOMINATIONALISM ❖

In 1861 William Booth (1829–1912), a Methodist pastor, and his wife, Catherine, began a mission in east London which he named the Salvation Army in 1878. The society was run with military ranks and discipline, and Booth appointed himself its first general. Although his temperament and methods were autocratic, Booth had succeeded in spreading the evangelistic and social work of the Salvation Army *(see caption, left)* to more than 50 countries by 1912.

The Salvation Army was only one of a number of non-denominational organizations that sought to reach out to the workers of the cities. In 1844 George Williams, a London draper, formed the Young Men's Christian Association during a prayer meeting in his lodgings. The unique mission of the YMCA – to evangelize by combining spiritual activities such as prayer meetings and Bible study with temporal interests like athletics and educational opportunities – grew rapidly around the world, particularly in the United States. A sister organization, the Young Women's Christian Association, was organized in 1894.

❖ DEVELOPMENTS IN THEOLOGY ❖

Partly because of the success of such nondenominational societies, the many foreign missions which adopted similar principles, and the vast inter-denominational mission conferences of the turn of the century *(p. 197)*, the Protestant churches gave increasing thought to reconciling the fragmented body of Christ. These meditations were to lead to the full-blown ecumenical movement that became prominent in the twentieth century *(pp. 214-15)*.

Less positively, much energy was taken up with a series of heated debates. Liberal theology *(pp. 178-80)* was opposed by conservative Christians because it often diluted or abandoned basic Christian beliefs; nevertheless it made steady inroads into the Protestant churches. The poverty of urban workers led to major disagreements about the social dimensions of the gospel *(p. 191)*, while an even bigger argument was sparked off by a book, *The Origin of Species*, in 1859. This work, by English biologist Charles Darwin, led many to question the biblical view of Creation. Some posited instead a solely material universe with all spiritual elements banished, others declared the biblical account of Creation a nonhistorical text. The debate was still rumbling on in the 1990s.

REACTIONS TO EVOLUTION
The theories of evolution put forward by Charles Darwin (1809–82) suggested that humans had simply evolved from apes, hence cartoons such as the one above showing Darwin as an ape. The reaction from theologians and clergy was mixed. Some, including the archbishop of Canterbury, Frederick Temple, the influential American clergyman Lyman Abbott, and the Scottish biologist and minister Henry Drummond, preached that evolution was a sign of God's providence and ongoing work in his creation. Most Christian leaders, however, denounced the growing acceptance of evolutionary theories.

❖

"SUNDAY SCHOOL CLASS" BY ISAAC MAYER
Having begun in c. 1780 with the aim of educating boys and girls from impoverished homes (p. 181), Sunday schools soon became (as the State began to provide universal education) a source of religious training for children of all classes and circumstances, which remained their role in the 1990s.

WORLD EVANGELIZATION

AFTER 1850 THE SPREAD of missionary activity was such as to make it a truly global enterprise, affecting almost every country on earth. As well as the fact that, in the churches of the West, missionaries had become heroes of the age, attracting great support, one new development was that women began to be accepted by missionary societies, and by 1900 they far outnumbered men. European power gave its peoples access to every country. Even China, defeated in war, was forced by treaties signed in 1844 and 1860 to allow foreigners in, and after that virtually no country was closed to Westerners.

❖ TO THE HEART OF AFRICA ❖

One of the greatest missionaries of the nineteenth century was David Livingstone. Born into a poor Scottish family in 1813, Livingstone was almost entirely self educated before he entered the University of Glasgow in 1830 to study theology and medicine. Although he originally wanted to be a missionary to China, that country was closed to foreigners because of the Opium War, and so the London Missionary Society sent him to South Africa. Livingstone was a progressive thinker for his era and decried the

LIVINGSTONE'S AFRICA
Livingstone's campaign against the slave trade led him to try to increase commerce to give African leaders an alternative source of income. Unfortunately, this paved the way for exploitation by British merchants and the settlers who followed in their wake.

THE WHITE FATHERS IN AFRICA
Founded by Cardinal Lavigerie in 1868, the missionary priests known as the White Fathers evangelized much of North and West Africa, along with many other new Catholic missionary orders.

treatment of blacks by white settlers. He maintained that African converts should be involved in the propagation of the gospel. He also believed that the tribes and villages in the northern countries of Africa were not being reached by missionaries. In 1852, after sending his wife, Mary, and children home to England, Livingstone began a perilous four-year quest that took him thousands of miles across the continent.

❖ THE SLAVE TRADE ❖

When news of Livingstone's explorations and discoveries reached England he became a hero. His views on the slave trade in central Africa, however, put him at odds with many influential members of British society. After his wife died in 1861, Livingstone focused his energies on African missions, returning in 1865 to Africa, where he spent the last eight years of his life. His disappearance during this time sparked the famous expedition by Henry Morton Stanley of the *New York Herald* who, upon discovering Livingstone in 1871, tried unsuccessfully to persuade him to return home. Livingstone died in 1873, while kneeling at his bedside, praying, and was buried in Westminster Abbey after making one more incredible journey – this time through the efforts of his native assistants, who lovingly carried his body more than 1,500 miles to the African coast, from where it could be shipped home.

❖ MISSION TO CHINA ❖

James Hudson Taylor was born in 1832 into a devoutly religious Methodist home in Barnsley, Yorkshire, and went to Shanghai, China, as a missionary in 1854. Taylor had an early interest in Chinese missions – he felt a direct call from God at the age of 17 – and began learning the Chinese language by studying a copy of Luke's Gospel that had been translated into Mandarin. His early experiences of sharing what little money and provisions he had with the poor and needy built within him a confidence that God would provide a way for him to fulfil his missionary vision without seeking funds from others.

Taylor had great respect and love for the native population and adopted their dress and customs so as to fit better into the local culture. This was common practice for Catholic missionaries (*p. 147*), but a new development in Protestant work. Also, like Livingstone, he had a keen desire to reach beyond the coastal regions. When the ill health that had plagued him since childhood forced him to return to England, he spent the next five years translating the New Testament into the Ningpo Chinese dialect for the British and Foreign Bible Society.

In 1866 he returned to China with his wife, Maria, their children, and a group of fellow missionaries. Together they formed the China Inland Mission. Although he suffered other setbacks, including the death of his wife from cholera, Taylor lived to see more than

800 missionaries from many denominations join his efforts. By the time of his death in 1905 at Changsha, over 500,000 Chinese had accepted Christianity through Protestant missions. Among these was Sun Yat-Sen, soon to be the first president of the Chinese Republic – a remarkable feat in a country with its own ancient religious traditions and where foreigners were generally viewed with suspicion.

❖ CATHOLIC MISSIONARY WORK ❖

The Catholic church was also very active with mission and relief efforts during this period. New missionary orders such as the Marists (founded in 1817), the Society of Missionaries of Our Lady of Africa, the Holy Ghost Fathers (founded in 1848), the Salesians of Don

THE BOXER RISING
By 1900 Chinese resentment of Western imperialism was at boiling point. It led to the formation of secret nationalistic societies known as the Boxers. In 1900 the Boxers suddenly rose up and killed every European they could find, including hundreds of missionaries, as well as between 20,000 and 30,000 Chinese Christians. Shortly afterwards, however, mission work began again, and church life continued stronger than before, with thousands of Western missionaries at work, and steadily growing numbers of Chinese Christians.

❖

SUFFERING FOR THE GOSPEL
The picture above shows persecution in Vietnam in 1838, at a time when Emperor Minh-Mang was trying to stamp out Christianity. In 1836 he had ordered, "Those who refuse to trample the Cross underfoot are to be beaten without mercy, tortured, and put to death."

❝ *There is a living God. He has spoken in the Bible. He means what he says and will do all he has promised* **❞**
JAMES HUDSON TAYLOR

One part of the world in which such missionary zeal appears to have been largely lacking was Latin America. Catholic leaders there were often preoccupied with politics, as a number of anti-clerical governments enforced the separation of church and state and encroached upon the Catholic church's traditional rights. President Rodriguez of Paraguay made himself the head of the church; in 1851 the president of Colombia even tried to appoint parish clergy. At the grass-roots level, popular religious fervor remained very strong, but it mixed Christianity with folk religion as freely as ever.

❖

" The evangelization of the world in our generation "

SLOGAN OF THE WORLD MISSIONARY CONFERENCE OF 1910

MISSIONS IN AFRICA
By 1914, missionaries were active in the greater part of Africa (above). Nearly one in ten Africans professed Christianity, although many of those still practiced folk religion.

Bosco (1859), and the Jesuits were active in many lands. By 1900 there were over 44,000 nuns alone working in mission lands. From France, in particular, which was experiencing a Catholic revival *(pp. 198-99)*, missionary orders multiplied. As the century progressed, large numbers of Catholic missionaries began to come from Belgium, Ireland, Germany, England, the United States, and Canada.

In North Africa, leadership was provided by the great missionary statesman, Cardinal Lavigerie (1825–92), archbishop of Algiers. He himself led by example, and the spread of French power over North Africa was followed by zealous spiritual work.

There, however, as in the' Muslim world, the evangelists had little success, but in sub-Saharan Africa, particularly in Uganda and the Congo, and in parts of Asia, notably China, Sri Lanka, and Korea, they began to build flourishing churches. In Japan, Catholic missionaries rediscovered the remnants of the Japanese church of the 1600s *(p. 151)*, whose survivors had gone underground to avoid terrible persecution: 10,000 of these underground Christians joined the Catholic church. In Vietnam a small Catholic church already existed. It was to be subjected to horrendous persecution by the emperors of Vietnam from 1833 to 1841 and from 1856 to 1862, when up to 300,000 Christians may have died, yet it grew rapidly thereafter.

❖ ON EVERY CONTINENT ❖
In 1800, part or all of the Bible had been translated into some 70 languages. By 1900 the complete Bible had been translated into over 100 languages, and substantial parts of it into another 400. Churches had been founded in almost every country, often with startling and explosive growth. Only a few examples can be given here.

A YOUNG CHINESE CHRISTIAN IN ABOUT 1900
There were 1,430,000 baptized Catholics and over 500,000 Protestants in China by 1912, although for many, the profession of the Christian religion was linked to the desire to benefit from the power and wealth of the foreigners.

In India several popular movements among oppressed social groups had seen the number of Protestant Christians increase tenfold between 1851 and 1890, while in Indonesia, the Batak people of Sumatra had accepted the Christian gospel "en masse," as had the populations of many of the islands of the South Pacific. Despite 26 years of severe persecution on the island of Madagascar between 1835 and 1861, the number of Christians quadrupled. Across Africa, millions had become church members.

Hundreds of thousands of Chinese were converted, while in Korea both Protestant and Catholic missions saw remarkable responses, and thriving, independent-minded Korean churches were founded. Progress was slower in Japan, but the one percent of the people who became Christians exercised great influence on their nation.

The missionaries did far more, however, than bring the gospel to the peoples of the world. Thanks to their efforts, in many countries modern medicine and agriculture, schools, and a written language became available for the first time. The hungry were fed, the status of women was enhanced, children were given shelter in orphanages, and the nefarious practices of slavery and the opium trade were decried and diminished – all through the dedicated efforts of men and women who believed that Christ's command to his original disciples to evangelize all peoples was a personal mandate for all Christians in every era.

"IF CHRIST BECAME MAN AND DIED FOR ME, THEN NO SACRIFICE CAN BE TOO GREAT FOR ME TO MAKE FOR HIM"

C.T. STUDD, ENGLISH MISSIONARY TO CHINA

An unplanned by-product of the missionary explosion was the beginning of the ecumenical movement – the coming together of different denominations, mission and Bible societies, and relief organizations, to work and worship in harmony. The ecumenical conferences they held were often the precursors of a new spirit of cooperation among their parent churches. One of the most significant was the World Missionary Conference held in Edinburgh (Scotland), in 1910. From it sprang the International Missionary Council, then in 1925 the Life and Work movement, which brought Christians from all denominations together to try to apply Christianity to social, economic, and political life.

At the beginning of the twentieth century, one of the most pressing issues facing the new churches was the creation of indigenous leadership. All the missionary organizations made some efforts towards this end, with ordained national Christians working in their ranks, but in each, ultimate leadership still rested with Europeans in 1914. The Catholic church in China was better than many: in 1912, of a total of over 2,200 priests, more than 800 were Chinese. Unfortunately, there were no Chinese bishops as yet. Christianity was half-way to becoming a global religion, but much remained to be achieved.

> **"** *The Church has not yet seriously attempted to bring the living Christ to all living men* **"**
> **AMERICAN METHODIST JOHN R. MOTT IN 1910**

THE IMAGE OF THE MISSIONARY
Missionary work attained a kind of glamour. This Catholic picture of c. 1900 from Munich, Germany, depicts a romanticized vision of baptism and evangelization in far away lands, with the baby Jesus looking on in approval. Missions drew so many enthusiastic Christians to their ranks that some suggest they weakened the leadership of the churches within Europe.

FORTRESS ROME

> **66** *You tell me to have confidence in the emperor [Napoleon III of France], but I repeat to you that I trust only God and that he is my own support* **99**
>
> **POPE PIUS IX**

THE MID-NINETEENTH CENTURY saw the Catholic church experiencing a remarkable revival of spiritual enthusiasm and missionary energy *(pp. 194-97)*. Pope Pius IX reigned as pope from 1846 until 1878, the longest pontificate in history. He was perhaps both the most popular and the most unpopular pope the world had yet seen.

❖ CHARISMATIC CONSERVATIVE ❖

A man of immense charisma and charm, Pius began his reign with a program of reform until the revolutions of 1848 *(p. 177)* convinced him that liberalism and democracy led to revolution and destruction. He henceforth supported the established monarchies against all political liberals and rebels. The newly united Italy absorbed the Papal States in 1861 and Rome itself in 1870, but Pius never accepted the loss of either, even though the government handed over to him the right to appoint all 237 of Italy's bishops (Italy had far more bishops than any other country). Combined with an enormous increase in the numbers of missionary bishops *(p. 183)*, this made papal control of episcopal appointments begin to seem the normal practice.

❖ INFALLIBILITY AND POPULARITY ❖

Pius was never unduly concerned about being diplomatic. In 1864 Europe was shocked by his "Syllabus of Errors," which seemed to condemn much of the modern world. Then in 1870 the First Vatican Council defined papal infallibility.

This appeared to Protestant ears to make the pope into a fount of new revelation, although it only defined two traditional Catholic beliefs: that the Holy Spirit would not allow the church to fall into error on an essential point of faith or morals, and that the Holy Spirit guided the church through the papacy. While unpopular with political liberals and Protestants, Pius

POPE PIUS IX BLESSING THE TROOPS OF THE KING OF NAPLES IN 1849
When he first became pope, Pius IX was idolized as a political liberal who would support the unification of Italy. In fact, he gave his blessing instead to the emperor of Austria and the king of Naples, who crushed the first attempt to reunify Italy. Pius's popularity plummeted, and he decided that liberalism and democracy led to blood-soaked revolution.

was simultaneously adored by ordinary Catholics around the world in a way that would have been impossible for his predecessors. With the advent of newspapers in the 1860s, and cheap books, the image of the pope, once a remote figure, seen by few, became ever less distant. New color printing technology made it possible for all Catholics to have a picture of the pope in their homes, and many did.

There was also a continuing revival in Catholic piety, especially in France. The popes encouraged this, and their authority benefited from it. Literally dozens of new religious orders were founded. By 1877 there were over 30,000 men and nearly 130,000 women living under a religious rule of life in France alone. Pius created over 200 new bishoprics or apostolic vicariates, and usually had the final say in the appointment of bishops. Perhaps more importantly, the growing churches of Africa, Asia, and the Americas tended to look to the pope for their spiritual and ecclesiastical leadership; in European terms, they were Ultramontanes *(see side column)*.

At the same time, the opposition between the church and all forms of progressive politics appeared to be set in stone. This conflict was epitomized at the time of the 1870 revolution in France, when the republican leader Jules Ferry declared that he wanted a humanity "without God and without kings," and the Catholic leader Count Albert de Mun responded, "The church must kill the Revolution or the Revolution will kill the church." It seemed that Pius IX had declared war on the modern world.

✧ CONSERVATIVE RADICAL ✧

Pius's successor, Leo XIII (r. 1878–1903), rapidly made peace. Although he blamed the Protestant Reformation for ushering in the many religious conflicts and anti-Christian philosophies that had plagued the church since, he made an earnest attempt to mend fences with world leaders and to address the ills that afflicted society.

Leo swiftly negotiated an end to Germany's *Kulturkampf,* "culture war," which had been waged against Catholic education and religious orders by Germany's "Iron Chancellor" Bismarck since 1872. He also tried to reconcile French Catholics with the Republic. In

POPULAR PIETY
The Feast of Corpus Christi at Fiesole, Italy, in 1902 (above), shows the public aspect of Catholic piety at its best: a community united in a festival of faith.

this he failed, as in his attempt to end their anti-Semitism, which was displayed at its most virulent in the Dreyfus case (1894–1906), in which a Jewish officer was unjustly accused of treason.

Leo's most important work was an encyclical of 1891, *Rerum Novarum*, which became the basis for modern Catholic social and political teaching. Expressing deep reservations about both capitalism and communism, Leo began to map out a Christian "third way" between the two, saying that the State should protect the rights of the poor workers, outlaw dreadful working conditions, allow trade unions to exist, and ensure that everyone received a living wage sufficient to enable them to save and acquire property of their own. Leo taught that socialism was a false cure, depriving individuals and families of independence.

POPE LEO XIII IN EXALTED COMPANY
This mural, designed to teach young Catholics about the papal claim to have inherited authority from the apostle Peter, shows Pope Leo XIII with Christ and the apostles. Both Leo and Pius IX had a great sense of the dignity of their office. They always ate alone, for example, and brooked no contradiction from anyone.

PAPAL AUTHORITY
Ultramontanism, which literally means, "beyond the mountains," was the most influential Catholic movement of the nineteenth century. Its adherents advocated increased papal authority. Its opponents wished the national churches within the Catholic church to have greater autonomy from the papacy. The Ultramontanes half-triumphed with the definition of papal infallibility, although this definition was limited to rulings on essentials of "faith and morals" only. The pope was not licensed to create new doctrines but, under the guidance of the Holy Spirit, to make explicit that which was already implicit in the original Christian revelation.

✧

FACING THE NEW CENTURY

BRIDGING THE DIVIDE

A prolific writer, respected theologian, and popular minister, P.T. Forsyth (1848–1921) was the most prominent moderating voice between Liberal theology and traditional Protestant conservatism at the turn of the century. As principal of New College, London, and chairman of the Congregational Union of England and Wales, Forsyth had a platform that made him influential on both sides of the Atlantic. Works such as *The Justification of God*, *The Person and Place of Christ*, and *Positive Preaching and the Modern Mind* reflect many aspects of the Liberalism of the day, while holding to the evangelical position on the divine nature and redemptive work of Christ.

❖

AS THE NEW CENTURY DAWNED, optimistic Liberal Theology was at its height in Europe and America. Convinced that Christian orthodoxy was outmoded, Liberal Protestant critics and Catholic Modernists sought to focus religion on man and the here and now, not on God and eternity. The most dramatic religious figure of the time, Dr. Albert Schweitzer (1875–1965), musician, Protestant theologian, and missionary doctor, confidently rewrote Christian doctrine, and was much admired.

❖ ORTHODOXY AT BAY ❖

In both the Catholic and the Protestant churches, defenders of orthodoxy fought back. The Catholic church was led by the traditional beliefs of Pius X (r. 1903–14). Venerated as a saint in his lifetime and canonized in 1954, Pius was a man of deep compassion for the poor (born a peasant, he was called the "peasant pope"), and a much-needed stabilizing force. His greatest challenge came from Catholic Modernists, who reflected the skepticism of Liberal Protestant theology.

Emphasizing process over origins and pragmatism over creeds, they had lost the traditional Christian belief that Christ's message was one of atonement, thinking that it was only to act and serve in the here and now. In 1907 the movement and its tenets were condemned by the pope, and a number of Modernists were excommunicated, including Alfred Firmin Loisy and Edouard Le Roy. Unfortunately, the Modernists were crushed in a particularly harsh manner, which created a climate of fear that also impeded orthodox scholarship. In other matters, Pius was gently pastoral, trying to deepen his flock's spirituality by encouraging frequent communion, allowing children to make their first communion at seven, reforming the liturgy, and improving teaching both in seminaries and in the parishes. He also had the code of canon law revised, inserting a new rule that all bishops must be nominated by the pope. While the pope fought Liberal theology in the Vatican, American Protestants were fighting similar battles in their churches.

"The Fundamentals," a 12-volume series of 83 articles published between 1910 and 1915, gave its name to a movement that tried to defend orthodox Protestant Christianity against all forms of Liberal Theology. Over three million copies were distributed. Of the six main fundamentals defended, all but one were doctrines, such as the divinity of Christ, common to all Christians, whether Catholic, Orthodox, or Protestant. The exception, the literal six-day reading of the Creation story in Genesis, caused huge controversy.

A NEW CHRISTIAN VISION IN BARCELONA
The Spanish architect Antonio Gaudi (1852–1926) expressed his fervent Catholic faith by designing perhaps the most remarkable cathedral ever, a fantasy in stone, begun in 1884 and still unfinished a century later.

❖ PROTESTANT ❖ DENOMINATIONALISM

By 1900, Protestantism had fragmented into many denominations. The largest – the Lutherans, the Anglicans, the Methodists, the Baptists, the Congregationalists, and the Presbyterians – all experienced factional disputes and renewal movements, and were to experience more in the next half-century. The Methodist church in the United States, for example, spawned various denominations, including the Disciples of Christ, the Wesleyan church, and the African Methodist Episcopal church (a group formed in 1816 in protest against racial segregation in the Methodist Episcopal church), and influenced many more.

Two denominations that grew rapidly in the nineteenth century were the Baptists and the Congregationalists. The Congregationalists benefited from their active participation in a number of revivals, while the Baptists' emphasis on missions and evangelism made them one of the largest and most powerful groups of believers in the world. Baptist denominations included, in England, the Baptist Union of Great Britain, formed in 1891. In the United States various new churches arose after disputes over such issues as national backgrounds, organization, and doctrine.

As Protestant denominations proliferated, so in some ways their differences became less important, and members of most denominations would cooperate with those of others on a number of issues, such as social action. "Para-church" non-denominational organizations, such as missionary societies and the Salvation Army, one of the major new phenomena of the nineteenth century, were increasingly numerous and important. Dynamic preachers and spiritual leaders were heroes far beyond their own churches, and spiritual revivals were no respecters of denominational boundaries.

THE BIBLE AND LITERARY FORMS

Form criticism seeks to apply scientific methodology to the history of literary forms. It was largely developed in Germany in the later nineteenth century by the biblical scholars Julius Wellhausen and Johannes Weiss. Wellhausen's theories were brought into disrepute by twentieth-century archaeological discoveries, but subsequent scholars, most famously Martin Dibelius and Rudolf Bultmann, have continued to use the tools of form criticism to build complicated (and unverifiable) theories about the origins and authorship of the Bible.

❖

AMERICAN APOCALYPTIC

Dispensationalism, the areas of salvation, history, and theology concerned with the end of the world, has been largely an American phenomenon. Many evangelicals and Fundamentalists built complicated theories about the "end times" preceding the end of history from the books of Daniel and Revelation. One of the most popular theories was codified in the notes to the best-selling *Scofield Reference Bible*, first published in 1909.

❖

SERVANTS OF A HEAVENLY KING
Whatever the challenges facing the Church, there has never been a time when devotion to Christ has dried up within its ranks. Here, new priests prostrate themselves in token of their desire to serve Christ, at the Cathedral of St. John Lateran, Rome, in 1907.

" GOD HAS BEEN DRIVEN OUT OF PUBLIC LIFE "

POPE PIUS X

❖ MOVE OF THE SPIRIT ❖
In 1906 an abandoned Methodist church at 312 Azusa Street in Los Angeles, California, became the center of a Pentecostal revival that would sweep the United States and the world. Inspired by the efforts of an African-American preacher named William J. Seymour, the revival lasted for three years from 1906 to 1909, and became an international sensation with newly inspired participants spreading the revival's

emphasis on the gifts of the Holy Spirit (p. 224). The Azusa Street Revival exhibited remarkable racial harmony and gender equity for its time. It was the first major stirring of what was to become the Pentecostal movement, one of the major Christian movements of the twentieth century (pp. 224-25), which would bring excitement, joy, and hope to churches in all the denominations. It would be much needed. The nineteenth century had been a tumultuous period; what lay ahead, however, would shake the foundations of the world.

WHERE IT ALL BEGAN
Like many other revivals, the Pentecostal movement began far from the centers of church power with the humble and poor. In this building in Topeka, Kansas, the home of Charles Parham's Bethany Bible College, Parham taught from 1900 that the mark of baptism in the Holy Spirit was speaking in tongues. One of Parham's students was William J. Seymour.

The Global Church

1914–1999

THE TWENTIETH CENTURY saw a transformation in the Christian church. The new churches across the continents of Asia, Africa, and South America became self-governing and grew so rapidly that soon they were more numerous and dynamic than the European churches. In fact, Europe was the one continent where Christian churches declined. Increasingly, important Christian movements, such as the charismatic and evangelical movements, became international in their scope. American Christianity remained vibrant, disunited, and vastly influential, especially in the Protestant churches.

By the end of the twentieth century, despite two world wars, genocide, and revolution, the church has not only survived but has endeavored to reflect changes in society and adapt to the needs of different Christian denominations. At the beginning of the third millennium Christians believe that the global church is still called by Christ to offer his support and assurance to humanity.

A church service in Kongor, southern Sudan

A WORLD AT WAR & A NEW THEOLOGY

THOMAS JEFFERSON'S WORDS, "I like the dreams of the future better than the history of the past," came to epitomize the belief held by many European and North American politicians and intellectuals in the early years of the twentieth century that humanity was about to enter a new age of peace, prosperity, and achievement. The churches, on the other hand, were divided on the future of Christianity. Conservative church leaders were alarmed at what they perceived to be a growing trend toward the secularization of culture. Liberal theologians embraced the notion that this would be the great "Christian century" of universal love and justice.

This ideology of love and justice was to be obliterated by one of the bloodiest wars in history. Called "the Great War" because it was the first war to involve most of the world's great powers, World War I was caused by national – rather than any religious – interests related to economics, military strength, and territorial rights. Christians displayed their patriotism by identifying with these national interests. Church leaders on both sides affirmed the nationalist view that their countries' actions were justified and righteous and offered up prayers for their armies to return victorious. Pacifists' views (*see side column*) were mocked.

✤ THE EFFECTS OF WAR ✤

Of the churches, the Catholic church suffered the greatest hardships. Such staunchly Catholic nations as Belgium, France, and Italy were decimated by the war. The fiercely Catholic Hapsburg-controlled Austro-Hungarian Empire ceased to exist. Germany, which had seen a revival of Catholicism before the war, was besieged by internal and external problems, and religious affairs were banished to the margins of national life.

> "CHRISTIANITY AND PATRIOTISM ARE SYNONYMOUS TERMS"
>
> BILLY SUNDAY, AMERICAN EVANGELIST, 1917

Although his calls for peace went unheeded, Pope Benedict XV took a lead in using church resources to bring relief and aid to those who suffered in the war. Protestant denominations contributed greatly, putting aside sectarian differences to minister to the wounded, comfort those families whose lives had been devastated, and provide basic human needs. The human toll was tremendous, with an estimated 10 million killed and millions more wounded. The war and the revolutions it spawned had a dramatic impact on the political landscape: new governments and monarchies formed; and the Russian Empire became a socialist state, the USSR.

BENEDICT XV: A WORKER FOR PEACE
Giacomo Della Chiesa (r. 1914–22) was elected pope as war broke out. From the start, he protested against the inhumanity of warfare. Although he did much good work, his desire to be impartial led him to call for a compromise peace – something a number of Catholic leaders did not endorse.

MIDNIGHT MASS IN THE WAR ZONE

The optimism of nineteenth-century Liberal theology, and its confidence in human nature, bled to death in the First World War. Soldiers on the Western Front found greater comfort in the timeless promises of a traditional communion (above) than they did in the Liberal theologians' optimistic belief that humanity was inevitably progressing toward peace and perfection.

> **" The gospel falls upon man as God's own mighty Word, questioning him down to the bottom of his being, uprooting him from his securities and satisfactions "**
>
> KARL BARTH

❖ THE RISE OF A NEW THEOLOGY ❖

Following World War I, an attempt, called Neo-orthodoxy, was made to revive the Protestant churches in Europe and the US. This powerful new theological movement was a radical departure from the now-discredited Liberal theology that had dominated much of modern Protestantism until that point (*pp. 200-201*). The movement also came to be known in Europe as "crisis theology," referring to the crisis of human culture epitomized by World War I and the critical state of Christianity in Europe after the war.

Although the movement was not an organized one, and had no precise definitions or boundaries, it was most closely identified with the German Karl Barth (1886–1968), considered one of the most significant twentieth-century theologians. Barth, a pastor in the Swiss Reformed church, denounced Liberal theology and sought to rediscover the fundamental teachings of the Bible and the main principles of the Protestant Reformation. Liberal theology had focused more on humanity than on God; Neo-orthodoxy returned to the God of the Bible. Barth believed that "God is not an abstract category…. he who is called God [in the Bible] is the one God, the single God, the sole God."

Other young theologians soon became involved in Neo-orthodoxy, including Friedrich Gogarten (1887–1967), a Lutheran pastor from Germany, and the Swiss Reformed Church theologian Emil Brunner (1889–1966), who said that the "most important thing we know about God is that we know nothing about him except what he himself makes known."

❖ A MULTI-FACETED MOVEMENT ❖

Although Barth and the other founders of Neo-orthodoxy affirmed the central Christian doctrines, they also accepted the main tenets of Liberal biblical criticism (*pp. 178-80*), which included a skepticism about the historicity of much of the Bible. As a result, they tended to separate their faith from Christian tradition, biblical history, and apologetics.

This left the way open for later Neo-orthodox theologians – such as Paul Tillich (1886–1965), who tried to reconcile secular and Christian beliefs – to embrace radical viewpoints far from traditional Christianity. A group of disenchanted ex-Barthians even taught a "death-of-God" theology in the 1960s. Nevertheless, Neo-orthodoxy was a serious attempt to bring traditional Christian beliefs to life in a contemporary culture.

KARL BARTH

Barth initially labored with a fellow pastor, Eduard Thurneysen, to bring meaning to the spiritual lives of their respective congregations during the war, publishing a book of sermons in 1917 entitled *Seek God and You Shall Live*. Barth's intense study of the Bible, particularly Paul's epistles, resulted in his *Commentary on Romans* in 1919, detailing what Barth later called "the Godness of God."

❖

THE ORTHODOX CHURCH IN COMMUNIST RUSSIA

PROMOTERS OF THE ATHEIST CAUSE

Lenin *(above left)* and Stalin *(above right)* considered religion an enemy that had to be controlled. Yet even after 36 years of persecution under their dictatorship, it became clear that Christianity was still a vital, living faith among the Russian people. As one Russian emigrant wrote: "In every place where the faith has been put to the test, there have been abundant outpourings of grace."

✦

❝ *The [Communist] Party cannot be neutral towards religion. It conducts an anti-religious struggle against all and any prejudices* **❞**

STALIN

T HE APPALLING LIVING conditions that developed in Russia during World War I sparked a revolution that set the stage for much of the social upheaval of Eastern Europe during the twentieth century. The Russian Revolution of 1917 also brought with it a new Communist regime that implemented one of the most anti-Christian programs in history.

✦ RADICAL REVOLUTION ✦

Inspired by the materialist and anti-religious writings of Karl Marx *(p. 191)* and Friedrich Engels, two communist revolutionary factions emerged in Russia by the turn of the century: the moderate Mensheviks; and the Bolsheviks, led by Lenin (1870–1924). He defeated his moderate rivals, ignited a revolution that deposed the czar, and established an absolute dictatorship. Ruthless in its intolerance, the new Communist Party wasted little time in trying to destroy the one institution it feared would divide the hearts and minds of the people: the Russian Orthodox church.

IN THE HOUR OF PERSECUTION
Once Stalin had gained power, the Communists' suppression of Christianity accelerated on a massive scale throughout the 1920s and '30s. Religious icons were torn down (above), *and church closures and persecutions of Christians increased.*

Within a few short years of the Communists coming to power, more than 1,000 bishops and priests had been executed, hundreds of monasteries destroyed, and much of the church's treasure and property seized. St. Tikhon (1866–1925), the leader of the Russian Orthodox church and patriarch of Moscow, condemned the revolution and excommunicated its leaders. Other church leaders led protests and called for a return to monarchical rule. As a result of their actions, the patriarch was imprisoned, and the state completely disestablished the church. The Communists attacked Christianity and other religions with their "anti-God" propaganda, forcing Christians, Jews, and Muslims to endure state oppression. It also became a criminal offense to teach religion to anyone under the age of 18.

❖ A WAR AGAINST RELIGION ❖

Conditions worsened under Lenin's successor, Joseph Stalin (1879–1953). Stalin was a former seminary student who, in a bitter irony, abandoned the orthodox church in favor of Marxist ideology. Under his harsh dictatorship, thousands more clergy were imprisoned and killed. Other denominations were persecuted by the Communists to the point of extinction, including Lutherans, Baptists, and Catholics.

In the 1930s Pope Pius XI condemned Communism and asked for worldwide prayer for Russian Christians. As a response to the pope's criticism, the Soviet government established the Militant Atheists International, a group that headed a vast, anti-religious campaign.

Conditions for Christians improved somewhat during World War II because of the support the church gave the Soviet government in wartime. Parish life briefly became easier in many areas. Stalin permitted a restructuring of the church: monasteries, theological academies, seminaries, and 20,000 churches were reopened, although priests were prevented from undertaking any social work or teaching religion to children.

After World War II the "Iron Curtain" descended as Communist oppression was extended to the churches across Eastern Europe. When Nikita Khrushchev (1894–1971) came to power in Russia in 1959, he launched an attack on the church that saw two-thirds of all churches closed, and priests and nuns arrested and imprisoned on fabricated charges. In 1914 there had been 51,000 clergy; by 1988 there were fewer than 7,000. The now silent suffering of the church was immense, despite the impression of outward calm given by the state authorities. Yet the Orthodox church survived, and after the fall of the Iron Curtain and the end of the USSR in 1991 it flourished again (p. 226).

AN END TO CENSORSHIP AND OPPRESSION

While Communism existed, Orthodox priests were prevented from undertaking charitable work or making social calls, and visits to the sick were limited. Sermons were recorded by the secret police, and study groups, parish libraries, pamphlets, and Bibles were all forbidden. With the new openness of *perestroika* in the 1980s, however, and the advent of religious freedom, the church could at last show its public face again (*above*).

❖

CRITIC OF COMMUNISM

Alexander Solzhenitsyn's novels, which include *The Gulag Archipelago*, led to his arrest and exile from the Soviet Union in 1974. His works express the belief that the root causes of the inhuman excesses of the Soviet regime were atheism and a rejection of traditional Christian values. Solzhenitsyn settled in the US until 1994, when he was allowed to return to Russia.

❖

SEIZE THE DAY
Revolutionary posters with powerful messages, such as this one of c. 1917, were a popular form of Communist propaganda.

THE WEST BETWEEN THE WARS

MOVEMENTS IN LIBERAL THEOLOGY

One of the key movements in twentieth-century Liberalism was the "Chicago School," which led radical American Protestant Liberal Theology from c. 1890–c. 1940. Its members believed that whatever cannot be accounted for through science and experience should be rejected. Within the evangelical tradition, Liberal evangelicals stressed the Bible's revelation of God in Christ as opposed to its infallibility, and the redeeming love of God, the value of scientific enquiry, and a commitment to social justice.

❖

AFTER WORLD WAR I, Communism, Nazism, and the Great Depression cast their shadow over the 1920s and '30s, and Christians became preoccupied with the churches' response to these threats. Church attendance and influence was weak across most of Western Europe, and evangelicals in particular were largely eclipsed. While strict traditionalism reigned in the Catholic church, in Protestant denominations Neo-orthodoxy (p. 205) gradually superseded the formerly dominant Liberal theology.

The Catholic church sought to secure and stabilize its position after the war. As an advocate of peace, Pius XI (r. 1922–39) worked to develop the church's social teaching and initiated a number of concordats with countries such as Poland, Italy, and Germany in an attempt to secure freedom for the church and halt the secularization of Europe. Not all of these negotiations were successful. The agreement with Hitler in 1933 provided the Nazis with more credibility, and ultimately required no more than a series of empty promises on Hitler's part; Nazi persecution toward Christians intensified. Pius was more successful in guiding the Catholic church in the developing world (p. 213), and was the first pope to communicate with Catholics around the world via radio.

❖ THE RISE OF FUNDAMENTALISM ❖

The 1920s in the U.S. saw a clash between two extremes, Liberalism and Fundamentalism. Liberal theology (pp. 178-80) at this time was still popular in the U.S., promoted by such influential advocates as Harry Emerson Fosdick (1878–1969), a Baptist minister and a popular writer, broadcaster, and speaker.

Fundamentalism, a movement that is most closely associated with the U.S., essentially holds to traditional Protestant orthodoxy. It began as an attempt to defend the fundamental doctrines of the Christian faith (p. 200). In mixing morality and patriotism with conservative issues such as the literal interpretation of Scripture, he Fundamentalists began to define their convictions more clearly and, after World War I, began to separate themselves from mainline Christianity.

❖ ADVOCATES OF ❖ FUNDAMENTALISM

By the late 1920s, Fundamentalists were losing ground to the various forms of modernism they opposed, and so either formèd their own groups – such as the Independent Fundamental Churches of America (1930), the General Association of Regular Baptist Churches (1932), and the Presbyterian Church of America (1936) – or came to dominate their own denominations, such as the Southern Baptist Convention. The intellectual leader of the Fundamentalists was Gresham Machen (1881–1937). His defense of biblical conservatism led him to found an influential new evangelical school of theology, Westminster Theological Seminary, in 1929.

A more effective form of opposition to Liberal theology came from two brothers, Reinhold (1892–1971) and Richard (1894–1962) Neibuhr. Both were Neo-orthodox theologians: Richard focused on the relationship between Christ and culture; Reinhold addressed the social and political challenges of the age. Their work meant that Neo-orthodoxy had become the most influential theology in the U.S. by the middle of the century.

THE MONKEY TRIAL
In a made-for-radio media trial in 1925, John Scopes, a school teacher from Tennessee in the U.S., was found guilty of teaching evolution to his class. Although the defense lawyer, Clarence Darrow (above), lost his case, not all American Christians were convinced by the Fundamentalists' separation of "biblical" truth and "scientific" truth.

CHRISTIAN THINKERS IN A SECULAR WORLD

IN 1947, the US news magazine *Time* printed a picture of an English academic on its cover. The headline underneath ran: "Oxford's C.S. Lewis: his heresy, Christianity." Only 50 years earlier such a headline would have been unthinkable. Lewis (1898–1963) had written popular books advocating the Christian faith, and was heavily criticized by his fellow academics for doing so. For the first time in a millennium, Christian thinkers in twentieth-century Europe found themselves existing outside the intellectual establishment.

> " *Joy is the serious business of heaven* "
>
> **C.S. LEWIS**

At a popular level, Lewis was the most influential Christian critic of modern secular beliefs. He felt that the modern world had replaced the Christian vision of life with a shrunken materialistic world view, and argued that society was obsessed with money, sex, and power, and had lost sight of the attraction and excitement of genuine goodness, love, and joy. He was also convinced that materialism had given modern thinking a diminished view of the value of the individual person: "There are no ordinary people. You have never talked to a mere mortal." Lewis believed that the way forward was to return to Christian orthodoxy – not just at a dry, rational level, but by engaging all of the imagination and soul.

> " *Christianity has died many times and risen again* "
>
> **G.K. CHESTERTON**

Many of Lewis's arguments were foreshadowed by the English journalist and writer G.K. Chesterton (1874–1936), an agnostic who converted to Catholicism. Chesterton felt that the modern world had lost the balanced framework of values provided by Christian orthodoxy. He satirized the idealization of skepticism, doubt, and tolerance so characteristic of the twentieth century. In his book *The Everlasting Man*, Chesterton argued that the revolutionary and liberating doctrine of Christianity was unique among the philosophies, myths, and religions of humanity.

T.S. ELIOT
Eliot expressed concern over the state of modern culture from a Christian perspective.

C.S. LEWIS
Lewis, a convert from agnosticism to Anglican Christianity, was one of the greatest communicators of his faith.

FRANÇOIS MAURIAC
Mauriac was a French Catholic writer who examined the ugliness of much of modern life in the light of eternity.

The Nobel prize-winning Anglo-American poet and critic T.S. Eliot (1888–1963) was a prestigious literary figure when he embraced the Anglo-Catholic faith. After his conversion his poetry focused on the place "between the concrete and the sky," where the spiritual and material worlds met "at the still point of the turning world."

Other important Christian literary figures included the French poet and playwright Paul Claudel (1868–1955) and the French novelist François Mauriac (1885–1970), who was preoccupied with the idea of the religious soul in conflict with sin, grace, and salvation. He depicted characters in drab, bourgeois settings, deprived of love.

> " *There is no ground anywhere that is not holy ground* "
>
> **FREDERICK BUECHNER, AMERICAN AUTHOR**

A number of French and Italian thinkers, concerned more with the social and political realms, laid the basis of a political movement, Christian Democracy (*p. 217*). Among their leaders was the philosopher Jacques Maritain (1882–1973) and his wife Raisa, who led a group that sought to help people live a fuller, "truly human life," and to suggest how society might be changed to enable this to happen. Among the most influential Christian thinkers in the U.S. were Francis Schaeffer (*p. 222*) and Carl F. Henry (b. 1913), who lectured and wrote on such issues as ethics, apologetics, and theology. Henry also co-founded the Fuller Theological Seminary, and in 1956 he became the first editor of the American evangelical magazine, *Christianity Today*.

> " *Christian monotheism laid its axe at the root of all my superstitions* "
>
> **TOYOHIKO KAGAWA**

The horizons of European and North American Christian thought were enlarged by the contributions of Christian thinkers from developing countries, such as Toyohiko Kagawa (*p. 216*) and Kanzo Uchimura (*p. 212*) of Japan. Collectively, these intellectuals brought an authentically Christian vision of life to the modern world, challenging the marginalization of religion and the dominance of secular views.

WORLD WAR II & AFTER

T HE WORLD HAD BARELY caught its collective breath after World War I when it was thrust into another global conflict, with even more devastating effects. The churches responded to this new crisis in ways both noble and ignoble.

❖ PRELUDE TO WAR ❖

The peace treaties signed after World War I had left a sense of brewing hostility in Germany. This gave Adolf Hitler the chance to rise to power in Germany in 1933. He nullified all existing treaties and imposed the political ideology of Nazism, which insisted on the absolute unity of the people with its leader. At first, German Christians remained passive despite Hitler's clear belief in racism, his hostility to Christianity, and, above all, his anti-Semitism. Most Christians chose not to defy Hitler; some conservative Catholics actively endorsed the regime, fearing that Communism was the only alternative. Those Catholic movements that did oppose the Nazis were soon dissolved or severely repressed. A Protestant movement of openly Nazi "German Christians" was established, whose philosophy was summed up by one of its leaders, Pastor Leutheuser: "Christ has come to us through Adolf Hitler … we have only one task, [to] be German, not Christian." A small group of Protestant Germans including Karl Barth (*p. 205*) and Dietrich Bonhoeffer (*below*), and led by Martin Niemoller, united as the "Confessing Church" in 1934 to oppose the German Christians and reject any belief in Nazism. Several members of this small church subsequently suffered and died at the hands of the Nazis for their beliefs.

❖ THE FIGHT AGAINST EVIL ❖

Hitler's invasion of Poland in 1939 initiated World War II and gave rise to the greatest evil committed by the Nazis, the Jewish Holocaust. Hitler claimed that even Christianity was a Jewish plot, declaring, "The heaviest blow that ever struck humanity was the coming of Christianity … [an] invention of the Jew."

THE COST OF DISCIPLESHIP

✠

M ORE Christians have been persecuted in the last 100 years than in any previous century. In developing nations, Third World countries, Communist regimes, military dictatorships, and Islamic kingdoms countless Protestant, Catholic, and Orthodox Christians have been imprisoned, tortured, and killed.

THE BLOOD OF MARTYRS

The scale of Christian martyrdoms has been massive – more than one million Armenian Christians were killed or exiled by the Turks in World War I, for instance.

Many German Christians were persecuted by the Nazis. One such martyr was Dietrich Bonhoeffer (1906–45), a German theologian and Lutheran minister who joined with other anti-Nazi German evangelical Christians to fight for religious freedom and who became a member of the Confessing Church. Although he was banned from Berlin and forbidden to teach, he continued to write. During World War II,

DIETRICH BONHOEFFER
Bonhoeffer once said of Christian suffering, "A Christian is someone who shares the sufferings of God in the world."

Bonhoeffer supported Christian attempts at resistance by becoming a member of the Kreisau Circle (*see right*). Although his involvement with the conspirators against Hitler was marginal, he was nevertheless executed by the Nazis.

In China Nee To-Sheng (1903–72), otherwise known as Watchman Nee, spent the last 20 years of his life imprisoned on false charges because of his active ministry establishing house churches and writing Christian literature. John and Betty Stam, a young American missionary couple serving the China Inland Mission, were beheaded by Chinese Communist guerrillas in 1934. Their courage inspired many people to become missionaries.

After many attempts on his life, the archbishop of El Salvador, Oscar Romero (*p. 212*), was finally murdered in 1980. Despite the dangers he faced, Romero often declared that, if God saw fit, he would be willing to "offer [his] blood" for the sake of his country.

The sheer scope of World War II, involving nearly 60 nations, had an impact on nearly every facet of civilization. Catholic and Protestant churches alike were devastated by the destructive force of war. In most of the Nazi-occupied territories – including France, Holland, Poland, and Denmark – churches and monasteries were closed down, and nuns and priests were imprisoned, tortured, and killed. Christians were strictly controlled and sometimes persecuted, particularly those of Jewish origin.

PRAYING FOR GOD'S PEACE IN THE MIDST OF CONFLICT
Using the hood of an army jeep as an altar, a Catholic priest celebrates Mass with American soldiers on a Normandy beach at the inauguration of an American cemetery, D-Day, 1944.

Although many German Protestant and Catholic leaders supported Hitler, Christian opposition survived in the form of movements such as the Kreisau Circle. Noted German laymen and clergy, both Catholic and Protestant, belonged to this movement, which plotted the failed attempt to assassinate Hitler in 1944. For this, most of the Kreisau Circle were tried and executed.

❖ AFTER THE WAR ❖

At the close of the war, the German churches also lay shattered. Many German cities were reduced to rubble, and the country was divided into occupied zones. Ecumenical efforts were made to raise aid, rebuild some of the churches, and provide relief programs to war-torn areas. In the face of such suffering, many turned to Christianity; yet after the war, growing affluence bred a materialistic spirit that perhaps damaged Christianity in Europe far more than the war. As a result, Europe became the most secular, least religious continent.

SAVING GOD'S PEOPLE

A devout member of the Dutch Reformed church, Corrie ten Boom (1892–1983) became active in the Dutch underground movement during World War II. She and her family hid their Jewish neighbors from the Nazis in their Amsterdam home, but in 1944 they were betrayed by an informant and sent to concentration camps in Holland and Germany. Released due to a clerical error one week before all women her age were executed at Ravensbruck, Corrie returned to Amsterdam, began to speak out about her life and faith, and wrote a best selling book, *The Hiding Place.*

❖

> ## "WE SHALL NOT REST UNTIL WE HAVE ROOTED OUT CHRISTIANITY"

HEINRICH HIMMLER, NAZI LEADER

While small groups of defiant Christians showed their outrage, the leaders of Christendom, particularly Pope Pius XII, were criticized for remaining passive about the Holocaust – something Pius XII's supporters argued was a mask for discreet diplomacy.

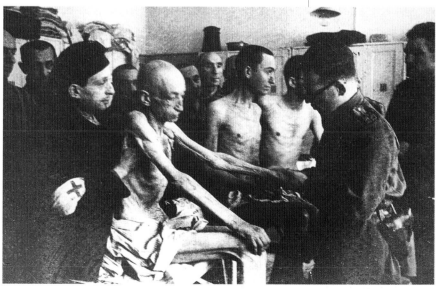

THE PAPAL REACTION TO NAZI ATROCITIES
Pope Pius XII faced a dilemma when he heard of the atrocities against Jews (above) and Catholics. Should he denounce Nazi crimes or remain silent? Pius XII had no sympathy for the Nazis, but he believed that public announcements would increase the scale of Nazi outrages. Thus he mobilized Vatican funds for rescue measures and organized refuge shelters for Jews – even sheltering 5,000 Jews in the Vatican at different times during the war – but resisted public denunciations until 1942.

DEVELOPING CHURCHES

> **" A new missionary era has dawned … a growing partnership of churches will develop and the universal character of Christ's Church will be more clearly exhibited "**
>
> THE LAUSANNE COVENANT, INTERNATIONAL CONGRESS ON WORLD EVANGELISM, 1974

THE DEVELOPING NATIONS of Africa, Asia, and Latin America became fertile ground for the spread of the Christian gospel during the twentieth century. However, during this same period some of the worst persecutions of Christian believers took place across these continents.

❖ TRANSFER OF LEADERSHIP ❖

The limit of Western missionary vision at the turn of the twentieth century was summed up by the Anglican Bishop Tucker of Uganda at the turn of the century. He desired a church in which foreign missionaries and an indigenous ordained ministry would work together on an equal basis and in the same spirit. Yet by 1914 the Catholic church, for example, still only had four non-European bishops, all of whom were in India. While there were indigenous priests and other ministers in many developing nations, ultimate leadership remained with foreign missionaries.

In 1919 Benedict XV (r. 1914–22) issued the historic decree *Maximum Illud* demanding greater recruitment and promotion of clergy from developing nations. His mission-minded successor, Pius XI (r. 1922–39),

THE ZION CHRISTIAN CHURCH ANNUAL PILGRIMAGE IN SOUTH AFRICA
The main traditional Christian denominations – Catholic, Protestant, and Orthodox – have been supplemented by an enormous variety of Christian movements and independent churches in the twentieth century. This is particularly true in Africa, where charismatic and Pentecostal worship (pp. 224-25) by such churches as the Zionist Christian church is very popular.

enforced this decree, overriding the prejudices of many European clergy. The first six Chinese Catholic bishops were ordained in 1926. By 1939, there were 40 indigenous bishops and over 7,000 priests in developing countries, although when training was conducted in local languages, the availability of any Christian literature was often woefully inadequate. In 1945 the pope created the first non-European cardinals.

Parallel progress was made in Protestant churches, which attempted their own programs to increase indigenous leadership. In the Anglican community the first Chinese bishop was appointed in 1918, the first two Japanese bishops in 1922, soon followed by bishops in West Africa and Asia. Developing Anglican churches were allowed more independence and responsibility, with their own constitutions, canons, rules, and revised prayer books. Thus by the 1960s the situation had been transformed: the bishops and other leaders of the churches in the developing nations were overwhelmingly indigenous. Christianity was no longer a primarily European faith but rather a world church.

✦ WORLD GROWTH ✦

Africa experienced some of the most rapid growth in Christianity in the twentieth century. In 1900 just under one in ten of the estimated 108 million population identified itself as Christian. By 1990 almost half of a population that exceeded 800 million belonged to Christian churches. This growth arose partly through the efforts of foreign and indigenous Christian missionaries, doctors, and social workers to provide relief and stability to those regions hit by natural disasters, political chaos, persecution, and warfare.

> ❝ LET US BE CONVERTED SO THAT CHRIST MAY LOOK UPON OUR FAITH AND HAVE MERCY ON US ❞
>
> **OSCAR ROMERO**

Christianity also grew across Asia, with countries such as South Korea experiencing a Christian revival from the 1940s onward (*p. 227*). Chinese Christians, numbering about five million in 1949 when the Communists came to power, increased dramatically despite severe persecution. In 1952 foreign missionaries were expelled, and Christian repression reached a peak during the

PALM SUNDAY MASS IN SALVACION, PHILIPPINES
The Philippines has embraced Christianity in an astonishing way: approximately 90 percent of the highly populated country is Christian. It is the only country in Asia with a Catholic majority, and thus the Catholic church exerts a strong political influence.

Cultural Revolution (1966–76). Yet Christianity continued to grow via unofficial house churches, local revival movements, and itinerant preachers, and by 1992 Chinese Christians numbered about 80 million.

Catholics and Protestant denominations initiated many positive efforts in Latin America; after the 1960s, Protestant churches saw a dramatic increase in their membership. Making Latin America a priority, Pope John Paul II made numerous visits there. The center of gravity of world Christianity now seems increasingly to lie with the churches of these developing nations.

DESMOND TUTU

BORN in South Africa in 1931, Tutu became an international symbol of Christian courage and dignity. He was ordained an Anglican priest in 1961 and became one of the most visible opponents of the racist system of apartheid. Best known as the archbishop of Cape Town, he was also assistant director of the Theological Education Fund of the World Council of Churches, general secretary of the South African Council of Churches, and president of the All Africa Conference of Churches. In 1984 he received the Nobel peace prize.

> ❝ *It would be illusory, useless, and even blasphemous to claim to bear witness to God without engaging in practical activity to repair creation* ❞
>
> **JON SOBRINO**
> **LATIN AMERICAN**
> **LIBERATION**
> **THEOLOGIAN**

ECUMENICAL MOVEMENTS

MISSIONARY ACTIVITY at the turn of the twentieth century was marked by strong yet declining competition between churches. Each wanted to win converts to its own particular style of Christianity. A number of the Reformed churches began to question the futility of this division and considered the possibility of uniting. This was the beginning of the ecumenical movement. "Ecumenical" means universal, and the movement's hope was that one day all churches would be united as one.

❖ A WORLD COUNCIL OF CHURCHES ❖

In 1910 an assembly of 1,200 delegates from 160 Protestant missionary societies, called the World Missionary Conference, met in Scotland (*pp. 196-97*). Further ecumenical initiatives followed, notably the formation of the Life and Work movement (*p. 197*) and, in 1927, the Faith and Order movement, which considered questions of church unity.

These two movements came together in 1948 at Amsterdam to form an umbrella group called the World Council of Churches, in order to foster links between Christian communities and to seek ways of overcoming prejudice. World War II had ended in Europe only three years previously, and this provided a boost for the movement toward unity. The council agreed not to make binding decisions on its members but rather encourage joint activity on such issues as poverty, justice, racism, doctrine, liturgy, charity, and politics. The group's aim was to offer Christian reflections on several issues facing humanity.

❖ CATHOLIC ❖ ECUMENICISM

The Catholic church at first had little time for ecumenicism. It adopted the position that since all Reformed churches had broken away from Catholicism, it was up to them to return. Between 1923 and 1927, a group of

Catholics and Anglicans met to discuss the possibility of reunion at Malines in Belgium. Pope Pius XI was not interested in the meetings and eventually advised the Catholic party to withdraw. In 1928 he published an encyclical letter, *Mortalium Animos*, which poured cold water on Protestant efforts to foster reconciliation and asked the difficult question, "Can we endure that the truth of God be made the subject of negotiations?" The pope also condemned Protestant movements as "false Christianity." It would be another 36 years before

> ## " RELIGION MEANS BINDING TOGETHER "
>
> GONVILLE FFRENCH-BEYTAGH,
> ANGLICAN DEAN OF JOHANNESBURG

Catholic bishops meeting at the Second Vatican Council would extend an olive branch to Protestants – whom they welcomed as "separated brethren." In 1959 Pope John XXIII encouraged Protestants and Catholics to meet and pray for unity, with mixed success – although in Liverpool, England, for instance, the Anglican and Catholic bishops established a close working relationship.

❖ SIGNS OF HARMONY? ❖

The Orthodox churches also engaged in ecumenical dialogue with the Catholic and Reformed churches, enriching discussions with their venerable traditions. In 1961 the Russian Orthodox church joined the World Council of Churches, and most of the other Orthodox churches then followed.

Progress toward unity was slow, however, partly because the smallest difficulties were often the most difficult to resolve. Pope John Paul II attempted to advance the unity of the Christian communities while trying not to raise false hopes. "The divisions of centuries," he realistically observed, "cannot be wiped out in a couple of decades."

BROTHER ROGER

A GROUP of Catholic and Reformed brothers who set up a community to follow a monastic way of life in the French town of Taizé, outside Lyons, have attracted thousands of visitors each year. The community was the idea of Brother Roger (b. 1915), a Swiss monk who settled in France shortly after World War II. His aim was that the community should be a welcoming center of ecumenism where the brothers would explain the Scriptures and pray together, accompanied by simple chants in which all could join. Pope John XXIII referred to Taizé as "a little springtime in the church."

MODERN CHRISTIAN ART AND ARCHITECTURE

FROM the nineteenth century onward, churches no longer dominated the skyline, nor were necessarily built in the main street of a town; from being the most visible focus of a community, many Christian churches became one of several religious meeting places in an area. Twentieth-century Christian artists and architects working in this climate tried to interpret their faith as a shared international religious experience, creating a unique form of Christian art and architecture out of the fusion of streamlined, refined function and technology and a style that was universal in its simplicity.

A CHANGE IN FORM AND FUNCTION

By the second half of the twentieth century, churches were designed to emphasize God's immediacy and intimate presence rather than accentuate the traditional

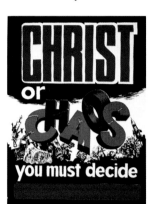

POSTER WITH A MESSAGE
This church poster, with its strong graphics and message of "Christ or chaos, you must decide," is one means of drawing Christian believers into the building.

"mysterious" nature of God. Minimal decoration, and unusual planes and split-levels became a feature of many church building designs. After the Second Vatican Council *(pp. 220-21)*, Catholic church designs also became simpler in their style and content.

Some Fundamentalist movements enthusiastically embraced twentieth-century advances in building techniques: several American televangelists, for instance, created the most magnificent edifices where the emphasis is on the preacher of the Word of God. These churches were purposely built using light, modern materials such as plate glass, with great attention paid to comfortable seating and perfect acoustics. Thus, as in the past, the aim of Christian artists and architects is that their work may speak to new generations of Christians through the developing artistic and technical challenges available to them.

MODERN CHURCH, MAURITANIA
Many contemporary church designs have attempted to match the timeless truths of Christianity with local or national cultures. The striking appearance of this uniquely shaped church, which conveys a sense of calm and simplicity, was achieved through the use of modern materials such as concrete and advances in technology.

SOCIAL ISSUES & ACTIVISM

FROM ADDRESSING THE ILLS of poverty, abuse, and alcoholism to protesting against injustice, greed, and warfare, the Christian church has stood as a moral beacon throughout the twentieth century. The social activism of the church has long been an integral part of its role in society, with missionary groups and charitable organizations taking a leading role in countering everything from the plight of workers and their families during the Industrial Revolution to igniting the abolition movement against slavery in the United States. Activism has also uniquely brought together liberal and conservative Christians who have united under the common banner of Christ's mandate to "love one's neighbor as one's self,"

WORSHIP IN THE WAR ZONE
In many war-torn parts of the world today Christian churches such as this one have become more than just places of worship, often providing material aid as well as spiritual comfort.

> **❝** When a poor person dies I want them to die in the arms of somebody who loves them. I want them to be able to look for the last time into the eyes of somebody who cares for them **❞**
>
> **MOTHER TERESA OF CALCUTTA**

MOTHER TERESA (1910–97)

BORN to Albanian parents in the Macedonian Republic, Teresa (born Agnes Gonxha Bojaxhiu) entered the order of Our Lady of Loreto in Ireland. After taking her vows she was sent to India, where she taught for many years. One day, while on a train, she felt that she heard the voice of God urging her to devote her life to the poor. Accordingly, she began caring for the sick, the poor, and the abandoned in the gutters of Calcutta. Mother Teresa soon had many volunteers helping her and founded a new order, the Missionaries of Charity, which grew rapidly.

although their perspectives and goals are typically divided by a wide theological gulf. Many, like Dietrich Bonhoeffer and Oscar Romero (*pp. 210-12*), have paid the ultimate sacrifice for their convictions.

As the world's population mushrooms, poverty and deprivation increase and Christians everywhere have found themselves challenged to respond to urgent needs. Whether it be a small local charity group or an international Christian organization, there is a need for practical help. Almost all such charities help where there is dire poverty, regardless of creed or denomination. Several churches have nationally organized charities, which coordinate overseas projects. Some of these simply provide emergency funds, but more often the emphasis is on education in order to aid further development.

❖ POLITICAL DEVELOPMENTS ❖

In the political realm, there has been a vast difference between the U.S. and Europe in the post-war years. Both American and British Christians have been affiliated to all the major political parties in their countries and might be placed at any point on the left-right political spectrum. In continental Europe, on the other hand, Christian thinkers and leaders from a number of countries not only created a new political philosophy, Christian Democracy, based on Christian values, but put it into practice. Building on the pioneering thought of such influential philosophers as Jacques Maritain (p. 209), Alcide de Gasperi, Jean Monnet, Conrad Adenauer, and others created political parties which gave new hope to war-torn Europe. Their primary concern was to structure society to protect individuals, families, and communities from war, and from both the abuse of State power and the inequality and insecurity of uncontrolled capitalism.

The Christian Democrats and their allies became the strongest political force in post-war Italy, Germany, Belgium, the Netherlands, and even for a time in France and Spain, rebuilding nations shattered by war and working together to form the European Union. Critics have suggested that over time their initial Christian focus became blurred, and they have tended to become conservative center-right parties. In Italy, some of the leaders of the Christian Democrats became embroiled in corruption in the 1970s and 1980s, bringing the party into disrepute. Nevertheless, even if it appears to be past its heyday, Christian Democracy has changed Europe in remarkable ways and has shown how in the social and political sphere the church can still influence modern society for good.

❖ THE STRUGGLE FOR SOCIAL JUSTICE ❖

In 1968, at the Conference of Latin American Bishops in Medellín in Colombia, the bishops declared the poor to be their primary concern and proclaimed their aim to awaken the consciences of the world to the needs of the marginalized. These words inspired many Christians to fight against such oppression, sometimes with violent consequences. They took comfort in reading the story of the Jewish people who met so many tribulations before they finally entered the Promised Land. A number of theologians taught "Liberation Theology," which encouraged the poor to act for themselves. Sometimes, it was argued, violence was needed to restore peace.

In 1971, the Peruvian priest, Gustavo Gutiérrez, published his influential theological work A Theology of Liberation. All over Latin America communities were formed where the poor were helped to overcome their problems by mutual sharing. Conservative opponents argued that the Christian activists were more inspired by Marxism than by the gospel. A particular worry was the clergy's involvement in political reform. Liberation Theology seemed under threat from conservative forces within the Catholic church, and, for a time, it seemed

DOROTHY DAY

The American Dorothy Day (1897–1980) was a former Socialist and convert to Catholicism. As a journalist, she founded The Catholic Worker in the 1930s, a monthly newspaper that made workers and employers aware of their rights and obligations. Drawing heavily on papal encyclicals on social justice, the paper did much to alleviate distress among the working-class people of America. Day was passionately interested in issues of justice, and also campaigned against nuclear arms. Her great friend Peter Maurin, who helped her found Homes of Hospitality for the homeless and the elderly, is regarded by some as a modern-day St. Francis.

❖

A PAPAL MESSAGE TO WORLD LEADERS

In 1967 Pope Paul VI published an encyclical in which he urged the developed nations to help the poor. Rather than use the current political terms East and West, he spoke of the divide between the rich North and the poor South. Paul challenged the status quo, which allowed structures of oppression to remain in place. Governments, he believed, must be willing to cancel debts that risk crippling poor, developing countries.

❖

HELPING THE HOMELESS IN ATLANTA, GEORGIA
As social problems have grown, unemployment has risen, and the number of homeless living on the streets has escalated. The church has found itself one of the most important institutions that reach out to the needy in a way that government bodies often do not.

MARTIN LUTHER KING AND THE AMERICAN CIVIL RIGHTS MOVEMENT

❖

MARTIN Luther King, Jr. (1929–68) was the most prominent and revered civil rights leader during the struggle for racial equality in America. King's message that the evils of racism are destructive to both the victim and the victimizer incorporated themes of pacifism, idealism, and justice from sources ranging from the Bible to Gandhi. A minister's son, King studied at Morehouse College, Crozer Theological Seminary, and Boston University. He became pastor of the Drexler Avenue Baptist Church in 1954 in Montgomery, Alabama. His career as a social reformer began with the Montgomery bus boycott of 1955 and 1956, which successfully ended the city's racial segregation on its public transport systems through a Supreme Court order. Blacks had been expected to give up their seats to whites.

In 1957 King helped to form the Southern Christian Leadership Conference (SCLC), which soon became a prominent force in

MARTIN LUTHER KING LEADING A FREEDOM MARCH TO SELMA, ALABAMA, IN 1965
King's message to white opposition included the words, "Do to us what you will, and we shall continue to love you …"

civil rights issues. He was a key figure in the march on Washington in 1963, when he gave his well-known "I have a dream" speech, and was instrumental in organizing and leading a famous march from Selma, Alabama, to Montgomery in 1965, along with less publicized demonstrations in such states as Mississippi and Florida. His efforts gave a vital impetus to the campaign which brought about legislation guaranteeing blacks civil rights in the US. In 1964 he was awarded the Nobel peace prize.

Later in the 1960s, King's opposition to the conflict in Vietnam and his endorsement of China's admission to the United Nations brought him into conflict with the US government. And, as other civil rights leaders called for more confrontational measures to bring about reform, King increasingly received criticism for his steadfast adherence to pacifism and non-violence. In 1968 King's life was tragically cut short by an assassin's bullet in Memphis, Tennessee.

that Pope John Paul II was against it on the grounds that it was too overtly political. On returning from a pastoral visit to Brazil, however, he made his feelings clear by stating that while he did not agree with the Marxist element of Liberation Theology, he firmly supported its fundamental aim of helping the poor.

Pope John Paul II also visited his native Poland on several occasions, each time addressing a particular doctrinal issue. His trips in the 1980s were criticized by Communist officials for inciting workers to strike, ultimately bringing about the fall of the Communist party in Poland. The Catholic church has countered that the Pope's desire for his people is justice and mercy, and he only asks that they respond to their governments in accordance with the example of Christ.

❖ THE FIGHT FOR PEACE ❖

Pacifist movements and the outcry against governmental injustice were not often organized or widely supported by the church during the first half of the century. Since the 1960s, however, religious groups have played key roles in political causes – from demonstrating against warfare to toppling Communist regimes. The World Council of Churches (WCC) drafted a statement in 1966 that, while rejecting

ANTI-VIETNAM WAR PROTESTERS OUTSIDE THE WHITE HOUSE, WASHINGTON, D.C.
Since terrible images of war have been brought into our homes through the development of photographic journalism and television coverage, Christians everywhere have become deeply involved in issues of peace and justice all over the world.

absolute nonviolence, stated that recourse to military action should only be a last resort. The WCC has consistently denounced the proliferation of nuclear arms and attacks on civilians and nonmilitary targets. Vatican II established the Roman Catholic position by praising those who renounced violence.

In the United States, the most prominent figure in the civil rights movement was Martin Luther King, Jr. (*see box*). The efforts of King and countless others produced the Civil Rights Acts of 1964 and 1968 and also inspired similar movements in the US and around the world to aid oppressed or disenfranchised groups.

Prison ministries have also flourished during the twentieth century. One organization, Chuck Colson's Prison Fellowship, has spread from the United States to form chapters around the world to bring redemption to those whose actions have placed them outside society and inside prison walls. Other issues related to the sanctity of life have led to the creation of ministries which provide a voice for those who cannot otherwise speak for themselves. These issues include the death penalty – many Christians have campaigned for its abolition – and the rights of the unborn – Catholics and U.S. evangelicals have joined hands on behalf of unborn children in the "Pro-Life Movement."

Saharan Africa too, from South Africa and Zambia to Congo, Uganda, and Kenya, church leaders led their people in campaigns for justice in the name of Christ in the face of corrupt governments.

> ## " ... WITHOUT JUSTICE AND RIGHT THE KINGDOM OF GOD WILL NOT BE ESTABLISHED "
>
> LEONARDO BOFF, BRAZILIAN LIBERATION THEOLOGIAN

JESUITS AMONG THE HOMELESS IN MANILA
Jesuits in the Philippine capital, Manila, have devoted themselves to working among the poor and homeless. Many have been inspired by the work of Cardinal Sin, who wrote these devout words as the foreword to a book on prayer: "We must be set apart from the world before we can be united into the Church. But while these truths are somewhat difficult to understand, we must continue pondering them in our hearts with the simplicity of children. Simple prayer is the key to progressive simplicity, which in turn leads us to a deeper faith."

❖

❖ EXAMPLES OF COURAGE ❖

Two dramatic examples of individual Christians whose moral authority alone helped change the course of politics in their countries are Jaime Cardinal Sin and Laszlo Tokes. Cardinal Sin, the archbishop of Manila, stood up to the corrupt regimes of both Ferdinand Marcos and Fidel Ramos in the Philippines in the 1980s. Along with fellow Catholic Corazon Aquino, Cardinal Sin was the nation's most vocal and courageous advocate for social reform and democracy.

Laszlo Tokes was a Protestant pastor in Timisoara, Romania, who, during the brutal reign of the Communist dictator Ceauçescu, had bravely sought to preach the gospel and bring revival to his land. In 1989, when it became known that the secret police were about to arrest Tokes, thousands rallied to his support – an uprising many credit with launching the revolution in Romania.

Examples such as these inspired other Christians in Eastern Europe and East Asia to fight oppressive regimes. In sub-

POPE JOHN PAUL II AND LECH WALESA IN POLAND, 1979
The first pope to go behind the Iron Curtain, John Paul II empowered a people in their struggle for freedom on his 1979 visit to Poland. One-third of the population turned out to see him. Lech Walesa, a devout electrician from the shipyards, led trade union campaigns against an unjust government with the full support of the pope. The Catholic church had become the country's only national symbol after centuries of foreign occupation and oppression.

CHANGING CATHOLICISM

WHEN THE ELDERLY Pope John XXIII (r. 1958–63) decided to convene a general council of the Catholic church, many thought he was mad. The pope explained that he wanted to call the bishops of the church together in order to "bring the church up to date," explaining that "the substance of the ancient deposit of faith" was unchangeable, but "the way in which it is presented" was another matter. Pope John had a passionate desire to improve relations not only with other Christian churches but with religions in general. He urged the participants in the Council "to seek what unites, rather than what divides." After lengthy preparations, which included wide consultation, nearly 3,000 of the world's Catholic bishops, along with lay Catholics and observers from other churches, met at the Vatican in October, 1962, for a council that was to last three years.

❖ THE SECOND VATICAN COUNCIL ❖

The Council declared that "the hopes and joys, the fears and worries of the world are equally those of the church," which wanted to preach the message of Jesus Christ to all humanity. The bishops, advised by senior theologians, reoriented the Catholic church's teaching on issues as diverse as the church's self-image, the Jewish people, modern technology, education, war and peace, atheism, and the education of the clergy. In particular, they took a new, positive attitude to other Christian churches and to the secular world, calling the Catholic church to work "with all men towards the establishment of a world that is more human." They decreed that the liturgy should normally be celebrated in vernacular languages and no longer in Latin, with more lay involve-ment. The Council also reversed the Catholic church's traditional opposition to religious liberty for non-Catholics, declaring that everyone has a right to such freedom.

All was not smooth sailing, however. Pope John did not live to conclude the Council, as in June 1963 he died after a painful struggle with cancer. He left behind him bishops who were deeply divided on several issues. John's successor was the archbishop of Milan, Cardinal Montini. The new pope, who took the name Paul VI (r. 1963–78), was left with the task of reconciling the

> **"** One of the gravest errors of our times is the dichotomy between the faith which many profess and the practice of their daily lives **"**
>
> THE SECOND VATICAN COUNCIL'S PASTORAL CONSTITUTION ON THE CHURCH IN THE MODERN WORLD

"GOOD" POPE JOHN XXIII

BORN Angelo Guiseppe Roncalli (1881–1963), John grew up in a poor community in Italy. Apart from short periods as a bishop's secretary and military chaplain, most of his life was spent as a Vatican diplomat. During World War II he played an important part in the rescuing of Jews in Hungary, Bulgaria, and Turkey. Elected pope in 1958, John went on to become the century's most beloved pope, winning the hearts of people around the world. He was deeply concerned for the poor, and his encyclicals urged nations to defend human rights. John also did much to erase anti-Semitism in the Catholic Church.

VATICAN II
The opening session of the Second Vatican Council was held on October 11, 1962. Fewer than half of the 2,800 bishops who attended came from Europe. This was truly a world Catholic council.

various groups – a difficult goal to achieve since some wanted radical change, others no change at all. The changes to the liturgy proved the most vexing to many conservative Catholics.

❖ THE PROCESS OF ADJUSTMENT ❖

The Second Vatican Council is seen as a watershed in the history of the Catholic church. After several years of uncertainty and division, the decisions of the Council have gradually been accepted and absorbed by the majority of Catholics. Vatican II did much to heal divisions between the Catholic church and other Christian communities, and both Paul VI and John Paul II (pope from 1978) continued to encourage discussion and co-operation with other Christian denominations.

In 1967 Pope Paul continued John's attempts to confront the problems of the modern world by publishing an encyclical letter on human rights and the needs of the poor (*p. 217*). A year later, he published another encyclical on the value of human life (*Humanae Vitae*). Despite its positive teachings on life and marriage, it condemned all artificial forms of contraception, which sparked a crisis within the church. Many Catholics refused to accept this teaching.

John Paul II has continued to affirm traditional Christian beliefs, even where modern Europe rejects them, denouncing modern materialism as a "culture of death" and calling for a "new culture" based on a reverence for life and a "preferential" love for the poor.

EAST AND WEST EMBRACE

Apart from improving Christian-Jewish relations, Vatican II also sought to heal the 900-year rift with the Greek Orthodox Church. On December 7, 1965, Pope Paul VI and Patriarch Athenagoras issued a joint declaration regretting the terrible events that led to the final schism in 1054 (*p. 103*). "A day will come," said Pope Paul, "when all Christians will drink from the same chalice." The photograph above shows the two religious leaders embracing in St. Peter's Basilica, Rome, in 1967.

❖

MODERNIZING WORSHIP

Following Vatican II, the Catholic church made several changes in its forms of worship. The most notable was that the Mass, which for centuries had been celebrated in Latin, could now be held in the local language of the people. This decision was resented by a small but vocal group of conservatives. Some Protestant churches also made major changes, bringing the liturgy more in line with modern times. The church of England, for instance, abandoned the old-fashioned language of the *King James Version* of the Bible and the *Book of Common Prayer*. Only the Orthodox church steadfastly refused to change and conserves its form of worship as it has done for almost 1,500 years.

❖

THE NEW EVANGELICALS

CULTURAL CRITIC

In 1948 the American Francis Schaeffer (1912–84) and his wife, Edith, founded a Christian community called L'Abri, meaning "shelter," in the Swiss Alps to help young people who were struggling with various issues and difficulties. The center became an internationally recognized gathering place and intellectual haven. Schaeffer also produced wide-ranging, biblically based critiques on the moral and spiritual decline of society.

❖

THE TERM "evangelical" derives from the Greek *euangelion*, meaning "joyful news" or "gospel." The worldwide evangelical movement in the twentieth century has been marked by an emphasis on the study of the Bible, on missionary outreach, and on the basic doctrines of the faith. These include an orthodox position on the person and work of Jesus Christ, a recognition of the Scriptures as the inspired word of God, the sovereignty of God over his creation, and the imminent return of Christ. Evangelicals are present in every denomination, although many prefer their own independent churches. All feel called to deliver to the world the gospel message of salvation by Christ through their words and actions.

❖ THE EVANGELICAL SPIRIT ❖

While the evangelical movement is often considered a modern Protestant phenomenon dating from the revivals of the 1700s (*pp. 164-69*), it is in many ways an integral part of the mainstream churches' ongoing traditions. From the Apostolic Fathers, the early monastics, and medieval reformers through to key figures of the Reformation, the Great Awakening, and nineteenth-century revivalists and missionaries, the evangelical spirit has often been the impetus behind the focus and direction of all the churches.

In the early twentieth century, however, the evangelical movement suffered a period of relative impotence. Faced with challenges from secular science, humanistic

BILLY GRAHAM: MISSIONARY TO THE WORLD

Although he has occasionally been criticized for his friendships with world leaders, for his crusades behind the Iron Curtain, and for his combination of theological conservatism and ecumenical spirit, Billy Graham has preached the Christian message of salvation to more people in more countries than anyone else in history, and he has become the symbol of evangelicalism. In 1989–90 alone, his "Mission World" campaigns were linked simultaneously by satellite to 59 countries.

CRUSADERS IN THE SPIRIT

✢

No one individual has defined the evangelical movement in the US and around the world more than Billy Graham. In 1949 he conducted a series of revival "tent" meetings, which gained extensive media coverage. Graham quickly became one of the best-known religious figures in the world; by 1997, he had spoken to an estimated 210 million people in 185 countries, and to hundreds of millions more via television and radio.

BILLY GRAHAM CRUSADE
This enormous gathering in the Metrodome Stadium, Minneapolis, is typical of the modern-day tent meetings Graham and others have evolved for preaching their message of evangelism.

THE WORLDWIDE MOVEMENT
Around the world, some of the greatest evangelical leaders of the twentieth century include the Ugandan archbishop Festo Kivengere and the South African evangelist Michael Cassidy, who together founded the organization African Enterprise – one of the first authentically African missionary enterprises – "to evangelize the cities of Africa by word and deed." In England John Stott became instrumental in maintaining evangelical dialogue with and influence on other traditions. He wrote and traveled much, encouraging evangelicals to engage with the intellectual issues that concerned their secular peers, and developed training for young evangelical leaders from every continent. The evangelist Luis Palau preached to hundreds of thousands of primarily Hispanic audiences around the world, and holds the distinction of attracting the largest crowd to hear an evangelical minister in Latin America: estimates of more than 500,000 people were reported during a crusade in Guatemala City in 1982.

In 1974 and 1989 evangelicals from every continent attended conferences on world evangelism. The first, at Lausanne in Switzerland, was attended by participants from about 150 nations; the second, in Manila, by 4,297 people from 166 countries – reflecting the impact of evangelicalism across the world in the latter part of the century.

philosophies, and two world wars, the churches were regularly confronted with cynicism, skepticism, and open hostility. In addition, Liberal theology and Fundamentalism (p. 208) polarized the Protestant churches and marginalized the more moderate convictions of evangelical believers.

> ## ❝ IT SEEMED TO ME, PERHAPS BECAUSE OF THE WAR, THAT THE WHOLE WORLD WAS RIPE FOR THE GOSPEL ❞
>
> **BILLY GRAHAM**

After World War II, the modern evangelical movement started to take shape, especially in Germany, Britain, and, most importantly, the US. The American evangelicals asserted their prominence by forming organizations such as the National Association of Evangelicals, the National Evangelical Anglican Congress, and the Conference of Confessing Fellowships, as well as two key institutions: the Fuller Theological Seminary, which was founded in 1947; and the magazine *Christianity Today*, established in 1956. Perhaps most importantly, American evangelist Billy Graham began his international ministry in 1949 (*see above*). In 1947 Harold J. Ockenga, the first president of Gordon-Conwell Theological Seminary, coined the term "new evangelicalism" to express the movement's youthful leadership and vitality.

Theologians distanced evangelicalism from Fundamentalism by asserting that the latter's separatist mentality, narrow worldview, and anti-intellectual spirit contrasted sharply with biblical Christianity. By initiating ecumenical dialogue with other Christians while remaining true to their own convictions, evangelicals have continued to flourish, and have established innumerable evangelistic efforts, mission and relief organizations, schools and seminaries, and publishing companies throughout the globe.

> ❝ *Christianity is unique, it is peerless* ❞
>
> **JOHN STOTT**

PREACHING THE MESSAGE
The growth of evangelical churches in Latin America in the twentieth century has been remarkable. Possibly as much as one third of the population of this continent is now affiliated with an evangelical or charismatic group.

THE PENTECOSTAL MOVEMENT

THE MODERN PENTECOSTAL movement began in the 1900s *(p. 201)*, although its roots can be traced back to nineteenth-century holiness movements that existed in the United States and Britain and which stressed sanctification, or sinless living. It was in the 1900s that a small group of Christians in the United States embraced and practiced the "gifts of the Holy Spirit," including speaking in tongues, prophecy, and healing. Originally spurned by mainstream churches, they formed their own denominations, which grew very rapidly. After 1960, however, many mainstream Christians began to experience these "gifts of the Spirit." These latter Pentecostals, also known as charismatics, are now part of every denomination.

POWERFUL MODERN MEDIUM
American Pentecostal preachers and evangelists such as Oral Roberts and his son, Richard (above), have been remarkably successful in spreading their message via television.

" *For that is spirituality – thinking, feeling, and acting in love, and singing praises to our Divine Lover. When we sing love-songs we may use the classic scores of Scripture or tradition, or we may make our own improvizations. But the themes are universal* **"**

FRANCES YOUNG, BRITISH THEOLOGIAN

Perhaps the most distinctive feature of the charismatic movement is its emphasis on enthusiastic, often spontaneous worship. The practice of the gifts of the Holy Spirit – considered controversial by some – is very important, and charismatic Christians are also renowned for their strict morality, keen evangelism, and whole-hearted discipleship.

✦ HISTORY AND SPREAD ✦

The most significant growth for the movement began after World War II. In 1947 the first World Pentecostal Conference was held in Zurich, Switzerland, and the following year the Pentecostal Fellowship of North America was organized in Des Moines, Iowa. Also in 1948, the Full Gospel Business Men organization was initiated, which helped to bring the movement respectability in the U.S.

Clergy from such mainline denominations as the Lutheran, Baptist, Presbyterian, Anglican, and Mennonite churches, and even the Catholic church, introduced charismatic elements into their ministries in the 1960s and '70s. Today, Pentecostals represent the

ON A MISSION TO LONDON
Charismatic and other churches are so strong in the developing nations that traditions have reversed: missionaries are now being sent to work and evangelize in Europe (p. 213). Here, a Nigerian nun brings the Eucharist to an English woman at home.

largest distinctive group in the Protestant community. In addition, over 50 million Catholics identify themselves as charismatic believers.

Worldwide, the charismatic movement has been especially successful in Latin America, where approximately 75–80 percent of evangelicals are Pentecostal. Pentecostal churches are also flourishing in Africa, Asia, Europe, and the former Soviet bloc. The various denominations across the world include the Pentecostal Holiness church, the Church of God in Christ, the Assemblies of God, the International Church of the Foursquare Gospel, the Open Bible Standard church, the Elim, Ichthus, and Apostolic churches, and the Church of God. Many charismatic congregations prefer to be independent, however, affiliated to no denomination.

✦ A GROWING MOVEMENT ✦

Perhaps the clearest indication of the extent of the movement came in 1991, when charismatic leaders gathered in Brighton, England, to discuss world evangelization. The conference, attended by the archbishop of Canterbury, George Carey, reported that there were by then about 390 million charismatics in over 100 nations around the world. By 1998 the movement had an estimated 500 million adherents, making it the fastest-growing part of the global church.

POPULAR FEELING
Pentecostal and charismatic groups have grown rapidly both within and outside the mainstream churches, reversing, in some cases, the decline of certain denominations.

PENTECOSTAL MUSIC
Music became particularly important to Pentecostal, charismatic, and evangelical Christians in the latter half of the twentieth century. A diversity of forms developed, including Southern Gospel music, which grew out of rural Appalachian communities; Black Gospel music, which often combines the gospel message with themes of social justice; and contemporary Christian music, which arose out of the Jesus Movement in California in the 1960s. A thriving industry has arisen to support the enthusiasm Pentecostals, as well as other evangelical Christians, have for expressing their faith through musical praise.

✦

WORLD CHRISTIANITY

AS THE CHURCH moves into the twenty-first century, it faces many challenges and opportunities. On the one hand, the global church is growing at a rapid pace, broadcasting and publishing organizations are bringing the gospel message to all but the remotest and most restricted regions, many spiritual and social ministries are thriving, and the Bible has been translated into virtually every tongue, with millions of copies distributed freely and widely. More than one-third of the world's population identify themselves as Christian. Yet problems abound. Many Christians are "biblically illiterate," and have only a vague understanding of the roots of the Christian faith and its essential doctrines. This is true even in the U.S., which is flooded with churches. Membership of various cult groups grows yearly, and in the developing nations human survival often takes precedence over eternal considerations. Ministry organizations must tend to basic local needs such as food and shelter before they can share their faith. The pattern of growth in the global church is also very uneven. In Africa, parts of Latin America, and much of Asia the global church is growing at an astonishing rate. Yet in Europe, long the bastion of the Christian faith, the story is quite different.

✦ EUROPE, RUSSIA, AND THE US ✦

Attendance at church services in Europe has fallen so dramatically in the second half of the twentieth century that it is now estimated that only one tenth of the population are regular churchgoers. Even many church members now feel free to disagree with their churches' teachings. Millions of Catholics, for instance, refuse to accept the church's teaching on a range of sexual and moral ethics including homosexuality, remarriage after divorce, artificial birth control, and euthanasia.

By contrast, Christianity in Russia has experienced a tremendous rebirth since the lifting of the Iron Curtain. This new openness was signaled when the Soviet government passed a law granting freedom of religion in 1990, fulfilling a pledge made by its leader, Mikhail Gorbachev (b. 1931), to Pope John Paul II the year before. Millions of Bibles and Bible tracts have been handed out with the approval of the Russian government, and Christian ministries have been permitted to work and evangelize in Russia. Surprisingly, one opponent of this new freedom has been the Orthodox church. Fearful that religious tolerance will bring unchecked proselytizing by cult groups, it has opposed the sanctioning of any religious bodies other than its own.

The vast majority of Americans still claim Christianity as their faith, and up to 40 per cent of the population can be found in church at weekends. There are challenges, though: many American Catholics state that they disagree with the pope on such issues as birth control, and the death penalty; religion is regularly legislated out of public life, particularly in schools where those who enforce the separation of church and state are ever vigilant to ensure that faith is not conveyed in a meaningful way. Despite this, the

PUBLIC DISPLAY OF FAITH
For 70 years the Communist party sought to eliminate religion in Russia, and all open expressions of faith were forbidden. Now that the country has religious freedom, Christianity flourishes.

BIBLE STUDY IN THE PHILIPPINES
Although many Catholics in the Philippines are still practicing Animists and Spiritists, charismatic revival and the study of Scripture have touched hundreds of thousands of believers. There has also been a dramatic growth in Protestant churches since 1974.

> **" Our old history ends with the Cross; our new history begins with the Resurrection "**
>
> WATCHMAN NEE
> (NEE TO-SHENG),
> CHINESE EVANGELIST

church in America remains vital and active and continues to be the single greatest source of funding for evangelization and ministry around the globe. Specialist ministry organizations in the U.S. – including the Promise Keepers (*p. 229*), Athletes in Action, Youth with a Mission, Focus on the Family, and numerous others – meet spiritual needs and are key to initiating spiritual renewal among their target groups.

Numerous local congregations are also active in winning converts and creating programs that bring revival to their churches – typically with well-organized campaigns that feature specific themes. Perhaps most important of all, the strong cultural familiarity Americans have with religion makes it relatively easy for Christians to share their faith with their friends, families, and neighbors.

✧ CHRISTIANITY IN ASIA ✧

Over one-half of the world's population lives in Asia, and Christianity is thriving there despite much opposition. The traditional Catholicism of the Philippines has had new life breathed into it (*see caption, above*), as has that of Vietnam. The Evangelical Church of Vietnam, too, flourishes: it has grown to about half a million members. The shipment of Bibles into the country was resumed in 1992, and ministry efforts among Vietnamese refugees in Cambodia and Hong Kong have shown

significant results. Both Catholics and Protestants have seen remarkable church growth in South Korea. Here, the success of sustained evangelistic efforts, including crusades by Billy Graham, has produced a nation that, by some estimates, is over 40 percent Christian. South Korea is now home to the largest church congregation in the world: Paul Cho's Full Gospel Central Church in Seoul has over 600,000 members.

Christianity continues to grow in many other Asian countries with about 6 percent of the population in Taiwan and 20 percent in Singapore Christian. Despite

CHRISTIAN PROCESSION, PAPUA NEW GUINEA
Ethnically and linguistically, Papua New Guinea is one of the world's most complex cultures. Despite this, the gospel message has been spread throughout the country over the past 120 years, and the country is now permeated by Christian values. As much as 96 percent of the population today claims to be Christian.

CHRISTIANITY AND TECHNOLOGICAL ADVANCES

With the advent of media, radio, television, and now the Internet, Christian groups can reach out to more people than ever. In the United States, in particular, Christian radio stations and television channels have grown enormously. By 1985, US spending on religious television program had reached $600 million per year. Religious figures have found that these media allowed them to reach far wider audiences than would otherwise have been possible. In the 1950s, for example, an American Catholic bishop, Fulton Sheen (1895–1979), had a weekly audience of over 30 million for his "Life is Worth Living" television show.

✧

violence against Christians on the Indian subcontinent by adherents of other religions, and restrictions imposed by the government on missionaries, there are over 6,500 indigenous missionaries active in India, Tibet, Bangladesh, Nepal, Myanmar, Pakistan, Bhutan, and Thailand, and nearly 5 percent of India's population profess Christian faith.

The fast-growing churches of China face continuing opposition. The government has created its own churches, which it can easily influence and even control. These organizations are the Catholic Patriotic Association and the Three Self Patriotic movement for Protestants. The independent Protestant and Catholic churches, meanwhile, continue to suffer harassment. The Japanese churches face no such opposition, but have seen little growth – fewer than 4 percent of Japanese identify themselves as Christian.

In the Muslim world there have been mass conversions in parts of Indonesia – today more than one in eight Indonesians are Christian – and mission agencies report slow but steady progress in countries such as Iran, Afghanistan, Iraq, Pakistan, and Kuwait. For now only in Saudi Arabia, more than in any other nation, has Christianity been utterly stifled.

❖ THE AFRICAN CONTINENT ❖

Reports from mission organizations suggest that by the year 2000 the African continent south of the Sahara will be largely Christianized; by 1990, approximately half of all Africans were church members. From predominantly Muslim nations such as Mali, to war-torn nations such as Ethiopia, the gospel is being preached, and thousands are converting to Christianity. Some nations, in fact, are overwhelmingly Christian, including the Central African Republic, Kenya, Congo, and Lesotho, which are all more than 70 percent Christian. Even in Sudan, which has suffered from years of genocide and other horrors, the church is growing rapidly as people seek spiritual comfort in the face of human depravity. Tragically, persecution and oppression can still exist within Christian communities: in 1994 nominally Christian Hutu and Tutsi tribes in Burundi and Rwanda slaughtered each other, with clerics and nuns accused of actively taking part in these massacres.

❖ LATIN AMERICA ❖

Latin America has traditionally been identified with the Catholic church, with over 90 per cent of the population professing to be Catholic. However, the proportion of nominal Catholics has sunk to perhaps two-thirds as evangelical Protestantism has successfully taken root in the last two decades. Pentecostals account for approximately 75 percent of evangelical Christians in Latin America. Increasingly, they belong to indigenous Pentecostal churches, such as the Universal Church of the Kingdom of God, established by Edir Macedo de Bezarra in 1977. Other well-known Protestant leaders include Argentine evangelist Luis Palau, whose ministry has extended beyond the Americas to include missions in Europe.

❖ THE FUTURE ❖

All the churches acknowledge their many faults. In 1996 Pope John Paul II admitted that some of the Catholic church's institutions needed to be adapted in the future. Even the papacy, he said, needed to be re-examined to see how it could be more a focus of unity, and less a stumbling block for other Christians. The dogmas and doctrines of the Catholic church can never be changed, but the manner of presenting them can always be improved. The Protestant and Orthodox churches, too, are taking stock, admitting past errors and looking for spiritual renewal.

At the same time, the traditional view of the churches' mission remains the same as ever: to preach the gospel until Christ's return, and not to be distracted by the difficulties and challenges that arise along the way. Jesus gave his disciples the essence of their task: "When the Holy Spirit has come upon you, you will receive power and will tell people about me everywhere … to the ends of the earth" (Acts 1:8).

THE GLOBAL SHIFT IN CHRISTIANITY

Statistics show that in 1990 almost two-thirds of the world's Christians came from the developing nations. As recently as 1960, about 60 percent of professed Christians lived in the West (Europe, North America, and Australasia); in 1999, that percentage had halved.

❖

CHINESE CHRISTIANS AT PRAYER
Since the demonstrations and massacre in Tiananmen Square in 1989, the Chinese government has taken a hard line toward the church and arrested hundreds of pastors and other religious leaders, especially those who belong to unofficial house churches. Many Christians have been imprisoned and tortured for their faith. The government has also tried to suppress Christian radio broadcasts.

THE PROMISE KEEPERS RALLY IN WASHINGTON, D.C., 1997

Since their first gathering in Boulder, Colorado in 1990, the Promise Keepers, an evangelical ministry to men, has filled football stadiums at rallies all across the United States – an estimated one million gathered at the Washington, D.C. rally shown above. Spiritual renewal, family responsibility, and racial reconciliation are the movement's key themes.

> *" Only love lasts for ever. Alone, it constructs the shape of eternity in the earthly and short-lived dimensions of the history of man on the earth "*
>
> POPE JOHN PAUL II

THE WORLD'S MOST POPULAR BOOK

By 1997 the Bible had been translated into 349 different languages. A further 841 languages had the complete New Testament, and another 933 had at least one book of the Bible. More copies of the Bible have been produced than any other book, religious or secular, since the advent of printing in the fifteenth century and Johann Gutenberg's first printed Bible in 1455.

GLOSSARY

A

ABSOLUTION The forgiveness and release of an individual from their sins. Catholics believe it has to be formally given by a priest or bishop; Protestants believe it comes directly from God.

ADOPTIONISM Heresy originating in Spain in the eighth century, which claimed that Christ is only a man adopted by God.

ALBIGENSIANS/ALBIGENSES Heretics who believed that the worlds of spirit and matter are separate, and hence denied the Incarnation and the SACRAMENTS. Flourished in southern France in the twelfth and early thirteenth centuries before being suppressed.

AMISH/AMISH MENNONITES Church founded by Jakob Ammann in 1693 after he broke away from the Mennonite Church. Amish communities first settled in Europe but most migrated to the U.S. in the eighteenth and nineteenth centuries. Its doctrine and church government are similar to that of the Mennonites.

ANABAPTISTS *from the Greek for* rebaptizers. Various radical Protestant groups that evolved during the Reformation and commonly shared a belief in the baptism of adult believers only. Anabaptists are identified not only by their radical discipleship but also by their simple lifestyles and their refusal to abide by any state laws.

ANGLICANISM *from the Latin for* English Church. A consequence of the Reformation by which an English law (the Act of Supremacy, 1534) declared Henry VIII to be the head of the church in England instead of the pope. The doctrines and character of the church were not defined and agreed upon until the reign of Elizabeth I. Today the term Anglicanism is used as an all-encompassing term for the practices and character of over 30 autonomous Anglican churches worldwide, all offshoots of the original Church of England.

ANTINOMIANISM The heretical belief that true Christians need not follow moral laws.

APOCRYPHA Term used by Protestants for 14 books in the Septuagint but not in the Hebrew Bible. Some, called deuterocanonical books, are included in Orthodox and Catholic Bibles.

APOSTOLIC FATHERS Distinguished church leaders in the period immediately after the New Testament, e.g., Clement of Rome, Ignatius, Polycarp, and Papias.

ARIANISM Fourth-century movement named after its founder, the priest Arius. Arians denied the true divinity of Jesus, believing that he was merely a human created by God. Although condemned as heretical by the Council of Nicea, Arianism remained popular for over a century.

ARMINIANISM Influential school of Reformed theology developed by Jacobus Arminius (1560–1609) in the Netherlands. In opposition to Calvinism, Arminianism stresses human free will and God's desire to save all human beings.

ASCENSION Christ's rising up into heaven, as witnessed by the apostles. According to Acts 1:3, this happened 40 days after the Resurrection.

B

BAPTISM The act of acceptance into the Christian church, practiced by all denominations. In some cases a blessing with holy water symbolizes the believer's admission into a church.

BAPTISTS Protestant family of denominations originating as a breakaway group from the Church of England led by the Puritan Separatist John Smyth in 1609, when he made baptism the basis of church fellowship. Today there are over 40 million Baptist members globally.

C

CALVINISM The theological doctrine of the Protestant church reformer, John Calvin, which was adopted by various bodies and individuals during the Reformation. Calvinism places a strong emphasis on the sovereignty of God at the center of Christian life, on the authority of the Bible as a guide for living the Christian faith, and on predestination.

CANON *from the Greek for* rule. The word is used to denote the list of books in the Old and New Testaments (canon of Scripture); the central part of the Mass (canon of the Mass); and the body of ecclesiastical laws that govern all areas of faith, morals, and discipline (canon law).

CAROLINGIAN RENAISSANCE The revival of education, art, and religion in the reign of Charlemagne (late eighth-early ninth centuries).

CATHOLIC MODERNISTS School of theologians who introduced LIBERAL THEOLOGY into the Catholic Church.

CHARISMATIC Modern movement that derives from PENTECOSTALISM, and which focuses on the presence of the Holy Spirit not just personally, but corporately. Emphasis is on the gifts of the Holy Spirit – healing, prophecy, and speaking in tongues – although these do not define the movement in the same way that they do Pentecostalism. Charismatics' approach to worship and prayer has influenced Christians who would not define themselves as charismatic.

CHRISTIAN DEMOCRACY Post-World War II political movement established in France, Germany, Italy, and in the Low Countries, based on Christian philosophy and values.

CHURCH COUNCIL Formal assembly of bishops and other church representatives which can be local or general. General councils consist of bishops convened from around the world to regulate church doctrine and identify any need for discipline. The seven authoritative councils considered the most important are (dates in parentheses): Nicea (325), Constantinople I (381), Ephesus (431), Chalcedon (451), Constantinople II (553), Constantinople III (680–81), Nicea II (787). Since splits within the Church, no council has had representatives from all parts of the Christian world, although the Catholic church still considers its general councils to be universal and authoritative. Three Catholic church councils have been convened since the Reformation: Trent (1545–63), Vatican I (1869–70), and Vatican II (1962–65).

CONFESSING CHURCH Protestant church founded in Germany in 1934 in reaction to Nazi policy towards Christians. Initially its name was derived from the act of confession, or affirmation, of the Christian faith, but as its members began to suffer Nazi repression, they saw themselves as a church of persecuted "confessors," or martyrs.

CONGREGATIONALISM One of the main REFORMED CHURCH traditions, in which a local church congregation is independent and self-governing.

COPTIC CHURCH Ancient Christian church of Egypt and still influential there today. Its name derives from the ancient Egyptian Coptic language.

D

"DEATH OF GOD" THEOLOGY An attempt to claim that God is either an irrelevant or meaningless concept. Its most influential proponent was the atheist philosopher Friedrich Nietzsche.

DEISM System of religion, popular in the seventeenth and eighteenth centuries, which held that God set the universe in motion but is no longer actively involved with it.

DONATISM Fourth-century heresy that split the church in North Africa. Donatists would not accept anyone into church leadership who had any connection, no matter how indirect, with Christian persecutors and said that sacraments celebrated by unworthy ministers were invalid.

E

EMPIRICISM The philosophical doctrine that all knowledge derives from experience.

ENLIGHTENMENT A movement of ideas in seventeenth- and eighteenth-century Europe which secularized much of European thought. Its leaders distrusted all forms of authority and tradition, aiming to follow only reason, observation, and experiment.

EUCHARIST *from the Greek for* thanksgiving. Term for commemorating Christ's Last Supper by the consecration of bread and wine. Other names for the Eucharist are the Lord's Supper, the Mass, and the Holy Communion. It is known in the Eastern Church as "the Divine Liturgy."

EVANGELICALISM Movement defined by members' belief in personal conversion, in the authority of scripture, in salvation by faith in Christ's atonement, and emphasis on evangelism.

F

FUNDAMENTALISM Protestant movement distinguished by its members' faith in the literal truths and teaching of the Bible.

G

GNOSTICISM Umbrella term for the beliefs of second-century religious sects that claimed to have a secret knowledge or revelation of God. They included parts of the Christian story in their beliefs and claimed to be the only ones to have the true understanding of it.

H

HERESY The doubt or denial, either erroneously or deliberately, of any authoritative doctrine of the Church.

HOLY SYNOD Established by Peter the Great in 1721, this religious body of priests and bishops governed the Russian church. The committee was set up to replace the patriarch. The Holy Synod was abolished in 1917 and the position of patriarch reinstated.

HUGUENOTS French Calvinists, persecuted in Catholic France before 1598 and again after 1685. The denomination was formally legalized in 1802.

I

INDEX, THE List of books that the Catholic Church forbade its members to read or possess, created in 1557 and which ceased to have a place in ecclesiastical law by 1966.

INDULGENCE The reduction, granted by God through the Catholic church, of the time that forgiven sinners would spend in Purgatory. Even after sin has been forgiven, penance is needed to make good its effects in the sinner, and indulgences enable the rest of the church to assist the sinner in this penance. Indulgences are now granted only by the pope.

INQUISITION, PAPAL, THE Organization to detect and pass heretics to the state for punishment. It was begun in the early 1200s in southern France; at its height an average of three people a year were burned for heresy. It was moribund in the 1400s and was revived in the Reformation, but was only effective in the Papal States.

INQUISITION, SPANISH, THE Modeled on the PAPAL INQUISITION and founded by the Spanish monarchy in 1478 to operate in its territories. It inspired great fear but was in decline by the late 1500s. It was finally abolished in 1834.

J

JANSENISM Seventeenth-century Catholic movement named after Cornelius Jansen, who attempted to revive the teachings of Augustine.

JUSTIFICATION The process by which humans are forgiven by God was traditionally thought to be attainable by grace through faith and good works. In the sixteenth century Martin Luther taught that justification was possible through faith *alone*, thus launching the Reformation.

K, L

LIBERAL THEOLOGY Cross-denominational movement begun in the nineteenth century with a tendency to focus on human freedom and humanity's power to perceive God by reflecting on human experience, rather than through Christian orthodoxy.

LIBERATION THEOLOGY Theological movement, originating in South America, which believes that Christianity has a commitment to change social and political conditions wherever there is oppression or exploitation.

LUTHERANISM Movement derived from the teachings of Martin Luther. Lutherans believe in justification by faith alone and in the authority of the Bible.

M

MENNONITES Protestant denomination founded by the former Anabaptist Menno Simons in the sixteenth century. Mennonite communities, which now exist in Germany, the Netherlands, Russia, North America, Zaire, India, Indonesia, and Mexico, all believe in adult baptism and in a symbolic interpretation of the Lord's Supper, although each congregation is independent.

METHODISM A Protestant denomination founded by John Wesley (1703–91). It was originally a part of the Church of England but had effectively become a separate denomination by the time of Wesley's death.

MONARCHIANISM A second- and third-century heresy concerning the relationship between God the Father and God the Son. It took two forms: one school of Monarchians tried to make Jesus less than God; the other united him to God the Father so closely that his distinct personhood was lost; both were trying to protect the unity (*monarchia*) of the Godhead.

MONASTICISM A form of Christian living in which those individuals who seek God through a life of asceticism and prayer live either as hermits or in religious communities. All lead a celibate life in varying degrees of seclusion from the world, focusing on prayer, reading, and monastic work. Monastic communities, or orders, include the Benedictines, Carmelites, Jesuits, Franciscans, Carthusians, Cistercians, and Dominicans. Communities undertake specific activities, such as education (Benedictines), missionary work (Jesuits), preaching and study (Dominicans), vows of poverty and manual work (Franciscans), and contemplative living (Carmelites).

MONASTIC RULES Codes of rules giving spiritual and administrative guidance for religious communal living. The first rule was devised by Basil the Great from a collection of questions and answers on monastic life, including asceticism, set tasks and manual work, daily liturgical prayer times, education of children, and poverty and chastity. Benedict's Rule covers issues such as practical organization, daily liturgical prayer times, and discipline, stability, and obedience.

MONOPHYSITISM The doctrine, declared heretical in the fifth century, advocated that Christ had only one divine nature and not two (human and divine). The Coptic, Ethiopian, Armenian, and Syrian Orthodox churches split from the rest of the church over this issue.

MORAVIAN BRETHREN Group of Bohemian Protestants driven from their homeland during the Thirty Years' War (1618–48). Scattered all over Europe, one group of refugees settled in Saxony on the Pietist Count von Zinzendorf's estate, which was given the name *Herrnhut* ("Lord's Watch"). Most Moravians now reside in the U.S.

MYSTICISM A personal spiritual experience of God, often emotional, in search of Christian truths and contemplation beyond the bounds of logical understanding.

N

NATURAL THEOLOGY The part of theology that deals with knowledge attainable by human reason without the aid of revelation.

NEOORTHODOXY Twentieth-century school of theology rejecting nineteenth-century Liberal theology and returning to the authority of the Bible and the centrality of Christ in the Christian faith.

NESTORIANISM Fifth-century doctrine, named after the priest Nestorius, claiming that Christ had two separate "persons," human and divine, and denying any union between the two.

NICENE CREED Authoritative statement of the main beliefs of the Christian church first issued by the Council of Nicea in 325. It affirmed that God the Father and Jesus the Son are of the same essence and upheld the divinity of the Holy Spirit. (Creed is from the Latin *credo*, " I believe.")

O, P

PAPAL BULL A formal and important official document issued by the pope.

PATRIARCH (i) Biblical: the father, or ruler of a tribe. The name is usually applied to Abraham, Isaac, Jacob, and the twelve sons of Jacob. (ii) Title given to the bishops of the ancient sees of Constantinople, Antioch, Alexandria, Jerusalem, and Rome. Today the title is also used for the heads of the Russian and Bulgarian churches.

PENTECOST The Greek name for the Jewish Festival of Weeks, used to commemorate the descent of the Holy Spirit on the apostles. Also known as Whitsunday.

PENTECOSTALISM Protestant movement with a distinctive emphasis on the gifts of the Holy Spirit, the authority of the Bible, the sovereignty of God, intense emotion, and spontaneous worship.

PIETISM Protestant renewal movement aimed at breathing new life into the Lutheran church in the late seventeenth century.

PREDESTINATION The belief that people are chosen by God for eternal salvation. Some controversial forms of belief in predestination hold that, while some are chosen for salvation, the rest of humanity is predestined to damnation.

PRESBYTER *from the Greek for* elder. A priest, or an elder in the early Christian Church or in the Presbyterian Church.

PRESBYTERIANISM Form of church order and doctrine emerging from the Protestant Reformation. Presbyterian church order relies on the ministry and authority of church elders. Presbyterian doctrine derives from John Calvin's teaching and recognizes God's sovereignty and the authority of the Bible above all else.

PURGATORY According to Catholic belief, it is a state or place where those who are on their way to heaven but not yet ready for it are purified through suffering.

PURITANISM Movement that emerged in England in the sixteenth century when some Protestants were not content to worship under Elizabeth I's ANGLICAN church settlement. They distanced themselves from the Church of England and all its associations (such as church ornaments, surplices, organs, etc.) in search of a purer form of church worship.

Q

QUIETISM Form of religious mysticism originating in the late seventeenth century. Quietists believed that in order to attain perfection, people must, through prayer alone, become totally passive to God's will.

R

REFORMED CHURCH Often used of all churches derived from the Reformation, the term "Reformed" applies more specifically to those churches that adopted Calvinist, rather than Lutheran, doctrine.

RESURRECTION OF CHRIST, THE Christ's rising from the dead three days after his crucifixion, death, and burial.

S

SACRAMENT One of the central Christian religious ceremonies, such as baptism and communion. Seven sacraments are recognized by the Catholic and Orthodox Churches.

SCHOLASTICISM The dominant school of philosophy and theology in Western Europe in the Middle Ages.

SEPTUAGINT Influential Greek translation of the Old Testament from the original Hebrew, probably completed by 132 BC, and used by the early church.

SHAKERS Religious sect that grew out of the Quaker revival of 1747 in England. Led by Ann Lee, a small group went to the U.S. where they settled near Albany, N.Y. The group earned their name from their ecstatic shaking while under the influence of spiritual exaltation.

T

TRANSUBSTANTIATION A term which refers to the Catholic understanding of the Eucharist, or Last Supper, according to which the bread and wine actually become the body and blood of Christ, not just symbols of it.

TRINITY, THE God in three persons, the Father, the Son, and the Holy Spirit. This is a central doctrine of the Christian faith.

"TRUCE OF GOD" The temporary cessation of hostilities, such as acts of violence and theft, ordered by the medieval church on particular days and church seasons, e.g., Lent.

U

ULTRAMONTANISM *from the Latin for* beyond the mountains. Catholic movement to promote the authority of the pope, at the expense of national or episcopal independence.

V, W, X, Y, Z

WALDENSES/WALDENSIANS Medieval heretics, seen by some as harbingers of Protestantism. The movement began in the late twelfth century in southern France.

INDEX

Picture Information

Jacket: Front cover bc: (please refer to p.62t); **tl:** (please refer to p.215b); **cla:** (please refer to p.85bl); tr (please refer to p. 12/13); **Front cover inside flap:** Shrine of the Book Temple Scroll, Israel Museum; **Back cover: tl:** (please refer to p.44tr); **cla:** (please refer to p.51b); **cra:** (please refer to p.27b); **tr:** (please refer to front inside flap); **bl:** (please refer to p.24b); **br** (please refer to 41tl); **1:** (please refer to p.41tl); **2:** Tony Stone Images/Paul Chelsey; **3c:** The Burrell Collection/ Andy Crawford; **4t:** (detail) (please refer to p.12); **4c:** (detail) (please refer to p.54/ 55); **4bl:** (detail) (please refer to p.56/7); **5cl:** (detail) (please refer to p.104/5); **5cra:** (detail) (please refer to p. 172/3); **5bc:** (detail) (please refer to p. 132/3); **5crb:** (detail) (please refer to p. 202/3); **5cra:** (detail) (please refer to p. 172/3); **5tr:** (detail) (please refer to p.154/5); **5tl:** (detail) (please refer to p.83t); **5b:** Sygma/B. Ausset; **6tl:** Centre panel from the lid of the *Holy Cross Reliquary*, c. 965, (detail), (gold, enamel cloissoné, precious stones), Byzantine, Cathedral Treasury, Limburg an der Lahn, Germany, AKG London/Erich Lessing; **7tr:** Mary Evans Picture Library; **8bl:** Reliquary bust of Charlemagne, Aachen, Germany, AKG London/Erich Lessing; **8tr:** *Pilgrims at The Tomb of a Saint*, 14th Century, by Master of St. Sebastian, Galleria Nazionale d'Arte Antica, Rome, Italy, Scala; **9tr:** *Puritans Going to Church in Colonial America*, by George H. Boughton, Peter Newark's American Pictures; **10tl:** *The Grace* by Jean-Baptiste Simeon Chardin, (1699-1779), Louvre, Paris, France, Bridgeman Art Library, London/New York; **10b:** Magnum/Bruce Davidson; **11t:** (please refer to p.218t); **11tr:** Man praying during 'Tinkat', Ethiopian Easter, Sygma/B. Ausset; **12/13:** *Adoration of The Magi (with self portrait of the artist)*, 1423, by Gentile da Fabriano (1370-1427), Uffizi Gallery, Florence, Italy, et.Archive; **14bl:** Robert Harding Picture Library/Richard Ashworth; **15cr:** Sonia Halliday Photographs/T.C. Rising; **15t:** *Abraham Prepares to Sacrifice Isaac*, (detail), 6th Century, (mosaic), Beth Alpha Synagogue, Zev Radovan; **16l:** *Moses Receiving The Ten Commandments on Mount Sinai*, 14th Century, illustration from the *Sarajevo Hagada*, Zev Radovan; **17cr:** *Idol of The Storm God Baal*, Bronze Age (c. 1350-1250 BC), bronze and gold, from Syria, Bridgeman Art Library, London/New York; **18bl:** *Head of a Persian King (Median or Achaemenian ruler or Cyros the Great)*, 5th century BC, marble, Ancient Persian, Achaemenian, Louvre, Paris, France, AKG London/Erich Lessing; **18t:** *King Shalmaneser III Receiving the tribute of King Jehu of Israel*, c. 825 BC , Panel from the Black Obelisk of King Shalmaneser III, from Nimrud, Zev Radovan; **19bl:** Sonia Halliday Photographs/Barry Searle; **19tr:** Shrine of the Book, (detail), BC, Israel Museum, Israel; **19br:** Zev Radovan; **20bl:** *Judith and Holofernes*, bronze, by Donatello, Piazza della Signoria, Florence, Italy, Alison Harris; **21tl:** Head of Alexander The Great, mid-2nd Century AD, (marble), found at Pergamom, Architectural Museum, Istanbul, Turkey, Bridgeman Art Library, London/New York; **21br:** *The Triumph of Judas Maccabeus* by Peter Paul Rubens (1577-1640), Musée des Beaux Arts, Nantes, France, Giraudon/Bridgeman Art Library, London/New York; **22/23:** High aqueduct built under Herod the Great, 1st Century AD, (partial view), Caesarea (Israel), AKG London/ Erich Lessing; **23tl:** *The Three Kings From The East Follow The Star of Bethlehem; The Three Kings Before Herod*, c.1315-20, mosaic, Byzantine, Kariye Camii, former church of the Chora Monastery (built C11th - early C14th) AKG London/Erich Lessing; **23tr:** Sonia Halliday Photographs; **24b:** *Flight into Egypt I*, 1979, by Gillian Lawson, Private Collection, Bridgeman Art Library, London/New York; **24tl:** Tony Stone Images/Tim Brown; **25br:** Sonia Halliday Photographs/Laura Lushington; **25t:** Zev Radovan; **26tr:** Mount of Beatitudes and the Lake of Gennesaret, photo, Israel, AKG London/Erich Lessing; **27br:** *Healing of The Palsied Man*, 2nd half of the 12th Century, Byzantine book illumination from a codex with the four evangelists, Ms93, folio 97r, Iveron Monastery, Mount Athos, AKG London/ Erich Lessing; **28b:** *The Isenheim Altarpiece: The Crucifixion* (central panel) *St. Sebastian* (left), *St. Anthony* (right), *Entombment* (predella), 1512/13-15, by Matthias Grunewald (Mathis Nithart Gothart), (c. 1480-1528), (oil on panel), Musée d'Unterlinden, Colmar, France, Bridgeman Art Library, London/New York; **28tl:** Zev Radovan; **29tr:** *The Resurrection of Christ and the Holy Women at the Sepulchre*, 1442, (fresco), by Fra Angelico (Guido di Pietro), (c.1387-1455), Museo di San Marco dell'Angelico, Florence, Italy, Bridgeman Art Library, London/New York; **30bl:** *Pentecost*, (detail from the Verdun Altar), 1181, Klosterneuburg, Lower Austria, AKG London/Erich Lessing; **31tl:** *Conversion of St. Paul*, 15th Century, by Hildesheim, Niedersachrisches Museum, Germany, et. Archive; **31cr:** St. Paul (detail), (fresco), 3rd Century, Ursula Held; **33t:** Engraving by J. Rogers, Mary Evans Picture Library; **33b:** *Arch of Titus*, panel from the Arch of Titus depicting Roman soldiers in triumphant procession carrying the Golden Menorah and other artefacts looted from the Jerusalem Temple before its destruction, Zev Radovan; **34b:** Sonia Halliday Photographs/Paul Milner; **35cr:** John Rylands Library, University of Manchester, UK; **35cb:** Stained glass, 1525 AD, Victoria and Albert Museum, London, UK, Sonia Halliday Photographs; **36/37:** (please refer to p. 54/5); **38tl:** *Egyptian statue of the Goddess Isis and the Child Horus*, late period (664-332 BC), (bronze encrusted with gold), Louvre, Paris, France, Bridgeman Art Library, London/New York; **38t:** Mary Evans Picture Library; **39b:** *The Torches of Nero*, 1876, Henryk Siemiradzki, Museum Narodowe, Krakau, AKG London/Erich Lessing; **40bl:** Christian History Magazine; **41tl:** Catacombe de Priscilla, Rome, Italy, Archive PCAS, Ikona; **41tr:** Zev Radovan; **42b:** Group of Gnostic amulets, late Byzantine period, Zev Radovan; **43cr:** *Mithras Sacrificing The Bull*, Roman, 2nd Century, marble relief, Museo Archeologico, Venice, Italy, Bridgeman Art Library, London/New York; **43tl:** *Isisi, Attis and Cybele*, (fresco), Roman, Museo Nazionale di Napoli, Naples, Italy, Scala; **44tr:** Mary Evans Picture Library; **44b:***The Christian Martyr's Last Prayer*, by Jean-Léon Gérôme, The Walters Art Gallery, Baltimore, USA; **45b:** *Diana or Christ?* 1881, (oil on canvas), by Edwin Long (1829-91), Blackburn Museum and Art Gallery, Lancashire, UK, Bridgeman Art Library, London/New York; **46bl:** Mary Evans Picture Library; **46cr:** Christian History Magazine; **47b:** Marcus Aurelius making a sacrifice, (stone relief), Roman, Alinari/Mus. Capitoline, Rome, Italy, Photographie Giraudon; **48tl:** Mary Evans Picture Library; **49tr:** Scenes from the Old Testament, from Dura Europos, built c. 200 B.C., National Museum, Damascus, AKG London/Erich Lessing; **49cl:** Yale University Art Gallery, (Dura Europas Collection), U.S.A; **50bl:** Catacomb of St. Callistus, Rome, Italy, Ikona; **50tl:** Catacombs via Latina, Italy, Ikona; **51t:** Catacomb of St. Priscilla, Italy, Ikona; **51b:** Catacomb of Via Latina, Italy, Ikona; **52b:** British Museum, London, UK; **53cr:** Sonia Halliday Photographs; **53tl:** Sonia Halliday Photographs/John Reynolds Library; **54clb:** *The Four Tetrarchs* (ruled 3rd Century AD), porphyry Sculpture on the Facade of the Treasury of St. Mark's, St. Mark's Square, Venice, Italy, Bridgeman Art Library, London/New York; **54/55 b:** *Martyrs in The Catacombs* (oil on canvas), by Jules Eugéne Lenepveu (1819-1898), Musée d'Orsay, Paris, France Réunion des Musées Nationaux Agence photographique/Jean Scholmans; **56/57** (please refer to p.76/77); **58bl:** *The Dream of Constantine* from *The Legend of The True Cross* cycle, c.1390, (fresco) by Agnolo Gaddi (c.1350-96), Santa Croce, Florence, Italy, Bridgeman Art Library, London/New York; **59cr:** Statue of Julian the Apostate, 4th Century, (marble), Louvre, Paris, France, AKG London/Erich Lessing; **59tl:** Map of Constantinople, 1422, British Library, London, UK, Bridgeman Art Library, London/New York; **59bc:** *Romans of The Decadence*, Thomas Couture, Musée d'Orsay, Paris, France/Philippe Sebert; **60bl:** *Ecumenical Council at Nicea*, (16th Century), Aghiosminas, Heraklia, Crete, Sonia Halliday Photographs/Michael Damaskinos; **61b:** MS Grec. 510f.367v, Bibliothèque Nationale de France, Paris; **61t:** Codex Sinaiticus, Add.MS 43725, ff.244V-245, British Library, London, U.K; **62b:** *Christ in Glory in the Tetramorph*, (tapestry), (detail), designed by Graham Sutherland (1903-80) for the Lady Chapel behind the High Altar, 1962, Coventry Cathedral, Warwickshire, UK, Bridgeman Art Library, London/ New York; **62t:** *Ecce Homo* by Antonio Ciseri (1821-1891), Galleria d'Arte Moderna, Florence, Italy, Scala; **63:** *Icon of The Holy Trinity* by Cretan (17th Century), University of Liverpool Art Gallery & Collections, Liverpool, UK, Bridgeman Art Library, London/New York; **64bc:** Pigmented stone (tufo) figure of St. Ambrose, mid-14th Century, Italian, Victoria and Albert Museum, London, UK, Bridgeman Art Library, London/ New York; **64bl:** Chi-Rho symbol on early Christian sarcophagus, Vatican Museums, Vatican City, CM Dixon; **65t:** Central nave of Santa Sabina Church, Rome, Italy, Scala; **66b:** *St. Anthony Visits St. Paul The Hermit* c. 1513, by Mathis Gothart Gruenewald, Colmar, Unterlindenmuseum, AKG London/Erich Lessing; **66tl:** *St. Martin of Tours*, c. 1415, produced by the circle of the Limbourg Brothers, illuminated in Paris Breviary of John the Fearless, Harl 2897f. 435, British Library, London, UK, Bridgeman Art Library, London/New York; **67br:** *St. Benedict* (c. 480-c. 550) *Preaching to His Disciples Near Montecassino*, illuminated by Jean de Stavelot (1388-1449), Flemish, MS 738/1401 f. 130rfrom a collection of writings on St. Benedict, (1432-37), Musée Conde, Chantilly, France, Giraudon/Bridgeman Art Library, London /New York; **67tl:** Corbis UK Ltd; **67tr:** St. Simeon stylites, 14th Century, (mural), Hagia Sophia, Trabzon, Turkey, Sonia Halliday Photographs; **68bl:** Saint Augustine (fresco), Rome, Italy, Ikona; **69tc:** Pope Pelagius I, Cavallieri, 1588, Mary Evans Picture Library; **70b:** The Forum, Rome, Italy, Robert Harding Picture Library; **71tl:** *Plundering of Rome by The Vandals*, wood engraving, No. XX, after drawing 1865, by Heinrich Leutemann, Pictures of Antiquity, Munich, AKG London; **71br:** *Pope Leo I Repulsing Attila* by Raphael (Raffaello Sanzio of Urbino) (1483-1520), Vatican Museums and Galleries, Vatican City, Bridgeman Art Library, London/New York; **71tr:** San Apollinare, Ravenna, Italy, et.Archive; **73c:** *Christ Pantocrator*, panel from the cover of a lectionary, Byzantine, late 10th Century, (ivory), M. 13. 1904, Fitzwilliam University of Cambridge, UK, Bridgeman Art Library, London/New York; **74c:** John Chrysostom, (mural), on apse wall of Kariye Camii, Dumbarton Oaks, Washington, DC, USA; **75tr:** Sonia Halliday Photographs/Jane Taylor; **76tl:** Empress Theodora, Byzantine, 1042-1050, (gold with enamel), Budapest National Museum, Hungary, No. 99/1860, AKG London/Erich Lessing; **76/77b:** *Emperor Justinian I and his Retinue of Officials, Soldiers and Clergy*, c.547 AD, (mosaic), San Vitale, Ravenna, Italy, Bridgeman Art Library, London/New York; **76bl:** Medallion commemorating the conquest of Justinian I, (reverse side), replica of gold medallion, 524 AD, Constantinople, Bibliothèque Nationale, Paris, France, Sonia Halliday Photographs; **77tr:** Hagia Sophia, completed in 360, Constantinople, AKG London/Erich Lessing; **79br:** *Clovis, King of The Franks and Alaric II, King of The Visigoths* from *Chroniques des Rois de France*, (early 15th Century), MS 869/522f. 17v, Musée Conde, Chantilly, France, Bridgeman Art Library, London/New York; **79tl:** Sonia Halliday Photographs/Jane Taylor; **80/81:** (please refer to p. 83tr); **82 tl:** *Pilgrims of St. John*, 14th Century, miniature, Jean-Loup Charmet; **82b:** *Stories of Queen Theodolinda of The Lombards*, (fresco), by Zavattari Family (fl. 15th Century), St. John Basilica, Monza, Italy, Bridgeman Art Library, London/New York; **83t:** *The Baptism*, French, *Collection of Treatise on Devotion*, (c. 1371-78), PEC 9177 MS 137/1687 f. 45, Musée Conde, Chantilly, France, Giraudon/Bridgeman Art Library, London/New York; **83cr:** *August: Coopering* from *Hours of The Duchess of Burgundy* (c. 1450), Musée Conde, Chantilly, France, Giraudon/Bridgeman Art Library, London/New York; **84b:** Robert Harding Picture Library/David Lomax; **85tr:** Canterbury Cathdedral, UK, St. Augustine chair, c.1210, Sonia Halliday Photographs; **85bl:** St. Bede, (detail), (stained glass) from The Benedictine window (20th Century), Norwich Cathedral, UK, Sonia Halliday Photographs; **86l:** Staatsbibliothek Bamberg, MSC. Lit: 1. 126r; **87b:** Stave Church at Fagusues, Borgund, Norway, 1150 AD, Werner Forman Archive; **87tr:** National Museum, Copenhagen, Denmark, Werner Forman Archive; **88l:** *Ascent of The Prophet Muhammad to Heaven*, Persian, 16th Century, by Aqa Mirak, OR2265, British Library, London Bridgeman Art Library, London/New York; **89br:** St. Paul's Monastery, (exterior dates from 4th Century, Egypt, Sonia Halliday Photographs; **89t:** The Great Mosque at Damascus (1715), The courtyard looking NE, Angelo Hornak; **90bl:** *The Coronation of Emperor Charlemagne* (742-814) *by Pope Leo III* (c. 750-816) *at St. Peter's, Rome in 800*, from *Grandes Chroniques de France* (late 14th Century) PF2826 f. 106r, Musée Goya, Castres, France, Bridgeman Art Library, London/New York; **91tr:** British Library, UK; **91b:** British Museum, UK; **92b:** Musée de L'Oeuvre, Notre Dame, Strasbourg, Sonia Halliday and Laura Lushington Photographs; **93t:** *Historiated Initial 'C'* (Cantate Domino), with three clerics singing and a musician playing the viol, English, from the *Vaux Psalter*, MS233 f. 145v, (early 14th Century), Lambeth Palace Library; Bridgeman Art Library, London/New York; **93b:** detail from *Utrecht Psalter*, MS. 32, f. 83r, University Library, Utrecht; **94b:** Beginning of St. John's Gospel from the Arnstein Bible, 1175, British Library, London, UK; **95tl:** Bibliothèque Nationale de France, N.A-Lat 1390 fo7, Paris, France; **95br:** *Le Pape Formose et Etienne VI*, 1870, by Jean-Paul Laurens, Cliché H. Maertens, Musée des Beaux-Arts de Nantes; **96b:** The Consecration of the Church at Cluny, from *Chronicle of the Abbey of Cluny* (12th Century), Lat 17716 f. 91, Bibliothèque Nationale, Paris, France, Bridgeman Art Library, London/New York; **96tl:** MS, Musée de Cluny, reproduced in *Les Arts Somptuaires* vol 1, Mary Evans Picture Library; **97cr:** Onyx chalice, Treasury of St. Mark's, Venice, Werner Forman Archive; **97t:** From a Book of Hours for Parisiens showing different monastic orders, 15th Century, Latin MS1176, Bibliotèque Nationale, Paris, Sonia Halliday Photographs; **98b:** *St. Nicephorus the Patriarch and the Holy Father: both examining iconoclasts breaking an image*, illuminated by Theodorus of Caesarea, Greek, *Studion* or *Theodore Psalter* (1066), Add H352 f. 27v, British Library, London, UK, Bridgeman Art Library, London/New York; **99b:** Byzantine icon of St. Gregory, Archbishop of Thessaloniki (tempera on papel), Pushkin Museum, Moscow, Russia, Bridgeman Art Library, London/New York; **99t:** Cretan Icon of the Mother of God of the Passion, mid-17th Century, attributed to Emmanuel Tsanes, Christie's Images; **100t:** *The Slav Apostles, Cyril and Methodius*, (detail), 1865, from *Illustrierte Zeitung*, vol.41, no.1047, Leipzig, p.69, AKG London; **100b:** Biblioteca Nationale, Madrid, Spain, Sonia Halliday Photographs; **101br:** from *Radziwill Chronicle*, end of 15th Century, St. Petersburg, AKG London/Erich Lessing; **102b:** Silver Rhia Paten, metalwood, 565-78, Dumbarton Oaks, Washington, DC, USA; **104/5:** *Lincoln Cathedral From The West* by Joseph Baker (d.1770), Lincolnshire County Council, Usher Gallery, Lincoln, UK, Bridgeman Art Library, London/New York; **106l:** Mary Evans Picture Library; **107cl:** *Madonna Sheltering the Order of Citeaux*, (oil on panel), by Jan II Provost (1465-1529), Musée de la Chartreuse, Douai, France, Bridgeman Art Library, London/New York; **107t:** *Chartreuse and The Resurrection of The Dead* from the *Coronation of The Virgin*, (detail), completed 1454 by Enguerrand Quarton (c. 1410-66), Villeneuve, Avignon hospice, Anjou, France, Bridgeman Art Library, London/New York; **108/9c:** *The First Crusade of Peter The Hermit*, illuminated by Sebastian Marmoret, from *Passages Fait Outremer* (c.1490), Fr5594f.19, Bibliothèque Nationale, Paris, France, Bridgeman Art Library, London/New York; **108b:** *The Taking of Jerusalem in 1079*, XIV edition of William of Tyre's History, Sonia Halliday Photographs; **108tl:** Robert Harding Picture Library/P. Hawking; **110bl:** British Library, UK; **111cr:** St. Denis, the High Altar and apse, Paris, France, Sonia Halliday Photographs; **111bl:** Michael Crockett; **112bl:** *The Apotheosis of St. Thomas Aquinas*, 1631, by Fransisco de Zubaran (1598-1664), Museo de Bellas Artes, Seville, Spain, Bridgeman Art Library, London/New York; **113cr:** Corbis UK Ltd /David Lees; **113tl:** *St. Thomas Aquinas*, 1491, by Domenico Ghirlandaio, Santa Maria Novella, Florence, Italy, Sonia Halliday Photographs; **114l:** *St. Francis of Assisi Preaching to The Birds* by Giotto di Bondone (c. 1266-1337) Louvre, Paris, France, Bridgeman Art Library, London/New York; **115cr:** *Christ Welcomes Two Dominican Friars* (detail), (fresco), by Fra Angelico (Guido di Pietro) (c.1387-1455), San Marco, Florence, Italy, Bridgeman Art Library, London/New York; **115tl:** *The Stigmata of St. Francis* by Bonaventura Berlinghieri (fl. 1228-74), Galleria degli

Uffizi, Florence, Italy, Bridgeman Art Library, London/New York; **116tl:** *The Last Sacrament*, from 14th Century Book of Hours, South African Library, Cape Town, Sonia Halliday Photographs/Antionia Dees; **116b:** *Canterbury Pilgrims*, by Alfred George Webster, Bridgeman Art Library, London/New York; **117br:** *The Neville Family at Prayer* by the Master of The Golden Legend in *Munich Neville Book of Hours* (1430-35), Bibliothèque Nationale, Paris, France, Bridgeman Art Library, London/New York); **117t:** *Monks and Nuns Conducting a Vigil*, from a 14th Century Book of Hours, South Africa Library, Cape Town, South Africa, Sonia Halliday Photographs/Antonia Dees; **118b:** *St. Dominic Presides Over The Burning of The Heretics*, by Pedron Berruguette (1450-1504), Prado, Madrid, Spain, Bridgeman Art Library, London/New York; **118tl:** Bibliothèque Nationale de France, Paris; **119t:** *The Plague of Tournai in 1095*, 1883, by Louis Gallait (1810-87), Musée des Beaux-Arts, Tournai, Belgium, Bridgeman Art Library, London/New York; **119bl:** *St. Eligius Making a Shrine; St. Eligius at an Anvil* by the Rohan Master and workshop (use of Paris) French Hours (c. 1418), T. 2616 MS 62f.215r Fitzwilliam Museum, Cambridge, UK, Bridgeman Art Library, London/New York; **120tr:** View of the entrance facade of the palace, 14th century (photo) Palais des Papes, Avignon, France, Peter Willi/Bridgeman Art Library, London/New York; **120bl:** *John Wycliffe reading his translation of the Bible to John of Gaunt*, 1847-8, by Ford Madox Brown (1821-93), Bradford Art Galleries and Museums, West Yorkshire, UK, Bridgeman Art Library, London/New York; **121b:** *September: Return of The Pilgrims From Santiago da Compostela* from *Hours of the Duchess of Burgundy* (c. 1450), Musée Conde, Chantilly, France, Bridgeman Art Library, London/New York; **122bl:** *The Conquest of Constantinople* by Jacopo Palma, Palace of the Doge, Venice, Italy, AKG London/Erich Lessing; **122tl:** *The Taking of Constantinople by The Turks , April 22nd 1453*, from *voyage D'Outremer*, by Bertrand de la Broquiere, MS. FR. 9087fo7, Bibliothèque Nationale, Paris, France, Sonia Halliday Photographs; **123tr:** Robert Harding Picture Library/Ellen Rooney; **124l:** Illustration to *The Wheel of Fortune* by Petrarch, French, 1503, Bibliothèque Nationale, Paris, France, Bridgeman Art Library, London/New York; **125b:** *The Day of Judgement* by Fra Angelico, Corbis UK Ltd; **126bl:** *The School of Athens*, 1508-11, Raphael, Stanza della Segnatura, Vatican, Vatican City, AKG London/Erich Lessing; **126tl:** Portrait of Christopher Columbus by Anonymous, Private Collection, Bridgeman Art Library, London/New York; **126tr:** Robert Harding Picture Library/Peter Scholey; **127c:** Sistine Chapel ceiling, 1508-12 (fresco) (post restoration) by Michelangelo Buonarotti (1475-1564), Vatican Museums and Art Galleries, Vatican City, Bridgeman Art Library, London/New York; **128/9:** (please refer to p.132tr); **130:** *Sale of Indulgences* by Jorg Breu from *L'Histoire des Moeurs* vol. 1, p. 297, XVIC, Mary Evans Picture Library; **131t:** Portrait of Erasmus by Holbein, Philip Mould Historical Portraits Ltd, London, UK, Bridgeman Art Library, London/New York; **131br:** Guttenberg Museum, AKG London/Erich Lessing; **132tr:** *Martin Luther and 95 Theses at Wittenberg*, 1517 by Auguste Blanchard after P.A. Labuchère, Mary Evans Picture Library; **132/3b:** *Luther's Sermon*, detail from a triptych, 1547, (oil on panel), by Lucas Cranach the elder (1472-1553) Church of St. Marien, Wittenberg, Germany, Bridgeman Art Library, London/New York; **133c:** Corbis UK Ltd; **133 tr:** Corbis UK Ltd; **134tl:** Corbis UK Ltd; **135b:** Corbis UK Ltd; **135tr:** Title page, *Luther Bible* (c. 1530), Bible Society, Bridgeman Art Library, London/New York; **136tl:** Portrait of Johann Calvin, Flemish School, Bibliothèque et Universitaire, Geneva, Switzerland, AKG London/Erich Lessing; **136b:** *Calvinists Destroying Statues in the Catholic Churches*, 1566, (engraving), Flemish School, Bridgeman Art Library, London/New York; **137t:** *Jacob Fugger in His Office*, 1518, drawing from the costume designs of M. Schwartz, Herzog Anton Ulrich Museum, AKG London; **138bl:** Mary Evans Picture Library; **139t:** Corbis UK Ltd; **140bl:** *The Surrender of Breda* (1625), (detail), c. 1635, by Diego Rodriguez de Silva y Velasquez (1599-1660), Prado, Madrid, Spain, Bridgeman Art Library, London/New York; **141cr:** *Mary, Queen of Scots and John Knox*, by Sidney Samuel (1829-96), Towneley Hall Art Gallery and Museum, Burnley, UK, Bridgeman Art Library, London/New York; **141t:** *Interior of the church St. Cunera in Rhenen*, 1655, by Pieter Jansz Saenredam, Dien Haag, Mauritshius, AKG London/Erich Lessing; **142bl:** Frontispiece of *The Book of Common Prayer*, 1549, (engraving), (b&w photo), Private Collection, Bridgeman Art Library, London/New York; **142br:** *Ego et Rex Meus* (Henry VII and Cardinal Wolsey) by Sir John Gilbert (1817-97), Guildhall Art Gallery, London, UK, Bridgeman Art Library, London/New York; **143bc:** *The Bartholomew's Day Massacre, 1572*, German, 16th Century, (woodcut), Anonymous, Giraudon/ Bibliothèque de Protestantisme, Paris, France, Bridgeman Art Library, London/New York; **143tl:** *Thomas Cranmer Being Burnt at The Stake* from Fox's *Book of Martyrs*, 1776, Mary Evans Picture Library; **144bl:** Oliver Cromwell, after the official portrait by Samuel Cooper, 1708, (enamel on vellum), by Christian Richter (1678-1732), Wallace Collection, London, UK, Bridgeman Art Library, London/New York; **145:** From *Christian History Study Guide: Survey: From the Reformation to the Present*; **146bl:** *St. Charles Borromeo*, (1538-84), by Carlo Dolci (1616-86), Palazzo Pitti, Florence, Italy, Bridgeman Art Library, London/New York; **146c:** Institut Amatller D'Art Hispanic, Barcelona, Spain; **147tr:** Mary Evans Picture Library; **148bl:** *The First Chapter of The 25th Council of Trent*, c.1630 by Italian School, Phillips, The International Fine Art Auctioneers, Bridgeman Art Library, London/New York; **148tl:** Mary Evans Picture Library; **149t:** *Processione delle Fanciulle del Sablon a Bruxelles*, Antonio Sallaert (1590-c. 1657), Galleria Sabauda, Torino, Italy, Scala; **150tl:** Illustration from *Conquest of The Incas* by Guaman Doma de Ayala, 1620, South American Pictures; **150tc:** Santa Maria de Tonantzintla, Cholula, South American Pictures/Tony Morrison; **151t:** Henrion, *Missions Catholiques*, vol. 4. 365 plate CX, Mary Evans Picture Library; **153cr:** Interior of St. Peter's Basilica, Rome: crossing with dome and baldachin (1624-33), by Gian Lorenzo Bernini, AKG London/Erich Lessing; **153tl:** Mary Evans Picture Library; **154/5:** *Wesley Preaching From His Father's Tomb, City Temple, London*, (engraving), et. Archive; **156bl:** *Sir Isaac Newton* by Van der Bank, Hulton Getty; **157tr:** Mary Evans Picture Library; **158/9b:** Hulton Getty; **159tr:** Blaise Pascal, 1785, (marble), by Augustin Pajou, Louvre, Paris, France, AKG London/Erich Lessing; **160bc:** *Courtyard of a House in Delft*, 1658, (oil on canvas), by Pieter de Hooch (1629-84), National Gallery, London, UK, Bridgeman Art Library, London/New York; **161t:** University of Halle, Germany, Bildarchiv Preußischer Kulturbesitz, Fürsorgeheime, Dtld., Gehäude; **162bc:** Mary Evans Picture Library; **162tr:** *Old Woman Reading From Lectionary* by Gerard Dou, Rijksmuseum Foundation; Amsterdam, The Netherlands; **164bl:** *John Wesley* (detail) by Nathaniel Hone, Peter Newark's American Pictures; **165t:** *Village Choir* by Thomas Webster (1800-86), Victoria and Albert Museum, London, UK, Bridgeman Art Library, London/New York; **167c:** *George Whitefield Preaching* by John Collett (1725-80), Private Collection, Bridgeman Art Library, London/New York; **168b:** *The Shakers Near Lebanon*, (litho), by N. Currier (1813-88) and J.M. Ives (1824-95), Private Collection, Bridgeman Art Library, London/New York; **168t:** *Johnathan Edwards* (1703-91), by Nathanial Hone, Peter Newark's American Pictures; **169c:** Title page of the Massachusettes Indian Bible, translated by John Eliot and published by Cambridge Press, 1663, Peter Newark's American Pictures; **169tr:** Carving by Guarani Indians with Jesuit influence, XVII, South American Pictures/Tony Morrison; **170br:** *Portrait of Peter I* (The Great) (detail), 1775, State Hermitage, St. Petersburg, AKG London/Erich Lessing; **170tl:** Robert Harding Picture Library/G.R. Richardson; **171t:** *Mount Athos, The Monastery of St. Paul*, 1858, by Edward Lear (1812-88), The Fine Art Society, London, UK, Bridgeman Art Library, London/New York; **172/3:** Camp meeting in Tennessee 1850 in *L'Illustration*, Mary Evans Picture Library; **174b:** *The Declaration of Independance*, taken from the painting by John Trumbull, Peter Newark's American Pictures; **175t:** *Thomas Jefferson*, 1800, by Rembrandt Peale, Peter Newark's American Pictures; **175br:** *Thomas Paine* (1737-1809), contemporary cartoon, Peter Newark's American Pictures; **176b:** *Pope Pius VI Blesses The Venetians*, 1782, by Francesco Guardi, Gemaldegalerie, Dresden, AKG London; **177b:** *Allegory of The Universal and Social Republic*, by F. Sourrieu, Musée Carnavalet, Paris, France, Jean-Loup Charmet; **178b:** Portrait bust of Friedrich Daniel Ernst Schleiermacher, 1829, sculpture, (plaster), by Christian Daniel, Berlin National Gallery, Germany, AKG London; **178tl:** *Portrait of Felix Mendelssohn-Bartholdy*, 1829, (watercolour), by James Warren Childe (1778-1862), Mendelson Archive, Berlin, SMPK, Staatsbibliothek, AKG London; **179c:** *The Wanderer Over The Sea of Clouds*, 1818, by Caspar-David Friedrich (1774-1840), Kusthalle, Hamburg, Germany, Bridgeman Art Library, London/New York; **180tl:** *Portrait of William Wilberforce* (1759-1833), 1828, (oil on canvas), by Sir Thomas Lawrence (1769-1830), National Portrait Gallery, London, UK, Bridgeman Art Library, London/New York; **180/1b:** *Bark Slums*, 1823, cartoon, by Cruikshank, Bibliothèque des arts décoratifs, Jean-Loup Charmet; **181tr:** Mary Evans Picture Library; **182b:** Mary Evans Picture Library; **182tr:** Mary Evans Picture Library; **183t:** Cook's ship *Endeavour*, from Murray Smith's *Arctic Expeditions*, 1877, Mary Evans Picture Library; **184/5b:** *Camp Meeting*, 1852, Mary Evan Picture Library; **185tr:** Christian History Magazine; **186bc:** *Final Emancipation Proclamation*, issued 1st January 1863, contemporary souvenir print, Peter Newark's American Pictures; **187bc:** 19th Century engraving, Mary Evans Picture Library; **187t:** *Prayer Meeting of Fugitive Slaves*, 1861/5, by William L. Sheppard, Mary Evans Picture Library; **188b:** *A Religious Procession in The Province of Kursk*, 1880-83, by Ilya Efimovich Repin (1844-1930), Tretyakov Gallery, Moscow, Russia, Bridgeman Art Library, London/New York; **189tl:** *Portrait of Fyodor Mikhaylovich Dostoyevsky*, (detail), 1872, by Wassili Grigoryevich, Tretyakov Gallery, Moscow, Russia, AKG London; **189br:** Corbis UK Ltd; **190b:** Illustrated London News Picture Library; **191t:** Bibliothèque des Arts Décoratifs, Paris, France, Jean-Loup Charmet; **191b:** *Mines at Blanzy*, watercolour, by I.F. Bonhommé, c. 1860, Musée du C.N.A.M, Paris, France, Jean-Loup Charmet; **192b:** *The Salvation Army*, (oil on panel), by Jean Francois Raffaelli, (1850-1924), Private Collection, Christie's Images, Bridgeman Art Library, London/New York; **193br:** *Sunday School Class* by Issac Mayer (Max Michael) (1823-91), Gavin Graham Gallery, London, UK, Bridgeman Art Library, London/New York; **193tr:** *Professor Darwin, 'This is the ape of form' Love's Labour's Lost, Act V, Scene II, Charles Darwin as an Ape*, 1861, (colour litho), by English School, Natural History Museum, London, UK, Bridgeman Art Library, London/New York; **193tl:** Bibliotèque des Arts Décoratifs, Paris, France, Jean-Loup Charmet; **194bl:** *The White Fathers of Monseigneur Lavigerie in Africa*, cover of a school book, c. 1880-90, Jean-Loup Charmet; **194tr:** David Linvingstone from *The Period*, 1870, Mary Evans Picture Library; **195tr:** *Massacres in China, The Boxer Rising*, 1900, (engraving), Private Collection, Bridgeman Art Library, London/New York; **195b:** *Martyrs in Annam in 1838, Missions Européens*, Jean-Loup Charmet; **196tr:** *Chinese Christian*, 19th Century, Lauros, Giraudon, Bibliothèque Nationale, Inv. Est, **197br:** Jean-Loup Charmet; **198b:** *Pope Pius IX Blesses the Bourbon Troops in Naples, 9th September, 1849*, by Achille Vespa, San Martino Museum, G. Dagli Orti; **198tl:** Henry Edward, Cardinal/Archbishop of Westminster from *Vanity Fair*, Mary Evans Picture Library; **199br:** *Catéchisme Mural*, 1900, Jean-Loup Charmet; **199t:** *Feast of Corpus Christi at Fiesole*, by R.C. Goff, 1902, Mary Evans Picture Library; **200tl:** Library of Congress, Corbis UK Ltd; **200b:** James Davis Travel Photography; **201tr:** Corbis UK Ltd; **202/3:** Panos Pictures/Crispin Hughes; **204bl:** Jean-Loup Charmet; **205tr:** Hulton Getty; **206/7c:** Mary Evans Picture Library; **206bc:** David King Collection; **206tl:** Sygma; **207tr:** Hutchison Library/Audrey Zvoznikov; **208bl:** Brown Brothers; **209t:** Hulton Getty/John Chillingworth; **209c:** AKG London; **209bc:** Magnum/Cartier Bresson; **210bc:** Topham Picturepoint; **211t:** Magnum/Steve McCurry; **211br:** Sygma; **212cra:** Corbis UK Ltd; **212b:** Sygma/Brooks Kraft; **213tr:** Andes Press Agency/Carlos Reyes Manzo; **213br:** Sygma/Patrick Durano; **214bl:** Rex Features/Vladimir Sichov; **215tc:** Topham Picturepoint; **215b:** Topham Picturepoint; **216c:** Hutchinson/Crispin Hughes; **216bc:** Sygma; **217b:** Sygma/J.Van Hasselt; **218t:** Magnum/Bruce Davidson; **218bl:** Magnum/Burri Reno; **219br:** Sygma; **219tr:** Sygma; **220/1br:** Vatican Museums, Ikona/Carrieri; **220bl:** Sygma/Keystone; **221tr:** Hulton Getty; **222b:**Brown Brothers; **223t:** Andes Press Agency/Carlos Reyes Manzo; **223br:** Magnum/Abbas; **224tr:** Rex Features; **225tr:** Magnum/Carlos Reyes Manzo; **226bl:** Popperfoto/Viktor Korotayer; **227t:** Andes Press Agency/Carlos Reyes Manzo; **228br:** Hutchison Library/Dave Brimicombe; **228:** Sygma/Brooks Kraft; **229:** Magnum/Stuart Franklin.

Acknowledgments

MATTHEW PRICE'S DEDICATION:
My parents are active, sincere, devout Christians. As were their parents, all four of them. As were my eight great-grandparents, or so I've been told. I'm not sure how the numbers add up beyond three generations but I'm confident the roots of my family's faith run very deep. Yet, somehow, despite my pious lineage, as a young person I had absolutely no interest in religion. None whatsoever. It wasn't until I was in college, at the age of 20, that I finally, suddenly, embraced Christianity. I certainly don't want to diminish the importance of the many prayers offered on my behalf, but my epiphany came while taking an elective course in church history. As the rich tapestry of the past was unfurled before me, I was amazed and humbled by the towering intellects and selfless martyrs who believed that a life centred purely around temporal pleasures and concerns was both shallow and shortsighted. They were men and women who had changed the course of history, and had done so in the name of an otherwise obscure Jewish carpenter who was, as some have written, either a madman or truly the Messiah: I realized that the weight of history lay entirely on the latter verdict. Thus I was delighted and honored when Sean Moore, the category publisher for religion at DK Publishing, asked me to participate in this project. My experiences from the beginning with the DK staff, and others who have labored on the book, have been uniformly positive. I would like to thank Anna Kruger who guided the early stages of the outline and David Pickering who, along with Susannah Steel and Caroline Hunt, provided keen insight and a steady editorial hand throughout. The marvelous layout of the interior pages are the handiwork of two gifted designers, Dawn Terrey and Claire Legemah. The dedicated efforts of Joanna Bicknell, assisted by Jonathan Wright, in the UK and Cliff Johnson, aided by Jim Bolton and Claudia Volkman, in the U.S. have given this project an excellent chance to achieve a wide audience around the world. Providing invaluable assessment and commentary was Mark Galli from *Christian History* while insight into certain key evangelical figures in American church history was supplied by my parents, Paul and Barbara Price. And, of course, I leave this project with the highest esteem for my Catholic coauthor, Michael Collins, whose wit, wisdom, and warmth made serving as the Protestant voice a delight. Finally I would like to thank my wife, Jeanie, and our children, Savannah and Harrison, for their patience and encouragement during the six months I spent evenings and weekends writing and rewriting. To paraphrase Solomon in the book of Proverbs, a supportive family is worth far more than rubies. It is to them I dedicate this book.

MICHAEL COLLINS' DEDICATION:
I would like to dedicate this book to my wonderful parents, Helen and John Collins, as well as my great brother and sisters, David, Paula and Geraldine. I deeply appreciate all the love and affection we have for each other. I want to dedicate this book also to my Italian family, Angelo, Rosanna, Filippo, and Lorenzo Balducci, who have been so incredibly good to me. And finally to my great friend Andrea Piras, for his constant support and affection. I want to express my gratitude and respect for the DK team who are responsible for this book. First and foremost thanks to Sean Moore, who commissioned this book, and to Anna Kruger for choosing a super team to work with. I was in almost daily contact with David Pickering, the senior editor, who oversaw my contribution to this book, and made great suggestions. Susannah Steel and Caroline Hunt made the task so much easier than I could have imagined. The beautiful illustrations of the book are due to the talented team of picture researchers. Although a lot of hard work went into this book, it was worth every minute. Matt and I worked together in perfect harmony, and I learned so much from his clear, precise, and fluid style. Finally I thank all the teachers I have had along the path of my life who have given me a love for learning, none more than the Faculty at the Pontifical Institute of Christian Archaeology in Rome. Primary thanks go to John O'Connell of Mac Publishing for his introduction to DK, and his constant help throughout the project.

DK Publishing would like to thank:
Andreas Piras for taking the photograph of Michael Collins; Nicky Thomasson for editorial assistance; Kirstie Sobue for research assistance; Mary Ann Jeffreys of *Christian History* magazine and Carla Bertini for picture research assistance; Dave Robinson for design assistance; Deirdre Headon, Jake Woodward, Nicky Powling, and Sanjay Patel for creating the jacket.